DECLINE OF DONNISH DOMINION

DECLINE OF DONNISH DOMINION

The British Academic Professions in the Twentieth Century

A. H. HALSEY

CLARENDON PRESS · OXFORD
1995

Oxford University Press, Walton Street, Oxford OX2 6DP

Oxford New York
Athens Auckland Bangkok Bombay
Calcutta Cape Town Dar es Salaam Delhi
Florence Hong Kong Istanbul Karachi
Kuala Lumpur Madras Madrid Melbourne
Mexico City Nairobi Paris Singapore
Taipei Tokyo Toronto
and associated companies in
Berlin Ibadan

Oxford is a trade mark of Oxford University Press

Published in the United States
by Oxford University Press Inc., New York

First published 1992
First published in paperback 1995

British Library Cataloguing in Publication Data
Data available

Library of Congress Cataloging in Publication Data
Halsey, A. H.
Decline of donnish dominion: the British academic professions in
the twentieth century / A. H. Halsey.
Includes bibliographical references and index.
1. Education, Higher—Social aspects—Great Britain—History—20th
century. 2. College teaching—Great Britain—History—20th century.
3. Education, Higher—Great Britain—Aims and objectives
History—20th century. 4. Educational sociology—Great Britain
History—20th century. I. Title.
LC191.8.G7H35 1992 378.41—dc20 91-39741
ISBN 0-19-827376-2
ISBN 0-19-827973-6 (Pbk)

Typeset by Pentacor PLC, *High Wycombe, Bucks.*
Printed in Great Britain
on acid-free paper by
Biddles Ltd., Guildford and King's Lynn

PREFACE

WAR and famine and economic boom and slump are always staples of television and newspaper. But in domestic affairs by 1992 schools and colleges had risen to near the top of political concern in Britain. It is therefore an appropriate moment to reflect on the past and present problems of higher education. The literature is vast but its character, especially in the last three decades, has changed dramatically, not only in scale but also in the degree to which it has entered into the arena of public discussion. Before the 1960s there was little sustained public examination of higher education in this, or to my knowledge, any other country. In Britain the discussion did not break out of narrowly academic circles until after Robbins reported in 1963. Up to that time the journalistic portrayal of university life was confined to the staid pages of *Universities Quarterly* and the reporting of appointments, deaths, boat races, and rugby football results from Oxford and Cambridge on the appropriate page of *The Times*. Nevertheless, behind and outside the academic scenes from the end of the 1950s, recognition of the need for expansion of higher education was accompanied by a stirring of self-consciousness among the progressive, usually socio-logically minded, dons. *Encounter* carried a series of articles on intellectuals. Edward Shils began to edit *Minerva* in 1962. The Society for Research on Higher Education began in 1964, *Higher Education Review* in 1968, and *Higher Education* in 1972. Meanwhile, and signalling full acceptance of higher education into the higher and middle journalism, the *Times Higher Education Supplement* (*THES*) published its first number in October 1971.

Thus, during the 1960s and 1970s, discussion became more widely shared. The growing number of graduates swelled that branch of the mass media industry which supplies more or less entertaining and informative ephemera to itself in the 'up-market' weeklies and supplements. The discussion also became more explicitly political, partly because higher education developed into an avid consumer of the financial patronage of the state, partly because universities and polytechnics came to vie with the hustings and the workplace in bids to displace parliament as the forum of political argument, and partly also because of the continuing role of colleges and universities as recruiting-grounds for political and administrative leaders of the future.

Hence debates on higher education, national and international, continue weekly if not daily. In the process, what has been called traditionally the 'idea of the university' has changed fundamentally. Thus, for example, before the 'events' of 1968 only the most extravagant social science fiction could have portrayed the university campus as did the French professor of sociology, Alan Touraine, in terms analogous to those used by Marx in describing the nineteenth-century class struggle in the new industrial towns. My major preoccupation in this book will be with sociological writing. Yet the larger literature of which the sociology of education forms part is not itself sociological. It is, in the main, a depository from the labours of European scholarship with its self-conscious history since medieval times. There are innumerable histories, biographies, memoirs, and novels which offer material to the sociologist who wishes to analyse the evolution of teaching, research, and administration in higher education. Some of the histories are of a general kind like H. Rashdall's three volumes on *Universities of Europe in the Middle Ages* (1936); some treat a particular institution as do the recent and forthcoming volumes of the *History of the University of Oxford* or W. H. G. Armytage in his *Civic Universities* (1955). There are anthropological monographs like Tony Becher's *Academic Tribes and Territories* (SRHE, 1990), quasi-anthropological novels like Kingsley Amis's *Lucky Jim* or Malcolm Bradbury's *The History Man* and quasi-historical memoirs like Sir Maurice Bowra's *Memories* or Noel Annan's *Our Age* (1990), and there are quasi-scientific analyses of the research culture like James Watson's *Double Helix*. Discussion of 'the idea of the university' as launched by John Henry Newman continues, for example, in Ronald Barnett's *The Idea of Higher Education* (SRHE, 1990). There is the even more voluminous debris of official reports and statistics from the Oxford and Cambridge commissions of the 1850s to the Leverhulme Report of the 1980s. All have made their greater or lesser mark on the developing idea of the university. The problem for me is to derive from them a convincing sociological interpretation.

When Jean Floud and I reviewed the literature at the end of the 1950s we wrote that 'modern sociology is a product of industrialism and the modern university has been profoundly modified in its nature and functions by the same forces. The explicitly sociological study of higher learning, therefore, has the consequences of industrialism as its context' (Floud and Halsey 1958). Add the extraordinary recrudescence of economic liberalism in the reformation of social policy since 1979, and the literature of the last thirty years seems to me to offer no good reason to revise this central judgement. I noticed at that time that two publications might properly be thought of as the foundation addresses to the modern sociological discussion of higher education. They both appeared in 1918, they are both of undiminished relevance today. One was a speech delivered by Max Weber in Munich on science as a vocation (Gerth and Mills 1947). The other was by the Norwegian-American sociologist Thorstein Veblen—an ironic protest against 'the conduct of universities by business men' (Veblen 1918).

Independently, and with distinctive contrast of style, these two sociologists set the stage for the debate which has become a staple of parliaments, common-rooms, and the weekly papers—the adaptation of corporate structures of feudal origin to the economy of modern countries. Any Secretary of State for Education and Science, at least from James Callaghan's famous Ruskin speech of 1976, might have used them. Weber put his emphasis on the demand set up by a modern economy for highly trained specialist manpower, the advance of bureaucracy in all forms of social organization, and the 'proletarianization' of the university research worker and teacher. He also adumbrated a major theme of interpretation of the European universities, namely, the role of America as a portent of the European future. In the Germany of his day the career of the *Privatdozent* was still 'generally based upon plutocratic prerequisites'. Veblen, too, saw the scholar as a member of a thwarted class. In his analysis of the power structure of higher learning in America he stressed the function of the university as itself a business enterprise in competition with other universities, bureaucratically organized under its president or 'captain of erudition' in pursuit of the aims of 'notoriety, prestige and advertising in all its branches and bearing' at the expense of scholarship and to the accompaniment of a vast competitive waste of resources. Does Veblen also describe our present discontents?

I shall try to answer partly from the history of higher education, partly from personal experience as an undergraduate at LSE in the 1940s, a redbrick lecturer in the 1950s, and an Oxford don from the 1960s. I can also draw on many visits to OECD countries in Europe and America over the same period. Most particularly, I can use three surveys of the British senior common rooms in 1964, 1976, and 1989.

My debts to colleagues are numberless. My colleague at Berkeley, Martin Trow, deserves first mention: he is a never-failingly patient reader and critic. Together we wrote *The British Academics* on the basis of our 1964 survey. I repeated the survey in 1976 and again in 1989. This third 'sweep' was made possible by the generosity of the Spencer Foundation, to which I am sincerely grateful. I was also given the opportunity in the summer of 1989 to deliver the Radcliffe lectures at Warwick University and so to essay a first version of the outline of this book.

I would like to thank my colleague Jane Roberts for her work on computing tables, my Research Officer Muriel Egerton for her authorship of Appendix 2 and contribution especially to Chapters 9 and 10, and my student Alison Park for allowing me to extract parts of her master's dissertation to include in Chapter 10. My thanks also go to Brian Harrison who, as editor of the twentieth-century volume of the History of Oxford University, has allowed me to include amended versions of my two chapters in his work as Chapters 3 and 7 in this book. With respect to the 1989 survey and the collection of official statistics I am indebted to Cynthia Holme at the University Statistical Record in Cheltenham, to Angela Skrimshire, to Sir Maurice Shock, Clive Booth, and Sir Christopher Ball, and most especially to Lindsey Brook at Social and Community Planning for the data collection described at Appendix 1. My thanks are also due to Elaine Herman for her skill and astonishing speed with a word processor.

Above all I am grateful to the nearly 5,000 colleagues in the polytechnics and universities who have had the patience to answer yet another, and in this case elaborate, questionnaire. Well over a thousand gave me also substantial comments on the survey questions. Some were extraordinarily friendly, even complimentary, others more candidly rude, all were instructive and reminded me of the limitations of the survey method. Despite widespread discontent, amounting often to despair, the British academics still believe in their calling. I salute the ideals by which they live.

CONTENTS

FIGURES

TABLES

ABBREVIATIONS

AUT	Association of University Teachers
BMA	British Medical Association
CAT	College of Advanced Technology
CDP	Committee of Directors of Polytechnics
CNAA	Council for National Academic Awards
CNRS	Centre National de la Recherche Scientifique
CPEC	California Postsecondary Education Commission
CVCP	Committee of Vice-Chancellors and Principals
DE	Department of Employment
DES	Department of Education and Science
ESRC	Economic and Social Research Council
GCE	General Certificate of Education
GCSE	General Certificate of Secondary Education
HEFC	Higher Education Funding Council
LSE	London School of Economics and Political Science
NAB	National Advisory Board for Public Sector Higher Education
NATFHE	NationalAssociationofTeachersinFurtherandHigher Education
NEC	National Commission on Education
NUS	National Union of Students
OECD	Organization for Economic Co-operation and Development
PCFC	Polytechnic and Colleges Funding Council
SCPR	Social and Community Planning Research
SRHE	Society for Research into Higher Education
SSRC	Social Science Research Council
THES	*Times Higher Education Supplement*
TLS	*Times Literary Supplement*
UCCA	Universities Central Council for Admissions
UFC	Universities Funding Council
UGC	Universities Grants Committee
WEA	Workers Educational Association

INTRODUCTION

THE British senior common room today presents a spectacle more interesting than joyful. My purpose in this book is to trace some major trends in the behaviour and opinion of university and polytechnic staff—what Harold Perkin aptly dubbed 'the key profession' (Perkin 1969)—and to examine the fortunes of the institutions of higher education from the exuberant innocence of the Robbins expansion plan through the anxious disillusion of the 1970s to the renewed expansionist declarations of the Secretaries of State for Education (Mr Baker and Mr Macgregor) in the late 1980s and the competitive resolve of the new Secretary of State, Kenneth Clarke, and his Labour shadow Jack Straw, to put education at the top of the political agenda in the 1990s.

To this end I am able to rely on three surveys of British academic staff. The first survey was conducted in 1964/5 at the beginning of the period of expansion associated with the Robbins Report of 1963, making possible a book on *The British Academics* which put Robbins into historical context (Halsey and Trow 1971). The second survey was carried out in 1976 after Robbinsian expansion (Halsey 1979; Clark 1983). The third survey took place in 1989, a decade after the decisive shift in British higher education policy ushered in by the Thatcher government.

My intention then is to revisit the British academic professions and to analyse their changing structure and functions in the quarter of a century since the Robbins Report. The three surveys yield a unique set of trend statistics on the changing state of 'the key profession'. They are arrayed in barest outline at Appendix 1. They offer the basis for a systematic account of the changing disciplinary composition, material conditions, status, attitudes, orientations, and morale of the staff in British higher education since Martin Trow and I wrote in 1971. At that point it was possible to look back at the evolution of a highly restricted provision for higher education as it had evolved out of earnest Victorian efforts to adapt to the demands of an advanced industrial society. But, of course, both the world and the academic professions have changed dramatically in the last two decades. The position of the academics in relation to state funding, salary levels, research facilities, staff–student ratios, public respect, and indeed every dimension of professional status, had deteriorated by the end of the 1980s to the point where both domestic and foreign observers regarded the British higher-education system as in crisis.

A London arts professor spoke for at least a substantive minority in commenting on the 1989 survey. 'I do not recall anything like the present demoralisation of the university professions. This has, of course, to do with practicalities—cuts in funding etc. But above all else it has to do with the present government's sustained disparagement of intellectual life, its denial that it is an inherent good, part of the life of a civilised society.'

Yet, paradoxically, the alarm coexisted in 1990 with a poll of European university teachers involved in the European community action scheme for the mobility of university students (Erasmus), conducted by the French magazine *Libération*, which gave top place to a British university in seven out of eleven mainstream academic subjects. Crisis in Britain apparently coincides with a judgement that British universities are the best in Europe. There is much here to explore and explain. A secondary theme will therefore be to set the British case into comparative context and particularly to draw comparisons with the academic professions of the United States as they have developed over the same period.[1]

But why should academics study themselves? Professor Burton Clark has offered a succinct reply.

For many reasons the academic profession ought to arouse our curiosity and elicit serious study. It trains the members of an increasing number of leading fields outside the academy; its ideas speak to economy and politics, to social order and culture; and its leading scientists produce knowledge and technique in such world-transforming fields as atomic energy, biotechnology and computerization. In so many ways, and more than before, it touches the lives of the general public. Yet, in the face of such

---

[1] Burton Clark has contributed to closing the knowledge gap with a notable landmark of publication in his study of the American academic professions (Clark 1987), as well as in bringing together a set of essays on these professions in Europe and America based on the conference held at Bellagio in Italy in 1984 (Clark 1986). This compilation includes a valuable essay on the UK professoriate by Harold Perkin as well as chapters on the US by Walter Metzger, W. Germany by Wolfgang Mommsen, and France by Gerhard Friedberg and Christine Musselin. See also the latest contribution to transatlantic discussion, Berdahl, Moodie, and Spitzberg 1991.

importance, how much do we know about the development of this profession in other than simple numerical terms? What does it mean for a profession to be a loosely coupled array of disciplines and professional fields, each having a history, a sense of nationhood, and a momentum that makes it a going concern in its own right? Observers have long noted that academicians study everything but themselves, a remarkable failing in an estate composed of scholars and researchers devoted to the task of assisting others to understand the natural and social phenomena that make a difference in shaping the modern world. Of this we can be sure: the academic profession makes a difference. We can hardly know too much about it. In the mid-1980s we still know little. (Clark, 1986)

THE EXPANSION

Senior common rooms have been transformed first and foremost by expansion. Higher education before Robbins was a reference to thirty British universities but, when the UGC was wound up in 1989, there were fifty-two institutions on the University Funding Council list as well as eighty-two polytechnics and colleges under the umbrella of the Polytechnics and Colleges Funding Council. In 1964 there were some 19,000 British academics. Subsequently the university sector has expanded to over 46,000 full-time staff in universities including nearly 17,000 working on funds provided from elsewhere. The growth of the polytechnic sector is still more striking. We have counted 18,000 in the English and Welsh polytechnics and the analogous Scottish central institutions, excluding occasional teachers who are not fully on the payroll. Meanwhile, the number of full-time students in higher education as a whole has grown from 130,000 to over 600,000 and there are also over 350,000 part-timers—a total approaching 1 million. Altogether 55 per cent of British higher-education students are in the polytechnics and colleges, 9 per cent in the Open University, and 36 per cent in the universities.

Revisiting the common room after an interval of twenty-five years, the sociologist can hardly fail to notice these expansionary changes. But there are other trends of no less importance. The university monopoly has gone, the binary line is nominally no more, and polytechnics are free to rename themselves. There are more women, their proportions having grown from 10 per cent to nearly 20 per cent in the universities (20 per cent in the poly-technics). The members are older, their average age was 38 before Robbins and is 44 now, and the younger ones are disproportionately non-tenured 'soft-money' staff, typically on research contracts. Moreover, the old stereotype of pure arts or pure science, which had in any case already become rather outdated in the 1960s, is now patently a thing of the past, and the majority are engaged in some natural or social-science based applied teaching and research. The atmosphere is different. It is both busier and more apathetic, newer and more neglected, more impersonal, more fragmented. It could be a high-tech factory boardroom or an airport lounge rather than an academic club room. The architecture at Bath or Brunel or Oxford polytechnic reflects amalgamation of the professional classes in business and administration rather than the monastic echoes of a combination room in a Cambridge college or the gothic revival milieu of Manchester or Durham. Erstwhile dons are now the managers of the higher-education industry.

The expansion of higher education in Britain started from a tiny base at the beginning of the century, with an accelerated growth in the 1960s and 1970s associated with the Robbins Report. By the end of the 1970s a binary system had evolved, the universities forming a top tier of prestigious centres of higher learning, the polytechnics and other 'public sector' colleges forming a second tier: but both together offering higher education to no more than a sixth of the relevant age-group. The binary system, though now in its last years of formal divide, is and is likely to remain an organized social differentiation of both staff and students in terms of social background and educational qualifications. And even within the university sector there is further institutional differentiation as between the Oxford and Cambridge colleges and the rest. From one point of view the system is meritocratic. From another it is a reflection of the changing class and status hierarchy. Like other systems of higher education the British universities and colleges illustrate the subtle accommodation of ascription to achievement in the reproduction of classes through meritocratic educational selection.

At the same time it has also become painfully clear that in the 1970s the modest expansion associated with the Robbins Report was dependent overwhelmingly on financial support from the state (Carswell 1985). This is true just as much for the 'autonomous' universities as for the 'public sector' institutions. When, therefore, a Conservative government came to power in 1979, determined to cut public expenditure, it was inevitable that higher-education budgets would come under severe pressure. There was in fact what Maurice and David Kogan have described as a systematic governmental attack on higher education (Kogan 1983). Between 1980 and 1983 the universities had to reduce their budgets by approximately 15 per cent, and there were further resource cuts in subsequent years. Level funding in real terms became and remained a dream—a utopia nostalgically preserved from the quinquennial past. In 1984 and 1985 the Department of Education and Science produced forecasts into the mid-1990s (in the only system among developed countries where the universities had actually contracted since the mid 1970s) which were hotly disputed by the Royal Society as well as the Association of University Teachers (*The Development of Higher Education into the 1990s*, Cmnd. 9524). In consequence some revision of governmental policy was made. In the White Paper of April 1987 (*Higher Education: Meeting the Challenge*, 1987, Cmnd. 114) the projections were raised by some 10 per cent. The new plan for the proportion of the age-group entering higher education as a whole took it from 14.2 per cent to 18.5 per cent by the end of the century. But as Sir Claus Moser commented, this was 'unambitious' and, he went on, 'I would urge the government to think in terms of a massive increase in higher education opportunities, with a target of the order of 25 to 30 per cent by the end of the century, with close on half of that allocated to the universities' (Moser 1988). Moser went further as President of the British Association for the Advancement of Sciences, calling in 1990 for a Royal Commission (Moser 1990). In the meantime the then Secretary of State, Kenneth Baker, had assumed a 30 per cent target for the end of the nineties. In May 1991 the Conservative party, in the context of competitive electioneering, announced plans for achieving a one in three enrolment in higher education for the twenty-first century and proposed to have a single funding agency in England, in Scotland, and in Wales for the whole of higher education. If plans become realities a new era is dawning.

On this perspective the post-Robbins story has to be seen as a failed thrust towards mass higher education. Robbins can be interpreted as the last expression of Victorian expansionism with its tacit assumptions that higher education was a finishing school for the sons and perhaps daughters of the élite, that occupational and social places for each new generation of the educationally elevated were separately assured, that the university was a decoration rather

than an engine of economic growth. Yet, given its economic
marginality, albeit combined with high social significance, the
university had a right to autonomy, to govern itself, and to receive
funding from the society it adorned, through state mechanisms
unencumbered by democratic parliamentary scrutiny. Hence the
royal charter, the University Grants Committee, the academic
senate, the gentlemanly (though austere) character of student
support with nominal fees and a maintenance grant. Hence the
absence of discrimination in salary between faculties, with clinical
medicine an exception to prove the rule that gentlefolk make their
claims through social status rather than through market strength.
Hence also the autonomy of the system of external examining of
students by dons and for dons; and the management of the
university finances without inspection by the parliamentary Public
Accounts Committee.

This too simple sketch of the world which Robbins perfected
brings out the essential features of a Victorian/Edwardian system
which now in 1992 has passed on. It is, to be sure, a caricature. The
exact form of post-industrial modernity has to be found in a more
elaborate and realistic description. There had been talk about the
need and the potential of education as the engine of economic
progress at least from the time when Victorians became aware of
German advance in the chemical industry and of the utilitarian
disposition of the American land-grant colleges. And there was a
renewed impetus given to the claims of merit whatever its social
origins by the social egalitarians and radicals after the slump years
of the 1930s and by the new hopes for social reconstruction of the
Second World War. Yet Robbins, for all that he was an eminent
economist, gave no precise economic justification for expanding
higher education. Instead he, in effect, described an article of faith.
Having talked, for example, to the Soviet authorities and having
been assured that short-term deductions from manpower requirements were basically irrelevant in that 'in the Soviet Union there
would always be use for people who had been trained to the limit of
their potential ability' (Robbins 1963: 74), he affirmed that 'We do
not believe that the Soviet Union is the only country that can make
full use of the brains of its people. This country above all must do
so . . .'.

So much for the supply side. On the demand side the basis of
Robbins's calculation was even more attenuated from economic

analysis. It was a social demand estimate of the qualified output of the secondary schools, buttressed only by a quotation from the Analects of Confucius asserting that 'it was not easy to find a man who has studied for three years without aiming at pay' (Robbins 1963: 6). In other words the Robbins Committee assumed that pecuniary or career motives would be adequate and the demand for places in universities and colleges could be basically estimated by the number of boys and girls emerging from the secondary schools with the traditional minimal requirement for matriculation. The problem was on the supply side, where it was anticipated that expansion would meet the nation's needs best if more science places were provided. Robbins made an over-optimistic forecast, reflecting the dominant influence on his committee of Philip Morris and the leaders of higher education with their urbane confidence in the expansive capacity of the universities and their unrealistic knowledge of the barriers, especially to girls, of secondary-school science choices and courses. At all events, as Carswell has demonstrated, the result was a serious gap between 'programme and performance' in the first Robbins decade—a gap filled by expansion of arts and social sciences (Carswell 1985: 169–72).

Even more remarkably, no account seems to have been taken of the implications for student support of the Anderson Committee (*Grants to Students*, 1960, Cmnd. 1051). Indeed as Carswell (1985: 25) points out, Anderson's Report was not even referred to in the Robbins Report. The new universities were built, like the medieval cathedrals, for ever, to the glory of God, and for the admiration of the peasantry without regard to their public pocket. I remember my friend and colleague Martin Trow touring the Sussex campus where he gazed sceptically at low-density, high-cost architecture and complained decisively that 'neither we nor you can afford to build like this for a mass system of universities.'

The British university professions are therefore of critical international interest. British higher education, after a remarkable burst of energy and expansion in the two and a half decades following the end of the Second World War, has entered a period of great stress, most markedly in the past decade. As Martin Trow put it in 1988, 'the problems, which taken together we can properly call a crisis, have developed largely in the public life of British higher education—in its finance, governance and organization—rather than in its private life, in the areas of teaching and learning. A crisis of this magnitude, however painful to those immediately affected, can be instructive and enlightening to the observer, as it wrenches old patterns and relationships awry and makes suddenly problem-atic what has long been assumed.' It is my purpose in this book to use the three surveys as an empirical base for testing Trow's appraisal of the crisis (Trow 1988).

Much current comment in the literature tends to interpret the crisis in terms of hostile government policy. A more fundamental explanation lies in the structure of British higher education itself, where the strains and difficulties reflect an attempt to develop a system to serve the varied requirements of an advanced industrial society and at the same time to maintain the élite character and size of the existing arrangements. On this view the problem lies in the British conception of the nature of a university and its relation to the wider society in which it exists. An examination of these conceptions appears in Chapter 2 below.

THE OUTCOME

A preliminary assessment of the outcome in the 1990s must begin by recognizing the experience of relative affluence among universit-ies over the thirty years of post-war boom ending around 1974. A common mistake in the years before Robbins was to assume a law of history which would progressively expand the universities into systems of higher education and draw more and more people into the world of science and scholarship. It was widely believed in the 1950s that there would be no end to the continued upward trend of enrolment and increasing allocation of resources. The idea, in other words, was that a modern rich society would develop a universal demand for the highest forms of education. Looking back over the period from the middle of the nineteenth century there appeared to be successive phases in an assured progress towards universal higher education. Martin Trow expressed the trend as one of stages of educational expansion from élite to mass to universal. This development was also held to reflect the changing relation between the universities and the economy. The economy of an advancing industrial society would require more educated people, who would be highly productive and so in turn provide the resources required for their own augmentation.

More abstractly, the theory asserted that demand for higher education was potentially infinite and would create its own supply either through governments or through the market. But with the end of the post-war period in the 1970s, the assumed expansion began to falter. Part of the difficulty was demographic. In some countries the actual numbers in the relevant age-group, which is roughly 18–21, began to decline. Also, apart from a diminution in absolute numbers, the rate of transition out of secondary schools into the tertiary system faltered, or in some cases actually fell. Japan is an exception to the general rule.

Now that history has demonstrated the falsity of post-war expectations it is necessary to produce a better theory to explain the expansion of the 1960s, the recession of the 1970s, and the renewed expansion under adverse conditions in the later 1980s. Such an improved theory must consider three things—the demand for education which comes from people, the development of the market for education, and the regulating role of government. It is to these three things that we must look for an explanation of both expansion and recession. Their implications for the structure of the academic professions, for the life of scholarship and its rewards and discontents, will then be more clear.

Beneath these economic and political forces lie a set of social attitudes towards higher education. There was a switch from confident expansion to adversity after the mid-1970s which may be partly explained by folk memory of the events of 1968, 1969, and 1970. At the high tide of expansion the image of the university student changed. Popular respect for the student as an earnest young man or woman who would advance social progress through economic productivity gave way to widespread suspicion of an irresponsible subversive who believed that revolution could be effectively conducted by persons aged 18–21. The importance of this change of image, when one considers the attitudes of people, particularly taxpayers, towards the education of other people's children, should not be underestimated. The effects on public respect for university teachers, and indeed for teachers generally, are still apparent.

Then, second, with respect to markets, we have to notice that the differential expectations in earnings and life-earnings of those with higher education began to decline. The rate of return to the highest education started to fall in most countries in the 1970s. In Britain there was a decline in the average rate of return for male university graduates compared with males obtaining any A levels between

1971 and 1984, with a trough in 1980 and 1981 followed by a partial recovery. To be sure there are difficulties about the calculation of social or private rates of return (not least that the earnings data are inescapably historical). Most economists would regard a decline in rate of return as a good predictor of a fall in demand. But the difficulty is that this can be argued in precisely the opposite way: that under certain conditions the tightening of the graduate labour market may increase competition for entry into the highest form of education. For education is a *positional* as well as an investment good. The surveys described in the following chapters throw light on how intensified competition for status leads institutions to differentiate themselves. An analysis of opinion and experience among university and polytechnic staff compared and contrasted with the earlier material from the period of Robbinsian expansion also illuminates present standards and expectations for students, for research, and for the academic succession.

With regard to the State, it is in this same period that governments, under pressure to raise more and more revenue to meet growing social and educational demands, were beset by falling rates of economic growth. In both Europe and America people became increasingly reluctant to vote themselves higher taxation. Higher education is only one of the possible contenders for state spending, and there was increasing competition with defence, housing, health, and social security which made it more difficult for the upward trend in government allocations to continue. Education in Britain particularly has failed to develop a strong political constituency. This is another significant facet of an élitist system in a political democracy. Glennerster and Low (1990) have shown that 'university and polytechnic spending relative to the age group of 18–24-year-olds fell by a quarter from 1973/74 to 1986/87.' By contrast the universities and colleges of the United States, by their expansion and democratization, are described by Martin Trow as a central force working 'to legitimate the political and social order by rewarding talent and effort . . . ' (Trow 1988). In Britain the establishment, as Ted Tapper and Brian Salter saw as early as 1978 (Tapper and Salter 1978), was divided by two conflicting policies for expansion. The older aristocratic and liberal élite followed the mild line of Robbinsian expansion as cultural progress. A newer élite, seeing polytechnics and universities as essentially a service to the economy of a competing nation, conceived of the system as an economic, human-capital, machine. Not social integration but economic efficiency was the justification for higher learning. This contrast of priorities underlay the subsequent dispute, and the war of attrition, especially between government and the universities, has remained unresolved to the present day.

THE BRITISH IDEA OF A UNIVERSITY

Britain is the most extreme case of expansion of universities in terms of a particular idea of what a university is and should be. The history of this self-conception of British academic people is described in some detail in Chapter 2 below. This idea was heavily laden with the conceptions of an earlier stage of the evolution of the university, when it was a straitened system from the point of view of access. It was restricted partly by its priestly origins which implied that those who entered must be totally immersed in learning. Under the working principle of commensality, professors and students must live together as in a kind of educative family separated from the rest of the world. The consequences included the most generous staff–student ratios in the world, some of the most beautiful buildings, and widely admired standards of teaching and scholarship.

After the medieval period, and superimposed on the priestly tradition, came the aristocratic assumption that anyone who went to a university was a person of independent means. In the twentieth century, if students were not of independent means the State had to make them appear to be so by giving financial support—a scholarship, and maintenance and tuition—which would enable them to conduct themselves as gentlemen. So in the 1980s, with the most expensive system of residence in the western world, Britain had only seven students in the universities for every 1,000 of population, the lowest proportion in Europe, less than half that of Japan (fifteen or sixteen), and about one-sixth of that of the United States of America.

On the other hand and for the same reasons, this extravagant system of total immersion in gentlemanliness looks better on the output than on the input side. The actual output of graduates as a proportion of the total number of students is higher in Britain than in any other country in the world. The British universities graduate 25 per cent of their students every year. The graduate population in Britain in the 1980s was 1.58 per 1,000, which compared well with other European countries, and was not all that far behind the Japanese proportion of 1.85.

From this standpoint the British system was efficient. But despite recognizing its efficiency, British governments after the end of the post-war period were alarmed by its cost. The alarm is understandable because the bill, including the student support bill, seemed likely to rise for ever. In response recent governments imposed a quota on the number of home students allowed to enter the universities. And it is significant that a distinction was made in the British system between UK students and those who come from overseas. In the case of the home students it was a political quota, in the case of the overseas students it was a market. In still more recent years the struggle has begun to overturn altogether the status of the student as a state pensioner and to move towards minimal government surveillance of a market with students on loans and institutions of higher education competing with prices for courses.

These shifts and strains of government policy illustrate an adaptation which has at its root the question of how far the provision of higher education can be managed politically, and how far it can be allowed to work itself out in the market. The development of the universities, or rather of post-secondary education, in the United States of America is a historical demonstration of the power of the market to produce a system that is responsive, flexible, and embraces large numbers, though it also has a curriculum—a range of studies—which no traditional European aristocrat would have recognized as part of a university education. The outstanding feature of the American experience, and the reason why the recession of the early 1980s had less impact than some, including Clark Kerr, anticipated, is that the market dominates. It shifts the determination of what is taught in universities away from professorial power towards student demand power, and what is researched from autonomous disciplinary interests towards the service of industry, government, and the practising professions.

The consequences for the academic career are profound. Burton Clark's analysis shows that power ebbs away from the professoriate to the sources of demand for courses and for research products (Clark 1987). There is a decline of donnish dominion. The academic professions proliferate in their specialist fields of knowledge, become more disparate in prestige and remuneration, and scatter in their professional schools, universities, and colleges. And in the meantime there is added stress as a struggle continues to admit women to the graduate class and the academic professions on equal terms with men. The three surveys enable me to describe these interrelated movements in the academic way of life and to offer empirically grounded explanation of the special case of Britain.

FROM ÉLITE TO MASS

Mass higher education still strikes the British academic ear as a self-contradictory absurdity. On his retirement as chief executive of the Universities Funding Commission, and addressing a conference on 'Quality in Higher Education' organized by the Birmingham Polytechnic jointly with Birmingham University in January 1991, Sir Peter Swinnerton-Dyer asserted that no country had successfully solved the problem of instituting a high-quality system of mass higher education. I questioned the generalization by pointing, for example, to contemporary California (Halsey 1990). He saw that particular American state only as a possible exception to the rule that contemporary governments show no willingness to provide the funds necessary to an adequate conception of quality as we have traditionally known it.

Expansion had its Victorian champions, but only in the context of tiny numbers; and Bruce Truscot, for all that he wrote from inter-war Liverpool, stayed firmly in the élitist tradition, while Flexner visited Europe from America only to endorse it. A fully developed description of the expansionist idea of a university came eventually as an import in 1963 from Clark Kerr, the then President of the University of California. What happened in Britain after the Second World War was that meritocratic impulses took a mildly expansionist turn in the hands of the traditional liberal establishment of Noel Annan's *Our Age*, and were stimulated by the experience of a socially eccentric wave of ex-service undergraduates. There was, to repeat, a failed thrust towards mass higher education.

Opinion shifted in the 1950s towards a more generous social conception of the educability of the population. None the less, at that time, it could be no more than support for growth from a highly restricted numerical base. For this reason the expansionist cause in Britain in the 1950s did not discriminate among those who thought of themselves as progressives. 'Pool of ability' conservatism required more skill in debate than its proponents could muster against those who chose irreverently to point to the continuing inequalities of educational opportunity in schools and the fact of a 5 per cent entry to universities. The Robbins programme was tacitly on the agenda from Sir Walter Moberly's time as Chairman of the UGC after the Second World War, stridently demanded by some of us from the mid-fifties, and coolly arithmetized in the Robbins back-room at the end of the decade.

Yet still it was all contained within élitist assumptions, and in this sense the Robbins Report was more a consolidation of Victorian expansion than the beginning of mass higher education. Looking back, in the light of American experience, what strikes me most is the timidity of the radicalisms of thirty years ago. Thus when John Fulton went to Sussex as the first architect of the brave world of new universities the optimal size was thought to be a student body of 3,000. No native analyst had dared to conceive of a university umbrella over all forms of post-secondary education. And even as late as 1963, when Clark Kerr published his *Uses of the University*, the British reaction, even among progressives, was as towards some tale from the lunar regions, more irrelevant than either shocking or amiable.

According to Kerr's account, the University of California

had operating expenditures from all sources of nearly half a billion dollars, with almost another hundred million for construction; a total employment of over 40,000 people . . . ; operations in over a hundred locations, . . . and projects abroad involving more than fifty countries; nearly 10,000 courses in its catalogue; some form of contact with nearly every industry, nearly every level of government, nearly every person in its region. Vast amounts of expensive equipment were serviced and maintained. Over 4,000 babies were born in its hospitals. It is the world's largest purveyor of white mice. It will soon have the world's largest primate colony. It will soon also have 100,000 students—30,000 of them at the graduate level; yet much less than one-third of its expenditures are directly related to teaching. It already has nearly 200,000 students in extension courses—including one out of every three lawyers and one out of every six doctors in the state. (Kerr 1963).

NEW UNIVERSITIES

Of course, there can be no return to Kerr's Berkeley of 1960 and far less to Humbolt's Berlin or Newman's Oxford. But it is now more than a quarter of a century since David Daiches edited *The Idea of a*

New University: An Experiment in Sussex (Daiches 1964). The following two decades confirmed both the success of the subtitle and the impossibility of the title. Once the European medieval universities were established there could be only two directions of newness in the idea of a university: one with respect to who should enter, the other with respect to what he or she should learn. On this view the seven new English universities of the 1960s were never new. They accepted established definitions of the conditions for entry and they chose curricula and a balance of learning between research and teaching from within the practices current in the existing western universities.

On the same view, a history of newness in ideas of the university in England would have three main chapters. The first one would be devoted to the incorporation of science and therefore concentrated on the end of the nineteenth century with its 'redbrick' monuments in London, Manchester, Birmingham, and Leeds and its reform of the hitherto arts and Anglican Oxford and Cambridge. The second would be devoted to that single and singular innovation of the twentieth century, the Open University. The third would tell the story of the polytechnics as a confused attempt to offer opportunities to new students in subjects held to be both relevant to advanced industrial society and also amenable to governmental influence. Thus the first chapter would refer to new learning, the second to a new vision of who might learn, and the third to both. In American perspective such a commentator as Martin Trow would probably add a fourth, to tackle the question of which among all the groups and institutions in society a polytechnic or university is trying to serve. It was the nationalization of funding which undermined the old redbrick and technical college concern for local industrial needs. New stringencies and devolutions may well in future make possible a wider variety of 'missions' for particular institutions of higher education.

Meanwhile to enter caveats against misinterpreting the significance of the new universities is in no way to belittle them. If the idea of higher learning in terms of which they were conceived was not new, their organizational history was certainly to be contrasted with that of their redbrick predecessors in the earlier expansion from the end of the nineteenth century which incorporated science, provided an education for the sons of the provincial bourgeoisie and the expanding 'new' professions of a maturing industrial society. In the earlier years of the twentieth century the redbrick universities, together with the dependencies of that large administrative and examining body which was London University, limped along from year to year in perennial anxiety about student admissions, fitful private philanthropy towards halls of residence, and minuscule state support of research and library facilities. In Manchester in the 1930s there was anxious analysis of the reasons for declining admissions. It was not until the 1980s that the universities had to face again the characteristic inter-war outlook of an uncertain future without firm prospect of expansion.

The perspective from Brighton Pier in 1961 was of an unquestioned expansionist horizon. In that year fifty students arrived to join a handful of founding dons, and by the end of the decade the senior common room could boast over 500 denizens and thus a membership within a decade which a redbrick university or 'provincial' university college had taken half a century to attain. By all the standards of previous experience the new universities moved with astonishing rapidity. They carried an optimistic atmosphere of higher education, modern and triumphant. They were youthful, democratic, and eager to demonstrate high capacity for teaching and research. They depended on their sister universities to supply new professors and old skills, but soon they would repay the debt with interest through a flow of able and productive graduates. The disaster of the 1968 events, which came close to destroying the University of Essex, was fortuitous rather than germane to the conception of the new universities.

As an idea, however, they were essentially stationary. Nor is this necessarily to condemn them. It is hard to imagine how they could have fundamentally changed the definition of the professor, the student, or the curriculum. The prevailing nostrum was that higher education was tertiary: it meant the successfully selected boy or girl from secondary education going on to claim the rights and privileges of an extended schooling on the same terms as those enjoyed by previous generations. Given that the 'output' of attested claimants had been rising and given the post-war birth-rate bulge, new universities in the trivial sense were simply an alternative to the expansion of the ancient and modern institutions inherited from the nineteenth century. Moreover, given the source of educational inspiration which drew so heavily for its vice-chancellors on people like Fulton (Sussex), Sloman (Essex), and James (York), who were products of Oxford and Cambridge and who had been deeply impressed by the merits of Oxford Greats or Modern Greats, it was natural that their major curricular inclination was to move from the inflexibilities of the single-subject Honours degree associated with redbrick towards the older organization of multi-subject Schools in which they had themselves been nurtured at Oxford and Cambridge.

Such was the grip of the ancient over the modern in all realizations of the idea of the university in England. It does not matter. They all turned on a convergence course in the next ten years. To walk through the campus at Warwick or Lancaster in 1990 was to experience the same international airport impressions that were to be found at Leicester or Exeter, or even at Birmingham if one turned one's gaze from the Aston Webb buildings across the extended campus in the Calthorpe estate, and to encounter a shared sense of governmental lack of sympathy, dearth of new academic recruits, and attenuation of resources for teaching and research. The achievement of the new universities had been to demonstrate the continued vitality of Victorian ideas and in the process to make the label they received in the 1960s meaningless.

THE OLD AND THE NEW

What, then, is the fate of the British academics and their institutions of higher education? No great expectations can be justified. But there is one essential continuity. All societies have arrangements for making, storing, and retrieving intellectual products. Since to be human is to live by culture there is always teaching and hence the possibility of 'men of knowledge'. Where there are specialized virtuosi of the more highly skilled and prized elements of a culture we have the prototype of the academic in his or her guise as sage or shaman, literatus or expert. The university is one among many possible arrangements for his or her incorporation. In the most general terms the university is the realization of a single idea—the idea of a social institution to ensure the continuity of intellectual work. But thought is incorporated into all social institutions: the family, the workplace, the church, the town hall are also bearers of intellectual continuity. Hence the university is in principle substitutable. It has a monopoly of nothing. The debate as to its proper form and function therefore turns on the changing social context of intellectual life and the components of that life which are most appropriately nurtured and maintained in a university rather than in some other form of social organization. In other words, the debate has been not so much about the quintessential idea of a university as about the relations between the shape and purpose of intellectual activity.

If, then, the debate took a new turn among the Victorians it was a reflection of contextual change in the intellectual dimensions of social life. The European university was born in medieval Christendom. But the age of renaissance and enlightenment was an age in which intellectual discovery became the agent of social change and therefore gave rise to the possibility of new 'men of knowledge'. Such men established the intellectual bases of industrial and 'modernized' society. They slowly and eventually found their place in the university but had little prominence as academics *per se*. They laboured to create new knowledge in the natural sciences and, later, to apply natural and social science to livelihood, leisure, and government. It fell to the Victorians to reform their idea of a university in the light of a changing social context. Newman stood, even at that late stage, as the champion of the older 'men of knowledge', while a succession of modernists ending with Clark Kerr insisted on tipping the balance of the idea towards the claims of the 'people of new knowledge'.

Thus a developing intellectual culture engendered a struggle between alternative emphases in cultural transmission, between the preservation and the creation of knowledge. But it is not, and never has been, only a question of what is to be sought and taught. The other great question in the idea of a university has been that of who should learn. The key to this second dimension may be found in Durkheim's remark that 'to find an absolutely homogeneous and egalitarian education it will be necessary to go back to prehistoric societies in the structure of which there is no differentiation'. In other words, the existence of higher learning presupposes a degree of complexity in the division of labour and a level of economic and political development that affords the possibility of 'idleness' for a scholarly class. Consequently universities have always played a role in social stratification, controlling access to highly valued cultural elements, differentiating the capacity of individuals to enter a hierarchy of labour markets, and therefore being intrinsically inegalitarian institutions. Beginning with Mark Pattison among the Victorians, there has been a continuous expansion in the definition of the potentially educable and, in consequence, an unfinished debate as to the place of the university in a system of higher education based on populist rather than élitist presuppositions.

This latter aspect of the debate has dominated discussions since the Second World War. Pressure to move along the path from élitist through mass to universal higher education has by no means spent its strength, though its momentum faltered when the post-war period ended in Britain and Europe. After the 1980s the nightmare of an educationally polarized society has become more vivid. It must be dispersed if the social order is to remain viable. Western industrial society did not break under the weight of the polarization of ownership of material capital. It was saved in part by the widening of educational opportunity. High-technology or post-capitalist society now threatens a new polarization in the ownership of cultural capital. Again education cannot be the sole antidote: but a widely inclusive educational policy seems more than ever necessary to ensure an integrated society. The question then arises of the position of the university in a vast system of higher education which maintains and extends an intellectually powerful culture and is the main agent of occupational and social placement of individuals in each new generation. It is in this sense a purely organizational question, a problem of setting 'the key profession' of academics in the context of universal education. The traditional and familiar face of the university could vanish under the manifold forms of a learning society. But the essential idea of a university will remain and find new expressions, probably with new structures, wherever civilization exists.

PART I
BEFORE ROBBINS

2

IDEAS OF THE UNIVERSITY

THE modern university, and indeed the polytechnic, began with the Victorians. I have mentioned Weber and Veblen, who published highly relevant essays in 1918. But further back, in 1873, there appeared two views of educational expansion, the one Catholic and clerical, the other Protestant and secular, by John Henry Newman on *The Idea of a University* and Alfred Marshall on 'The Future of the Working Classes' (A. Marshall 1925).

Calendar dates, of course, give false clarity to the ebb and flow of ideas; otherwise, in these two discourses we might identify 1873 as the end of the ecclesiastical and the beginning of the lay conception of education. A truer chronology would note that Marshall stood on the shoulders of John Stuart Mill, modernizing the chapter from the latter's *Principles of Economics* on 'The Futurity of the Labouring Classes'. Newman began his work in 1851, published the first half in 1853 as *Discourses on University Education*, a second volume five years later entitled *Lectures and Essays on University Subjects*, and a combined and revised edition of both in 1873 (Newman 1853–73). Indeed, so slow was the tide on his own view that he saw the office which occasioned the *Discourses*—his Rectorship of the Catholic University of Ireland—as resting on the millenial authority established by St Peter.

Our concern at this point is with the Cardinal, not the Professor. Yet it is right first to couple them, for they both experienced and interpreted the evolving liberalism of nineteenth-century thought—the Oxford divine as traditionalist critic, the Cambridge economist as progressive champion. To point only to their differences would be to distract attention from their common inheritance. Thus Marshall's biblical allusions are no less intrusive than Newman's, and Newman's claim for educational opportunity on behalf of Irish Catholics was not fundamentally different from Marshall's advocacy of the educational cause of the English working class. Moreover, it could have been Marshall just as plausibly as in fact it was Newman who wrote:

The view taken of the university in these discourses is the following: that it is a place of *teaching* universal *knowledge*. This implies that its object is, on the one hand, intellectual, not moral; and on the other, that it is the diffusion and extension of knowledge rather than the advancement. If its object were scientific and philosophical discovery, I do not see why universities should have students; if religious training, I do not see how it can be the seat of literature and science. (Newman 1959)

Newman's view of a place for teaching universal knowledge, in other words, was in no way original. Indeed, it was a consensual commonplace. The reason why the term university had originally come into medieval usage is not known. (In Roman law it meant a corporation.) But Newman offered no new definition on behalf of Catholicism. Samuel Johnson in the previous century had entered the university in his Dictionary as 'a school where all arts and faculties are taught'. Even the emphasis on teaching would have commended itself to Marshall, to Cambridge, and to colleges throughout the English and American territories where the German challenge on behalf of research and discovery had as yet made no serious impact.

The crucial difference, however, may be put in a short over-statement. Marshall succeeded and Newman failed to persuade their successors. Marshall's faith in education to bring rising wealth, cultural progress, and narrowing income differentials has since provided the orthodoxy of educational reform for more than a century. His adroit marriage of high-mindedness to material prosperity through educational expansion encouraged state patronage of schools and universities beyond all Victorian dreams. That, *ambulando*, his theory has falsified itself has yet to become fully appreciated. No matter that the original text has gone unread: Robbins rewrote it and more. No matter that the utility of the educational programme is more revered than its egalitarianism: the march towards universal higher education continues and its standard-bearers are Marshallian.

Newman's failure was that he addressed himself not to the abstractions of the *universitas* but to its practicalities. Teaching universal knowledge—'such is a university in its *essence*, and independently of its relation to the Church. But, practically speaking, it cannot fulfil its object duly, such as I have described it, without the Church's assistance; or, to use the theological term, the

Church is necessary for its integrity. Not that its main characters are changed by this incorporation: it still has the office of intellectual education; but the Church steadies it in the performance of that office' (Newman 1959: 7).

There are two arguments here, neither of which have convinced or been resolved by the modern university. The first is an inference from the idea of universal knowledge. If theology is knowledge and the university is what it claims to be, then it must have chairs of theology. Newman elaborates this case at length and with passion, particularly against the pretensions and predications of the first Oxford professor of economics, who, in his introductory lectures, asserted that in the course of a few years political economy would 'rank in public estimation among the first of *moral* sciences in interest and in utility'. Newman's reply was that 'if theology is not allowed to occupy its own territory, adjacent sciences, nay, sciences which are quite foreign to theology, will take possession of it . . . It is a mere unwarranted assumption if . . . the political economist [says] "easy circumstances make man virtuous". These are enunciations, not of science, but of private judgement; and it is a private judgement that infects every science which it touches with a hostility to theology, a hostility which properly attaches to no science in itself whatever' (Newman 1959: 125).

The first argument has had no theoretical solution. In practice it has been resolved by compromise and by that most idle of unintellectual means which expansion affords to institutions—simple neglect. But the second practical thesis advanced by Newman is less easily set aside. It is the problem of how to justify the power and privilege required for the exercise of the academic role. Newman put forward his view in the context of the foundation of a new Catholic university. In its more general form it is the question of the authority and organized purpose which makes a university possible. The liberal tradition has appealed directly to the values of reason and tolerance. Thus, for example, the University of Chicago rests its viability as an institution—i.e. as something more than an aggregate of researchers and teachers—on adherence to these values. It follows that all appointees should possess the requisite 'academic citizenship'. 'Appointive committees . . . must expect that those whom they appoint will enjoy the protection of academic freedom and that they will also be the guardians of that freedom.' These are noble and necessary commitments. But what they lack and what Newman offered is a moral authority on which to base them.

Newman was the Vice-Chancellor of a new Victorian university, who took his authority from the Church. His successors to the vice-chancellorships of the present century are creatures of the State. It is highly improbable that we can return to the one, but no less hazardous to expect that we shall always be sustained by the other.

A legend survives from 1845 that had he not missed the coach from Oxford to Birmingham, Mark Pattison would have accompanied John Henry Newman to Rome. Instead he stayed, first as perhaps the most perfect exemplar of that new model of the inspired working tutor which has served ever since as an alternative to the professional and professorial hierarchy in the English idea of a university, and second to produce an agenda for university reform which embodied a radically different alternative to both the tutorial model and to the purpose of higher education propounded by Newman. His was the prototype of the research university with open entry and exit, and his the most direct English translation of the German idea of a university—translated that is by direct experience and not as imported later to the provincial redbrick universities via Scottish and American example.

Pattison's journey from the first to the second of these two major Victorian positions, which in mutual adaptation evolved as the bases of the distinctive English idea of a university, at least until the Robbins Report, was, on one view, personally idiosyncratic.[1] Pattison can hardly be said to have travelled hopefully. He was privately obsessed with the fear of hereditary insanity. His academic career was a process of embittered frustration, including failure to be elected Rector of Lincoln in 1851 under circumstances and in relation to persons vastly more implausible than those invented by C. P. Snow in *The Masters*. If he finally arrived at the Lincoln Rector's Lodge in 1861 it was to enter a marriage in which love was denied to him by Emilia Strong (who transferred herself to Sir Charles Dilke as soon as Pattison was dead), to look out on an Oxford he thought made worse by the reforms he had advocated to the 1850 Commission, to see his second advocacy rejected by the Salisbury Commission of 1877, and to die in 1881 before publishing the major work on which he had spent most of his life.

[1] The story is well told in John Sparrow's Clark lectures at Cambridge in 1965 (Sparrow 1967) and in V. H. H. Green's *Oxford Common Room*, (1957) which comprises a convincing account of Pattison's college, Lincoln.

Though Pattison wrote one of his last letters to Newman as 'your affectionate son and pupil', the two men were antithetical figures. Pattison's arid pilgrimage had carried him steadily further, first from Canterbury, then from Rome, and finally to a religious scepticism beyond Christianity. Oddly to us, but characteristic of the Victorian definition of appropriate locations and 'media', his *Suggestions on Academical Organisation* (1868) were adumbrated in sermons delivered from the pulpit of the University Church earlier in the 1860s. As John Sparrow puts it, 'he did not advertise his religious scepticism or allow it to affect his everyday life. To renounce Holy Orders would have been ridiculous; besides, it would have meant giving up his position and its emoluments—a crippling sacrifice that would have served no useful purpose. So he continued to the end of his days to officiate, and to administer the Sacrament, in the college chapel' (Sparrow 1967: 57).

Yet it would be utterly misleading to suggest that the Victorian debate was pivoted on the alternative conceptions of two personalities. There were other voices—Matthew Arnold and Benjamin Jowett at Oxford; Sedgwick and Seeley, who have been described as equivalent figures at Cambridge by Sheldon Rothblatt (1968); John Stuart Mill in London; and, indeed, a sizeable proportion of the intellectual aristocracy of the day. Nor was the debate confined to a choice between a teaching and a research conception of the university. No serious contributor, then or now, would settle for either end of this crude dichotomy. It was never, in other words, a simple option between either the don as transmitter of 'universal knowledge' or the professor as creator of new knowledge. The idea of a university has other dimensions and its modernization was seen as a multi-faceted problem of political, religious, and economic as well as educational reform.

The essence of Pattison's ideas was to create conditions for 'the close action of the teacher on the pupil', with its accompanying 'beneficial reaction of the young on the ageing man' resulting in a mutual search for 'mental culture'. He thus implied criteria for the recruitment of dons and students and for the content of higher education which fused what to us now appear as elements from conservative and radical thought. The apparent conservatism was expressed in his evidence to the 1850 Commission as a plea for the college against the professorial system: 'the perfect idea of the Collegiate system proposed to take up the student from quite tender years, and conduct him through his life till death. A college was not divided into tutors and pupils but . . . all were students alike, only differing in being at different stages of their progress . . . The seniors were at once the instructors and example of the juniors, who shared the same food, simple life, narrow economy, looking forward themselves to no other life' (Rothblatt 1968: 194). The apparently radical element could scarcely have a more modern ring. He wanted to do away with both entrance requirements and examinations.

But these are apparent rather than real truths about Pattison's ideal for the organization of higher learning. In fact he held a general view which is radical in a timeless sense. This is that the university ought to be a sanctuary reserved only for those who are so single-minded in their resolve to know the world and themselves to the utmost limit of available knowledge and their capacity to master it that they are willing to give up all the material rewards that otherwise accrue to such a sustained effort of intellectual labour.

In the 1840s this view necessarily expressed itself in antipathy to old Tory Oxford, with its largely exclusive recruitment from the aristocracy and the gentry whose sons had little inclination or encouragement to scholarship, to the corrupted traditions of almost all the colleges with their irresponsible wealth, donnish hierarchy, neglect of the university and of science, and their inefficient teaching. Above all, it meant condemnation of the system of closed fellowships.

By the 1870s Oxford had been transformed by the efforts of the liberal dons among whom Pattison had stood before the 1850 Commission. Honours degrees and strict examinations were becoming central to the undergraduate career. Religious tests were abolished. Science had begun to flourish. There were intercollegiate lectures. The university was governed by a democracy of dons and, most important, fellowships were awarded in open competition on merit. Yet Pattison came to see it all with a jaundiced eye as a system of over-tutoring both the apt and the inept for the degree stakes rather than as a realization of the 'close action of teacher on pupil' for which he had hoped. He retained the original conception but its application was redirected. Rothblatt suggests that his abandonment of the college ideal was connected with 'the improbable circumstances that deprived him of the headship of Lincoln' (Rothblatt 1968: 194). Certainly in the twenty-five years between the two Commissions, he switched his allegiance from college to university, from tutor to professor, from education to learning. The disastrous election of 1851 perhaps precipitated the process. He resigned his college tutorship, took no part in university administration, and spent much time abroad. His wanderings took him to Germany in the 1850s and there he gained crucial experience of a type of university life which was totally different from that of Oxford. An organized professoriate occupied the frontiers of the whole range of knowledge, pushing back its boundaries and instructing willing students through seminars and lectures. The ex-tutor was converted from his Oxford collegiate to a German university ideal.

In consequence, his submission to the Salisbury Commission included a recommendation which might have come from an Oxford student 'sit-in' in the late 1960s—the abolition of the colleges and their fellowships. The corporations were to be dissolved and their endowments transferred to the University. Nine colleges were to become the centres of the nine faculties. The rest were to be halls of residence and, no doubt, the modern radicals could have had one for a central student union. Entrance examinations were to be abolished. The cost of an Oxford education was to be nominal and no one would be forced to take degree examinations. Pattison thus qualified himself for rediscovery as a prophet for the student radicals of the 1970s. Except perhaps that his underlying motive was not to create a power base for social revolution, though he held uncompromising contempt for Oxford and Cambridge as finishing-schools for the upper classes. His passion was to make over the university not to youth, nor to professional training, nor to the social life of the high-born or highly connected, but to those who were consumed with the purest love of learning.

Newman and Pattison were illustrious figures who failed to make either the Catholic University of Ireland or Lincoln College amount to much. Jowett, on the other hand, was the embodiment of Victorian success and Balliol was the leading university institution of Victorian England. There had been worthy predecessors in the Mastership—Parsons (1798–1819) and 'the Old Master' Jenkyns (1813–1854)—but by the time Jowett had reigned for the last quarter of the nineteenth century the college was virtually identified with his name.

Balliol came into prominence with the decline of Oriel which had dominated the Oxford scene after the Napoleonic wars. Newman was an Oriel tutor in the 1820s and Pattison entered as an undergraduate in 1832. Jowett entered Balliol in 1835, was elected a Fellow while still an undergraduate, became one of the three Balliol tutors when he was 25, and stayed there almost to the end of the century, as Regius Professor of Greek from 1855, as Master from 1870, and as Vice-Chancellor of the University from 1882 to 1886. He died in 1893 at the age of 76.

Balliol has never lost the fame which Jowett consolidated for it. Only the direction changed, the college 'becoming concerned for the cure of a sick society rather than the improvement of a healthy social order' (Faber 1957: 32). This apt phrase is Geoffrey Faber's and he was presumably referring to the generation to which Archbishop Temple and R. H. Tawney belonged. Jowett's young men passed and continued to pass with 'effortless superiority' into *Who's Who*. They attained high imperial office at home and abroad, wrested pride of place in the All Souls prize fellowship examinations from Christ Church, colonized other colleges, and occupied the heights of the educational establishment throughout Victorian, Edwardian, and Elizabethan expansion. Charles Morris, for example, was the inter-war doyen of the Vice-Chancellors who carried Balliol to Leeds. John Fulton founded 'Balliol by the Sea' in Sussex.

For an appraisal of Jowett's life the obvious comparison is with Pattison. Nor is comparison here all contrast. They were contemporaries. Both were Oxford classical scholars, both exemplary tutors, both influenced by German experience (Jowett was the first Englishman to read and understand the work of Hegel). Moreover, both were first rejected and later elected to be head of their colleges, and the parallel runs even further here in that both first reacted to electoral disappointment—Pattison in 1851 and Jowett three years later—by withdrawal from the life of their senior common rooms.

Subsequently, however, their lives diverged. Jowett went on with his tutorial devotion to gain reputation and influence among the highest levels of British society through an ascendancy over the younger men and an indefatigable involvement in their graduate careers. His steady, triumphant march through Victoria's monarchy seems somehow, and faithfully, to reflect the confident progress of an imperial nation. Moreover, his personal life was largely free of the miseries endured by Pattison. He remained faithful to that peculiar brand of stern evangelical childhood which, in nineteenth-century England, fitted men for bachelorhood and dedication to work. Unlike Pattison, he entered on no disastrous marriage and, though he too acquired enemies, he developed a genius for friendship, including a platonic and protracted love for Florence Nightingale, which has practically disappeared from middle-class life in our own day.

Post-Freudians have learned to dismiss this type of character as 'homosexual', and to debunk its expression in sustained personal intimacy without carnality as 'sublimation'. Yet it is open to doubt whether this peculiar style of life and personality has ever been fully appreciated in its significance for the idea of a university which made the accomplishments of Oxford and Cambridge in the second half of the nineteenth century such a puzzle to foreign observers. The sexual institutions of Victorian Oxford gave firm if unplanned support to the tutorial idea of a university for recruits to the imperial ruling class. For example, the 'reading party', which, if he did not invent, Jowett developed to the highest level of personal comradeship in learning, was a typical manifestation of the potentiality of 'libidinal energy' to support a distinctive vision of university purposes. The abolition of the celibacy rule signalled the slow death of tutorial relations which set out not merely to instruct the mind but to fashion the character of the undergraduate and to absorb him into a lifelong nostalgia for his college years and a loyal membership of the educated élite. Today the tutor who carries on that tradition is a demographic and psychological oddity, weakly supported by his collegiate traditions and strongly rejected by the heterosexual compulsions of both his colleagues and his students. If Balliol still has devoted tutors it is despite the fact that the spouses and children of North Oxford continually call them away from collegiate commensality. Not so for Jowett. His marriage was to his college. He was undisputed master in his own house and the union spawned half a century and more of Britain's most glitteringly successful children.

As with sex, so too with the institutions of authority. There were multiple reasons in the anthropology and politics of the day which made Jowett a nationalist in an assuredly hierarchical nation. From this point of view the Church of England appears as another social foundation for the English idea of a university. It gave an ideological form to the education of an élite as well as an occupational destination for large, if decreasing, numbers of Oxford and Cambridge graduates. Newman, Pattison, and Jowett, it must be remembered, were all in Orders, and theology was Jowett's primary intellectual concern. The education of under-graduates, both its content and the social organization of its experience, had to be justified in relation to Church doctrine and Church authority.

Jowett never challenged that authority. He remained a believer all his life, though he moved from the characteristically evangelical outlook of his youthful contemporaries to a 'liberalism' which took him on a sharply different course from that of Newman and which, at least for his successors, eventually permitted reason to under-mine faith. Today it would be inconceivable for the Head of a House in Oxford or Cambridge to emulate Jowett's autocratic self-confidence without revolution in both the senior and junior common rooms. The modern authority of science and reason has to take more democratic and anarchical form.

It was Jowett's liberalism, expressed in his contribution to *Essays and Reviews* (1860), that constituted the one major blunder of his career. His views on the interpretation of scripture were ahead of his time. Today those few who could bring themselves to be concerned at all over that old doctrinal conflict would, in almost every case, support him. The details are a minor episode in the history of the advancement of scientific authority. But for Jowett it was more a failure to judge the temper of Church authority, and he never afterwards repeated the error. What is interesting for us about the affair is the light it sheds on the utterly different notions of authority which were still current in Victorian Oxford. In 1863 the Vice-Chancellor's Court issued a 'monition' which 'com-manded the Yeoman Bedell of Law to cite the Rev. Benjamin Jowett to appear before our Vice-Chancellor . . . concerning the reformation and correction of his manners and excesses, but more especially for infringing the Statutes and privileges of the University by having published . . . certain erroneous and strange doctrines . . . contrary to and inconsistent with the doctrines of the Church of England . . . ' (Faber 1957: 268).

Admittedly, *The Times* referred to the Vice-Chancellor's jurisdic-tion as 'a rusty engine of intolerance' (Faber 1957: 269) and Jowett was not in the end forced to appear. But what the episode underlines for our understanding of the idea of a university is that scientific authority is a precondition of the research university. Jowett stands as the last champion of an earlier idea, first because of the particular social context of Victorian Oxford and second because for him not science but the Church and the imperial hierarchy were the integrated sources of his theory of higher education.

But what was the fate of democratic access to higher education in all this? Seventy years ago Albert Manbridge described 'a general labourer, and an ardent socialist, (who) could not restrain his tears as, standing upon New College Tower, he gazed on the incomparable beauty of Oxford. "I want my comrades to see this", he said; he really meant that, in season and out of season, he would strive with all his power to make the dingy, gloomy crowded town in which he lived as near to the ideal of beauty as ever it was in his power to do' (Mansbridge 1923: 185). In 1973 a student minority of a minority spoke with a different proletarian voice: having been repulsed by a collection of elderly clerks from an attempt to break and enter the offices of the Indian Institute in Oxford, they described their unwilling hosts as 'hired thugs'.

Two generations separated two opposing views of Oxford, but both claimed to represent working-class interests. This can be put in the context of the evolving conception of a university in which I have described Pattison and Jowett as the radical luminaries of Victorian higher education, though some modern radicals would dismiss this harking back to them, and even more to Newman, as an antiquarian and suspect salutation of élitists.

Thus the French sociologist Alan Touraine, after the May Events, sketched a view of the university as a polarized factory of intellectual production, owned, managed, and controlled in the interests of the ruling class. He saw the modern campus, at Nanterre or Santa Barbara, as Marx saw the industrial town in the nineteenth century with its central factory and its dormitory annexe for the proletariat. Deans and professors were the managers of the new industrial-academic knowledge factories, halls of residence the equivalent of the dormitory annexe, and the products were technology and technologists for the 'military-industrial complex' and the mass media (defined to include the compulsory school as well as all the other organs of press, television, and radio which together make up the formidable modern means of propaganda). Universities maintained a modernized system of class exploitation by their socially selective 'intake' and their 'output' of men and knowledge for the service of the status quo. They reflected the structure of the national and international society in their internal regimes of 'repressive tolerance' and cosmopolitan culture. Student revolutionaries believed that the values of the ruling class per-meated down from the top and determined what was to be considered academically permissible in teaching and research. Pattison's or Jowett's idea of a university here finds expression only as a qualification to the description of an institution fundamentally dominated by class interests.

What happened to the idea of a university between 1868 and 1968 or between New College Tower and the Indian Institute? From a study of the century before 'student power', Martin Trow and I distinguished four general views of the university from the denizens of the senior common room. On one dimension academic men and women inclined either towards élitist or towards expansionist views of the functions of the university in society. On a second dimension they were inclined to stress either the function of preserving and transmitting knowledge to the students under their care or the task which was given such powerful impetus in the nineteenth century by the German universities—the search for new knowledge. They tended, in other words, to occupy one of four positions in their conception of the university: they were élitist teachers, élitist researchers, expansionist teachers, or expansionist researchers.

There can be no doubt that Newman, Pattison, and Jowett were élitist teachers. Admittedly, both Pattison and Jowett had expan-sionist sympathies and both used the expression 'unnational' to describe the Oxford of their day and to refer to its religious, sexual, and class exclusiveness. But the measure of their expansionism has been put into context by John Sparrow, who points out that Pattison's 'ideal of a national university . . . ' as . . . 'co-extensive with the nation' meant in practice that he wished to 'draft in five hundred, say three hundred, students (additional) from a class whose education hitherto terminated with the national school, or the commercial academy' (Sparrow 1967: 38), whereas the number of 'additional students' planned to be 'drafted' in the twenty years after Robbins was 350,000.

The expansionist teacher idea of the university none the less has Victorian origins. The reference here is not so much to the London University, Josiah Mason College in Birmingham, or Owens College in Manchester, which were institutions created by and for the sons of a rising bourgeoisie, but to the university extension movement founded by the Cambridge professor James Stewart in 1873, which was a primary influence in the emergence of university colleges like those of Nottingham and Sheffield.

What, in retrospect, is so striking about the expansionist-teacher view is the failure of the national labour colleges (or any equivalent of the German *proletkult*) to offer a successful alternative conception of adult education to working men. The WEA was the monument to working-class acceptance of the traditional idea of the university, and Albert Mansbridge was its chronicler.

Mansbridge published his *The Older Universities of England* in 1923. He saw Oxford and Cambridge as venerable institutions slowly adapting, as would also the institutions of government and industry, to a democratic age. Belief in the power of democratic socialism to bring about peaceful revolution is nowhere more faithfully or more hopefully expressed. He saw the signs in the admission of women and the abolition of Greek as a condition of matriculation. Both innovations, in his judgement, had to be submitted to the test of reinforcing in the ancient universities 'the purity and power of their mind and spirit'. His concern was not to abolish classical education but to extend it. 'The English working man', he wrote, 'is interested in ancient Greece and Rome; left to himself he is attracted by it as by few other things' (Mansbridge 1923: 123). He looked forward not to changes in the definition of what ought to be taught but only to an extension of the definition of to whom it should be taught. 'The whole idea of university education is democratic, in the sense that anyone who has the capacity and the good will, no matter what his previous experience has been, or what his father was before him—shall have full free opportunity to develop his mental faculties. It is clear that the policy of providing university education for working men and women must not be taken as omitting others in the community' (Mansbridge 1923: 177). He then went on to argue that working men themselves wished ardently not to change Oxford but only to join it. And he cited the experience of the WEA (which began in 1903 as an 'association to promote the higher education of working men') and especially of the university tutorial class movement exemplified in Rochdale under R. H. Tawney's tutorship.

'The working man', Mansbridge tells us, 'fresh from his industrial city, was by no means a mere worshipper at the shrine of Oxford or Cambridge; he saw in them the promise of a fuller life which it was his duty to achieve for his comrades of the mine or factory . . . There was never any bitterness in their minds. To look forward with generous enthusiasm to the finer life to be is characteristic of the thoughtful English workman' (Mansbridge 1923: 185–6).

These views serve to remind us of a significant element in the social thought of our fathers and grandfathers. Not, of course, a majority voice, but still an authentic one which once informed the attitude of the labour movement to the British universities, but which has apparently been lost in the thought of the Labour Party since Robbins. A modern aspirant to the post of Secretary of State for Education is unlikely to have read either Mansbridge or the 'student power' literature. The older working-class idealism has no spokesman in a dominantly graduate House of Commons. But the modern proletarian 'realism' has its malign effects among both Labour and Conservative politicians. The modern parliamentary Left seems to have a tacit and diluted feeling of hostility to the élitist and allegedly unresponsive universities. The modern Right seems to offer a mirror reflection—suspicion and resentment that the universities offer an easy sanctuary to revolutionaries and subversives. Between them a noble idea of rational radicalism above the clash of class interests still struggles for life.

ÉLITISM AND UNIVERSITY EXPANSION

Élitist teachers fashioned the Victorian idea of the university in England. Newman, Pattison, and Jowett propounded more or less worldly and more or less qualified versions of the view which, for all the revolutionary implications of the industrial society in which they lived, did not differ essentially from ancient and medieval traditions. Max Weber in Germany summarized these traditions as a cultivation of young men in the humanistic outlook and style of life of the dominant strata. Charisma apart, he distinguished between two types of social personality as the products of higher education—the *cultivated* man and the *expert*, and the British Victorians had certainly made much of the correlative curricular distinction between *education* and *training*. Behind these distinctions Weber had identified two corresponding forms of power—the *traditional* and the *rational*—and the twentieth-century history of universities may be understood as a struggle between drives to express these underlying forms of authority in the curriculum and organization of the university and its claims to enter its alumni into positions of occupational and social authority.

The sociology of education is essentially a study of these issues. Weber's formulation of them has the merit of neither ignoring nor accepting a mechanical subsumption of cultural and organizational conflict as epiphenomenal to class warfare. In this way he invites us to recognize that what a society defines as knowledge, how that knowledge shall be distributed, in what form, and by what method, are not simply educational questions.

Answers require an appraisal of the political character of society. At the same time, Weber's approach leaves open the possibility of an interactive and indeterminate relation between, on the one hand, education (which is the process whereby knowledge is defined, distributed, and transmitted) and, on the other hand, the power structure of society.

Forms of society in which authority is sanctioned by custom and tradition have varied widely not in their common characteristic of restricting higher education to élites but in the cultural character of élite formations. The commonality and the variations include the education of Chinese mandarins, the minority leisure class of citizens in ancient Greece or Rome, or the gentlemanly strata of eighteenth-century Europe. Thus the aim of the university might have been to turn out a socially distinctive type of knight or courtier as in the case of the Japanese samurai or an educational scribe or intellectual as in the case of a Buddhist priest or a Christian cleric, or it might be the amateur gentlemanly administrator as in Jowett's Balliol.

Systems of education for membership in a cultivated status group have usually been under religious control. This is true of the Christian, Islamic, and Judaic traditions and it was, of course, to the first and third of these that Newman largely owed his idea of the university. But religious control has not been universal in such systems. The Chinese literati and the Hellenic schools of philosophy were important exceptions. Laymen taught laymen in ancient China, and the Hellenic schools were completely secular. Pattison and Jowett, for all that they were in Anglican Orders, felt the pull of Greek tradition.

However, what none of these three English pedagogues ever squarely faced was what Weber saw as the fundamental struggle, in the adaptation of education to industrialism, between the cultivated man and the expert—a fight which he saw as determined by the 'irresistibly expanding bureaucratisation of all public and private relations of authority and by the ever-increasing importance of expert and specialised knowledge' (Weber, in Gerth and Mills 1947: 243).

Thus the outmoded character of the authors I have been discussing consists of their failure to appreciate the reformist strength of the research conception of the university in either its élitist or expansionist forms. Though without benefit of a systematic expositor, the voice of the élitist researcher has probably been the most effective force for change in the twentieth-century English universities, as has been that of the expansionist researcher in the state universities of America.

The research orientation, however, has had a qualitative rather than a quantitative impact. It fostered the single subject honours degree more as a definition of the undergraduate as a potential recruit to the academic succession than as a trainee specialist for the scientific professions. It fostered at the same time a conception of intimate tutorial relations which led the 'provincial' universities to assimilate more to Oxford and Cambridge than to the demands of the industrial centres in which they were located. Consequently, the ideology of the élitist teacher was never seriously challenged. Research institutes never flourished and graduate study, at least in the first sixty years of the century, was never more than a minor appendage to the dominant undergraduate organization of the universities. Writing in the late twenties, the American Abraham Flexner observed that the English were 'curiously averse to recognition of graduate students as a group. They are excessively conscientious teachers: "it is our first business to teach", one hears again and again. Between 1882 and 1928 Manchester conferred 6,473 Bachelor's degrees but only 74 Ph.D's' (Flexner 1930: 222).

Indeed, the concern with 'excellence' on the part of élitist researchers strongly reinforced traditional opposition to expansion of numbers. Sir Eric (later Lord) Ashby entitled his essay for the Carnegie Commission on Higher Education *Any Person, Any Study* (1970), thus characterizing the system of mass higher education in America by reference to Ezra Cornell, whose intention it had been to 'found an institution where any person could find instruction in any study'. This always was and remains the antithesis of the English idea of the university which Flexner, writing in All Souls, could only applaud. At a time when the American universities and colleges had been through an expansion which the British univers-ities were not to match until the late 1960s, he deplored 'a wild, uncontrolled, and uncritical expansion . . . the quacks emit publications that travesty research and make a noise that drowns out the still small voice to which America should be listening . . . '. And he thought of the ancient English universities as 'seats of higher learning incomparably superior to anything that has yet been created in America' (Flexner 1930: 233–4).

Moreover, the opinion that more means worse maintained itself and even renewed its vigour as the Robbins programme of expansion proceeded; Terence Miller devoted a column in THES (25 Jan. 1974) to demolishing what he believed to be the false vision of mass higher education—'a great many people will, one hopes, remain able to observe that most people, in any nation, are simply not capable of the intellectual effort to take in the stuff of higher education and would therefore be much better off without being dragooned into it.' Thus did the director of a polytechnic in the 1970s echo Flexner, who was telling us in 1930 that 'the English show no signs of being converted to the American theory that college or university education is indiscriminately good for anyone who can make his way through high school. Such is, quite clearly, not the case; hundred of youths, eighteen to twenty-two years of age, can be better employed than in attending a university; and the English, by increasing provision of technical and other schools, try to give this host—the majority—what they need and can assimilate' (Flexner 1930: 227). The expansion of higher education for the working class had thus remained a dream.

Though Pattison in his later years moved towards it, there was no systematic English apology for the research conception of the university. That had to wait for a Professor of Spanish at the University of Liverpool in the 1940s, who wrote under the pseudonym of Bruce Truscot. This was the voice of the dominant English tradition. The research idea of the university was, of course, of German origin and taken up at the turn of the century with enthusiasm by President Gilman at Johns Hopkins and with still more vigorous flair by William Rainey Harper at the University of Chicago.

It was in Chicago in the 1950s that I first learnt to understand this most un-English conception through appreciative acquaintance with that beleaguered academic square mile in which the probability on any given day of an exciting conversation was, and possibly still is, greater than in any other place that I have known. Not surprising, then, that the classic advocacy of this idea of the university should have been written at Chicago by that rare American genius Thorstein Veblen under the title *The Higher Learning in America*: and no less surprising that it was practically unknown in England, at least in the first half of the century. Even Bruce Truscot, when writing *Redbrick University* (Truscot 1943), appears to have been unaware of his distinguished predecessor.

Veblen was the kind of man that legends are made of. 'The last man in the world to have known everything' is one part of his reputation. He was born in 1857 in the obscurity of an immigrant Norwegian farming community in Wisconsin and died, also in obscurity, in 1929 in a cabin in California. In the meantime this alien, gangling, and unfashionable man migrated between several American universities (Hopkins, Yale, Minnesota, Chicago, Stanford, Missouri, and the New School for Social Research in New York). The, perhaps apocryphal, story is told that at one point the President of his university informed Veblen with magisterial reproach that 'the Regents and I are not satisfied, Professor, with your marital arrangements.' 'No, sir,' replied Veblen sadly, 'neither am I.'

Nor was Veblen satisfied, to quote the subtitle of his book, with 'the conduct of universities by business men', whose behaviour he was prone to describe, as Richard Hofstadter remarked, in terms usually reserved for moral delinquents. He saw the ideal milieu for scholarship and science, like the frenetically productive society it reflected, as threatened and corrupted by the predatory ethics of business salesmanship.

For Veblen the possibility of a university was rooted in universal human nature as 'the instinct of workmanship' and the impulse to 'Idle Curiosity'. These impulses, he held, gave rise to esoteric knowledge in all known civilizations and therefore to a custodial function for 'a select body of adepts or specialists—scientists, scholars, savants, clerks, priests, shamans, medicine men'. The particular organization of highly valued knowledge varies from one society to another but always makes up the central substance of the civilization in which it is found. In the modern West, social evolution, as he saw it, had brought empirical and scientific knowledge to the highest point of prestige as the ideal aim and method of scholars. 'For good or ill, civilised men have come to hold that this matter-of-fact knowledge of things is the only end in life that indubitably justifies itself' (Veblen 1918: 15).

Here was where Veblen found the basis and justification for the modern university. The single distinguishing function unique to the university was the pursuit of knowledge, not for profit nor indeed for any utilitarian purpose but simply to satisfy idle curiosity. The university of the future, he thought, made this the only unquestioned duty incumbent on the university. He recognized, of course, that the advancement of higher learning involved two lines of work, distinct but closely bound together—scientific enquiry and the instruction of students. But, he argued, 'the former of these is primary and indispensable' (Veblen 1918: 16). The work of teaching properly belonged in the university only in so far as it facilitated the pursuit of new knowledge in science and scholarship. It had an appropriate place only in so far as it trained each rising generation of scholars and scientists for the further pursuit of knowledge. Training for other purposes was necessarily of a different kind and was best done elsewhere.

The university man, for Veblen, was a student, not a schoolmaster. The secondary school, the professional school, the British polytechnic, the American liberal arts college, and indeed pretty well any American university would have been denied the title by his exacting test. Oxford and Cambridge would have been similarly disqualified, for, 'while the lower schools necessarily take over the surveillance of their pupils' everyday life, and exercise a large measure of authority and responsible interference in that behalf, the university assumes (or should assume) no responsibility for its students' fortunes in the moral, religious, pecuniary, domestic or hygienic respect' (Veblen 1918: 201). It was characteristic of his ironical style of thought that he went on to accord the larger and more serious responsibility for preparing citizens and producers, not to the university, but to the lower and professional schools. He was adamant that the university could not be charged 'with extraneous matters that are themselves of such grave consequences as this training for citizenship and practical affairs'. 'These', he argued, 'are too serious a range of duties to be taken care of as a side issue, by a seminary of learning the members of whose faculty, if they are fit for their own special work, are not men of affairs or adepts in worldly wisdom' (Veblen 1918: 21).

The origins of the medieval university in vocational training for ecclesiastical and courtly hierarchies he dismissed as irrelevant evolutionary stages in the evolution of barbarian civilizations. Technologists and medical men could only be corrupted by incorporation. Unless housed in separate establishments, doctors, lawyers, and engineers would be placed in a false position and unavoidably led to court 'a specious appearance of scholarship, and so to invest their technological discipline with a degree of pedantry and sophistication . . . '. 'Doubtless', he added, 'the pursuit of scholarly prestige is commonly successful, to the extent that it produces the desired conviction of awe in the vulgar, who do not know the difference; but all this make-believe scholarship, however successfully staged, is not what these schools are designed for . . . Nor is it what they can do best and most efficiently. It is the quest for knowledge that constitutes the main interest of the university. Utilitarian impulses and applications are alien to that purpose' (Veblen 1918: 31).

Veblen's vision was never realized. The American road was to lead to the 'multiversity'. Perhaps the Princeton Institute for Advanced Studies, post-Franks All Souls College, or the Center for the Study of Behavioural Sciences at Palo Alto were his monuments. But even at those illustrious institutions a visit from Veblen in his customary role as the sardonic cultural anthropologist would have detected the diversion of energies into 'habitual parochialism . . . and the meticulous manoeuvres of executives seeking each to enhance his own prestige' by men 'picked though they may be with a view to parochialism and blameless futility . . . ' and therefore unable 'to forgo their habitual preoccupation with petty intrigue and bombastic publicity' (Veblen 1918: 58). It was always a Utopian dream, naïve, for all the erudition of its author, in the beguiling belief that human organizations can ever be single-mindedly concentrated on a single function: and no less naïve in the unrealistic if flattering Rousseauesque conception that the instinctive virtues of men are perverted only by the institutions of society.

The Victorian and Edwardian legacy of ideas about the nature, purposes, and organization of a university emerged from the struggles of our forebears towards a radical reinterpretation of medieval tradition adequate to the needs of their new industrial society. The redbrick universities early and the polytechnics later in the twentieth century were their major achievements. In the process ecclesiastical was increasingly displaced by secular authority in academic life; and uneasy uncertainty persisted as to what might constitute an appropriate modern curriculum. The writers I have discussed debated the distinction between education and training and anticipated the crisis vulgarized by C. P. Snow in the 1950s as the problem of 'the two cultures'. They discussed these issues as either élitist or expansionist in their view of the place of the university in society and as inclining to emphasize either the teaching or research side of its internal life.

Unhappily, Victorian social inventiveness exhausted itself with the creation of the industrial provincial universities at the turn of the century, and the inter-war years, which gave us Abraham Flexner's commentary, were bleak. Political attention was directed elsewhere, towards economic depression at home and the rise of the new secular religions of communism and fascism abroad. The major current of intellectual thought seemed to bypass the universities, and neither Marxism nor Freudianism had its roots in academic institutions. Looking back, it appears that intellectual activity was heavily and quietly concentrated in the natural sciences, where a few creative men and women with inadequate resources were constructing a body of physical and technological knowledge that was soon to transform the world beyond even their own imagination. The redbrick universities thus went through a generation of unambitious consolidation, completely overshadowed by the 'élitist teaching' conception of the university which gave Oxford and Cambridge their magic and lustre and consigned the civic newcomers to a drab and placeless social obscurity.

It is against this background that Bruce Truscot's *Redbrick University* may be reread. He was an unconscious successor to Veblen. Thus,

The primary aim of the university must be search for knowledge—research as we call it today: not merely actual discovery, not merely even the attempt to discover, but the creation and cultivation of the spirit of discovery. Imagine a group of men, in any age, retiring from the life of the world, forming a society for the pursuit of truth, laying down and voluntarily embracing such discipline as is necessary to that purpose and making provision that whatever they find shall be handed on to others after their deaths. They pool their material resources; build a house; collect books; and plan their corporate studies. This, in its simplest form, is the true idea of a university. (Truscot 1945: 69)

Veblen would have approved. But later in the book it becomes clear that Truscot would qualify his idea into something much more like the impure practicalities of the university as we know it. He ended by writing of 'two chief aims, research and teaching', which 'blend so frequently and at times so completely, that it is often more accurate to describe them as one single aim which can be regarded from two aspects'. Moreover, he included graduate teaching, having in mind the American type of organization of graduate schools, as part of the research interest.

There had been mild rumbles of complaint and suggestion, particularly from students, along these lines before the war, designed to redefine university courses across the boundaries of the arts and sciences. A new humanistic synthesis had been called for by several writers, including Walter Kotschnig in *The University in a Changing World* (Kotschnig and Prys (eds.) 1932) and Adolf Lôwe in *The Universities in Transformation* (1941). A debate also started in this period as to where, in the disciplinary sense, the new synthesis might lie. Some like Karl Mannheim argued for the social sciences, others like F. R. Leavis at Cambridge in his *Education and the University* (1943) saw a 'humane consciousness' as best nurtured in the schools of English. In the event, when expansion began in earnest in the 1960s, the palm went to the social sciences, and the consequences for the social consciousness of the current generation of educated men can hardly be exaggerated. The dicta of Durkheim, Weber, and C. Wright Mills became part of the common currency of the 'quality newspapers', and Alan Bullock, preparing a dictionary for the *TLS* reader in the 1970s, found it necessary to explain the meanings of the new words from 'anomie' to 'stochastic processes'.

POST-WAR NOSTALGIA

After Bruce Truscot and the Second World War the first major essay on the idea of a university came from Sir Walter Moberly.

Moberly was Chairman of the UGC in the early post-war years and steered its early movement along an exponential curve of state patronage of higher education which by 1980 appeared to have reached its end. While he was writing *The Crisis in the University* (1949), Treasury finance to the universities was being quadrupled. Yet whether out of confidence or lack of interest in the material future of the universities, Moberly identified the crisis as a spiritual one. We shall never know whether he envisaged the sweep of the curve which was to ascend from about £13 million to over £3 billion now. Nor does it matter. His eyes were turned not to the price of universities but to their value. Since that crisis of aim and purpose remains unresolved we may profit from his description of it.

The war, it may be remembered, had brought a convulsion of social consciousness, not only in the Whitehall corridors, but throughout the nation among both civilians and members of the armed services. Ordinary people had divined that war had brought the opportunity for new beginnings, that it had been fought over the principles and not only the expediencies of human relations, and that a return to civilian life ought to mean also a reconstruction of society on better foundations. Moberly argued that the universities reflected 'the crisis in the world and its pervading sense of insecurity'. Over a large part of Europe and Asia there was a lack of binding conviction and there was confusion, bewilderment, and discord. 'All over the world, indeed, the cake of custom is broken, and old gods are dethroned and none have taken their place' (Moberly 1949: 16). He set out to examine possible plans for a rejuvenation of the universities on the assumption that the essential contribution had to come from Christianity.

It was precisely because Moberly's standpoint was avowedly Christian that his book received scarcely a mention when all the talk turned on crisis at the end of the 1960s. Student movements all over the world phrased their protests, rebellions, and ideological revolutions in secular nostrums. Yet what Moberly had to say remains seriously persuasive, not because of his Christianity, which is subtle and as undogmatic as a religious creed permits, nor because of his thoughtful grasp of previous writings about the idea of a university, but rather because he analysed a problem which refuses to go away. The questions he asked—'What are universities for? What effect should they have on their alumni? What are their responsibilities to the outside world?'—are still with us.

Moberly's view was that, beneath the façade of development and hopefulness of his day, universities all over the world hid a peculiar malaise of impotence. They had little inner self-confidence because they lacked any clear, agreed sense of direction or purpose. As he saw them then, and as observers like Peter Scott continue to see them today, they shared rather than transcended the spiritual confusion of the age. For Moberly the problem had been accentuated by the moral collapse of the German universities under the Nazi regime. The tragedy for his generation was that these universities had occupied a position of the highest intellectual prestige and had been models to the rest of the world. In the next generation a similar disillusionment developed towards the American universities, which had appeared in the 1950s to lead the way towards a democratic amalgam of popular openness and Nobel-prize-winning excellence through the model of the University of California only to be shattered by the 'student troubles' of the following decade.

Already in the 1940s Moberly was setting down an anticipatory description.

The cultural failure of the universities is seen in the students. In recent years large numbers of these have been apathetic and have had neither wide interests nor compelling convictions. The active-minded minority have often been in revolt. A few years ago a shrewd observer at one of our older universities said that he was struck with the rarity with which undergraduates expressed or felt any deep respect for, or debt to, dons as having opened up for them a whole new attitude to life; though unless all the biographies are untrustworthy, such discipleship was not uncommon in earlier generations. This estrangement between the generations has come about largely because students feel themselves to be living in a different world from their teachers . . . If they find prophets at all, it is outside the university . . . out there in the street is something new in the making, which will shatter all the syllogisms and formulas of the schools. (Moberly 1949: 23)

Moberly arrived at his own solution by looking back and identifying three basic ideas of the university—the Christian-Hellenic, the liberal, and the technological-democratic. He saw nineteenth-century Oxford and Cambridge as embodying the Christian and Graeco-Roman tradition. He recognized Newman's *Idea of a University* as a picture of Oxford's characteristic excellences. Basically the same ideal was held by Jowett and had been expounded a few years earlier by Whewell at Cambridge (*On the Principles of English University Education*).

As Moberly put it, 'On this view the chief duty of the university is to produce good citizens. It should train an élite who are to be the future leaders in affairs and in the learned professions.' He appreciated its merits. In it, education is liberal as opposed to servile, general as opposed to specialized, and systematic as opposed to dependent on fashion or individual caprice. He also saw, as did Newman, the expression in nineteenth-century Oxford of the principle that the university, being a community of teachers and learners, has to be regarded as a family. Hence tutorial teaching, essay-writing, disputations, and, above all, 'the relation between the staff and students is regarded as being paternal on the one side and filial on the other. The student is under authority. The office of the teacher is to some extent a pastoral one. He has a responsibility towards his pupils as human beings which extends far beyond his formal obligations as an instructor' (Moberly 1949: 33).

An idealized, Newmanesque Oxford was Moberly's idea of the university for the future. But he recognized that the older medieval conception had already been displaced by liberal ideas in the nineteenth century and foresaw the displacement of the liberal inspired university by what he labelled a technological-democratic movement. His interest and purpose was to understand and thereby to modify both these ideas of the university so as to restore, in modernized and viable form, the Christian principles which had guided the traditional European universities before liberal ideas made the German universities such triumphant leaders in the development of higher learning for advanced industrial societies.

Moberly was at one with Jowett and the Victorian reformist churchmen whose naïve optimism actually welcomed liberalism as a potential emancipation of the Christian university from parochial narrowness and indefensible interference with free enquiry. He was almost as sanguine as his predecessors in taking for granted the capacity of a moral outlook to survive without institutional power. He even echoed the fashionable talk of the early post-war days about Britain's future in the world as a moral force which might be strengthened by loss of empire. At all events, he saw no possible return to direct ecclesiastical control of the life of scholars and sought to incorporate liberalism rather than to defeat it.

Accordingly, he emphasized that the liberal conception of a university stems historically from the Christian-Hellenic traditions but expresses some features of the older ideal rather than others. It was primarily based on the idea that investigation matters more than instruction. Liberalism characterizes the outlook of the élitist researcher. The liberal ideal stresses, second, that learning for learning's sake is the proper business of the university and, third, insists on 'the function of the university as a community of science and learning quite distinct from that of church or state, or commerce and industry, and never to be subservient to them'. It stayed away from current practical controversy in politics or religion. It eschewed partisanship. It was a place for thought rather than action. It followed Max Weber's distinction between science and politics as vocations.

Fourth, following Abraham Flexner, Moberly noted that the university which is liberal assumes a need to be highly selective in the subjects it embraces and the methods it employs. 'It should abhor mediocrity: its business is with an intellectual aristocracy.' And 'the criterion is not the social importance of the proposed faculty or subject but its inherent intellectual value. It is only the learned professions or those that have intellectual content in their own right with which the universities should concern themselves.' And finally, to the doctrine of *Lehrfreiheit* of the teacher corresponds that of the *Lernfreiheit* of the student (Moberly 1949: 42).

For Moberly both Flexner and Bruce Truscot reflected the liberal view which descended from the nineteenth-century prestige of the German universities and had been celebrated by Sir William Hamilton in his attacks on Oxford in the 1830s, by Mark Pattison in his writing in the 1850s, and by Matthew Arnold in the 1860s. Again, it had found a persuasive missionary in Lord Haldane at the beginning of this century and is probably still the idea of the university to which most senior academic people would subscribe.

But again, as Moberly saw, the twilight of the liberal university was at hand. His third contender was a form of higher education which would be technological and democratic. It was rooted in the rise of applied science and technology, the socially sensitive optimism of the post-war generation, and what he saw as the growing democratic character of the universities. The aim of the university endeavour on this view is predominantly practical and utilitarian; it is the conquest of nature for the satisfaction of human needs. This is the creed of the expansionist researcher. Its discipline is analytic; its political mood is Fabian. In Moberly's words, 'it requires clarity and precision, it steers clear of all that is cloudy, grandiose and emotionally coloured' (Moberly 1949: 45). It discriminates between fields and methods which promise practical results and those which do not. It is activist and optimistic. It gives a rationale to the entry of the university into the modern world of search for new and more efficient solutions to age-old human needs.

The democratic companion to the technological impulse needs no elaboration. These two influences together, as Moberly saw, were producing a new culture, differing sharply from university traditions, condemning liberalism as being aristocratic rather than egalitarian, detached rather than participatory, and 'as exalting a sterile scholarship rather than being frankly occupational and utilitarian' (Moberly 1949: 48).

However, Moberly accepted none of these three views nor the further approach which would emphasize expansion and teaching and which completes the fourfold Trow–Halsey classification. He turned instead to the possibility of a rejuvenated and modernized Christianity for the universities, rid of its ancient guilt over the *odium theologicum* and any attempt to shackle free enquiry with dogmatic orthodoxy. Against the modern hope for progress through pragmatic and positivist science, he argued that the fundamental aim of the university can never be fulfilled by intellectual gadgetry, however sophisticated. It is not enough to know how to apply physics or chemistry or even social science.

Curiously enough, at least some British academics were already ambivalently aware of this model of our educational future from the United States, which had already gone beyond the Robbins targets for 1980, having 3 million college students in 1960 and the expectation of doubling again in the next decade. Ambivalence heavily obscured awareness. Two years before Kerr delivered his lectures at Harvard, I travelled to California with Sir John Cockcroft to survey American educational growth. Cockcroft had formed his idea of a university in the 1930s at the Cavendish Laboratory in Cambridge and fascinated me with the story of his travelling (by train) across America to the Californian Institute of Technology to carry the news of his famous electrical exploits with the atom. We came to La Jolla, where there had been a tiny institute since the 1920s formed by a handful of oceanographers-cum-sailors to map the sea-bed: but now there was to be a new university campus, mounting rapidly on lovely hillsides to house 27,500 students. The Chancellor was appointed, an architect, and a few secretaries. The architect was delighted to see us. 'You people are from Oxbridge?' Sir John blinked a deprecatory nod. 'You have colleges there. We are thinking along the same lines. Tell me, how many guys do you put in these colleges?' Sir John turned nervously to me and I guessed that Christ Church at Oxford or St John's, Cambridge, would be among the biggest, about 500 each. 'Yeah', smiled the architect, 'That'll be the faculty, but how many students?'

Sir John blinked again and retreated towards the oceanographers. The next year, Clark Kerr produced his account of the multiversity. On Kerr's view the idea of a university in medieval traditions was a village with its priests; the idea of a modern university as the Victorians fashioned it was a town—a one-industry town—with its intellectual oligarchy; and the idea of a multiversity 'is a city of infinite variety'. He recognized it as a somewhat amorphous and anarchic place, pluralistic in its base but high at the apex in pursuit of academic excellence. For him, then, it was a city of intellect with a diverse citizenry but held together by a spirit of tolerance and generous conceptions of what was justifiable in the varied realms of teaching, research, service to the community, selectivity, and openness towards student admissions and bargaining for funds with governmental and private patrons.

The Californian vision as described by Kerr was an extravagant dream in Britain on the eve of the Robbins Report. Yet it was, if only a geographically remote reality, a possibly realizable plan for the future of higher education in Britain and Europe, at once germinated and constrained by the ideas of the past which the new social architects had inherited.

Robbins's recommendations had for the most part been accepted wholeheartedly by a Conservative government. But the signposts since 1968 have frequently read doom and crisis, alarm and despondency. Robert Nisbet tells us that 'no one seriously surveying the academic scene today can conclude other than that the American university is in an exceedingly precarious position. The lustre of even the most historic and distinguished universities is fading rapidly. For the first time in the history of this country there is valid reason for wondering whether the university will survive'

(Nisbet 1972: 197). In their final report in 1980 (Carnegie Council 1980), summarizing a minor library on American higher education, the Carnegie Commission began with a chapter describing decline from 'Golden Age to Time of Troubles'. They referred to political crises and financial depressions. They noted that the social idealism and social optimism that characterized the New Deal and the period following the Second World War had given way to cynicism and pessimism. 'A lack of confidence now exists in what is being done, in conceptions of what should be done in the processes for making changes . . . There has been a basic erosion of affection for and interest in education, including higher education.' This is a recurrent theme of American commentary of which Alan Bloom's best seller of 1987 is a characteristic late example (Bloom 1987).

On the other hand, the Carnegie Commission refused to be daunted. 'We do not believe', they said, 'higher education will decline, and we are convinced that it would be a tragedy for the nation if it did. We end our six years of study of higher education, in the time of its greatest trauma of self-doubt, with faith in its potential continued vitality and with a deepened belief in its essential value to American society.'

The work of the Carnegie Commission on Higher Education invites British comparison with the Robbins Report. The official British inquiry took place in the early 1960s, heralding an unprecedented spurt of expansion. The semi-official American study began in 1967, changed its name in 1974, and presented its final report in 1980, heralding an unprecedented decline. To compare, therefore, is mainly to contrast. In any case the American investigation was larger than the British in rough proportion to the number of students and colleges involved. Under Clark Kerr's indefatigable chairmanship, and supported by such notables as William Bowen, Ernest Boyer, David Reisman, and Martin Trow, a massive and detailed ethnography of American higher education was put together. It documents and analyses the final decades of an expansion of schooling unrivalled in any other country. It gives as complete a picture as any scholar or administrator could hope for of a system of higher education which grew from 1870 to 1970 at a compound annual rate of 5 per cent, taking its share of GNP from 0.1 to 2.1 per cent, and incorporating by 1980 some 8.5 million full-time equivalent students into over 3,000 institutions. As this vast increase of scale and scope appeared to be ending, the Council surveyed and advised on the future (Carnegie Council 1980). What will, and what ought to, happen to these 3,000 universities and colleges in the next twenty years? The answers, which assumed numerical decline, contained interest for European countries facing a similar fate.

American growth in the recent past had not, of course, been free of trouble. The student buffoonery of the sixties shook public confidence in universities, though Americans, by international standards, retained their traditional faith in a college education. The rising production of Ph.D.s had its impact on the labour market in the 1970s, reducing the personal rate of return on high qualifications and forcing down the real incomes of university teachers. The average quality of both entrants and graduates fell as the numbers increased. Financial difficulties multiplied in the later 1970s as the system became dominantly and increasingly one of the large public campuses, funded and increasingly regulated by the State. The aspirations of minority groups for equality of opportunity had not been fully met, the regularizing efforts through 'affirmative action' often clashed with the principle of individual merit on which excellence had traditionally depended. As expansion temporarily tailed off, the average age of university staff rose, defensive unionism grew, and a new generation of students made novel demands. An ageing and relatively impoverished teaching body had to unlearn the established habits of a period of rising budgets, and face students as a market of consumers rather than a guaranteed parade of potential recruits to the academic succession. In short, institutional survival had already come to depend on successful adaptation to an uncertain student market.

The future was dominated by these uncertainties, and the Council accordingly addressed itself first to the prospects for student enrolment. Decline was not inevitable and did not in the event materialize. It was, however, certain that the traditional college-going population of 18–21-year-olds would fall by 25 per cent between 1980 and the end of the century. Some optimists predicted correctly that the falling total would be more than offset by an increasing proportion of college entrants, particularly women and members of ethnic minorities. They argued, too, that as a personal investment in life earnings, the degree would become more rather than less important, and that the return, after falling by one-third between the mid-sixties and the mid-seventies, would rise. So one possible projection was for 25 per cent increase. At the other extreme a decrease of 40 per cent had been forecast. The Carnegie Councillors opted for a mild pessimism in the shape of a fall in undergraduate enrolments of between 5 per cent and 15 per cent between 1980 and 2000. After that, they postulated recovery on the assumption that fertility and/or immigration would increase to keep the total American student population in equilibrium.

What were the solutions? The Carnegie Commission offered nothing spectacular. In effect, they enjoined the universities, the State, the professors, the students, and the public to be their best selves. The federal government should provide ample funds for basic research. The public should be generous, should support tax laws facilitating private gifts, and maintain its enthusiasm. Students should pursue higher education, especially in the humanities, for its own sake as well as for its market advantages. The universities should redouble their efforts to be excellent, to be responsive to social needs, and exemplars of moral probity and devotion to science and scholarship.

These conventional wisdoms, calmly stated, are not to be dismissed. For they reflect the essential and essentially admirable idea of the university. The problem was to deliver them. In reality the staffing of universities is inflexible. Tenure is the prized norm and is tenaciously defended by men and women whose recent material affluence has been somewhat eroded. Academic men and women tend to see themselves as the natural proprietors of their institutions and therefore to be defensive against initiatives from other origins, whether government, unions, presidents, or their own administrators. The challenge was to retain self-government while overcoming its associated conservatism.

Meanwhile the most recent British contribution to discussion of ideas about higher education has been offered by Peter Scott, the editor of the *THES* (P. Scott 1984). It is a notable contribution to the sociology of education and not least because he argues that if there is a crisis, it is of higher education in a liberal-democratic secular society, and not merely of the British universities under a Thatcher administration. Any such argument requires diagnosis of historical trends, not only of the relative simplicities of numbers of students and resources, but also of the complexities of values, purposes, and principles which make up the intellectual culture of a nation. Scott sees the British universities as evolving from traditional through liberal and modern to a post-modern form or alternatively, in the context of post-secondary education as a whole, from élite through mass to universal provision. He refuses to place higher education simplistically into either interpretative framework and so to produce confident and naïve 'waves of the future' in a final chapter. Instead he leaves more questions than answers, more open challenges than closed facts.

He is tempted to declare his own long historical framework irrelevant by awareness that the contemporary British universities were largely created during the 1950s and 1960s, 'the product . . . of the Robbins' Committee blueprint for expansion that was so spectacularly executed during the 1960s and 1970s' (Scott 1984: 118). Had he yielded to that temptation, he would have saved himself the immensely more difficult task of deciphering the eidos and ethos of a tradition reaching back to twelfth-century Paris. He could have dealt with past, present, and future in pragmatic, unmysterious terms, judging achievement more or less numerically from the stated objectives of the UGC and the DES, and the news in the files of the *THES*. But he did not yield to such misleading superficial certainties, though he does include an informative account of the post-Robbins period.

Issue may well be taken with one aspect of his pragmatic interpretation—his flat assertion that 'of course another Robbins is impossible' (Scott 1984: 258). Professor Robin Marris subsequently argued exactly to the contrary (*THES*, 6 Apr. 1984) 'the economic return to the nation from university education is so high, that there is in fact an overwhelming case for a new massive expansion, for, in effect a "new Robbins"'. Marris arrived at his conclusion by strictly economic calculation. Scott, apart from anticipatory criticism of the basis of such arithmetic (for example, that if higher education acts in the labour market mainly as a sieve, its value to individual graduates is bound to decline as the production of graduates increases), devotes much more print to the social and political forces which shape opinion and decision in senior common rooms, boardrooms, and Cabinet offices. To this end he presents a summary recapitulation of the liberal and modern phases of the history of British higher education, attempting to distil their cultural essence as traditions which mould present thought and future possibilities.

This is not to say that his sympathies (or mine) are opposed to the general thrust of Marris's advocacy. It is to say, however, that Scott recognizes the power of inherited ideology; and in this sense the book belongs to the large literature on 'the idea of the university' which I have discussed in this chapter. Scott's interpretation of institutional history is also, in effect, a review and reflection of the ideas of Newman, Pattison, Jowett, Veblen, Mansbridge, Truscot, and (more explicitly) Robbins and Kerr.

From this long lineage of predecessors, Sir Walter Moberly is the most apt for comparison. To select him is at once to throw light on the dubious use of the word crisis: for Moberly's title in 1949 was *The Crisis in the University*. Perhaps the tiny difference of a preposition (from 'in' to 'of') signals a change in the thirty-five years between the two books in the emphasis on the 'public' rather than the 'private' lives of universities. Certainly Scott is more aware than was Moberly of the wider intellectual culture and of the existence of what came to be recognized as the binary line and a system of higher and further education as well as a 'knowledge industry', with which universities have manifold relationships.

But crisis is the conceptual continuity and the definition of it has not changed. Neither author describes crisis in terms of resources. Moberly was Chairman of the UGC in the early post-war years of burgeoning funds. Scott, by contrast, watched and recorded the use of the UGC, the National Advisory Board, and the Research Councils as agents of a governmental drive towards reduced public expenditure on higher education. Yet neither sees the economics of higher learning as crucial.

For Scott as well as Moberly the crisis was spiritual. 'There can be little doubt', he writes, 'that there has been a decisive shift towards pessimism in Britain since the early 1970s and higher education has shared in this mood and been a victim of it.' 'The different branches of knowledge find it increasingly difficult to regard the modern university as in any sense an organic academic society rather than simply as a shared bureaucratic environment' (Scott 1984: 115). Scott could even be held to speak for his pre-Robbins predecessor when he ends his book with the fear that higher education, and the values it embodies, may be condemned to 'marginality and erosion' and the demise of 'that configuration of belief and practice, typical of modern society, and the metaphor of a moral social order that is a guarantee of both freedom and progress' (Scott 1984: 271).

The questions and the crisis are, then, much the same. So, too, are the essential conceptions or 'ideal types' inherited from the past

—the traditional (what Moberly calls Graeco-Roman), the liberal, and the modern (Moberly's 'technological-democratic'). Both writers locate the liberal university in the period from the revival led by the eighteenth-century Scottish universities up to the first half of the twentieth century—roughly from Hume to Rutherford. In the three preceding centuries European intellectual life had passed out of the post-medieval university, which slept through the Renaissance, the rise of the Royal Society, and the spread of the Enlightenment. The liberal university was then awakened by the rise of natural and political science. Rationality was, and still is, the value which a university embodies. Reason is the timeless principle of the idea and organization of any university and sets the problem for Scott or any other interpreter of the fate of universities. But universities are also always mirrors of the age. In the case of the age of classical industrialism, Scott argues that there are identifiable social and economic forces which gave the liberal university particular character as the custodian of an intellectual tradition 'derived from the culture of an elite and the codification of scientific principles by a corps of academic experts' (Scott 1984: 31).

These two elements of tradition and pedagogy are our inheritance from the liberal university. They were exemplified in Edwardian Oxford and Cambridge, they modified and contained the 'redbrick' universities which developed in the great provincial cities from the end of the nineteenth century, and they continued to shape the self-conceptions of the new universities of the 1960s. But a new conception—the modern university—is thought of by Scott as based on an emerging redefinition of knowledge as product rather than process. A scientific rather than a cultural definition of knowledge emphasizes research more than teaching, intellect more than sensibility. A reconstruction of intellectual life displaces humanism by academicism; technology replaces education. The university is more fissiparous, less integrated, more eager to respond to external influences, less separate from the mainstream of profane life, and therefore more serviceable as well as more pliant to the power of the State. While central to society for the generation of new scientific knowledge as well as the distribution of occupational chances (at least to the more remunerated, more esteemed, and more powerful echelons of a modern division of labour), the university is also, by the same process, less independent of government and the pressures of industry.

Scott is less sanguine, more sophisticated, and much more forward-looking than was Moberly. He looks for a moral outlook in secular institutions, and the search leads him to a perspicacious discussion of the nature and organization of intellectual enquiry and its disciplines, the differences and similarities of 'cultural' and 'scientific' definitions of knowledge, and the social ethics of access to higher education. If he does not find any simple solution to the threat of academicism and instrumentalism or any guarantee for the preservation of 'cognitive rationality' and social justice in the future organization of higher education, at least he places these problems coherently and practically into the context of contemporary debate. His cautious canvassing of the strategy of a post-binary policy for higher education (including the universities, and designed to balance the need for diversity, efficiency, accountability, and freedom) makes up a short but lucid chapter which deserves and facilitates wide consideration.

Scott's advance on Moberly can also be described by reference to the four basic ideas of the university formed out of the élitist and expansionist teaching and research orientations that we have discussed. Moberly's imagination was confined to two conceptions —those of the élitist teacher and the élitist researcher. Scott's horizons are broadèr. They encompass the expansionist-teacher and the expansionist-researcher, and accordingly he addresses himself to the whole range of educational institutions beyond school. He wrestles with the problem of finding a place for all four views concerning the development and transmission of knowledge in an integrated system of higher education in Britain. The outcome is his post-binary policy.

For these reasons Scott's contribution is likely to 'stay in the literature' and inform future debate, whereas Moberly's book was but briefly remarked and quickly forgotten. And yet their common 'crisis' remains. A misnomer, perhaps, for a chronic peril, it may never be finally resolvable. For intellectual life, however serviceable to material production or civilized consumption, will always demand its freedoms and its privileges and must therefore remain vulnerable to suspicion from the populace and the powers.

3

THE EVOLVING HIERARCHY BEFORE ROBBINS

THE history of British higher education from Victorian times is one of evolving hierarchy. It is briefly traced here as a developing relation between Oxford and the system of higher education for reasons bluntly expressed by Edward Shils in 1955.

'If a young man, talking to an educated stranger, refers to his university studies, he is asked "Oxford or Cambridge?".' And if he says Aberystwyth or Nottingham, there is disappointment on the one side and embarrassment on the other. It has always been that way' (Shils 1955: 80). Whether in the pages of eternity twentieth-century Oxford was a 'good thing' is an open question; the cultural fact of its superior image is a closed one. Not only was it a famous university but frequently the symbol of all universities. And it was more than a university. It was an integral part of an ancient establishment along with the crown and the aristocracy. So members of Hebdomadal Council (the elected central committee of the university) would refer to each other as the Warden (of All Souls) or the Dean (of Christ Church) with the same ceremonious attribution of dignified office as was used in the House of Lords. University College, London was seen as 'provincial' while University College, Oxford was metropolitan. Of course, 'wherever two or three are gathered together' there also shall be a sociological commonplace: invidious comparisons will emerge.

The task in this chapter is to discover Oxford's position, not so much in a widening circle of British universities as in an emergent hierarchy of higher educational institutions. Oxford, with Cambridge, dominated an expanding system from a numerically declining share of teachers and students throughout the first three-quarters of the twentieth century (see Fig. 3.1–3). How and why is our question. The answer will involve a narrative of Oxford's reluctant incorporation into a developing national system as the older sister of Oxbridge. She remained the source of magic and moonshine that illuminated a distinctive ideal of university life which we have discussed in Chapter 2. She held sway over the minds of those who selected students and appointed staff. She maintained a persistent power to place people in positions of high political and administrative office, and finally, after the Second World War, she successfully reinforced her ancient assumption of status from social connection by strengthening her claims to merit, selecting students more and more systematically for academic promise, and increasingly encouraging productivity in her scientists and other scholars.

But first two key words must be clarified—*Oxbridge* and the *system*. Insiders know that there are many Oxfords. Outsiders believe that, culturally if not geographically, Oxford and Cambridge are the same place. Surveys of opinion and official statistics commonly use the term Oxbridge—a convenient if inelegant label originating in Thackeray's *Pendennis* (1850) which came belatedly into general usage after the Second World War, when 'the system' impelled the two ancient universities to present a combined interest. The alternative construction 'Camford' has never become popular.[1] Precedence goes to longevity in the British notion of seniority. Either term in any case may serve to diminish the real differences between Oxford and Cambridge, which are so beloved of migrant dons and were elaborated for the earlier decades of the century by Ernest Barker, who studied and served in both places (Barker 1953). Oxford was more convivial, more intercollegiate, more oriented to classics, church, and politics. Cambridge dons were more specialized, scientific, and puritanical. Nevertheless, consultation and interchange between the Cam and the Isis grew during the period.

The word *system* also has its difficulties. The Robbins Committee noted in 1963 that no system of higher education existed in Britain before the committee itself was formed. But this is an administrative rather than a sociological truth. From the Middle Ages there was a system in England constituted by Oxford and Cambridge, with the close connection of certain of their colleges to particular schools. The residues of that system survive to the present day, and Oxford and Cambridge maintain frequent, sometimes nervous consultation in their responses to external pressure. But industrialization inexorably enlarged the academic circle, uniting the kingdom, connecting science and scholarship to empire, to Europe, America, and the world. A new British system of higher education

[1] See e.g. Rose and Ziman 1964 (*Camford Observed*).

thus gradually appeared. As the civic universities, and later the Open University and the polytechnics, gained recognition, Oxford and Cambridge moved from monopoly to pre-eminence. 'The other place' remained the significant other, even though its definite article increasingly and embarrassingly misrepresented the reality of a national set of institutions.

The evolution of a national system was closely linked with the relation of higher education to the State, and even here the origins of support by the State reach back to royal patronage of Oxford and Cambridge in the Middle Ages. When England and Scotland united in 1707 the crown took over the Scottish government's financial grants, and parliament paid them after 1832. Later in the century parliamentary grants began to flow to the Welsh university colleges and eventually to other institutions of higher education in Britain. The University Grants Committee (UGC) was formed in 1919, and at this point a set of definable relations arguably became an official system. For in that year three bodies came into being: the UGC as the channel of state finance, the Committee of Vice-Chancellors and Principals (CVCP) as the body representing the interests of the universities, and the Association of University Teachers (AUT) as the body representing the academic staff of those institutions. Moreover a fourth body, the National Union of Students (NUS), was formed immediately after, in the early 1920s. Against this background Oxbridge may be seen to have moved from separated grandeur to incorporated stardom. And in transition Oxford remained the traditional symbol of university life, loved and loathed, extolled and condemned, as it had been down the centuries.

In terms of custom and conception the system was continuous. From the period of Victorian reform the English idea of the university gave a common stamp to universities in this country despite differences of age, size, and location.[2] There were norms in British universities which reflect a more or less unified conception of higher education: an idealized representation of Oxford. Was there any alternative to the Oxford English idea? In part perhaps yes: there was the civic pride and regional need of the industrial provinces; there was the imperial invitation to make London a central examining and research metropolis; there was a growing

---

[2] Elaborated in Halsey and Trow 1971. For the influence of this idea on the English new universities see Cross and Jobling 1969.

demand for high scientific manpower in an increasingly techno-logical economy. But these alternatives were assimilated to Ox-bridge dominance. There was also a fourth possibility. The Scottish model of democratic intellectualism had made its mark on the civic universities in the shape of professorial rule and departmental organization.[3] Yet it too was assimilated, and those who have tried to describe it as crushed by English hegemony or internal colonialism in the United Kingdom have written 'stirring stuff' but 'pretty poor history' (Slee 1987: 194).

Oxbridge met the Victorian challenge of classical industrialism and of religious nonconformity partly by reforming and expanding its own statutes and curriculum, partly by drawing in the sons of successful businessmen, and partly by the movement of Oxford and Cambridge dons to teach in the newly created universities (Rothblatt 1963: 86–7). As a result two traditions emerged. Oxford and Cambridge were national and residential federations of colleges connected with the national élites of politics, administration, business and the liberal professions. They offered a general education designed to mould character and prepare their under-graduates for a gentlemanly style of life. All the rest were provincial and, including London, aimed to meet the needs of the professional and industrial middle classes; furthermore they took most of their students from their own region. The percentage of students drawn from within 30 miles in 1908–9 was at Bristol 87 per cent, Leeds 78 per cent, Liverpool 75 per cent, Manchester 73 per cent, University College, London 66 per cent. The students at civic universities were offered a utilitarian training for middle-class careers in courses typically concentrated on a single subject and directed especially towards the newer technological and professional occupations such as chemistry, electrical engineering, teaching in state grammar schools, and the scientific civil service.

In the nineteenth century these two traditions existed side by side with little contact. But in the twentieth century a pyramidal structure evolved with Oxford and Cambridge at the apex and a widening array of civic and new universities and polytechnics at the base. Oxford thus occupied a commanding but numerically declining place among British universities in a period of unpreced-ented development of higher education. In 1900 the population

[3] Davie 1961. See also Davie 1986 and McPherson 1973 for a persuasive analysis.

numbered 39 million with 20,000 university students taught by
2,000 university teachers, of whom a third were at Oxbridge. By
1964 the British academic staff was equal in number to the students
at the beginning of the century. In the subsequent 'Robbins's
decade' further expansion raised the total of university students to
over a quarter of a million and the teachers and researchers to
40,000. Of these, less than 3,000 (7.5 per cent) were resident in
Oxford or Cambridge, teaching a much reduced proportion of the
country's undergraduates—from a third at the beginning of the
century to less than 8 per cent by 1980.

The chances for the members of the relevant age-group of
reaching a university grew from 1 in 60 between the wars to 1 in 31
in the middle of the century to a planned 1 in 6 by 1980.[4]

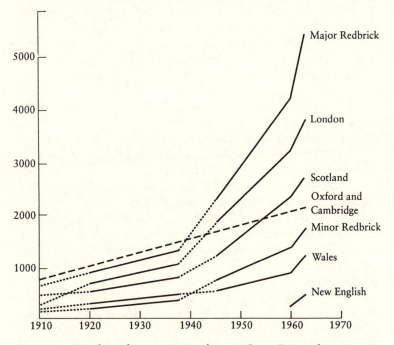

FIG. 3.1. *Number of university teachers in Great Britain by university
group, 1910–1964. Source: Halsey and Trow 1971: 145*

[4] For a detailed analysis by class of chances of entry to university over the period
from before the First World War to the 1960s see Halsey, Heath, and Ridge 1980:
ch. 10.

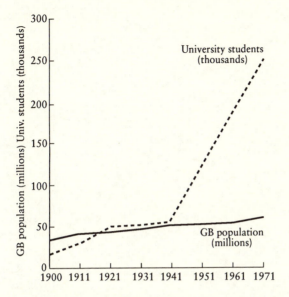

Fig. 3.2.   *Great Britain, population and university students, 1900–1971*

The two world wars stimulated growth for two reasons: they encouraged opinion favourable to reform, and to educational reform in particular, and thus increased the effective demand for university places; and they dramatized the utility of university research for military and industrial efficiency. Underlying these accelerating forces of war there was also pressure from beneath, stemming from the increasing number of grammar schools in a national system of secondary schooling after 1902. The proportion of 17-year-olds in full-time education doubled from 2 to 4 per cent between 1902 and 1938 and rose further to 15 per cent by 1962 and 20 per cent by 1970. At the same time the demand for graduates strengthened as the managerial and professional occupations expanded in government, in industry, and in the educational system itself. Managers and higher professionals grew from 4.4 to 13.6 per cent of all occupations between 1911 and 1971 (Price and Bain 1988: table 4.1(*b*), 164), and increasingly sought graduate recruits.

Expansion before Robbins had two phases. The first began in the late Victorian period with the foundation of the civic universities

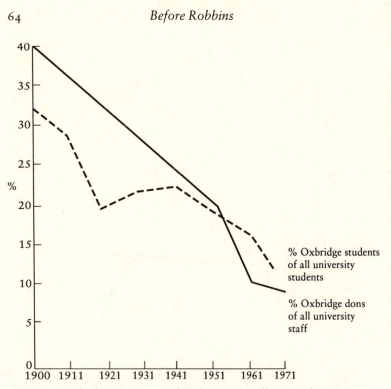

FIG. 3.3 *Oxbridge proportion of students and staff in British Universities,*
1900–1971

and continued after the First World War until it faded during the
depression years of the 1930s. At the beginning Oxford and
Cambridge were conspicuously preponderant numerically, as well
as academically and socially. By the end, just before the Second
World War, they had been surpassed in numbers of students and
staff by the major redbrick universities and overtaken by London.
Within the first decade of the century Birmingham, Bristol, Leeds,
Manchester, and Sheffield all gained charters as independent
universities and, together with Durham and its Newcastle constituent, they began to lead the expansion of the British university
system.

The second phase of growth began after 1945 and included the
granting of independent charters to the former London-dominated
provincial university colleges at Nottingham, Southampton, Hull,
Exeter, and Leicester. The last-named became independent in 1957,

bringing the total number of British universities to twenty-one. In 1949 the establishment of the University College of North Staffordshire at Keele, largely under Oxford influence and without tutelage from London, anticipated the much-publicized movement to found new universities with independence from the outset. The earliest of these, Sussex, admitted its first students in 1961. Subsequently East Anglia, York, Essex, Kent, Warwick, and Lancaster received charters and four new Scottish universities were formed—Strathclyde (out of the Royal College of Science) in Glasgow, Heriot-Watt in Edinburgh, and those at Stirling and Dundee. These new foundations contributed little to the second phase of expansion between 1947 and 1964, which mostly took place in the established universities in the industrial provincial cities, in London, in Wales, and in the ancient Scottish universities as well as in Oxford and Cambridge, whose numbers gently drifted upwards.

Social and economic developments after the Second World War surpassed all previous pressures towards growth. The change in opinion about the desirable provision of university and other forms of higher education after the mid-1950s was quite unprecendented.[5] At that time only a very small minority of radical expansionists was ready to contemplate 10 per cent of the age-group being in universities. By the time the Robbins Committee reported in 1963 middle-class opinion, including academic opinion nationally, accepted that some 20 per cent of the age-group should be educated to this level by 1980. Behind this shift lay fundamental changes of political and social outlook: aspirations to higher education came to be taken for granted in the middle classes and began to penetrate into working-class families, especially those in which the parents themselves had some experience of education beyond the minimum school-leaving age. And the old fear of industrial decline, with its invidious international comparisons and its acceptance of the theory that skill and training make the largest marginal contributions to the productivity of the economy, brought political support for the ever-growing higher-education budget.

Moreover, the older class-based conceptions of education, so strongly associated with Oxbridge, were challenged after 1945. Inequality of access to the universities became an almost commonplace illustration of distributive injustice. Economic growth required

[5] For a graphic description of the changing climate of opinion see Annan 1967.

the cultivation of all potential talent. The assumption of a restricted 'pool of ability' came to be seen as a rationalization for preserving class privilege. The traditional ideological defence of an Oxbridge system of universities for the élite was no longer tenable, and the development of higher education came to be seen more in terms of economic feasibility and a balanced regional distribution.

In the newness of their early urban beginnings the civic universities were not particularly preoccupied with matching the prestige of Oxford. There were formidable barriers to attaining the Oxford ideal. One indispensable requisite was that a university should be national rather than local. The nineteenth-century foundations in the industrial cities were creatures of a nonconformist and non-metropolitan culture, selecting their students, in the main, from the middle and lower middle classes of their own suburbs and region, while Oxford and Cambridge drew from the sons of those families who were able to use the national public schools.

Redbrick sought a different clientele. In the 1920s women took 30 per cent of the places, though their proportionate gains were halted in the slump years. In Oxford men outnumbered women by 5 to 1 and in Cambridge by 10 to 1 . The Oxbridge ratios were to persist until the 1960s when G. E. M. de Ste Croix led the move by New College to transform an ancient male preserve into a mixed college (Ste Croix 1964: 29). Oxbridge influence partly explains why the position of women was less favourable in England than in Scotland and Wales, where opportunities for scholarships were more evenly divided between the sexes. Oxford and Cambridge awards were biased towards men, whereas in the nationally maintained scholarships—State Scholarships and Royal Science Scholarships—and in most local awards, no such distinction was made between candidates of equal merit.

Another inter-war feature was the increased flow of students into the arts faculties. In 1930/1, while Oxford had 80 per cent, only 52 per cent of all British university students were reading arts—and of these a third were prospective teachers subsidized by the board of education. This government subsidy was especially important for women, nearly 75 per cent of whom were in the arts faculties in 1930/1 compared with 44 per cent of the men. Intending teachers also swelled the numbers registered for honours rather than ordinary or pass degrees. Scotland maintained the predominance of ordinary degrees, for in 1930/1 only 24 per cent of graduates in Scotland took honours, while 66 per cent did so in England; the percentage in Wales was 55 (Whiteley 1933: 27).

Graduate studies also made relative gains after the First World War. In 1919 the percentage of students engaged in research was 2. By 1930 it was 5. Of the 1,941 graduate students 173 were at Oxford, 237 at Cambridge, 237 in Scotland, 116 in Wales, 430 at the English provincial universities, and 748 were in London. At the time it was thought that London's place 'at the heart of national and international activities' and 'the provincial universities in close proximity to industrial enterprise' offered both support and incentive to research.

When the UGC assessed financial assistance to university students in 1928/9 it found that 50 per cent received some form of help. An Oxbridge place was privileged. Between them Oxford and Cambridge had £250,000 a year to award in scholarships, which was rather more than the total cost of scholarships maintained by the nation as a whole (Whiteley 1933: 29). State scholarships were keenly sought. Between 1919 and 1929 the number of applicants for the 200 available awards quadrupled. In 1931 there were 300 scholarships and 4,333 applicants, a ratio of 1 to 14. The state scholars had a decided preference for Oxford and Cambridge. In 1929/30 232 were holding their awards at Oxford and 177 at Cambridge, while 115 were at London, 94 at provincial universities, and 24 at the Welsh colleges (Whiteley 1933: 32–3).

But Oxbridge remained difficult of access to 'the poor student'. Though nearly two-thirds of the 642 state scholars in 1929/30 were at Oxford or Cambridge, only 11 per cent had been pupils in elementary schools compared with 15.6 per cent in London, 36.1 per cent in the provincial universities, and 54.7 per cent in Wales. A report presented to Nuffield College showed that eighteen leading schools (nine boarding and nine day) provided 40 per cent of the scholars and exhibitioners in the Oxford colleges between the wars. Winchester was the clear leader and also headed in the degree performance of its scholars. Only five of the eighteen were grammar schools not in membership of the Headmasters' Conference (Clapham and Brunner 1944).

Oxbridge could in principle have expanded to accommodate early twentieth-century demand for university education. Lord Curzon had included a chapter on 'The admission of poor men' in his 1909 report (Curzon 1909), noting that the question had been raised only to be dismissed by the commissioners of 1850. He himself distinguished between expansion of admission to Oxford and the expansion of Oxford's extramural activities in the industrial cities. Between Pattison in the 1850s and Jowett in the 1870s the extramural had largely displaced the intramural solution. And this evasion lay behind the twentieth-century distinction between 'undergraduates' tutored by 'dons' at Oxford and 'students' taught by 'university teachers' elsewhere. The extension movement so brilliantly led in Rochdale by R. H. Tawney was largely displaced by the provincial university colleges after 1918, by the Open University in the 1960s, and by the polytechnics in the 1970s.

Largely displaced but not wholly, for Oxford continued to boast the largest extramural staff and the extension impulse took a new turn in the 1920s under A. D. Lindsay's enthusiasm, which led eventually to the foundation of Keele University in the Potteries. Lindsay and his friends, including Kenneth Leys, Walter Moberly, David Ross, and J. L. Stocks, formed an 'Oxford Reform Committee' which drew up a memorandum for the Asquith Commission. Their aim was to make Oxford more accessible by reducing the bias towards boys from the public schools, by reducing the costs of being a student at Oxford, and by forging stronger and wider links with the educational system of the country as a whole. They wanted extramural work to be recognized as an essential part of the work of the university, with claims on its endowments, tutorial-class tutors as college fellows, and tutorial-class students as scholarship holders. They also sought university support for the summer schools pioneered at Balliol (D. Scott 1971: 89).

Balliol did in fact change its pattern of admission in Lindsay's time. In 1906 two-thirds of the fifty-three entrants were from public schools, including nineteen from Eton. In 1939 the numbers were half of the 104, including fourteen Etonians. In 1949, when Lindsay left, the public schools contributed 28 per cent of the 109 entrants, with only one Etonian. And a further indication of Balliol's influence in the academic world beyond Oxford is that while Lindsay was Master his college provided 250 professors to universities throughout the world (D. Scott 1971: 110, 118).

The relation of Oxbridge to the provincial universities between the wars is epitomized in the academic biography of the chancellor of Oxford elected to succeed Harold Macmillan in 1987, Lord Jenkins. Roy Jenkins attended the University College of Cardiff from October 1937 to May 1938, being not quite 17 years old when he started. He came with 'an indifferent Higher Certificate' from Abersychan County Grammar School, it being thought that 'if I was ever to get into Oxford I needed to be shaken out of this early staleness by some broader horizons'. His father had been at Ruskin College before the First World War and 'had conceived an almost romantic attachment for that shore'. His own 'object at Cardiff was therefore to learn some history and some French . . . to start some elementary economics and to try to prepare myself for Oxford scholarship and entrance examinations' (Jenkins 1983: 97–8).

All this heavily underlines Oxford's tentative response to the rise of the modern universities after the First World War. Keele was exceptional in its direct institutional connection between Oxford and a new university. Oxford's initial reaction to the expansion of the university system was isolationist. Oxford neither colonized nor incorporated the civic innovations. Before 1930, though paying its subscription, Oxford had held aloof from the Universities' Bureau of the British Empire and the Committee of Vice-Chancellors and Principals. The Vice-Chancellor rarely attended in person, nor did he send a deputy when absent. Instead Oxford cleaved more closely to Cambridge between the wars. For example, Oxford agreed privately and politely with 'the other place' not to disagree publicly over the bureau's articles of association. Both wanted to safeguard their common interest against any possible future domination of the bureau by the University of London. From 1931 the university's Hebdomadal Council regularly received reports of decisions of interest to Oxford taken by the CVCP, though the Vice-Chancellor still did not go to its meetings. An Oxford and Cambridge Standing Joint Committee was formed in 1935 and met regularly twice a year to discuss such matters as saving money by avoiding unnecessary duplication of academic courses and research, the age of call-up for war service, and the power of the two universities to alter the conditions on which trusts had been settled.

During the 1930s, however, it became clear that Oxford and Cambridge had to involve themselves with the CVCP, which was becoming a main channel of communication between the government and the universities. It was consequently agreed that the Registrar should attend meetings of the CVCP, and in fact both the

Vice-Chancellor and the Registrar normally did so. Suspicion of Oxford and Cambridge among the civic Vice-Chancellors declined, the Oxford and Cambridge Standing Joint Committee was an effective apparatus for presenting an Oxbridge common front, the other universities recognized the special position of their seniors, and the Oxbridge point of view could be transmitted to government through the CVCP without animosity. In the same period a network of alliances between Oxford and Cambridge colleges developed. The two colleges of Corpus Christi allied in 1926, Merton and Peterhouse in 1930, New College and King's in 1931, and others followed suit, in each case granting common-room rights to the fellows of the sister institution (Roberts 1935).

Still more important, individuals consolidated a powerful nexus. Graduates of the 1920s and 1930s moved between the two places. John Hicks in economics, Asa Briggs and John Habakkuk in history, and Frederick Dainton in chemistry are famous examples, each exemplifying interchange in research, each also playing an important part in the interactive development of the wider university system. Hicks held a chair at Manchester from 1938 to 1946, Dainton and Briggs held chairs at Leeds. Habakkuk was chairman of the CVCP, Dainton became chairman of the UGC. Habakkuk was vice-chancellor of Oxford, Dainton of Nottingham, and Briggs of Sussex; and all collected national honours in the course of their career spirals.

All in all, Oxbridge gradually became a real entity within the British university system after 1914. It was not only the ritual of competitive solidarity in the annual boat-race. It was an intricate network of institutional and individual exchange, born of common interest in perpetuating the Oxbridge ideal within a growing system that might otherwise have engulfed the ancient universities.

Yet the Oxbridge ideal had to yield to modern reform of the curriculum. For example, there was a national movement which aimed to bring higher technological education into the service of industry. It was inspired by fear of industrial competition from the Continent, by appreciation of the industrial benefits gained by Germany, France, and Switzerland from their polytechnics, and by admiration of the American land-grant colleges. This movement was naturally concentrated in the civic universities and in applied scientific courses. Oxbridge opinion was suspicious. Oxford's dons feared that technological education would lessen the spell of

Newman's lectures, Pattison's essays, and Jowett's teaching. 'It is not surprising, therefore, that they opposed the segregation of technological education into separate institutions. The manager-technologist must receive not only a vocational training: he must enjoy also the benefits of a liberal education; or at least he must rub shoulders with students who are studying the humanities.' On the other hand, there was also opposition in the same circles to the idea that the lower middle classes needed the cultural benefits of higher education and so, contrarily, 'the most powerful argument for the new university colleges was one based on their utilitarian value'.[6]

Thus technology first established itself in the civic colleges in Scotland and in London, spreading later to Oxford and Cambridge to become an integral part of the university curriculum. At the same time, however, technological and applied studies never gained the prestige accorded to them in either the separate technological institutions of Germany or France, or such American institutions as the Massachusetts Institute of Technology (MIT) or the California Institute of Technology, 'Cal. Tech.' Once established, the provincial universities tended everywhere to shift the scope and balance of their studies towards the norms of Oxford and Cambridge. But they lacked the wealth, the libraries and laboratories, the independence of cultural tradition, the social status, and the political connections to offer a serious challenge to the entrenched position of the ancient foundations.[7]

Moreover, Oxford was always able to raid the departments of the other universities to modernize its own research and teaching. Oxford science was built up after 1918 by importing professors and directors of research from elsewhere. For example, organic chemistry was heavily dependent on Manchester, which as a 'first-class waiting-room' yielded up both Perkin and Robinson. Oxford's external relations were, to repeat, interactive. Some developments, for example in philosophy with Austin and Ayer or in chemical kinetics with Hinshelwood or in zoology with Goodrich, were

---

[6] Ashby 1961: 220. 'The utilitarian argument', Ashby adds, ' was less persuasive in Wales. In Aberystwyth and Bangor it was the idea of a university as a place for liberal education which aroused public support.' See too Evans 1953.

[7] Their private endowments were modest, and by the end of the First World War were negligible by comparison with governmental grants. The income from endowments in 1919–20 was: Birmingham £7,500, Bristol £8,000, Leeds £7,100, Manchester £30,500. *UGC Returns 1919–20* (Cmd. 1263, HMSO). See Halsey and Trow, 1971: table 4.20, 92.

indigenous. In other areas Oxford graduates went elsewhere to learn—at Imperial College or Leipzig or MIT. In yet other cases the Jewish exodus from the Third Reich was exploited, for example by Lindemann at Breslau or, after a long delay, with the translation of Rudolph Peierls via Birmingham to the Wykeham chair of physics in 1963.

Oxbridge also initially held aloof from the nationally organized representation of university teachers and researchers, taking no part in the foundation of the AUT in 1919 and not forming a local association until 1939. Even then, and subsequently, the proportion enrolled as members of the AUT remained relatively small. In part this was because collegiate life was based on the democracy of fellowship, while the modern universities were departmental monoliths ruled by professors in their senates and by laymen in their councils. A co-operative of producers has no place for a union. The staff of civic universities, because of their contrasted organization, could appropriately see vice-chancellors and senates as employers. The dons of Oxford, however, were a self-governing corporation. In the 1920s the AUT represented above all the teaching staff of the civic universities.

Oxbridge influence on the AUT was none the less deep. As its official historian puts it, 'A.U.T. policy on university government was closer to the collegiate ideal of a community of scholars than to the civic tradition of a professorial-dominated hierarchy' (Perkin 1969: 64). A local association in Oxford had been mooted as early as 1921, and when it was formed finally in 1939 it had as its president the Warden of All Souls, Dr W. G. S. Adams, and as vice-president Professor E. R. Dodds, a long-standing member of the AUT's executive. Perkin describes the relation aptly in reference to 1947–8:

Oxford had only 103 and Cambridge only 18 members out of staff numbering over 800 and over 700 respectively. Their few members were very keen, and some of them, such as Professor E. R. Dodds of Oxford and Dr V. E. Cosslett of Cambridge, both sometime presidents of the A.U.T., played a very active role in the national Association. Nevertheless, the old tension between the Oxbridge tradition of a community . . . and the professional academics elsewhere with their natural penchant for professional organization, still polarized university teachers into Oxbridge sheep and redbrick goats. One of the jibes of the former against the latter was that the A.U.T. was really a trade union, and from time to time some members of the Association who were not automatically horrified by the notion have toyed with the idea of registering, or procuring a certificate, as a trade union in order to bring the universities and through them the UGC and the Treasury to arbitration in salary matters. (Perkin 1969: 143)

Oxbridge influence was again vividly illustrated in 1961 when the submission of the AUT to the Robbins Committee argued that Oxford and Cambridge were already too big, attracted too large a share of the best arts students, and should not be allowed to expand further or to develop into universities of graduate students. But at the council of the AUT in December 1961 the paragraphs critical of Oxford and Cambridge were withdrawn and replaced by a statement urging the need to examine the relation between the ancient and the modern universities (Perkin 1969: 218). So despite the decline in the proportion of Oxbridge graduates who become university teachers and the increased proportion of scientists and technologists who had been recruited from elsewhere, the ancient influence remained crucial in a vital expression of AUT policy.

As with the organized academic profession so also with the State. Nothing better explains the peculiar character of the UGC than the Oxbridge network of prestigious influence. The UGC's own account of its early days after 1919 refers to the concept of a 'buffer' which was advantageous to both sides. It relieved the government of assuming direct responsibility for the universities, and it safeguarded the universities from political interference. More positively, it was an earnest of the government's willingness to provide money for the universities 'without strings', and it enabled the universities to enjoy public funds without the fear that the gift might turn out to be a Greek one (UGC 1968: para. 554).

And the key to the working of the principle?

From 1919 until 1963 the University Grants Committee was the direct concern of the Treasury. Its staff consisted of Treasury civil servants. It was always clear, and totally accepted, that once they 'came to the University Grants Committee' these civil servants were the servants of the committee and not of the Treasury. But they knew the Treasury, its habits, its ways of thinking; and they knew personally the individual Treasury officials with whom they were dealing on the committee's behalf . . . The Treasury was deeply committed to the 'buffer' principle, and guarded most jealously the committee's independent status. A succession of highly paid Treasury officials, among whom the most determined was Sir

Edward (now Lord) Bridges, defended with all their acumen and experience the autonomy of the universities, and of the committee, against every attack from whatever quarter (UGC 1968: paras. 576–7).

So within the framework of a recently completed parliamentary democracy, Oxbridge retained its effective control of élitist institutions by like-minded members of the élite. It survived fifty years of Conservative and Labour governments because, as the committee put it, 'it has been rooted and grounded in one indispensable element, reciprocal confidence between the bodies concerned' (UGC 1968: para. 55). The tribute is more specifically to the extraordinary stability of the British system of recruitment from Oxford and Cambridge to positions of political and bureaucratic power.

Power and influence are carried by institutions and by people. Establishing an association between Oxbridge and educational decisions and positions is simple if tedious. There is ample evidence of close and comprehensive connection between experience in Oxbridge as a student or don and high office in the politics or administration of educational affairs. It is obvious that Oxbridge was a gateway to power. Most of those who passed through it imbibed and disseminated a set of ideas and assumptions reflecting the norms of the Oxbridge establishment. Of course others have been heretical; and those who have not been Oxbridge people may also have been either conformists or deviants. There is no mechanical processing of opinion by institutional experience. None the less the Oxbridge impact on educational thought and policy was highly significant if only because of the concentration of Oxford men and women in the relevant public offices.

There were thirty-one political heads of the Ministry of Education between 1914 and 1978,[8] seventeen were Oxford graduates, from H. A. L. Fisher (1916) to Shirley Williams (1976); five were from Cambridge, three from other universities, and six were not graduates at all. The first chairman of the UGC, Sir William McCormick, was a Scottish graduate, but the first full-time chairman, Sir Walter Moberly, was an Oxford man. So also was Keith Murray, who became chairman in 1953 and for the next ten

---

[8] i.e. President of the Board of Education 1911–44, Minister of Education 1944–64, or Secretary of State for Education and Science 1964–74.

years presided over a crucially important period in its history (Carswell 1984: 14).

While notables in the world of academic administration and leadership frequently had their origin or early career in Oxford, migratory career-patterns suggest that Oxford assumptions were also carried to other parts of the academic system. Thus Henry Hadow left Oxford in 1909 to become the Principal of Armstrong College, Newcastle and later (1919) the Vice-Chancellor of Sheffield University. J. L. Stocks vacated his fellowship at St John's in 1924 to take the chair of philosophy at Manchester and, in 1936, the vice-chancellorship at Liverpool. The Morris brothers became Vice-Chancellors—Charles at Leeds, Philip at Bristol. Sir Charles Grant Robertson went from All Souls in 1920 to be principal and later Vice-Chancellor at Birmingham. Sir Walter Moberly began as a tutorial don and ended as an academic administrator, becoming the Principal of University College, Exeter in 1924, Vice-Chancellor of Manchester in 1926, and Chairman of the UGC in 1934. Ernest Barker left Oxford in 1920 to become Principal of King's College, London. William Beveridge, after Balliol and Toynbee Hall, eventually became the Director of the LSE. John Fulton, another Balliol don, became Principal at Swansea in 1947 and the founding Vice-Chancellor of Sussex in 1959. A network of famous men linked Oxford to the other British universities throughout the period.

More widely there was a secure and comprehensive connection of Oxford and Cambridge with the world of 'top' people. In 1960 115,000 graduates of these two universities (20 per cent of the total) contributed half the entry to *Who's Who*, three-quarters of graduate MPs, and nearly all of those who entered the administrative class of the civil service and foreign service by method II, which includes a series of personal interviews. And even where initial entry to professions, business, and high scientific posts was open to all graduates, the freemasonry of school and college tended to publicize the abilities and accelerate the promotion of the public-school and Oxford or Cambridge man. A current resentment in the redbrick universities between the wars was that the civil service, the professions, and leading industrial enterprises systematically preferred graduates of Oxford and Cambridge to those of 'provincial' universities.

Moreover, Oxford and Cambridge continued to dominate the Royal Society, the British Academy (though less than in the early decades of the century), the upper echelons of the civil service and the older professions, and the vice-chancellorships (see Tables 3. 1–3). They also maintained their exchanges with the House of Commons, the House of Lords, and the major political parties. The average size of the Cabinet in the twentieth century has been 19.5, of whom 13.5 have been graduates and no less than 11.5 from Oxford and Cambridge. Over the same period a quarter of all ministers (inside or outside the Cabinet) came from Oxford, and nearly a half from Oxford and Cambridge together.

Student organization and sentiment mirrored that of the senior members. As the colleges' senior common rooms had stood aside from the AUT, so their junior common rooms were reluctant to join the NUS (Simon 1987: 189–203). Provincial students both gained and lost by national representation. There was a stronger voice and more national publicity for student needs, but the older universities tended to dominate NUS leadership, to patronize and misrepresent the newer universities, and to subordinate the interests of provincial students to the political agenda of the Oxbridge junior common rooms (Morse 1990). Even as late as the 1950s the separatist tendency of Oxford's undergraduates was still to be found and Anthony Howard, as president of the Oxford Union, failed to persuade his members to debate with their redbrick counterparts (Howard 1954).

The development of governmental policy, reflected in the UGC, the CVCP, the AUT, and the NUS was in effect a rising pressure towards standardization. One consequence was the nationalization of student entry with the formation of the Universities Central Council on Admissions (UCCA), another body which Oxford and Cambridge could bring themselves only half-heartedly to join in 1964 while preserving their separate admission procedures. Standardization through nationalization gave the system more substance and, in particular, created a national body of students. After the Anderson Committee reported in 1960, the redbrick universities attracted students from the whole country and also from abroad. The trend was towards national and international status for every university, and so Oxbridge lost one of its major distinguishing features. State scholarships freed students from the need to earn, and encouraged them to live away from home by offering a larger grant if they did so. Moreover, the new universities of the 1950s and 1960s were free to choose a model or image with a

TABLE 3.1. *Fellows of the Royal Society by university groups, 1900–1990 (%)*

	Oxford and Cambridge	London	Others
1900	36	32	32
1920	37	33	30
1940	34	34	32
1960	39	26	35
1970*	37	29	34
1980*	38	25	36
1990*	40	22	38

* The total association with any university represents 65% to 66% of the total fellowship. There were 1,060 fellows in 1990 of whom 690 had a university attachment.

Sources: Halsey and Trow 1971: 217; *Year Books of the Royal Society*; and *Who's Who*.

TABLE 3.2. *Fellows of the British Academy by university groups, 1900–1990 (%)*

	Oxford and Cambridge	London	Redbrick	Scotland	Wales
1910	74	8	6	12	10
1930	62	16	7	11	4
1961–2	63	24	3	7	2
1989–90	55	21	15	7	2

Sources: *Proceedings of the British Academy*; *Who's Who*.

TABLE 3.3. *Percentage of Vice-Chancellors and Principals educated at various universities, 1935–1981*

	Oxford and Cambridge	London	Scotland	Civic	Other
1935	66	5	18	5	6
1967	59	n.k.	15	10	n.k.
1981	60	11	8	26	3

Sources: Halsey and Trow 1971; figures for 1981 kindly supplied by Professor Sir William Taylor.

less regional colouring than was possible for their Victorian and Edwardian predecessors. The later foundations did not think of themselves as provincial, and the term itself was now less often heard in reference to any British university. All the forty-six institutions empowered to grant degrees in 1970 now had a cosmopolitan flavour.[9]

None the less Oxford and Cambridge continued to choose their students from the upper strata of the hierarchy of class and status of English society. Only 13 per cent of Oxford undergraduates in the 1950s came from the families of manual workers, compared with a third at universities like Manchester, Leeds, and Birmingham (Kelsall 1957: 9). Oxford students had fathers who were predominantly well-to-do, southern, professional and managerial, Conservative, and Church of England. Three-quarters of the entrants at that time came from public or direct-grant schools, whereas two-thirds of the redbrick entrants came from LEA-maintained schools. Secondary schools supported the hierarchy, in that the self-respect of grammar schools was firmly tied to the annual scholarship stakes for places in Oxford and Cambridge. Moreover, enquiring parents of sixth-formers soon discovered—if not from wireless and, later, television programmes from King's College chapel, then from headmasters and LEA officers—that student life at Oxford and Cambridge was blessed with much superior amenities. All Oxford undergraduates either lived in college or enjoyed common-room, library, and dining rights in a college. Only a quarter of the redbrick students lived in accommodation provided by their university, and the student union was widely judged to be no substitute for civilized collegiate life. In the brave pioneering days of the civic universities local philanthropists began to provide halls of residence, for example the Wills family at Bristol. But such provision waned in the depression years after 1929. The UGC provided exhortation but little cash. The results are shown in Table 3.4—a rise to a quarter in redbrick residences by 1930, but stagnation thereafter until the 1960s.

Between the wars redbrick universities lived through a demoralizing period of self-criticism and low esteem, poorly regarded by the national intelligentsia. There was a series of critical appraisals from Herklots in 1928 to Truscot in 1943. Truscot's principal anxiety

[9] For instruction on how to count universities in the UK see Carswell 1985: appendix III.

TABLE 3.4.   *Term-time residence of full-time university students in Great Britain, 1920–1980, excluding Oxford and Cambridge*

Academic year	% in colleges or halls of residence	% in lodgings	% at home
1920–1	10.2	37.5	52.0
1929–30	24.9	32.9	42.1
1938–9	25.1	33.2	41.7
1950–1	24.3	39.1	36.6
1960–1	27.4	50.7	21.9
1971–2	39.7	41.7	16.3
1979–80	46.4	35.0	14.6

Source: UGC returns.

was about the connection between redbrick and what Edward Shils later described as the Oxford–London–Cambridge axis. Truscot's book appeared at a time when idealism and utopian euphoria about 'post-war reconstruction' was sweeping through the Whitehall corridors and the Nissen huts, crew-rooms, and quarterdecks. It was a best-seller by the standards of the day and had to be reprinted. Truscot argued for 'an England in which there are no longer two large residential universities for those who are either well-to-do or brilliant, and nine smaller universities, mainly non-residential, for those who are neither'. He urged that there be eleven universities of approximately equal size, 'all in the main residential and each having certain schools in which each excels the rest' (Truscot 1943: 54).

This formulation retained Victorian Oxford's idea of a university as an élitist teaching institution. Truscot argued that the State should become a generous patron of what would be in effect a system of Oxfords, enlarged to educate an expanded professional élite. And there was essentially the same recipe of commensality. 'It should be an axiom that every university must have sufficient hostels to accommodate a very large proportion of undergraduates, and every student should be compelled to reside, either in one of these hostels, or in lodgings affiliated, as it were, with the hostels, and under strict university control . . . ' (Truscot 1943: 58). The restrictive character of this notion he noted, but dismissed.

The total numbers of students at the university would probably be reduced but that might not be a bad thing, for many think the present numbers too

high. The advantages are obvious. One has only to contrast the present
redbrick university situated in (or very near to) the slums to the redbrick
university city of the future, lying well outside the municipal boundaries,
with its Great Hall, its playing fields, and, above all, its Green Gates, its
White Gables and its Gold Crest, each creating traditions of its own and
gradually endowed by the benefactions of its own former residents—the
colleges, hoary with tradition, of centuries to come. (Truscot 1943: 59)

Truscot had in effect abandoned the modern urban conception of
the university which had motivated John Owens in Manchester and
Joseph Chamberlain in Birmingham. The result was that post-war
expansion came more as a threat than as a support to the civic
universities. Moreover, for all its merits, Truscot's call for reform of
the structure of university studies had similar effects. Leeds,
Liverpool, and Sheffield were devoted to the departmentally
organized, single-subject honours degree, and thereby lost cachet to
the new (if more anciently conceived) universities where, beneath
the superficialities of competitive advertising, there were attempts
to redefine university courses across the boundaries of the arts and
sciences.

There was, of course, a countervailing belief: the idea that
universities should provide high scientific and professional manpower for an increasingly affluent society. Yet the idea of a
university was still for the most part legitimized in the public mind
through its association with the magic of Oxford. Thus, though
there was solemn debate about the location of universities—with
arguments and counter-arguments over the availability of digs, the
crowding of cities, the need to take advantage of existing civic
amenities, and the desirability of missionary movements to civilize
new industrial centres lacking higher education—the policy that
eventually emerged could be plausibly pilloried as a comic pattern
of return to medieval symbols. York and Lancaster, Essex and
Sussex, Norwich and Warwick, were resounding names of places
which might have been Oxford and Cambridge but for the minor
accidents of our pre-industrial history. True, there was expansion,
but the Oxford model was sufficiently powerful to ensure that the
new English foundations were established in locations associated
with agrarian society rather than, as the Victorian universities were,
at the urban growth-points of population. Professor Armytage
proposed a university for Scunthorpe, but in the scramble for UGC
funds the cathedral town was preferred to the industrial area. Only
two of the successful applicants were from the industrial North.

It seemed to some critics and reformers at the end of the 1950s that the 'ancient' and the 'modern' universities might now compete for public esteem on more level terms. A more gloomy view envisaged a compromised form of meritocracy, anticipating that reform would strengthen the existing social hierarchy of learning by further legitimizing merit. On the other hand, room at the top of the professional and scientific world would clearly expand faster than the output of Oxford and Cambridge, which produced 25 per cent of the graduates in England and Wales in 1938 but less than 10 per cent in the 1970s.

Sir Charles Morris believed that in graduate studies the modern universities had already gone a long way towards establishing themselves as independently excellent—and certainly the views of their Victorian founders favoured the training of scholars for research and the pursuit of scientific research. But the primary emphasis of expansion, no doubt properly, was on undergraduate education in science and technology, and the major burden of this training of the new white-collar classes was to be borne by the redbrick universities. Though the traditions of the modern universities might have fitted them better for graduate education, in fact Oxford and Cambridge had more graduate students (2,842) in 1959 than did Manchester, Birmingham, and Leeds combined (2,526) (Halsey and Trow 1971: 75).

By the 1960s the civic universities were no longer regarded as new institutions. That label was appropriate, if ever, only to the first decade of the century. In the same sense the seven new English universities, founded in the enthusiasm surrounding Robbins, were, as we noted in Chapter 1, never new. They accepted established definitions of the conditions for entry and they chose curricula and a balance of learning between research and teaching from within the practices current in the existing western universities.

Oxford and Cambridge still represented the older social and educational ideals of the cultivated member of a governing class as opposed to the highly trained professional expert. They cultivated the ideal of an intimate relation between teacher and taught, maintained through the tutorial method, the shared domestic life of a college, and the separation of the roles of teacher and examiner. They were held up as examples of democratic self-government by academics who were themselves in charge of the administration. Above all they had the dignity of antiquity, riches, and architectural splendour to produce a calm assurance of secure status for intellectual life no matter what political or economic vicissitudes might assail their society.

It seemed possible in the early 1960s that a score of competing educational principalities might emerge to replace the old polarity between redbrick and Oxbridge, unleashing creative energy and stimulating change, and perhaps even subverting the relative popularity of Oxford and Cambridge (Halsey 1961). Yet Oxbridge preserved its predominance, and competition for places at Oxford became still fiercer. A stern meritocracy had emerged by the 1970s: whereas the proportion of undergraduates admitted with very high grades at A-level (AAA, AAB, AAC, or ABB) was stable for the British universities as a whole at about 22 per cent, in Oxford it was 58.6 per cent, and rose to 73.5 per cent by 1980. In our 1976 survey university teachers were asked 'Which is the best department in your subject?' The results are set out in Table 3.5 as 'league tables'. The question was asked in the light of expansion and the foundation of new universities after Robbins, by reason of which it was anticipated that particular 'centres of excellence' would develop in new places.

There was clear agreement as to university excellence in Britain. Among the seventeen subjects Cambridge led strongly in the sciences and Oxford equally strongly in the arts. Taking all votes, and not only those in the subjects tabulated, the ancient English universities secured 36 per cent of the total, with London second (27 per cent), and the major redbricks third (14 per cent).

To be sure, this was by no means the whole story. The London School of Economics had always been a strong challenger in the social sciences, and still held the highest number of votes in economics, in sociology, and in government and administration. Imperial College had a possibly more remarkable prestige in the applied sciences and engineering. Moreover, the solid worth of the Victorian foundations in Manchester and Birmingham, the enduring excellence of Edinburgh and Glasgow, the rise to prominence of Bristol, and the quickly established position of some departments in the new universities were all features of the university scene by 1976. The institutions which seem to have fared least well were the technological universities and the smaller redbricks such as Leicester, Hull, and Exeter. These formerly provincial colleges of London University attracted fewer votes than the new universities founded in the 1960s. They were too late to acquire the solidity of

TABLE 3.5. *Which is the best department in your subject? (% of vote given to institution in each subject, 1976)*

English		Physics	
Oxford	35.9	Cambridge	43.9
Cambridge	24.6	Oxford	14.7
UCL	6.3	Imperial	13.7
East Anglia and York	4.2	Bristol	4.1
History		Birmingham and UCL	2.5
Oxford	47.2	*Civil Engineering*	
Cambridge	21.0	Imperial	40.0
Edinburgh and LSE	3.7	Cambridge	36.2
Economics		Swansea	5.7
LSE	49.8	Leeds and UCL	3.8
Cambridge	20.3	*Government and Administration*	
Oxford	7.0	LSE	26.6
Edinburgh	3.0	Oxford	25.2
Warwick	2.2	Manchester	12.9
Law		Essex	7.2
Oxford	35.1	Birmingham	5.8
Cambridge	30.9	*Geology*	
LSE	8.2	Imperial	22.2
Edinburgh	4.1	Cambridge	18.5
King's (London)	3.1	Oxford	17.8
French		Leeds	11.1
Oxford	22.7	Edinburgh	6.7
Cambridge	13.6	Manchester	4.4
Manchester	10.6	*Mathematics*	
Bristol	9.1	Cambridge	36.9
Bradford	7.6	Manchester	13.3
Philosophy		Oxford and Imperial	9.4
Oxford	89.3	Edinburgh	4.0
UCL	2.7	*Chemistry*	
Geography		Cambridge	26.1
Cambridge	56.3	Oxford	20.1
UCL	14.8	Imperial	17.0
Bristol	5.9	Bristol	7.4
Durham	4.4	Leeds	3.1
Aberdeen and LSE	3.0	*Electrical Engineering*	
Sociology		Imperial	33.1
LSE	27.1	UMIST	9.6
Oxford	11.2	Leeds	4.2
Essex	9.8	Birmingham, Manchester,	
Manchester and Cambridge	6.5	and Queen Mary (London)	3.6
Biology		*Physiology*	
Cambridge	29.1	Cambridge	39.0
Edinburgh	10.3	UCL	28.0
Sussex and Glasgow	5.6	Oxford	13.4
Bristol and Liverpool	4.7		

Source: A. H. Halsey, 1976 survey.

such places as Durham and Leeds, but too early to benefit from the
excitement and adventure of the universities founded in the
following decade.

The 1 in 6 sample of academic staff were also asked whether they
agreed that 'Oxford and Cambridge have preserved their predominance in practically everything that counts in academic life.' There
was less accord in response to this bald assertion. Just over one-
third agreed, one-third disagreed with reservations, and nearly one-
third disagreed strongly. The percentages shown in Table 3.6 make
it clear that agreement about Oxbridge predominance was strongest among those connected to the ancient institutions by study or
teaching experience, among older academics, and in the arts and
pure sciences. Disagreement was strong among those whose careers
had not taken them into the orbit of Oxford and Cambridge and
among those who taught the applied, natural, or social sciences. As
the system widened, the Oxbridge connection narrowed, but still
roughly 12,800 (32 per cent) of British university teachers in 1976
had studied or taught in Oxford or Cambridge at some time.

The continued importance of the ancient universities within the
expanded national system of higher education is confirmed by the
fact that the number of migrants to other universities was much
greater than the resident members of Oxford and Cambridge. Still
more telling are the replies to a further question. 'Which of the
following posts would be most attractive to you personally:
university lecturer and college fellow at Cambridge, professor at
Sussex, professorial head of department at Leeds, or a reader in the

TABLE 3.6. *Percentage of academic staff agreeing that Oxford and
Cambridge have preserved their predominance in practically everything
that counts in academic life, 1976*

Oxford and Cambridge dons	54	Arts dons	44
London dons	35	Pure scientists	39
Redbrick dons	36	Applied scientists	35
Scottish universities	33	Medicine	35
Welsh universities	34	Social studies	32
New English universities	33		
The over-50s	39		
The under-50s	34		
All	36		

Source: A. H. Halsey, 1976 survey

TABLE 3.7. *First preference between university posts in 1964 and 1976 (%)*

Post	1964	1976
University lecturer and Fellow of a college at Cambridge	33	35
Professor at Sussex	30	27
Professorial head of department at Leeds	21	23
Reader in the University of London	16	19

Source: A. H. Halsey, 1964 and 1976 surveys

University of London? As may be seen from Table 3.7 the Cambridge post, although lowest in salary and formally the lowest of the four in rank, attracted most first votes in both years, and in fact rose from 33 per cent in 1964 to 35 per cent in 1976; the chair at Sussex, the chair at Leeds, and the readership in London followed in that order. In both years the respondents were asked whether they would prefer another university to the one in which they were presently serving. Nearly one-third wanted to move, and preferences were strongly for Oxford and Cambridge. On this measure, therefore, the attraction of Oxford and Cambridge was still very marked, if slightly reduced. Preference with respect to other groups of universities was fairly stable, the solidity of the major redbricks in Manchester, Birmingham, Bristol, and Leeds again being notable. In the light of such ambitions it is not surprising that Oxbridge was the most self-recruiting of the groups. The Robbins Committee found that, in 1961–2, 78 per cent of Oxbridge dons had graduated from Oxford or Cambridge, while self-recruitment in the civic universities was 40 per cent (with 26 per cent from Oxbridge) (Robbins Report: appendix III, tables 45 and 46). Our survey in 1976 showed that Oxbridge's self-recruitment had dropped to 59 per cent, while the figure of 39 per cent for civic universities was roughly where it had been in 1961–2 (with again 26 per cent from Oxbridge).

Satisfactions mirror aspirations. Compared with all other groups, Oxford and Cambridge dons were most satisfied with their present university, least interested in moving, and most contented with the standing of their departments or faculties. These satisfactions were in turn well grounded in favourable stipends, career success[10],

[10] We return to this question in Ch. 9 below.

library and laboratory facilities, opportunities for sabbatical leave, and the company of able and well-qualified colleagues and visitors. Over 40 per cent of Oxford and Cambridge dons had already been offered a chair in a British university compared with 15 per cent of their nearest rivals in London University. They lived in a more research-minded environment than their colleagues elsewhere. Two-thirds of them were more inclined to research than to teaching, compared with barely more than one-half of university staff generally. By the various measures of research activity—books and articles—they were the leading group, though only slightly ahead of London. Among their immediate colleagues 58 per cent held first-class degrees compared with 40 per cent in the redbricks and under 25 per cent in the former colleges of advanced technology. In short, the Oxford and Cambridge dons of the 1970s retained advantages of both market and working conditions. And they had meritocratic advantages in terms of academic selection and reputation. In 1976 as in 1964 they were relatively heavily recruited from the professional and managerial classes (59 per cent compared with 49 per cent for all university staff) and the private sector of secondary education (41 per cent against 30 per cent).

Was Oxford the triumphant defender then of a pre-industrial, even anti-industrial tradition? Lord Curzon told the Vice-Chancellor in 1909:

a greater injustice could not be done to modern Oxford than to represent it as the home of stationary forces or ideas. On the contrary, the spirit of reform is probably even more active inside the walls of the University than it is among the vast and scattered constituency of non-resident Oxford men. Our object accordingly should be to . . . convince the nation at large that Oxford is as capable now as ever—nay more so—of fulfilling its traditional part as the focus of the best educational activities, the highest civic aspirations, and the most advanced thought of the age. (Curzon 1909: 13–14)

At the end of the period after Robbins, despite Franks and before Thatcher, the question remained. From the dead the quick had inherited architectural surroundings of exquisite beauty, libraries of fabulous amenity, and standards of intellectual accomplishment to humble their achievements and inspire their dreams. The challenge now as then was to match privilege with responsibility in an age in which egalitarian claims, if denied, could quickly turn into ugly resentment.

In the past Oxford had carried academic excellence in a vessel of economic and social advantage. In the future it would have to justify the claims of its scholarship and science on public academic resources. A Leeds lecturer recorded his nightmare of an Oxford with full private status and charging economic fees.[11] To others too this idea was repugnant, because for them Oxford was a priceless national and international centre of learning. Responsibility had to be public for a public institution.

The Robbins Committee nationally and the Franks Commission locally raised the same issue in the 1960s. Indeed, Lord Franks discussed it publicly with Lord Robbins, who made his view clear in 1965:

The solution to the problem arising from excessive competition for places at Oxford and Cambridge is for the Government and private donors to see to it that other centres of learning are enabled to develop on such a scale and in such a way as to provide places which are not deemed so manifestly inferior as so many of the places provided hitherto have been. This is not something that can happen overnight. But the progress already made in some other universities, both old and new, suggests that, given a more deliberate adoption of this objective, it should not be impossible to achieve it over the next quarter of a century or so.[12]

Robbins's idea of British higher education included a place but no monopoly for the ancient universities. He went on to criticize Oxford for the obscurity of its statistics, its grasshopper vice-chancellorship, its open scholarships (which he wanted transferred to graduates), and its syndicalist approach to its own government. Finally he speculated on the future of Oxford and Cambridge, opposing both great expansion and their development as exclusively graduate schools. Nevertheless, within the general context of a more pluralistic system of competing centres of excellence, he envisaged the substantial enlargement of graduate studies at Oxford beyond 20 per cent as 'Something like manifest destiny'.[13] It was however still unclear in the 1960s how far British higher education, and Oxford within it, could follow the path which Robbins had sketched out for them.

---

[11] In *THES*, 6 Dec. 1974, 13.

[12] Franks Commission, *Written Evidence*, pt. XI, 174

[13] Ibid. 180. The proportion had in fact risen to 24% by 1981: not a dramatic destiny in the event.

In the event Oxford in the 1970s and 1980s remained a proud symbol and exemplar of the western university. Between the magnificent medieval masonry of the divinity school and the elegant twentieth-century concrete of Wolfson College there was a continuously evolving equilibrium of conservatism moderated by civility and of radicalism moderated by reason. From the middle of the nineteenth century, the pace of evolution had quickened as Oxford absorbed the sciences into the collegiate organization of a liberal university. After the Second World War the increasing financial intrusion of the State demanded further and faster adaptation. Oxford University had to find its place in the system of higher education as an administrative hybrid of public funding authorities and private colleges. It had to justify itself by merito-cratic admission of students and election of dons and it had to negotiate competitively with government departments and quasi-governmental agencies like the UGC and the research councils. The evidence is broadly that a successful adaptation was in train.

Yet uncertainty also persisted. Meritocracy had widened the social composition of senior, middle, and junior common rooms, and Oxford could be represented satirically as the best liberal arts college outside or inside America. But was even a successful realization of that reputation enough to honour the past and bequeath to the future? Some thought not. Their essential notion was that the future development of the 'system of higher education' would transform the traditional arrangement of universities admit-ting their students directly from secondary schools. Instead they envisaged a framework of continuing education which could not be confined to a narrow age-band in full-time, state-funded, study but would embrace a range of liberal or vocational studies beyond school for students of all ages. Oxford could of course ignore this possible future, which in any case would not prevent it from continuing its established teaching and research. If however Oxford were to respond, then its admissions, teaching methods, examina-tions, residence requirements, and fees would all have to face drastic change. In its relationship with the British system of higher education Oxford after Robbins was at yet another turning-point in the ceaseless debate which has to be carried on wherever men and women pursue educational excellence.

PART II
AFTER ROBBINS

4

EXPANSION SINCE ROBBINS

THE Robbins Report heralded further expansion in British higher
education. Ideas about development, as we reviewed them in
Chapter 2, and the evolving hierarchy as we traced it from its
Oxbridge apex in Chapter 3, are windows through which the
Report appears in historical perspective. In the following period
from 1963 to 1990 expansion continued in such a way as to
obliterate Robbins as a numerical landmark. Absolute numbers of
students in the higher education system rose every year. In 1962 the
total number of full-time students was 119,000. By 1988/9,
including part-timers in universities, the Open University, the
polytechnics, and other colleges offering advanced courses, it was
964,000.

Apparently therefore Britain has had, and indeed still has, a
record of successful development of its investment in higher
education through fluctuating economic fortunes and through
Labour and Conservative governments. In fact the story is less
simple and more interesting. Less simple because the numbers have
risen at varying rates. More interesting because the definition has
widened from the original conception with which Robbins began.
Higher education, in successive steps, invaded 'further' education.
The definition moved gradually, and continues to move, towards
the American conception of all post-compulsory or post-secondary
schooling as 'higher'. So the statistics I have cited begin as full-time
or sandwich-course students and end with all full-time and part-
time students in a wide range of colleges additional to the
universities. Thus Christopher Ball was able, for 1987/8, to
describe the higher education system in Great Britain as one in
which the polytechnics and colleges (including Scottish ‧central
institutions) contributed 55 per cent of the student total with the
Open University taking 9 per cent and what he labels as 'the other
universities' 36 per cent (Ball 1990: 18). Ball, perfectly properly in
administrative terms, depicts three sectors of higher education with
separate funding bodies—the Universities Funding Council (UFC),
the Polytechnic and Colleges Funding Council (PCFC), and the

Open University funded directly by the Department of Education and Science—with 'no single guiding intelligence' for the United Kingdom as a whole. Underlying this description lies the commitment to a unified mass provision of post-compulsory opportunities towards which educational reformers have been slowly moving for at least a century. At least nominally, the announcement of an end to the binary line in May 1990 brought the end of the process into clearer view. From that starting-point it is possible to examine the interaction of economic, political, and cultural influences which have produced the discontents of the senior common room and the population at large with their unflattering international comparisons and their conflicts between types of institutions, researchers and teachers, academics and politicians, educators and employers.

Looking first at the universities, it may be seen from Table 4.1 that full-time student numbers rose from 119,000 in 1962/3 to 334,500 in 1989/90. But the annual rate of increase was by no means steady. It was as high as 21.6 per cent in 1965/6 when the former Colleges of Advanced Technology were incorporated and when the Universities of Kent and Warwick opened their gates. These were direct consequences of the Robbins surge. But advance slowed down in 1972/3, and turned to retreat after 1981 when the Conservative government imposed severe cuts on the UGC. Absolute decline continued until economic slump gave way to boom in 1985, from which point growth accelerated each year to 1990, recapturing the expansion rates of the late 1960s and the early 1970s.

Economic and funding vicissitudes apart, a demographic and an educational factor underlie the trend of university numbers. The number of 18-year-olds peaked at over a million in 1965, fell to 800,000 in 1973, rose again to nearly a million in 1981, and then fell to nearly the 1973 level in 1990. These wide, even wild, oscillations were, however, evened out by the rising productivity of the secondary schools. The percentage of the age-group with two or more A-levels in GCE rose from under 8 per cent in 1962/3 to nearly double that proportion in the late 1980s (15.3 per cent of boys and 14.1 per cent of girls in 1984/5). Nine out of ten of those who enrolled in full-time degree courses became eligible for a grant towards tuition fees and maintenance following the Anderson Report of 1960, and the proportion of graduate students, though fluctuating, also rose slightly from 16.9 per cent in 1965/6 to 17.7 per cent in 1989/90.

TABLE 4.1. *Full-time student numbers in British universities, 1962/3 to 1989/90*

	Number (000s)	Annual growth (%)	No. of full-time staff wholly university-financed (000s)	% change over 5 years
1962/3	119.0	+5.2		
1963/4	126.9	+6.2		
1964/5	138.7	+9.7		
1965/6	168.6	+21.6	23.6	+65.4
1966/7	182.2	+9.6		
1967/8	199.7	+8.4		
1968/9	211.3	+5.8		
1969/70	219.3	+3.8		
1970/1	228.0	+4.0		
1971/2	235.0	+3.1	28.9	+22.4
1972/3	239.4	+1.9		
1973/4	244.1	+2.0		
1974/5	250.6	+2.7		
1975/6	261.3	+4.3		
1976/7	271.8	+4.0	31.8	+10.1
1977/8	280.5	+3.2		
1978/9	288.4	+2.8		
1979/80	292.7	+1.5		
1980/1	298.7	+2.0	32.8	+2.9
1981/2	300.2	+0.5	30.7	−4.3
1982/3	295.4	−1.6		
1983/4	291.7	−0.13		
1984/5	290.6	−0.4	29.6	−11.0
1985/6	295.5	+1.7	30.0	−10.0
1986/7	301.3	+2.0	30.0	−8.4
1988/9	317.6	+4.0	29.3	−2.8
1989/90	334.5	+5.3	30.0	+1.1

Source: UGC/UFC *University Statistics*, i, table A for the relevant years.

Note: There were *changes in classification of category of payment in 1989/90*: a number of clinical staff (paid by NHS) were reclassified to 'wholly university financed'. Inspection of table A suggests an estimate of at least 400 reclassified, whose removal gives the following figures:

Adjusted for 1989/90: N = 29,573; % change over five years = +0.2.

What were the consequences for universities and colleges as organizations? The effect of growth on the size and shape of universities is of interest in the light of the ideas of the university which we discussed in Chapter 2. By international, and especially American, comparisons the British university remains a small institution (Table 4.2). Even today only seven out of forty-six universities have more than 10,000 students. The average is 6,238 compared with 4,040 before Robbins, and twenty of them have less than 5,000 students. In this respect expansion has not seriously undermined the intimate scale of the traditional notion of a university.

As to the composition of the enlarged student body, the question arises as to whether quality has been maintained. For students in higher education as a whole there has been an increase in the age-participation ratio (defined as the proportion of first year home students under 21 years to the 18-year-old population of Great Britain in the year of entry). Before the Second World War it had been less than 3 per cent. Just before Robbins in 1962/3 it was 7.2 per cent. It rose

TABLE 4.2.　*Size distribution of British universities, 1961/2 to 1989/90*

Size (full-time students)	1961/2	1971/2	1981/2	1989/90
<1,000	1	1	1	1
1,000 to 1,999	12	4	—	—
2,000 to 2,999	4	15	6	—
3,000 to 3,999	3	11	9	11
4,000 to 4,999	2	2	9	8
5,000 to 5,999	2	4	8	8
6,000 to 6,999	2	3	2	3
7,000 to 7,999	—	1	4	2
8,000 to 8,999	1	2	2	5
9,000 to 9,999	1	2	2	1
10,000 and over	—	2	4	7
Average size	(4,040)	(5,000)	(6,390)	(6,238)
No. of institutions	28	47	47	46[*]

Note: London, London Graduate School of Business, Manchester Business School, Welsh National School of Medicine, and in 1989–90 UWIST are excluded. Newcastle, Dundee, St Andrews, and the constituent Colleges of the University of Wales are counted separately.

　* No figures for UWIST in 1989–90.

Sources: UGC *Annual Returns: Statistics of Education*, vi, and UFC, *University Statistics*, i, table 13.

steadily until 1972/3 but then the age-grade chances fell (to 12.7 per cent in 1977/8) and did not climb back to the 1973 level again until 1984 when they rose to 15.2 per cent, and further to 16.9 per cent in 1988/9 (Table 4.3).

TABLE 4.3. *Age-participation ratios (APR) for students in British higher education, 1962/3 to 1988/9*

	First year home students aged under 21 in higher education in GB (000s)	18-year-old population of GB (mid-year in year of entry) (000s)	APR (col. 1 as % of col. 2)
1962/3			7.2
1972/3			14.2
1977/8			12.7
1982/3			13.5
1984/5	138.4	912.5	15.2
1985/6	137.3	901.2	15.2
1986/7	137.1	873.2	15.7
1987/8	139.0	867.7	16.0
1988/9	141.7	839.9	16.9

Sources: DES *Statistical Bulletin*, Nov. 1990, and OPCS Population Estimates Unit.

But did more mean worse? Robbins had been confident that student quality had not declined and need not fall on the Committee's expansion plans. With respect to the universities we can now check this meritocratic optimism from the record of the A-level qualifications of accepted home candidates over the period from 1971. On the basis of that measure it is clear from Table 4.4 that standards were distinctly *higher* in 1989 than they were in 1971. They rose markedly between 1976 and 1984 and then levelled off. It cannot, of course, be maintained that the merit or the aptitude of candidates is exactly represented by A-level results which, in any case, have rather low correlation with degree results. But in the terms of the argument before and after Robbins there is no better practical calculus. The 'pool of ability' has yet to be exhausted. On the standards that obtained when Robbins reported there remains ample scope for university expansion.

For the higher education system as a whole the picture is less clear. Part-time students and older entrants with 'non-traditional'

TABLE 4.4.   *British university entrants: A-level scores of home candidates*
accepted through UCCA, 1971–1989 (% with various scores)

	Scores			
	3–8	9–12	13–15	
1971	28.0	46.7	25.3	
1976	29.8	43.9	26.2	
1981	24.2	45.7	30.0	
1984	14.8	49.3	35.7	
1988	16.6	48.5	34.9	(61,225)
	6–15	16–25	26–30	
1989	12.6	54.2	33.2	(70,219)

Note: Only candidates with three or more A-levels are included and the best three
counted with grade A=5, B=4, C=3, D=2, and E=1. The scoring system was
changed in 1989 to include the AS qualifications.

Sources: UCCA *Statistical Supplements*, 1987–8, table B5, 1988–9, table 2C.

qualifications have to be taken into account, along with higher-
degree candidates and students from overseas. The most direct and
simple measure of degree-seeking potential for the nation is the
profile of qualifications of successive school leavers. By 1987/8 16
per cent of both boys and girls were attaining two A-levels (or three
Scottish H Grades), while the age-participation ratio in that year, as
we have seen (Table 4.3), was also 16 per cent. Admittedly this is a
simplified assessment, not fully taking into account the diversity of
the routes beyond compulsory schooling, or the variety of courses
in different institutions, or all the shifts and potential shifts of
recruitable ability among social classes, ethnic groups, the sexes,
and the geographical regions. Nevertheless it is sufficient to our
present purpose. Other nations have developed bolder educational
ambitions, notably France with its plan for preparing 75 per cent of
its young people for university entrance by the year 2000, and
California, which already has a structure of post-secondary colleges
and universities accommodating the vast majority. Nearly three-
quarters of young Californians now graduate from high school and
well over a quarter attain the bachelor's degree (Halsey 1990).

University teachers have, on the whole, manifested optimism.
The quality of the young, as judged by examination performance at

the end of secondary schooling, had been rising gently since before the period of expansion ushered in by the Robbins Report. In 1965/6 12.9 per cent of boys and 8.6 per cent of girls obtained two or more A-levels in English and Welsh secondary schools. By 1985/6 these percentages had risen to 15.0 and 14.7 for the United Kingdom. Moreover, using the more stringent criterion of very high scores in three A-level subjects (AAA, AAB, AAC, or ABB), the proportion of high-flyers among university entrants has risen from 25.3 per cent in 1971 to 30.0 per cent in 1981 and further to 34.9 per cent in 1988.

The Robbins report in 1963 recommended that the proportion of 18-year-olds going on to full-time education in Britain, which was then 8.5 per cent, should rise to 17 per cent by 1980. In 1964 we asked our sample of university teachers what proportions they would like to see in Britain. Donnish opinion ran ahead of Robbins. About half the sample wanted a higher proportion than Robbins envisaged, though very few, one in eight, envisaged the kind of mass higher education with a third or more of the age-group in some form of higher education which already existed in the USA and the USSR.

Academic opinion shifted steadily upwards in subsequent years until by 1989 well over nine out of every ten university and polytechnic teachers wanted to see more than 20 per cent enrolled by the end of the century, and over a third of both university and polytechnic teachers wanted to go beyond 30 per cent. Meanwhile the growth of numbers, which had faltered in the universities in the 1970s, continued in the polytechnics, especially in the 1980s, so that expansion remained a normal feature of the higher education system as a whole.

Looking back in 1964 our university sample was overwhelmingly satisfied that past expansion had not reduced student quality. 'More means worse' was certainly not the collective view of the past. Indeed, only 1 per cent held such a view strongly, and over 75 per cent thought that expansion up to that point had either raised or left unchanged the average standard of matriculants.

Looking forward to what the Robbins programme entailed, however, the university teachers were more apprehensive. They were asked: 'if the number of students doubled in the next decade with the same staff-ratio, what would you expect to be the effect on the quality of graduates in your subject from your university?' In the event the rate of expansion was less, but not much less than doubling. Nevertheless, a useful comparison can be made between the forward look in 1965 and the backward look in 1976. It appears that experience was more comforting than anticipation. Two-thirds had anticipated a fall in the quality of students, whereas in retrospect, approaching two-thirds saw either no change or an improvement.

I repeated the question in 1989 to find that experience of still further expansion has resulted in still more cheerful opinion about the quality of students. Whereas in 1976 40 per cent of the university staff looked back on a lowering of student quality, in 1989 that proportion had dropped to 27 per cent, while in the polytechnics it was 38 per cent. In other numbers this means that the proportion of university teachers who thought that over the past decade student quality had remained the same or improved rose from 60 per cent to 64 per cent through the 1980s, while the proportion of those teaching in polytechnics who took the same view was 62 per cent. It may also be noted that when, in 1989, the academic staff were asked to assess the ability of students on graduation as distinct from admission, the proportion of cheerful responses (ie. no change or improvement in quality) rose from 64 to 84 per cent among the university teachers and from 62 to 82 per cent among the polytechnic teachers (Appendix 1, p. 276).

A further check on attitudes and apprehensions about student quality in an expanding system comes from the invitation to respondents in 1976 and 1989 to agree or disagree with the statement 'we have now reached the point where more or less all those school-leavers capable of benefiting from higher education have the chance to do so.' Agreement with this view fell over the thirteen-year period quite dramatically. Whereas in 1976 well over two-thirds of the university teachers were inclined to accept it, by 1989 less than one in five did so. And a very similar trend occurred in polytechnic opinion over the same period.

The general line of development is clear. At the time of Robbins the senior common room was looking cautiously towards modest expansion and envisaging a system of higher education not fundamentally different from the highly restricted access provided by the universities before the Second World War. Public discussion led by educational progressives and those who took optimistic views of the educability of the population joined with a growing conviction among industrialists and politicians that a much more highly educated younger generation was needed to ensure the wealth of the nation. Then experience of larger numbers in the post-Robbins decade encouraged more and more university teachers to believe that larger proportions of each new generation were capable of receiving what they had to offer in some form. The bulk of the expansion then took place in the polytechnics and colleges. In the process, it may be inferred, the boundary between higher education and further education was tacitly being shifted. Moreover, the 1989 survey, since it contains judgements of student quality at graduation as well as admission, suggests also that universities and polytechnics see themselves as capable of giving considerable added value to the ability of the students they admit from the secondary schools. These 'value added' numbers are set out in Appendix 1 (p. 276).

Returning to the characteristics of the universities it must be noted that staff–student ratios have deteriorated over the post-Robbins period. In Table 4.5, derived from Table 4.1, the ratio is defined in terms of full-time students and full-time staff who are wholly financed from university funds. So the measure is a crude one. It does, however, unequivocally describe decline, from 8.1 to 1 in 1971/2 to 11.2 to 1 in 1989/90. What are the implications? If we look at international comparisons, British universities merge as uniquely privileged from the point of view of intensive contact between teachers and taught, not only because of the ratio, which is typically 17 or 18 in comparable foreign

TABLE 4.5. *Staff–student ratios: full-time students to full-time 'wholly university financed' staff (GB)*

	Staff–student ratio
1971/2	8.1
1975/6	8.3
1979/80	8.8
1983/4	9.7
1987/8	10.2
1989/90	11.2

Source: UGF/UFC, *University Statistics*, i, table 2.30.

institutions, but also because of residential arrangements, student maintenance, and an entrenched culture of devotion to tutorial and pastoral relationships. The consequence, as we have noted, is that drop-out rates are low and graduate output compares better with other countries than undergraduate input. Furthermore, modern teaching techniques, especially capital-intensive methods of the kind used in the Open University, allow internal differentiation of staff-student contact adapted to the type of course or subject and the stage of education or training of particular students. So the question of teaching-quality must remain open. All we can say is that some retreat from the traditional ideal, and some reverse for the UGC's defence of the unit of resource, has been a feature of post-Robbins expansion.

At this point we are in a position to see the evolving institutional and opportunity pattern of developments since Robbins. The general pattern of expansion is disaggregated in Table 4.6 for the period from 1970 to 1989. It is there confirmed first that the total enrolment rose but the composition of the student body crucially shifted. The traditionally most prestigious form of higher education —the full-time male undergraduate in a university—was the one that rose most slowly, by 8.9 per cent. The lesser and least prestigious forms expanded more rapidly. The number of part-time female students in a polytechnic or in a college of higher education rose by 900 per cent. The Open University enrolment of under-graduates rose by 660 per cent, from 19,581 in 1971 to 60,500 in 1981 and 71,017 in 1989. Thus for the traditionalist the experience of higher education has been one of rapid devaluation through redefinition which is presented as expansion. For the reformer, on the contrary, access has widened (and should widen further) to opportunities appropriate for a modern economy and a universal citizenry. For the traditionalist more means worse. For the reformer more means different.

The expansion of opportunity for women may be regarded as a further complication of the same general pattern. The proportion of all students who were women was less than a quarter before World War Two, began to rise significantly after the mid-sixties, and became 42.8 per cent in 1989. By the early 1990s sexual equality with respect to undergraduate entry appears to have been achieved. Absolute increases invite satisfaction. Relative increases reinforce optimism. But differential relative increases incite resentment and

TABLE 4.6. *Expansion of British higher education, 1970/1 to 1988/9, for various categories*

	1970 (000s)	1988/9 (000s)	Absolute addition (000s)	% addition
University full-time undergraduates				
Male	128.3	139.7	11.4	8.9
Female	57.0	109.7	52.7	92.5
Polytechnic and college students, full-time				
Male	102.0	147.9	45.9	45.0
Female	113.1	146.7	33.6	29.7
Total full-time students from abroad				
Male	23.9	21.1	−2.8	−11.7
Female	8.0	14.0	6.0	75.0
Total full-time students	432.4	579.1	146.7	33.9
Part-time University				
Male	18.1	29.0	10.9	60.2
Female	5.7	21.1	15.4	270.2
Polytechnic part-time, day				
Male	69.8	118.5	48.7	69.8
Female	6.7	67.0	60.3	900.0
Polytechnic part-time, evening only				
Male	39.8	38.1	−1.7	−4.2
Female	5.0	26.5	21.5	430.0
Open University				
Male	14.3	45.0	30.7	214.7
Female	5.0	40.3	35.0	660.4
Total part-time				
Male	142.0	230.6	88.6	62.4
Female	22.7	154.9	132.2	582.4
Grand total part-time	164.7	385.5	220.8	134.1
Grand total HE, full-time and part-time	597.1	964.6	367.5	61.1

Sources: calculated from DES, *Statistics of Education*, iii, *Further Education* and vi, *Universities*.

the reminder that, historically, feminization of occupational roles
has been associated with diminished status. Those who consult the
facts will accordingly have mixed emotions. In the polytechnics
sexual equality of opportunity is established. And as is clear from
Table 4.6, full-time university undergraduate places have accommodated more women both absolutely (52,700 extra women
compared with 11,400 men) and relatively (92.5 per cent for
women compared with 8.9 per cent for men). Moreover, male postgraduates in universities have declined in number. But the evidence
of differential relative expansion is also there. Women have gained
on men but their advance has been disproportionately in the forms
of higher education that are of lower prestige. All part-time
categories have risen faster for women than for men over the two
decades.

For social classes the general tendency for inequality of educational attainment to persist in relative terms is well documented
(Halsey, Heath, and Ridge, 1980). In the post-Robbins period there
is some evidence of small advances towards less inequality
(Glennerster and Low, 1990). Nevertheless, there is an important
cross-national hypothesis which awaits rigorous test—that expansion in the post-war period has been accommodated by a pattern of
institutional development of the kind described in Table 4.6, such
that the most prestigious universities (the Harvards and Stanfords
in the USA, the Grandes Écoles in France, the ex-Imperial
universities in Japan) have actually narrowed their recruitment
on to the upper echelons of the professional, managerial, and
bourgeois classes (Windolf, 1985).

The possibility of this particular form of social polarization—the
'nightmare' to which I have referred[1]—cannot be ruled out.
Glennerster and Low have used General Household survey data to
show that the proportions of those entering higher education from
manual working families have *relatively* increased by comparison
with those from the professional and managerial classes. They
analyse the percentage who gained degrees from the universities
and polytechnics as a ratio to their numbers in the general
population. For degree holders whose fathers were professionals or
managers the ratio was 2.7 in 1974, i.e., they were graduating at
nearly 3 times the rate that would obtain if degree-holding were
randomly distributed. At the other extreme the children of semi-

---

[1] Above p. 19

skilled and unskilled workers had a ratio of 0.2 and the children of skilled manual workers 0.5. By 1985 these ratios had moved to 2.1, 0.4, and 0.5 respectively. The numbers of entrants to higher education from non-manual social origins had risen absolutely, but not relative to their numbers in the general population (Glennerster and Low, 1990: 71–2 and Table 3.14). This finding offers hope to egalitarians, and the evidence of polarization so far is inconclusive. But the movement from grants towards loans inaugurated in 1989 and the logic of education as a positional good might well produce greater class inequality in British higher education in the future.

Expansion, we should emphasize, was not a simple linear progression. Universities, and higher education generally, are always in competition for shares from the public purse and therefore vulnerable not only to shifts in national prosperity but also to both political priorities and arguments about the social return to educational investment. Against a general international background of pro-educational policies there have been ebbs and flows of public confidence as to the desirability of expanding post-compulsory schooling. Robbins caught a strong flow of the tide. But then came the student troubles of the late 1960s, the oil crisis of 1973, and the hostility of Conservative governments from 1979.

If we recall Adam Smith's remark that the word 'scholar' had been synonymous with 'beggar' in the medieval origins of the European university, we may thereby highlight the fact that in the debate leading to the Robbins Report, the perceived relationship between scholarship and society was virtually reversed. Scholarship had been a decorative dependency: now it became received opinion that society needed scholars and scientists to be productively and efficiently modern.

So it was out of conviction of its usefulness that higher education was justified in the 1950s and 1960s. The arguments, true or false, persuaded politicians and constituents that the policy must be expansion. The number of full-time and sandwich course students in higher education in Great Britain rose from 463,800 at the beginning, to 516,300 at the end of the 1970s, and further to well over 600,000 at the end of the 1980s. The previous two decades, the 1968 events notwithstanding, still belonged to the decades of rising expectations. Progressive opinion held that the rise of the graduate was to be of parallel historical importance to the rise of the gentry in the sixteenth century. Educational evolution was destined to pass by stages from élite through mass to universal higher education. Down the ages exemption from exacting, life-long labour had been the privilege of minorities, exploiting the gullibility, weakness, or subservience of the majority. But now, the higher literacy and numeracy of advanced society was to be extended to all.

The rich and privileged, of course, had always had more or less rigorous and lengthy education and training for their stations. These traditions, where they were priestly or military, represented education as an investment. Only for the aristocracy and bour-geoisie was higher education in any serious sense a consumption good. But now, with the authority of Robbins, it was increasingly possible to think of education as investment in human social capital necessary for a modern society, and appropriately undertaken by the State, with a wide social distribution of education as consump-tion an appropriate and desirable consequence. Investment educa-tion was to be distributed by merit, consumption education by democratic right.

Though Lord Robbins was an eminent economist, not until late on into the decade with Fred Hirsch's seminal *Social Limits to Growth* did education, expanded and democratized, come to be seen as a *positional* good, preserving scarcity and frustrating democracy. Expansion, it became clear, does not automatically admit everyone to the educational franchise. So long as jobs are allocated competitively according to certificates issued by educa-tional authorities, scarcity must persist. Education accordingly remained a competitive struggle for positions in the queue for more desirable jobs. Social determinants of educability retained their importance, along with a politics of education which was increas-ingly focused on the higher stages of schools and colleges.

Putting all this less portentously, it could be seen in the early seventies that the future at least offered a secure social base for 'quality' newspapers. Brian McArthur moved from *The Guardian* in 1971 to become the first *THES* editor, making the confident assumption that Robbins had underwritten a third Supplement: and he was right. Circulation viability was assessed in those days at 20,000. Even if the readership was to be confined to dons, there were already 30,000 of them, compared with 2,000 at the beginning of the century, and the numbers were planned to rise beyond 50,000 before *THES* would celebrate its tenth anniversary.

Expansion, moreover, not only guaranteed the readers, but also ensured the copy. Even the student troubles and American doubts about the graduate market, which might have given pause, were also sources of news. In any case there were virtually inexhaustible questions about higher education, so recently an obscure *rite de passage* in the late adolescence of tiny and irrelevant, if privileged, minorities. What, where, how, and to whom a vastly elaborated higher education was to be given were now larger and absorbing new questions. They came out of a society which was developing serious unease about the serviceability of its established institutions —economic, political, and educational—for a future without old external assurances of empire and economic superiority, or the internal solidarity of a United Kingdom.

THES inaugurated a weekly rehearsal of the education answers. Looking back over the two subsequent decades they seem to add up to something like a thousand lessons in disillusion: and the first of these was expansion itself. During the 1970s there were successive reductions in anticipated student numbers from their high point (835,000 by 1981/2) in 1970 to the target (later further reduced) of 560,000 by 1982/3, which was accepted in 1979. In the preceding decade of the sixties the age-participation rate had doubled from 7 per cent to 14 per cent; but in the seventies it fell back again to 13.4 per cent in 1975–6 and 12.5 per cent in 1980–1. Moreover, this waning attractiveness of education beyond school after the waxing hope and resolve of the later sixties portended ill for the eighties and nineties, given the reduced birth-rates of the post-Robbins period, and the advent of the Thatcher/Joseph doctrine of strength through starvation. Here, then, was perhaps the major disillusion of the seventies: the demolition of fond belief that universities and colleges had an assured and, for practical purposes, an unending growth.

Of course, it may reasonably be said, this encounter with reality for the dons only mirrored the experience of the nation. The Gross National Product had followed a similar course. Shirley Williams referred in 1975 to 'the end of the generation of prosperity'. Between 1950 and 1975 Britain had a quarter of a century of steadily rising prosperity during which the GNP per capita almost doubled. But, as with student numbers, the real income of ordinary people then began to slide back, so that by 1981 they were little, if at all, better off than they had been in 1971. A long previous history of steady growth, admittedly slower than in some other countries, and conspicuously so by comparison with Japan, West Germany, and Scandinavia, had made each generation feel wealthier than its parents and expectant of a still better future for its children. Then came the oil crisis of 1973 and the assumption of continuous progress was shattered.

Shattered is perhaps too violent a verb, for both British higher education and British middle-class society were cushioned, materially and psychologically, by an earlier start, the legacy of imperial spoils and established standards of educational living in Oxford and Cambridge as well as York and Sussex, which were the envy of the scholarly world. Moreover, the nation still had North Sea Oil and dons their 1:8 staff–student ratio. Nevertheless, rumours of recession, economic and academic, mounted from the middle of the decade, and became harsh reality by the end of it. In 1973 fewer than half a million were without jobs. By 1977 the unemployment rate was 6 per cent, giving a total of 1.4 million people in the dole queues, and at the beginning of the 1980s the prospect was 3 million, with redundancy entering even the senior common room.

Clearly, then, for the 1980s, either retrenchment or a sombrely revised programme of educational expansion with very different assumptions about the funding and working conditions of intellectual labour had to come. Such has been the post-Robbins history of the academic teaching professions. Growth faltered in the mid-seventies but the national income rose again, at least for the majority, in the 1980s. Educational expansion went on, partly by enlarging the definition of higher education, locating it in colleges which had been previously allocated and administered under the heading of 'further' education, and in the Open University, as well as in what came to be labelled 'conventional' universities. Part-time attendance and short courses multiplied as continuing education was partly absorbed into what was previously stereotyped as a full-time, three-year, residential system for young men.

Why did this expansion, albeit in the form of increased but also devalued opportunity for students and their teachers, continue and even become the first priority of both John Major and Neil Kinnock? Why, admittedly after dropping back to 12.5 per cent in 1979, did the participation rate for 18- to 19-year-olds rise to 16 per cent by 1989 and have targets of 33 per cent set for the end of the century? Taking a long view, the nature and significance of idleness,

I would suggest, is one key to interpreting the decades after Robbins both for British society and the colleges. Idleness has two closely related, but not synonymous, alternatives, leisure and unemployment. The point of economic growth is to achieve leisure, to avoid unemployment, and to profit from a special post-industrial form of idleness, that which was praised by Bertrand Russell, i.e., the release of scientists and scholars from mindless toil so that they might invent more powerful modes of human command over nature—material, aesthetic, and moral. Higher education, on this view, is a justified form of idleness without stigma. It is, so to say, the use of idleness to beget idleness, but the former is constructive research creativity, and the latter is the leisure of a consequently more civilized society: neither involves unemployment, except as failure.

Yet, the seventies in Britain saw a dramatic shift in our appreciation of idleness. On one view the nation may be said to have reaped the reward of past labour and past research, which is economic growth taken out in increased leisure. On another view the country entered a more conspicuously dangerous phase of the so-called British disease, which is idleness in the form of overmanning, the perpetual tea-break, sleeping-bags on the night-shift, etc. The parallel in the academy is clear. Both scientific productivity and literary inventiveness necessitate leisure (the 1 : 8 ratio again, the sabbatical, the long vacation, 'dons don't keep hours'), and the whole point of it all was to increase human domination of the universe so as to provide more leisure for more civilized use. Again unemployment meant failure.

Then from the mid-seventies, earlier in America and later in Britain, with decisive action under the 1979 Conservative administration, came strident challenges to the justification of higher education. It was bound to happen. Britain was adding more students in the quinquennium of the early 1970s than the total attending universities before the war, and £9 of every £10 was being provided directly by the State. Academics had persuaded politicians, employers, and philanthropists that their wares were a paying investment for the nation as well as for individuals. Education was reckoned to yield a higher rate of return than factories or machines. It was, moreover, claimed to be the source of still higher rates of return in the future, because the higher learning produced technological advance. These arguments justified Imperial

College. Parallel ones had claimed that professors could guide politicians to good government. Keynesian macro-economic demand management could be supplied to Westminster and Whitehall from Cambridge, and administrative intelligence could be recruited from the Oxford School of Modern History. These claims now received increasingly sceptical scrutiny as the bill for buildings, salaries, and student grants mounted, and finally came under direct attack especially on the weakest flank, that of the recently expanded social sciences. Arguments from utility had almost entirely displaced arguments from idleness. But a monetarist, market-oriented government, determined to reduce public expenditure, was temporarily unreceptive to both kinds of arguments, so that, for the first time, at least in living memory, the real resources of higher education, as traditionally defined, began to fall.

What is perhaps especially remarkable about the first post-Robbins decade was its illustration that 'the revolution of rising expectations' was not the irresistible force which it had commonly been supposed to be in the 1960s. Not only could utility arguments be questioned, and the Robbins social-demand principles shown to be by no means inviolable, but the attractiveness of higher education itself (as manifested in the demand for places from qualified secondary-school leavers) could decline. Somehow British society, by 1981, could find itself tolerating mass involuntary idleness on the scale of the 1930s, despite the continuation of social inequalities of access to universities and colleges which the 1944 Act and Robbins had been invented to eliminate. The last relevant statistic of the 1970s told us that only 6 per cent of state school leavers went on to higher education compared with 29 per cent from independent schools and 40 per cent from direct grant schools.

Unhappily, then, the seventies saw little progress towards the democratization of leisure which a modern system of higher or continuing education should represent. Instead the end of the decade saw governments, whether of the left or of the right, groping for solutions to external checks on economic growth, while the minority of the educated began to be more sophisticated about the nature of education as a positional rather than an investment or a consumption good, and the majority remained in blighted ignorance that education had anything seriously constructive to offer to either private or public life.

Nevertheless the story remains unfinished. Both economic

fortunes and political pressure moved in the later 1980s. On the economic front a much-disputed restructuring of the economy with an also disputed movement towards integration with continental Europe had educational consequences. The achievement of competitive advantage impelled renewed educational expansion. Invidious international comparison in the preparations for '1992' excited almost hysterical reorganization of training arrangements and reinforced pressure towards vocational education at all levels of schooling. From different standpoints and with different assumptions both the Conservative and Labour parties and the reformed Liberal Democrats began to share the view that a mass system of higher education was inevitable for twenty-first-century Britain. Whether a more open society would emerge in the shape of more equal opportunities for higher education for the children of all social classes and the translation of equalized opportunity into equalized relative chances of employment in the more attractive occupations remains an unsettled question.

As I write, the story is still unfinished and is further obscured by hectic electioneering. On 20 May 1991 the Conservatives, following the other parties, announced the beginning of the new educational era. Mass higher education would accommodate one school leaver in three (an extra 300,000 students over the next eight years), polytechnics could call themselves universities, the funding bodies would be dismantled and 'a single intelligence' would replace them, though with separate establishments in England, Scotland, and Wales. The CNAA would be abolished. Quality would be assessed by the new academic audit unit which had recently been set up by the universities.

It must be immediately added that plans for funding the new expansion remained vague. The drive towards increasing reliance on tuition fees will remain as a governmental stimulus of market forces. The government will also encourage universities and colleges to seek funds from the private sector, particularly from industry and commerce, benefactors and alumni. A fair share of public expenditure is guaranteed to higher education, but the final emphasis is on further efficiency, which the embattled dons will realistically interpret as a levelling down of standards and still further reduction of staff–student ratios. The struggle will doubtless go on beyond the election of 1992. But one thing is sure. The binary line has lost its official status and a post-binary system has begun. It is to that prospect that we now turn.

5

TOWARDS UNITARY HIGHER EDUCATION

A HURRIED declaration of post-binary higher education policy came out of the clamour of the hustings. Its scope and shape are yet to be clarified. Meanwhile, universities and polytechnics may still be thought of conventionally as the ancient and the modern in British higher education. How far these common conceptions represent historical realities can be debated. But such has been the pace of change that a unitary system is now officially in place. The immediate question in 1991 was the timing of the announcement of formal integration. It came in May. Under the aegis of the 1988 Education Reform Act, the UGC had given way to the UFC and the National Advisory Board (NAB) to the PCFC. These two short-lived funding bodies were in close interchange, though their constituents were still divided fundamentally over entitlements to research funding. The new higher-education funding councils for England, Scotland, and Wales will be the forum for a difficult allocation problem. The two sectors have been in a state of chronic reorganization virtually since 1970, when thirty polytechnics were formed and catapulted into rapid growth. Two sectors, it should be noted, was in any case a simplification of a complex arrangement of different colleges and universities. And integration oversimplified the position in Scotland where (as Scottish respondents are quick to remind one) the whole educational system is different and the Central Institutions were not strictly classifiable as polytechnics. The polytechnics had escaped the financial control of their founding local authorities and many of them had openly sought recognition as universities, in effect following the path of the Colleges of Advanced Technology which were born out of the Robbins Report and took their place in the university sector after 1966.

The essential starting-point in making sense of the history of expansion is to recognize that higher education was never coterminous with the universities as we have described them. Upthrust into something equivalent to university status is the major theme of the institutional story from before Robbins. The University of London had been open to matriculated candidates since 1900. In the 1930s about 11,000 external students were registered, and numbers rose by 1975 to over 35,000. In 1979 the polytechnics and other public-sector institutions took over the bulk of these full-time degree seekers. Within the varied provision of non-university institutions in 1966 there were thirty Area Colleges and twenty-five Regional Colleges already offering full-time degree courses to 12,000 undergraduates quite apart from their advanced and non-advanced work. They were waiting in the wings for recognition as part of the system of higher education, and it was out of the Regional Colleges that Anthony Crosland, as Secretary of State for Education and Science, recognized a distinctive 'public' sector alongside the 'autonomous' universities.

Boris Ford asked Lord Robbins in 1965 whether he would have modified his Report in any way in the light of what had then transpired. Robbins was forthright. 'If I had known that anything so reactionary and half-baked as the binary system was going to be propounded I certainly would have suggested adding a few paragraphs to the report, dealing with this as it deserves' (Robbins and Ford 1965: 13). But Anthony Crosland's Woolwich speech of that year and the White Paper of 1966 (Cmnd 3006) announcing the creation of thirty polytechnics established a binary division which has never subsequently ceased to be debated (Bronson *et al.* 1971, Robinson 1970, Pratt and Burgess 1974, P. Scott 1984, Stewart, 1989).

When Maurice Kogan talked to Edward Boyle and Anthony Crosland in 1970 he was given two different views. On the one hand Edward Boyle saw the binary system as 'inherently unstable . . . any attempt at precise articulation of the difference between what a university is for or what a polytechnic is for doesn't stand up' (Kogan 1971: 128).

Anthony Crosland on the other declared that when he had 'finally mastered the subject (he) became a passionate believer in binary and polytechnics . . . ' (Kogan 1971: 194). Crosland based his decision, or as he thought of it confirmation, in part on the view that the universities were not in a position to give the government what it needed at that time. They were, he thought, in the throes of post-Robbins expansion and they 'couldn't possibly have given us the yet further expansion of numbers that we needed', and, in any case, he believed that 'the urgent need was for an expansion of polytechnic-style rather than university-style higher education'. In the White Paper the government asserted its belief that 'the best results will be achieved by developing higher education along polytechnic lines wherever practicable'. And the policy was unbroken by electoral fortune. Mrs Thatcher's White Paper of 1972, *Education: A Framework for Expansion* (Cmnd 5174) endorsed the Labour policy and looked to the polytechnics to play 'a key role' in the expansion of the 1970s.

The Committee of Directors of Polytechnics responded with idealistic enthusiasm tempered by realistic demands. On the one hand they affirmed their confidence in the idea of a polytechnic as an 'enlightened and relevant form of higher education for the nineteen eighties and beyond' (CDP 1974). On the other hand they set out claims for practical support which they deemed essential for success. These demands, in short, were for parity with universities. They wanted a long-term programme for student accommodation, grants, staff ratios, salaries, and administrative and secretarial support which would steadily eliminate the established advantages of the universities in all these respects.

The debate continued. On the one hand stood the entrenched commitment to the independent selective and autonomous universities, cautious in their definition of vocational purposes, jealous of their self-government, and anxious for their material amenities. On the other hand the polytechnics accepted wider definitions of higher education, responsibilities towards local industry and commerce, a vocational mission, and opportunities for local people to pursue part-time courses below the academic level of undergraduate study. The polytechnics were understandably envious of the former CATs which had been given the chance of establishing a polytechnic milieu within the magic circle of the recognized universities, with all the advantages of independence, UGC protection, research funding through the joint support arrangements, and national funds for capital expenditure. The polytechnics at the same time were in practice obliged to distinguish themselves from the Area Colleges and the technical college tradition which was 'further' rather than 'higher' education. The Director of Manchester Polytechnic, Sir Alexander Smith, caught the spirit of a distinctive polytechnic policy in 1974 with his pamphlet *Many Arts, Many Skills*, stressing the flexibility of full-time and part-time courses in the application of the arts as well as the sciences to the needs of a modern industrial and urban society. The justification for social and business studies was also contained in Smith's formula, and with the addition of teacher training, the polytechnics could claim by the early 1980s that their mission of responsiveness and relevance as defined by Crosland had been fully met despite financial constraints, multiple sites, and local authority control. They had made a success of varied modes of student entry, validation by the CNAA, modular courses, and relative ease of transfer compared with the universities. Had they not now earned a fuller administrative recognition? As Maurice Peston argued, 'the public sector in higher education exists for historical reasons' and 'it is desirable to think the whole subject through again' (Peston 1979).

We can carry the discussion further here through empirical comparison of fact and opinion about the universities and the polytechnics from our surveys of teachers in both types of institution in 1976 and 1989. As will become clear there were significant differences of background, qualification, job content, and attitude as between university and polytechnic teachers. But in comparing proportions it is well to reiterate that the two types of organization are different in more ways than are captured by the labels of ancient and modern. In 1976 the university sector was much larger, with 286,000 students against 220,000 in the polytechnics; and there were 261,000 full-time students in the universities as against 100,000 in the polytechnics, of whom a third were doing work below degree level as were also two-thirds of the part-time polytechnic students. There were fifty-three universities and thirty polytechnics. The average size of a university in terms of student numbers was 5,250 and that of a polytechnic 7,000. In general, university students were more highly selected, more nationally recruited, subjected to broader curricula, so that, in an older terminology, they might be regarded as more educated than trained. They were more domestically and intimately taught in institutions which enjoyed superior physical amenities and a greater degree of self-government and autonomy.

Such differences might well have been held to warrant a description as binary. Nevertheless the debate was not over and the situation was not stable. Thus half the polytechnic teachers in 1976 wanted to see at least some polytechnics become universities, and a third of the university teachers agreed with them. Among the other half of the polytechnic teachers who did not want to see polytechnics given university status, the main reason was one version or another of the view that the polytechnics existed to serve different ends than those appropriate to a university. Yet when asked how they expected their own polytechnic to develop in future and given the opportunity of only one answer, well over one-third anticipated that their institution would become increasingly like a university.

By 1987/8 the numbers of full-time students were equal in the two sectors at rather more than 300,000 in each. There were 233,000 part-timers in the polytechnics and the Scottish Central Institutions, with only 41,000 in the universities and 86,000 in the Open University. Nevertheless the essential difference of student mix was still there. Thirty per cent of the polytechnic full-timers were at sub-degree level and 62 per cent of the part-timers. Comparisons are accordingly dangerous. Behind the expansion and shift came a slow blurring of the line between higher and further education which, as Britain finally began a fundamental reappraisal, destroyed the binary divide and opened the prospect of a genuinely unitary system along the lines, for example, of the arrangements in the leading states of the USA.

It cannot, however, be too heavily stressed that the effective transposition of American arrangements for higher education, as they define it, will require much more radical reform than has so far been envisaged by British policy. First and foremost it is insufficiently appreciated that American education, whether formally public or private, is massively subsidized by the State—a huge empirical fact that recent British Conservative governments have completely failed to recognize. Second, the successful pursuit of both wide popular access and high research excellence requires a firm legislative framework defining the 'mission' of different teaching and research institutions under the umbrella of higher education (Halsey 1990). Third, the demarcation between secondary schooling and higher education is quite different in the United States—the outcome of a populist history that contrasts markedly with that of Europe, including Britain. The community college is a uniquely American institution and much American undergraduate education is still the province of secondary schools on the eastern side of the Atlantic. But fourth, and most difficult, is the problem of transposing a culture as distinct from a legislative and financial framework. Education in America is akin to a secular religion whereas, at least in England if not also in Scotland and Wales, salvation, perhaps especially industrial salvation, has been held to reside elsewhere than in schools and colleges. The populist educational revolution in Britain has yet to dawn.

The history of the polytechnics has to be set in this broader context, and what follows in this chapter must not be allowed to illustrate the ancient Chinese saying that when small figures cast long shadows, the sun is setting. Recent changes in both the university and the polytechnic sector may be scanned in Appendix 1, where the main results of the surveys are recorded in the form of the 'marginals', i.e., percentage answers to the survey questions from the two bodies of staff. It is there apparent that, quite apart from the higher rate of expansion in the polytechnics, the scale of internal reorganization has been considerably greater. Asked in 1989 whether his or her faculty, department, school, or unit had been reorganized in the previous ten years it emerged that 92 per cent of the polytechnic staff had experienced such a change compared with 71 per cent of the university respondents, especially by amalgamation with other departments or facilities. Similarly 78 per cent of the polytechnic staff had seen an increase in the students of their specialism compared with 51 per cent of the university teachers. And the polytechnics remained relatively aggressively buoyant about the absorption of future, presumably more, students. They want, in half the cases, to move the balance of student numbers more towards their own type of institution, whereas university staff are inclined to preserve the existing balance. A vital underlying factor here is the scramble for students of high quality in which the polytechnics, as one polytechnic head of department commented in answering our 1989 questionnaire, are disadvantaged by the fact that 'virtually every student would rather be at a university'. Legislation alone is unlikely to overcome this deep cultural commitment to a binary conception of higher education.

We can use our 1976 and 1989 survey data further to track progress out of binary arrangements in terms of four questions: Who are the teachers in these institutions and how far are they already a unitary professional body? What do they do in their jobs? What is their conception of higher education? What has been their own answer to the alternatives of unitary and binary organization?

WHO ARE THEY?

There is nothing in the demographic and social composition of the two groups in 1976 or 1989 that suggests any insurmountable barrier to a unified profession of teachers in higher education. The biographies of university and polytechnic teachers show no crucial difference of class origin or schooling, though the university people are more likely to come from independent or direct grant schools. There is a similar mixture of political identifications and voting patterns, similar proportions of men and women, the women still very much in the minority especially in the senior posts. The university teachers are slightly more likely to come from middle-class families. But none of the differences are dramatic or significant.

There is of course a separate union membership and a different hierarchy of academic ranks both of which stem from separate organizational histories. The polytechnics are more unionized than the universities—78 per cent as against 63 per cent. Approximately two-thirds of university staff belong to the AUT. Slightly greater proportions of the polytechnic staff belong to either NATFHE or the Association of Polytechnic Teachers or both. The AUT and NATFHE work fairly closely together, and the latter has urged the former to consider a merger of the two (Warwick 1990: 9). Academic ranking, like union organization, is a product of separate organizational development. But it entails a crucial historical element in the binary division and one which the Committee of Polytechnic Directors has heavily stressed. There have been relatively more senior posts in the universities. Writing in 1974 the Committee pointed out:

For the education of 1,000 students in a university, there are nearly 40 people at levels of senior educational leadership—senior lecturers, readers, professors—whereas in the polytechnics there are only about five in that salary range.

One in every three members of the teaching staff in the universities is at the level of senior educational leadership—senior lecturer, reader, professor; in the same salary range in the polytechnics, the figure is one in about thirty. (CDP 1974)

The Houghton award and the bargaining misfortunes of the university teachers in 1975 did much to modify this picture. Our sample survey statistics in the autumn of 1976 indicated that, though the range was wider, the average salary in the universities was *lower* than in the polytechnics: £5,376 against £5,564. And the trend from 1976 to 1989 has been a reversal of the differential proportion of posts at senior lectureship level or above. University teachers holding chairs have declined from 10.2 per cent to 9.5 per cent while the heads of departments in polytechnics have risen from 4.0 per cent to 7.3 per cent and it is estimated that 500 professorships (as titles rather than salary brackets) were created in the three years from 1988 to 1990 (Walker 1991). Readers and senior lecturers now constitute 19.7 per cent of the university staffs, while principal and senior lecturers in the polytechnics make up half of the whole. The 15 per cent pay rise (albeit tied to reduced holiday entitlement and a guarantee of up to 18 hours of teaching a week) offered to the polytechnics in December 1990 was greater than the 9 per cent offer to universities in May 1990. So the two teaching bodies continue to converge, though towards a lower level of remuneration than in comparable professions outside higher education.

These externalities again offer no insuperable bar to unification, but there are serious differences between the two groups with respect to qualifications: 42 per cent of the university teachers secured a first-class honours degree from their first institution of higher education, compared with 16 per cent of the polytechnic staff, and while 69 per cent of those teaching in universities hold a doctorate, the percentage among the polytechnic staff is only 32. It is clear that any immediate assimilation of the two sectors into a single structure would involve a sharp reduction in the formal level of qualification beyond that which had already taken place during the expansion of the universities after the Robbins report.

WHAT DO THEY DO?

In our 1989 survey we went into some detail as to what functions of higher education were appropriately served by universities and polytechnics. The outcome (Appendix 1, Question 6) is a pattern of both agreement and disagreement between the staffs of the two sectors. Agreement is indicated where a majority or at least a substantial minority in both sectors sees the function in question as appropriately exercised by both universities and polytechnics. Opinion conforms to this definition with respect to the admission of mature students and those with non-traditional qualifications and the provision of access courses. Both sides also agree that graduate sandwich and part-time courses should be offered throughout the system. But this agreement is heavily modified when it comes to the question of granting doctoral degrees. Here three-quarters of the polytechnic respondents want no discrimination, even though a quarter believe the function to be particularly appropriate to universities. By contrast the university staff adopt the converse pattern—three-quarters want doctoral degrees to be a monopoly of their own institutions, though a quarter are willing to extend the privilege to the polytechnics. This finding has to be underlined in view of the fact that elsewhere, for example in the California master plan, the separation of this function as a province of the university as distinct from the polytechnic (usually called a state university) has been built into the constitution of higher education and jealously defended.

Similarly, while opinion in both sectors is in favour of locating research throughout the system, in that over two-thirds agree that the conduct of applied research and even more the development of links with business and industry are proper functions of both types of institution, disagreement shows itself with respect to funda-mental research. Here the university dons prefer overwhelmingly (79 per cent) to keep this activity in their own hands, while nearly half of the polytechnic staff see it as equally appropriate on both sides of the binary line.

In fact there are no broad types of study to be found in the universities which are not also carried on in the polytechnics (Table 5.1): and, ironically, the only exception is that the vocational studies of agriculture, forestry, and veterinary science are almost entirely confined to the universities. The idea that polytechnics would offer the modern vocations while the universities educated without specific regard to industry and the professions was always a myth. Any notion that the universities are confined to scholarly 'uselessness' or to basic science and scholarship while the polytech-nics pursue the application of science and letters to the vocational needs of an industrial society, founders on the facts. The differences are of emphasis not of categories of study.

Pure science dominates the modern university, while the compar-able giant of the polytechnics is social science, including adminis-tration and business studies. The professional mix as a whole is different (and of course also varies within the two sectors of higher

TABLE 5.1. *Subject area of university and polytechnic staff, 1976 and 1989 (%)*

	University		Polytechnic	
	1976	1989	1976	1989
Education	4.3	3.4	7.2	7.3
Medicine, Dentistry, Health	13.7	17.4	2.6	3.2
Engineering and Technology	12.9	8.3	20.5	14.2
Agriculture, Forestry, Veterinary Science	2.5	2.2	0.0	0.5
Science	31.3	26.6	18.5	25.6
Social Sciences, Administration, Business	17.7	21.6	27.9	30.9
Architecture, Professional and Vocational	1.7	1.0	7.3	5.9
Languages, Literature, Area Studies	9.4	10.3	5.6	5.0
Other Arts	6.4	9.3	10.4	7.4

Source: A. H. Halsey, 1976 and 1979 surveys.

education), but stems more from the circumstances of expansion—the technical colleges obviously brought in the relative weight of engineering and technology to the polytechnics, the older professions of medicine and dentistry were firmly established in the universities before the rise of the technical colleges; rapid expansion of polytechnics was partly effected through absorbing colleges of education, and the social sciences offered the cheapest form of growth.

However, when we turn from subjects to types of activity in relation to them, marked contrasts appear. University staff are much more involved with research than are their polytechnic colleagues. This basic difference of behaviour and outlook is reflected in both the activity and the orientation reported by our respondents in 1976 and in 1989. Admittedly there has been some convergence. There is more supervision of research students in the polytechnics now than then; there has been an increase in research work by polytechnic teachers and an increased publication rate throughout the system, even though both sectors have had their research and teaching time significantly invaded by administrative work and the wholesale internal reorganization of departments and faculties. The university academic spends a fifth and his polytechnic colleagues a quarter of his or her time on these activities.

Nevertheless, serious differences remain. In 1989 over three-quarters of the university teachers were supervising research students compared with less than a third of the polytechnic teachers. Nearly all university teachers were currently doing work expected to lead to publication compared with less than three-quarters of the polytechnic teachers. Over half of the former had published more than twenty articles whereas over a quarter of the latter had published none. And what is most telling about the institutional milieu is that the felt pressure to do more research than the respondent would ideally like is expressed by similar minorities of about a third in both sectors. Polytechnic teachers incline more towards teaching and spend more time on it—48 per cent of their working time compared with 34 per cent in the case of the average university teacher.

CONCEPTIONS OF HIGHER EDUCATION

These contrasts in style of professional behaviour suggest a binary division between researchers and teachers. But this is less a distinction between persons than between the emphases of institutional life. History generated the institutional difference. But self-selection may then perpetuate it and perhaps accentuate it. The survey data supports such a view. More than half of the university teachers specify a leaning of their interests towards research rather than teaching, compared with a quarter of the polytechnic teachers. There is more agreement among *both* university teachers and polytechnic teachers that 'an active research interest is essential if a person is to be a good university teacher'. And when asked what proportion of his or her time would ideally be spent on research, the average university teacher answers 40 per cent and the average polytechnic teacher 24 per cent.

It is congruent with this pattern of views and activities that when asked to evaluate their own department in relation to its equivalent in other universities (polytechnics), the university staff tend to see their departmental strength in research and the polytechnic staff to do so in undergraduate teaching. There is an increasing overlap of conceptions of higher education but the map remains divided, not so much into distinct territories as into two strata of prestige and attractiveness. The hierarchy can be seen from the data on ranking departments, subjective definitions of career success, and the patterns of choice in response to opportunities of shifting between the two sectors. When asked to name the best department in the respondent's own subject in Britain, first choices went overwhelmingly to the university departments, from both university and polytechnic teachers. In the minds of the university teachers the hierarchy runs from Oxford and Cambridge through the most famous London colleges (Imperial, LSE, and UCL) to Manchester, Edinburgh, Bristol, and Warwick. No other university department and no polytechnic at all gained as much as 2 per cent of first votes. Oxford and Cambridge attracted 34 per cent of the first university votes, London 22 per cent, and Manchester 4 per cent. From the polytechnic voters London got most acclaim with 19 per cent, Oxford and Cambridge second with 16 per cent, and Warwick third with 3.4 per cent.

Similarly, when asked to identify the post regarded as the highest professional achievement, the university claimed the overwhelmingly preponderant share of choices from both university and polytechnic staff. Almost no university teacher named a polytechnic post, and the university chair, especially at Oxford or Cambridge, was the majority choice. Among the polytechnic staff over half named a university post, usually a chair, and less than one-third named a lectureship, departmental headship, or directorship of a polytechnic. Again similarly, attitudes to shifting across the binary divide are markedly asymmetric. If offered the opportunity, two-thirds of the polytechnic staff would take it seriously at the same salary, and nearly a fifth at a lower salary. By contrast three-quarters of the university teachers would not consider going to a polytechnic at the same salary, and as many as 44 per cent would fail to be tempted by a higher salary.

THE UNITARY SOLUTION?

There has been glacially slow movement towards the abolition of the binary divide. In 1989 nearly two-thirds of polytechnic teachers wanted distinctions between their institutions and the universities to disappear. But more than three-quarters of the university staff were opposed. Underlining this pattern of opinion there are sharp differences of attitude between the senior common rooms of the universities and the polytechnics. It is agreed by nine out of ten of our respondents on both sides of the divide that there should be equal non-academic provision, for example, residential accommodation. It is also agreed by the majority on both sides that a division of function in which the universities restricted themselves to the traditional academic subjects, leaving the newer and more vocational subjects to the polytechnics, is not desirable.

But beyond that point the two sides radically disagree. A majority of polytechnic teachers want a common salary scale, while the majority, though admittedly a bare one, of the university teachers do not. They want instead, in a two-thirds majority, to have better staff–student ratios, and this is a view rejected by virtually all the polytechnic staff. Again, while the polytechnics want equal academic provision, for example of libraries and laboratories, a third of the university teachers would be unwilling to equalize in this respect. The majority of the polytechnic respondents do not think the polytechnics should become more like universities or that universities should become more like polytechnics, and both these views are even more heavily supported by the university teachers. Their views as to what will in fact happen are, however, all too realistically cynical. They represent an effective recognition that central directives will run counter to academic opinion. Most particularly, between two-thirds and three-quarters on both sides believe that the universities will, over the next decade, become more like polytechnics.

A lecturer in economics at one of the Scottish Central Institutions wryly summed up the position in 1989. 'Questions relating to what universities and polytechnics do best are difficult to answer. The reality seems to me that we offer higher education at lower cost, achieved by more facilities and by cutting out some high cost areas (e.g., medicine) and some specialisms that will always have small numbers of students due to limited job opportunities. The distinction into vocational and non-vocational is one of less importance.'

CONCLUSION

History gave us a binary system of higher education. Policy now aspires to unity. But neither can offer a separate but equal division of institutions with discernibly different functions. Neither existing practice nor the opinions of teachers in higher education offer any basis for any such functional division. The distinction is different. It is more a separation in higher education between levels of amenity, quality of staff, and concern with the advancement rather than the transmission of knowledge. Both universities and polytechnics teach, but the university adds a more pronounced effort in research and has the equipment, and still more the quality and interest of staff, to pursue it.

Opinion in the senior common rooms reflects these similarities and differences. The hierarchy is widely acknowledged. Career aspirations and conceptions of prestige clearly favour the university. There would have to be a massive switch of resources, especially resources for research, to shift the widely held preference for a university career. Equalization of salaries has not, and could not, by itself shift the awareness of a more attractive research milieu in the universities. Naturally enough, most polytechnic teachers want complete equalization of amenity, supporting staff, student ratios, salaries, and career opportunities. University teachers sympathize with respect to non-academic amenities but, equally naturally, they tend to resist the other demands, seeing themselves collectively as engaged in the same enterprise—higher education—but at higher standards, especially of research, through their higher qualifications and more selective recruitment.

The reality of the binary system, in short, is a blurred division of quality and not a horizontal division of educational function. Future scarcity of resources is unlikely to allow levelling up of the polytechnics to university standards. Levelling down is more likely, but further threatens the already endangered position of the universities in the international world of science and scholarship. The whole structure needs to be thought through again, in unitary terms. With a Higher Education Council throwing the protection of an umbrella over the UFC, the PCFC, and indeed all post-secondary education, we may at last look forward to the possibility of a coherent national policy with well-defined functions for collaborating colleges and a realistic system, flexible in its arrangements for student transfer, but firm in the resolve to provide for research excellence as well as massive opportunity.

6

GUILD, UNION, PROFESSION, AND PROLETARIAT

THE 'key profession' may have dug its own grave. It faces a future of mass higher education after a quarter of a century of adaptation to the consequences of its own successes. Survey at the time of Robbins showed *The British Academics* to be 'basically conservative; even those who are boldest and least conservative in their own intellectual lives want to preserve and strengthen the institutions which make their scientific and scholarly achievements possible. Expansion means change; change holds promise, but also a threat . . . ' (Halsey and Trow 1971: 465). The expansion has occurred, its scale if not its shape following and going beyond the target set in the Robbins report. What then has happened to the academic professions?

A first answer in 1992 must be that senior common room morale is low. In 1989 as many as 37 per cent of university teachers and 39 per cent of their polytechnic colleagues had seriously considered leaving academic life permanently: the comparable percentage among university staff in 1964 had been 23. The underlying explanation was, I believe, anticipated by the Weber and Veblen forebodings of 1918: the key word is a long and alien one—proletarianization. Yet the story is complicated, not least by the fact that expansion of higher education (and the professional classes to which it has added itself and which it serves) has been accompanied by further developments of institutional hierarchy and the recrudescence of market as opposed to guild conceptions of the academic calling.

There are basically three ways to provide time, place, and facilities for the pursuit of academic activity. The first is a status group, the second a market, and the third a professional bureaucracy. Elements of all three are to be found in twentieth-century Britain, but from the First World War to the 1970s, higher education evolved essentially from the first to the third form, with the State as the almost monopsonistic employer. In the 1980s governmental policy on funding and on the settlement of salaries, tenure, and conditions of work, took a new tack in the direction of fostering an academic market-place. The question therefore is whether these developments, old and new, represent a trend towards proletarianization.

Proletarianization may be defined as a threefold reduction of power and advantage in the work and market position of a class or occupational group: in autonomy of working activity, security of employment, and chances of promotion. All three have changed. We shall review this triple trend in order to decide whether and in what senses academic power and advantage may have been diminished in the course of expansion and the increasingly market orientation of the 1970s and 1980s. A further and related question may be illuminated by the same analysis. It was in the 1970s that the issue came to a head as to whether the AUT should affiliate with the TUC. Should, as many members would have put it, the AUT become a 'real' union?

Traditionally dons were gentlemen—a status group depending for their material existence on a gentlemanly class with power and inclination to support scholars as vicarious members. Ruling classes of priests have, historically, indulged these tastes more liberally than have those composed of soldiers or business men. Certainly the medieval European university was primarily a creature of the Church. Out of that tradition there emerged a system of fellowship in the Oxford and Cambridge colleges as the origin and model of an elevated pedagogy with its distinctive features of commensality,[1] concern for moral as well as intellectual curricula, and resistance both to mass instruction and specialized science. Fellows had not only this cultural foundation of solidarity but also the material base of autonomy through their share in the corporate ownership of college endowments, continually renewed by Church and State, and by bequests from the gentlemanly classes into which the colleges sent a significant proportion of their alumni. At least until the middle of the nineteenth century fellows did not constitute a professional cadre. Even the academic career was essentially transient; a youthful interlude *en passage* to marriage and a 'living'

---

[1] Celibate monks evolved elaborate forms of dining, deflecting their tastes from sexual intercourse into the sensualities of cuisine. A beneficial by-product was the refinement of conversational arts through wide tables and changes of seating in three different rooms as a dinner progressed.

controlled by the college in some more or less remote Anglican parish.

These quaint arrangements could not and did not survive into a modernized secular age. None the less they have had a deep influence on the self-conception of university teachers in general and on the development of the AUT in particular. They offered an alternative model to that imported from Germany—scholars organized in a federation of hierarchic departments on a university campus. They also offered an alternative to the American academic market-place, in which a wide range of academic enterprises compete for the employment of teachers and researchers by individual bargaining. Even today, in international comparison and mythology, the don remains an admired and resented model of academic privilege and autonomy. As late as 1930 Abraham Flexner visited from America to envy Oxford and Cambridge for their inestimable advantage possessing 'ample means of associating in worthy scholarly fashion with men of learning and distinction, not only an amenity but a source of profound spiritual stimulus. However modest the means of an Oxford or Cambridge scholar, he can without effort or sacrifice be host to a Minister of State, a great scientist or a philosopher' (Flexner 1930: 288).

Even in the 1980s Peter Scott was still emphasizing the distinctive character of the British academic professions compared with their counterparts on the European continent, stressing their solidarity of outlook and the autonomous conditions under which the British carried on their teaching and research. He remarked the relative equality of privilege and influence between junior and senior staff, their strong collegiate traditions, the unity of teaching and research, the ambiguity of status relations between professors and tutorial fellows in the Oxbridge colleges, and the general homogeneity of intellectual and cultural values that pervaded all ranks, all faculties, and all institutions, including the polytechnics as well as the universities.

Some of Scott's arguments may perhaps be challenged. By pointing to the 'gold standard' of externally examined degrees he played down the inequalities between institutions which I have sought to emphasize, especially in Chapter 3. He acknowledged the binary divide and the more hierarchical traditions of the technical colleges from which the polytechnics evolved: but he saw the development of polytechnic staff as assimilating to university habits and customs with the erosion of administrative power and hierarchical ethos. Most telling in a comparative context, he observed that:

No master plan has ever been envisaged that would assign precise educational roles to particular institutions. Indeed the Council for National Academic Awards, which validates degrees in non-university institutions has acted as a notable agent of synthesis, not only providing an avenue for polytechnics and colleges to undertake work all the way up to PhD level but also encouraging the development of common academic values across the system.

There are some signs of developing solidarity (which were examined in more detail in Chapter 5), but on balance, they are over-weighed by the forces that have placed the polytechnics on the lower levels of the modern pyramid of institutions of higher education.

At all events the old legacy of the academic guild, and the slow pre-Robbins expansion, favoured the rise of donnish power. In Britain, as Scott argues, distinctive conditions favoured state benevolence towards the universities—the higher education system was small and the UGC a product of Oxbridge connection to Westminster and Whitehall. And, what Scott most strongly emphasizes, 'the pragmatism of the British intellectual tradition inhibited the development of an oppositional intelligentsia which might make its natural home in higher education and so provoke the suspicion of established society' (Scott 1983: 249). On the contrary, pragmatism and distinguished work in the natural sciences reinforced the willingness of ministers to subsidize the universities and extended the quiet influence of academics in the higher reaches of politics and public administration. Both business and government actively sought the professional services of professors. Academics were reconciled to both the public and the private society that gave them their privileges.

Professionalism came slowly. The celibacy rules at Oxford and Cambridge survived into the 1860s. An academic meritocracy began only with the Victorians. By the end of the nineteenth century there were but 800 dons in the ancient English colleges, 500 teachers in the provincial redbrick universities, a similar number in Scotland, and 250 in London. Nevertheless, organized science was beginning to make its mark on university life and the two world wars increasingly attracted governments and industrial firms to its patronage. An even more important force for expansion and change was the slow unfolding of the logic of a political democracy with its intrinsic demand for popular access to the material and cultural advantages of education and for guaranteed programmes of economic growth. Both of these elements of modernization became political objectives. Competing political parties put forward alternative means to achieve them. Thus the State emerged as the principal provider and eventually threatened to become the sole controller of academic jobs, graduates, and research.

Expansion in Britain came late but with relatively dramatic speed. By the Second World War there were still only 5,000 university teachers, but after Robbins came the eightfold increase to 40,000 in the course of a decade, rising further to 70,000 by 1991. When the UGC was created after the First World War, universities had a total annual income of £3 million. Before 1945 university teachers lived comfortably on the margins of economic and political life. In the post-war generation they, by and large, enthusiastically supported the aggrandizement of their own interests under the patronage of government. Not until the 1970s was there serious questioning of the possibility of conflict between their and the State's interests. In the meantime it was the social sciences, the studies with the least secure claim to academic privilege in return for social service, that had grown disproportionately on both sides of the binary line.

When, after the First World War, Max Weber in Germany drew attention to the incipient proletarianization of intellectual labour, and Veblen in America inveighed against the subordination of universities to business interests, there was little echo in Britain. University teaching was strongly contained within the gentlemanly tradition. True, the redbrick employers tried at first to behave as market maximizers, striking individual bargains such that the range of salaries within the professoriate was greater at the turn of the century than is the range over all academic ranks now. And true there was exploitation of young recruits by professors who, sometimes employing assistants personally, would withhold tenure and substitute a cheap beginner every three years. Part of the drive towards founding the AUT came from these miseries. But almost from the beginning the union embraced the whole hierarchy of academic ranks and thereby muted internal conflict. This was at a time when, although professors earned four times as much as their assistant lecturers, the average university teacher earned four times as much as the average manual worker.

After the Second World War, government insisted on assimilating all university teachers into a national academic bureaucracy in respect of salaries. There was little opposition to the disappearance of direct market determination of stipends. Only the highly organized and highly connected medical fraternity got and kept a salary differential. The gentlemanly heritage sanctioned what was in effect a modern form of guild. The AUT expressed a rhetoric of internal hierarchical harmony. Gentlemen are not subjected to wages, hours, and conditions of work. They have no employer, no trade union, and no machinery of negotiation, arbitration, and conciliation. They receive remuneration, not a rate of pay. They follow a vocation rather than hold a job. All would, in any case, be well, it was widely believed, while the UGC played a 'buffer' role between dons and Treasury knights who had shared social priorities firmly anchored in their common upbringing in public schools and ancient colleges.

Under these circumstances the AUT was of little consequence. Moreover, expansion after the Second World War gave some scope for academic entrepreneurship within the framework established by the English form of the gentlemanly tradition. The tutorial heritage had justified the highest staff–student ratios in the world. Professionalism had added the modernized doctrine that half of a university teacher's time was for research. The resulting combination of light duties and personal autonomy relied on colleaguely reputation to ensure productivity. Such a framework of money and morals made it possible for some, to a greater or lesser degree, to use the university post as a base for further entrepreneurial earning through consultancies, advice to governments, journalism, and the like. The National Incomes Commission (NIC) tried to measure this entrepreneurship in the 1960s. The consequence which mattered was not the dubious accuracy of the measurement of supplementary earning so much as a weapon with which civil servants could reject the claim of academics for stipends comparable with those of their own upper echelons.

Thus the university teaching professions, which were originally neither professions nor confined to teaching, adapted their gentlemanly and collegiate origins to specialized professionalism and finally to bureaucratization as the State took over the management of higher education. Yet the accompanying prospect of proletarianization was differently viewed in Britain compared with America. In America in the 1970s Professor S. M. Lipset phrased the problem as one of unionization, growing rapidly in the United States in response to threats to 'the faculty', from students on the one hand, and on the other from niggardly state finance. The danger, as Lipset saw it, was one of threat to the individualistic opportunities and rewards of a meritocracy—the revenge of the mediocre. In Britain there was the marked difference of uniform salaries in a national academic guild, and the problem was accordingly formulated as one of threat to the total collective income of the guild. Was, then, a gentlemanly status group to be proletarianized? That was the issue which, in Britain's peculiar society, could appear as the question of whether academic salvation was to be found in the avuncular arms of the president of the Trades Union Congress, Len (later Lord) Murray.

Opinion in America at the time was running strongly in favour of unionization. A majority (61 per cent) were in support, even among the privileged and successful academics in those American research universities (which were equivalent to the contemporary British universities) whose members most strongly favoured salaries based on merit as distinct from age or seniority. Unionization, Lipset and Ladd ruefully concluded, was 'the wave of academia's future' (Ladd and Lipset 1976).

In Britain affiliation to the TUC was the subject of a ballot paper for the first time in 1971. The Council of the AUT sent out, with the ballot papers, a document which on balance advised rejection of affiliation on the ground that the machinery of negotiation used in the trade union movement was 'based on the model that there is a permanent and irreconcilable conflict between employer and employee', whereas the new negotiating arrangements for university salaries were superior—a quadrilateral corporatism with the UGC, the CVCP, and Government. The underlying reluctance, however, stemmed from a persistent attachment to the traditional guild ideas of academic self-government and autonomy. In the event resentment against relative reduction of academic salaries within the hierarchy of unequal pay, together perhaps with the hope that TUC solidarity would in the future somehow protect all 'workers', manual or non-manual, was sufficient to win the day and the guild tradition was still further attenuated.

By the 1990s it has become apparent that power or industrial 'muscle' remains elusive and the long secular deterioration of the class conditions of intellectual labour continues unchecked. The trend figures are shown in Table 6.1. The differentials by academic rank and by sex are given in Table 6.2 for 1988/9, linked to measures of the qualifications of the relevant categories. It appears that, within the trend towards lower relative average earnings, men and the higher academic ranks receive more than research staff or women. Decline is again accompanied by hierarchical differentiation.

Nevertheless it must be noticed that the salary variation is not large by comparison either with the history of academic remuneration or with the inequality of wages and salaries in the economy as a whole. From the records kept by the University Statistical Record of full-time academic staff in the British universities it appears that in December 1989 the average professor received 2.74 times more salary than the average research worker, 1.76 times that of the average lecturer, and 2.8 times the average of the lowest-paid category, the female research worker. We shall return to sex differences in Chapter 10. Here it may be remarked that though there are clear sex differences in chances of promotion between the academic ranks, at each rank there are no sex differences of pay.

As between the university groups the range of salaries is narrower than that between ranks—though it must be remembered that Oxford and Cambridge incomes from college employment are not included in the USR returns.[2] (The Franks Commission in

TABLE 6.1. *Average salaries of British academic staff, 1928–1989*

	1928/9	1938/9	1951/2	1956/7	1966/7	1988/9
A. All university teachers, average earnings (£ p.a.)	584	612	1,091	1,328	2,368	18,470
B. Average earnings, manufacturing industries (£ p.a.)	156	184	455	648	1,102	11,975
Ratio A/B	3.7	3.3	2.4	2.0	2.1	1.54

Sources: Halsey and Trow 1971, and A. H. Halsey, 1989 survey.

[2] There is currently (1991) agitated discussion in Oxford concerning wide disparities of pay between people of the same academic rank doing the same job but in different colleges. College emoluments may result in total salary disparities of £5,000 p.a.

TABLE 6.2. *Full-time university academic staff, 1988/9 (GB): rank, age, qualification, and salary by sex*

	No. in various ranks			Age 50+ (%)			Higher degree (%)		1st class 1st degree (%)			Mean salary (£000s)		
	Men	Women	All	Men	Women	All	Men	Women	Men	Women	All	Men	Women	All
Professor	4,008	126	4,134	61.4	62.7	61.4	84.8	77.0	40.3	33.3	40.0	28.8	27.8	28
Readers/Senior lecturers	7,813	706	8,519	41.2	39.1	41.0	77.2	58.4	31.9	23.4	31.2	23.8	24.6	23
Lecturers	19,658	5,141	24,799	12.7	8.2	11.7	65.7	62.3	30.3	24.6	29.1	16.6	15.4	16
Research staff	2,714	1,832	4,546	0.5	0.9	0.7	24.0	21.7	16.2	11.1	14.1	10.5	10.3	10
TOTAL	34,193	7,805	41,998	23.9	10.2	21.3	67.2	53.7	30.7	21.4	29.0	19.2	15.2	18

Source: USR Census of full-time staff at 31 December 1988.

Oxford in 1965 calculated the Oxbridge/non-Oxbridge differences as somewhere between 4 per cent and 18 per cent.) The average salary of full-time university academic staff in Britain as a whole in 1989 was £19,498.80 per annum. Indexing on this base produces the minor variations shown in Table 6.3. The dispersion between university groups, leaving aside the Oxbridge questions, is insignificant. There is only one system of national payment and such variation as exists is a function of differences in the faculty and rank structure of the eight university groups. Faculty variation in turn is wider but still small, varying from 115.2 per cent in the medical faculties to 91.0 per cent in the biological and agricultural sciences. It may, perfectly reasonably, be objected that the inequality is understated because the categories are heterogeneous, and it is true that, when further subdivided within university groups and faculties by age, rank, and sex, wider variation can be

TABLE 6.3.   *Salary variations, 1972 and 1989, by university group and faculty* (Indexed)

	1972	1989
Total average salary (£)	3,721	19,499
University Group		
Oxford and Cambridge	82.4	93.8
London and London Business School	105.6	101.9
Scotland	100.3	101.0
Wales	99.0	101.4
Old redbrick	101.2	101.8
New redbrick	101.1	98.3
New universities	95.5	98.9
Technological universities	107.0	98.1
Faculty		
Education	105.7	105.2
Medical, Dental, Veterinary	114.3	111.5
Allied to Medicine	97.6	96.9
Biological and Agricultural	92.2	91.0
Maths and Physical Science	96.5	96.0
Engineering, Technology, Architecture	105.2	93.5
Administration, Business, Social Studies	94.3	101.9
Language, Literature, Area Studies	96.0	100.3
Other Arts	98.7	104.4

Source: calculated from USR, Dec. 1989

discovered. Thus a more detailed breakdown shows that there is, for example, a small group of Oxbridge medical professors in the last ten years of their service with stipends of over £56,000 per annum and a similarly small group of female social science research workers in the older redbricks with salaries below £11,000 per annum. But the bulk of the university academic profession—the lecturers in all universities, all faculties, and both sexes in mid-career are paid between £16,500 and £19,000.

Moreover, it may also be noted from Table 6.3 that despite the moves towards a more market-driven determination of academic salaries which have been prominent in government policy in recent years, the *actual* dispersal narrowed from 1972 to 1989. London and the Technological Universities moved towards the national norm. The marketing drive is undoubtedly there, but has yet to show itself as conspicuous inequality. The 1 per cent grant for discriminatory individual awards initiated in the 1988 salary settlement seems to be establishing itself as a cumulating annual differentiation which will steepen the salary hierarchy in the 1990s. It met the vigorous resistance of gentlemanly minorities, carriers of the older guild spirit, in Oxford and Cambridge, but the edict prevails and a few, doubtless meritorious, professors quietly take an extra £4,000 to £8,000 to the bank each year. The major residual resentment is not so much internal as external—the fall of the donnish stipend by comparison with professionals and managers in other middle-class branches of the public and the private sectors of the economy.[3]

But discontent for the academic profession as a whole is linked more closely to loss of status and the deterioration of working conditions rather than market position. The vast majority of university and polytechnic staff are convinced that public respect as well as appreciation from politicians and civil servants has sharply declined over the past decade. How is this to be explained? One mundane but powerful factor must surely be expansion itself. The professor is no longer a rarity in society. Growing numbers of students must be expected, other things being equal, to have a depressing effect on academic salary levels. The academic empire

---

[3] It was reported in May 1991 that the Governor of the Bank of England accepted a 17 per cent pay rise (from £132,000 to £155,019, i.e. an increase greater than the total salary of the average academic) in 1990, while also recommending pay settlements at below the inflation rate.

has expanded all over the world in the twentieth century. Britain, as we have seen, began with rather less than 2,000 full-time university teachers at the beginning of the century. In 1966 there were 25,000. By 1970/1 it was 33,000 and, by the end of the 1980s, 46,288.

Expressed as percentage increases over the preceding five years, we find a quinquennial growth rate of 14.4 per cent in the early 1970s and 13.0 per cent in the later 1970s. There was a check in the first half of the 1980s (the numbers actually fell between 1980/1 and 1981/2) and then renewed growth at a 10 per cent quinquennial rate in the second half of the decade. In parallel it must be added that an even faster increase took place in the staff of the polytechnics, from about 13,000 in 1970 to 23,000 in 1989. This total of nearly 70,000 academic men and women in 1990 is indicative of loss of prestige. Status is now much less protected by social scarcity.

So the postulated trend towards proletarianization is first a consequence of expansion. Second, autonomy with respect to working conditions has declined. The proportion of all academic staff who enjoy the protection of finance wholly from university funds fell from 84 per cent in 1970 to 77 per cent in 1980 and further to 63 per cent in 1989. A growing minority were employed directly on outside funds for specific research projects, increasingly part-time and at the lower ranks. The government played its own part in the undermining of traditional security, successfully pressing universities to weaken the strength of tenure for those appointed after 1988. Promotion opportunities also deteriorated. The proportion who held professorial rank fell from 12 per cent in 1964 through 10 per cent in 1976 to 9 per cent in 1989. Then the screw was tightened further in both the universities and the polytechnics at the end of the 1980s when the Government withheld part of the grants passed through the UFC and the PCFC until evidence was produced to demonstrate managerial discretion in rewarding particular individual academics for productivity. Meanwhile staff–student ratios were forced down by receding levels of financial support which fell short of compensating fully for cost inflation.

Third, after 1981, restriction and reduction of capital grants led to an increasingly visible process of private stringency through declining relative salaries accompanied, outside Oxford and Cambridge, by public squalor in the common rooms and amenities of the redbrick universities and especially the polytechnics.

The majority of academics naturally deplore these developments. Some, however, actually desire their acceleration. Sir Douglas Hague of the Manchester Business School, and erstwhile Chairman of the Economic and Social Research Council, argues stridently for active governmental policy aimed at finally destroying the university (plus potential polytechnic) monopoly over the granting of degrees, for the abolition of national university pay scales and life tenure, for the reduction of the role of the UFC to, at most, providing grants to students, for the introduction of the American system of an October-to-June basic salary for academics so as to end the dual support system and separate teachers from researchers. He then envisages an unrestricted system of market competition between 'knowledge businesses' and the control of the teaching market by sovereign consumer student demand, made perfect by better information or 'Good University Guides', with money saved from the scaling down of funds from the State to the UFC. We will return to these proposals in Chapter 12 below. Here the point is that what is being proposed, among other things, is a final demotion of the rank-and-file of academic teachers and researchers to a proletarian role as non-tenured, peripheral, contract staff under the direction of a small élite of highly paid 'core' luminaries: 'The universities should pay twice the current salaries to half as many people' (Hague 1991: 18). Proletarianization in this form would extend to 'the knowledge industry' the structural features of modern dual labour markets. Perhaps that is the fate of the academic in the twenty-first century.

At all events, it appears that one important aspect of adaptation to expansion is indeed the gradual proletarianization of the academic professions—an erosion of their relative class and status advantages as the system of higher education is propelled towards wider admission of those who survive beyond compulsory schooling. In the transformation there are many casualties. The traditional guild of autonomous fellows is driven to the margins of the academic system, albeit at the top of the pyramid of institutional prestige. Managerialism gradually comes to dominate collegiate co-operation in the organization of both teaching and research. Explicit vocationalism displaces implicit vocational preparation— the Victorian distinction between training and education—as degree courses are adapted to the changing division of labour in the graduate market. Research endeavours are increasingly applied to the requirements of governmental or industrial demand. The don becomes increasingly a salaried or even a piece-work labourer in the service of an expanding middle class of administrators and technologists.

Meanwhile an underlying consensus at all points of the political compass holds that an enlarged investment in human capital is essential to competitive survival in the coming European and world economy. Britain is handicapped in this race in at least two ways— its waste of secondary-school-age pupils (the 16- to 19-year-old problem) and its lack of a co-ordinated system of post-secondary education.

Controversy over the two handicaps turns on two theories, the one emphasizing demand, the other supply. Demand has been curtailed by cautious definition of the educability of young Britons and the legacy of belief and policy that first-class minds have to be identified early and sponsored through a relatively fast and specialized higher education. The meritocratic conception of education beyond school has ignored expansionist alternatives. The Robbins expansion was accordingly a failed thrust towards mass higher education, the last extension of Victorian élitism: it has been found wanting. Reformers now urge, passionately and rightly, that policy must be directed towards manifold problems of both demand and supply. As they succeed, a new and different basis of respect and appreciation for the academic career in universities and polytechnics will have to be found.

Meantime morale is at a low ebb among the members of the senior common rooms who see public esteem, salaries (stationary in real terms, while other professions have risen by a third since 1975), research facilities, and career prospects in decline while, paradoxically, British higher education as a whole exhibits high productivity and rising standards of both teaching and research. Many British and foreign observers define it as a crisis. And a bigger one is looming—a shortfall in the supply of teachers and researchers against the rising demand for their services. The present government has encouraged a transformation based on the opinion that Britain recruited, in staffing the universities and the liberal professions, too many individuals of alleged amateur and gentle-manly predisposition with an 'Oxbridge' disdain for the entrepren-eurial spirit. The talented young have been severely pressed to seek their fortunes along other occupational channels in the past decade, and especially to strive to make money in the tertiary sector of financial services, the media, advertising, and public relations. Meantime those who have spoken for the traditional academic interest have bewailed a haemorrhage inadequately stemmed by new-blood posts.

A first test of these despondencies is to look at the survey record of qualifications among academic staff. Quality is of the academic essence, but defies exact measurement. Two formal measures—the proportion with doctorates and the proportion with first-class bachelor's degrees—point in opposite directions. On the basis of a careful assessment of data collected for the Robbins committee in 1961/2 with new data from 1969/70, Gareth Williams and John Bibby concluded:

> If we consider that a First has no importance but that PhD is a perfect indicator of 'quality' we should conclude that the quality of staff in general improved by nearly 20 per cent between 1962 and 1969. If, on the other hand, we consider the first class honours degree a perfectly accurate measure of intellectual ability and a PhD of no value we should claim a nearly similar decline in staff quality.

More recent and more reliable evidence for the universities since 1975 can now be obtained from the Universities Statistical Record. The figures show (Table 6.4) that, as judged by doctoral qualification, the quality of university full-time staff has risen very slightly since the mid–1970s while the proportion holding first-class bachelor's degrees has fallen. The movement in these contradictory trends over a fifteen-year period is, however, minuscule. The quality of polytechnic staff, it must be added, is distinctly lower. Our 1989 survey showed that only 17 per cent of them held firsts and 34 per cent held doctorates. The picture as a whole cannot be interpreted as a catastrophic decline in the quality of the higher teaching professions; it shows a smaller proportion of highly talented recruits perhaps, but also a continuing trend towards more advanced training for research among those who are recruited.

What these figures do confirm is that expansion has been accompanied by sharper hierarchical differences in the quality of the staff of different institutions. This is important in the context of the need and the declaration of intent to develop an integrated post-secondary system. I fully share the dominant view that policy should aim at a unitary and not a binary system, and indeed that all post-secondary education needs to be integrated. But at the same

TABLE 6.4. *Quality of university teachers, 1975–1989: doctorates and first class honours (GB) (%)*

	1975		1976		1983		1984		1988		1989	
	Doctorate	1st Class	Doctorate	1st Class	Doctorate	1st Class	Doctorate	1st Class	Doctorate	1st Class	Doctorate	1st Class
Oxbridge	42	39	41	39	41	35	44	40	50	39	49	38
London	48	25	48	25	48	24	47	24	42	22	42	21
Scotland	43	33	43	33	43	30	42	30	42	38	41	27
Wales	39	34	38	31	39	28	40	28	40	27	41	27
Old redbrick	44	26	40	27	41	26	41	25	43	25	43	25
New redbrick	42	34	43	33	42	30	42	29	44	27	45	26
New Robbins	42	38	43	37	43	34	43	34	44	32	44	32
Technological	38	23	40	23	41	22	41	22	43	23	44	22
TOTAL	42.4	29.9	42.3	29.9	42.7	28.1	42.7	28.0	43.3	26.8	43.3	26.1

Source: USR records

time we have to recognize a hierarchy in levels of academic excellence. The essential requirement is to ensure maximum flexibility of access and movement for students and staff rather than to equalize the distribution of academic talent between different institutions.

A prestige ranking of institutions had already emerged in Britain before Robbins which is reflected in the more recent career patterns of teachers in higher education and in the distribution of the more able. The structure has expanded in the past quarter of a century to create a wider variety of universities and to incorporate the polytechnics and the colleges. One possible plan for a centrally administered system would be to flatten the hierarchy by salary scales, senior posts, and capital grants to the lesser institutions coupled with drastic meanness towards Oxford, Cambridge, and the leading London colleges. Such a policy was actively canvassed in the discussions surrounding and following the Robbins and Franks reports. But it now seems unlikely to attract the energies of either politicians or administrators. A second strategy might be that of formally recognizing and appropriately funding different levels of the teaching and research system. Though explicit labelling of research universities, something in between, and teaching (or, in effect, liberal arts) colleges has not developed, the UGC/UFC research selectivity exercises have constituted a move in that direction, and the Secretary of State for Education in 1991 (Kenneth Clarke) has indicated that the bulk of research funds will continue to go to the (old) universities rather than the new (previously polytechnic) institutions.

Much more likely, at least in the contemporary climate of political opinion, is some kind of British variant of the American model, with government as the more or less interventionist market maker. The UFC, and in a slightly different way the PCFC, were moving in the direction of managing an academic market-place before they were absorbed into the new structure of higher-education funding councils. We cannot (in 1991) be more definite. Future development is impossible to decipher from governmental utterance on funding policy.

Meanwhile both the structure of the academic career and the preferences of the members of the academic professions reflect the history of an evolving hierarchy. It emerges from Table 6.5 that the dominant feeder institutions where academics gained their first

TABLE 6.5. *Career paths in British higher education of present staff 1989 (%)*

	Undergraduate origin		First job		Job now (1989)	
	Univ.	Poly	Univ.	Poly	Univ.	Poly
Oxbridge	31	9	7	0	9	0
London	17	17	15	1	16	0
Old redbrick	21	21	20	2	24	0
New redbrick	8	11	8	1	10	0
New Robbins	5	10	10	1	11	0
Technical Univ.	2	4	7	1	10	0
Scotland Univ.	10	7	12	1	14	0
Wales Univ.	4	5	5	0	5	0
Polytechnic	2	14	1	70	0	100
Other	1	3	12	23	0	0
Abroad	—	—	4	2	0	0
TOTAL	100	100	100	100	100	100

Source: A. H. Halsey, 1989 survey.

qualifications are Oxbridge, London, and the old redbrick universities. Only 2 per cent of present university teachers were students in polytechnics, and the vast majority of polytechnic teachers were not, perforce, 'home-grown' (14 per cent) but came originally from degrees in the redbricks, London, and Scotland. The net exporters are Oxbridge, especially to the universities; and London, the redbricks, Scotland, and Oxbridge again, to the polytechnics.

As to preferred destinations, our survey respondents were asked in 1964, 1976, and 1989 whether they would prefer another university, and if so which. The would-be movers, who increased slightly from 29 per cent in 1964 to 32 per cent in 1976 and 1989, expressed a stable and heavy preference for a post in Oxford or Cambridge—47 per cent in 1964, 42 per cent in 1976, and 47 per cent in 1989. Similarly, when asked to rank four academic posts in order of preference our respondents chose a university lecturer and college fellow at Cambridge, rather than a professorship at Sussex, a chair and headship of department at Leeds, or a readership in the University of London (Table 6.6). The attractiveness of the Cambridge position actually increased between 1964 and 1989, and remains the most preferred of the four posts specified, despite

TABLE 6.6.   *First preferences between university posts, 1964, 1976, and 1989 (%)*

	1964	1976	1989
University lecturer and college Fellow at Cambridge	33	35	40
Professor at Sussex	30	27	25
Professorial head of department at Leeds	21	23	27
Reader at the University of London	16	19	17

Source: A. H. Halsey, 1964, 1976, and 1989 surveys

the fact that it carries the lowest salary and formally the lowest academic rank.

It is questionable whether the development of an academic market-place raises individual mobility between institutions. Universities and colleges in the American system certainly do have higher rates of mortality as well as longer periods of gestation than has been typical of the more managed systems in Europe. In the British case the persistent feature is persistence. More recently institutional change, accompanied admittedly by frequent rumours of impending bankruptcy, has characteristically come about through mergers and, as in the cases of Brunel, Chelsea College, or Bedford and Royal Holloway, by geographical migration. Within that flux, however, an equally persistent feature has been individual immobility. Because of a national pay scale, virtually automatic tenure, and the custom of largely internal markets for promotion to a readership or senior lectureship or their polytechnic equivalent, movement between institutions in the main career grade (the lectureship) has been remarkably low. The career points at which movement takes place are almost exclusively the first appointment and the promotion into the professoriate. The career paths recorded in Table 6.5 reflect this pattern and also show its hierarchical form.

On the movement of individuals between universities we have evidence from four points in time. Between 1937 and 1938 1.3 per cent of university teachers translated from one British university to another; between 1967 and 1968 the comparable figure was 1.7 per cent (Halsey and Trow 1972).[4] The differences between 1937–8

[4] These figures were based on analyses of the entries in the Commonwealth Universities Year Books: a sample of names was selected from the first year and these

and 1967–8 is not statistically significant, even though the 1930s were a time of very modest growth while the post-Robbins sixties were a time of marked expansion.

For later years we find that 2.8 per cent of the population of University teachers—professors, readers, senior lecturers, and lecturers—moved from one university to another between 1975 and 1976, and 2.6 per cent between 1988 and 1989.[5] These estimates are inflated because they include movement between the separate colleges of the University of London. Thus there was no less—and probably no more—mobility in the mid-1970s or the late 1980s than in the post-Robbins years of 1967–8. We cannot wholly discount the possibility that this finding may be the result of different methods. None the less, the data are sufficient to make us doubt that the pause in expansion of the mid-1970s brought about any marked decrease in mobility between institutions, or that the more recent renewal of expansion increased it.

We can analyse the 1976 and 1989 data further. In Table 6.7 it appears that there is less movement among readers and senior lecturers than among professors or in the junior grades—lecturers and 'others' (a mixed category including large numbers of researchers). Readers and senior lecturers are normally internal promotions. Probably most movement at the professorial level is associated with promotion; at the very least, it represents movement to a position that is considered to be more desirable. Mobility in the 'other' category is more likely to be forced movement, as fixed-term appointments expire and force their holders to find other jobs. The rather unexpectedly high mobility at the lecturer level may well reflect a situation where people have taken up research fellowships and other temporary jobs in the universities prior to obtaining a lectureship; i.e. they were not moving between lectureships but to a first lectureship.

Table 6.7 also shows mobility by university group. Perhaps the most striking point is the greater mobility of University of London

names were checked against the entries in the second year. It would seem possible that this procedure may have understated change—either because entries in the Year Books were not properly updated, or through failure to locate movers. However, the procedure was identical for the two years.

[5] Our data for the years 1975–6 and 1988–9 come from a different source. The Universities Statistical Record is a computerized data bank on all senior members of universities. Tabulations supplied by USR allow us to calculate the amount of movement for the total university population between these two years.

TABLE 6.7. *Movement between British universities, 1937/8 to 1988/9*

	1937/8	1967/8	1975/6	1988/9
% of all staff who had moved	1.3[a]	1.7[a]	2.8[bc]	2.6[b]
% of non-clinical staff who moved			2.2	
% of staff from various universities who moved				
Oxbridge			2.1	2.6
London			7.4[d]	1.5
Scotland			1.8	2.4
Wales			1.2	3.1
Old redbrick			1.6	3.3
New redbrick			2.4	3.1
New English			2.2	3.0
Ex-CATs			1.7	2.6
% of staff of various ranks who moved				
Professors			2.5	3.6
Readers/Senior lecturers			1.9	1.0
Lecturers			3.2	3.1
Others			3.1	1.5

[a] Between 1937 and 1938, 5% left university teaching by death, retirement, etc.
[b] These figures include clinical medical staff.
[c] Excluding London the estimate is 1.8%.
[d] This London figure is inflated because it counts the constituent colleges of the University of London separately.

Sources: For 1937/8 and 1967/8, Halsey and Trow 1971: 228; for 1978/9 and 1988/9, University Statistical Record.

staff. If clinical staff are excluded,[6] mobility is greatly reduced, but is still more than twice as great as in any other group. In view of the fact that movement from one college to another in London is included, this finding may be dismissed as artefactual, but to the extent that mobility is associated with improving one's condition, the mobility of London teachers is a decided advantage for them. And to the extent that mobility into an institution brings about a new injection of ideas and different approaches, the institutions which recruit these London teachers—whether they be other London colleges or other universities—are the gainers. The Welsh colleges seem particularly marginal, judged in terms of the ability of

---

[6] This is not an unreasonable exclusion. Clinical staff have, in effect, two career ladders—one in the universities, and one in the National Health Service—between which they can move, and this makes their careers essentially non-comparable with those of other academics.

their members to move in the system. And the chances of Oxbridge teachers being 'imports' are not notably high, even though Oxbridge is, for its size, a relatively large supplier of staff to other institutions. We conclude that, although Robbinsian expansion and the further expansion of the system in the 1980s brought in many new teachers, there was little effect on the career mobility of recruits once they were in the system.

Does it matter? On the one hand it can be argued that the movement of ideas is more important than that of bodies, and that information flows more freely year by year as information technology is refined and journals, conferences, and international contacts proliferate. On the other hand creativity, through we do not know its defining circumstances, may often depend still on the intensity of face-to-face contact of colleagues in a laboratory or department or college. There are probably both upper and lower limits to the turnover of staff in an optimally creative milieu.

What we can say with greater confidence about the British experience of expansion within the hierarchical framework of institutional prestige is that particular departments or faculties have been vulnerable to raiding from above despite the low rates of total mobility that we have mentioned. In describing inter-war science in Oxford, J. B. Morrell, as we noted in Chapter 3, referred to Manchester as 'a first-class waiting room'. This is no isolated case. The Commerce and Social Science Faculty of the University of Birmingham, a group of about twenty-five people, was of outstanding quality in the 1950s. But in the early 1960s it lost a third of its younger members to Cambridge, Oxford, London, and the new universities, lured away partly by promotion but also by the remorseless pull towards the more metropolitan institutions. It is hard to believe that individualized market bargaining would have very marked general effects on mobility of this kind. It might, however, enable a polytechnic or a university to invest in excellence in a particular field or to defend its intellectual capital in such a field once it had been established.

In summary conclusion I would emphasize the unforeseen consequences of the expansion of British higher education. A highly restricted, relatively amateur, and small-scale guild-like system has responded with considerable reluctance to growing demand for wider access. That response precipitated a crisis in the financial relations between universities (including polytechnics) and government, which in any case exacerbated the longer run trend towards more proletarianized intellectual labour. The struggle for wider access has made considerable gains, especially for women, and was promoted from within the academic professions themselves. The claims of applied, vocational, or modern studies have also made irrevocable inroads into the curriculum of higher education. Dons are no longer set apart so clearly from the professional, administrative, and industrial classes. Their prestige, salaries, autonomy, and resources have been much humbled. Whether their quality as teachers and researchers has risen or fallen is an open question. Whether their creativity, in the past both celebrated and never fully understood, can be maintained into the future is a vital but unsolved issue.

PART III
THE ACADEMIC CAREER

7

THE COLLEGIATE ALTERNATIVE: THE CASE OF OXFORD[1]

IF we follow Max Weber we learn that classes are formed out of distinct market and work situations. The market position of academics in many countries, including Britain, has been increasingly defined since the end of the First World War by the power of the State as a monopsonistic employer. This does not mean, as for example in modern Germany, that dons have been official civil servants. Nor does it mean that work situations have been directly dictated by a central minister acting as the agent of government. Such developments were a threat largely unheeded until the 1970s. Threat has begun to approach reality only in the past decade with new legislation curtailing tenure. Over a longer period restriction on the proportion of senior posts in universities has reflected State financial interests and was a point of chronic conflict between the UGC, the CVCP, and the AUT from after the Second World War. The third component of class formation—autonomy of working conditions—is, however, different. Without it the still longer-run tendency towards proletarianization is accelerated, and the process is possible under State management as much as free market conditions because, as Weber insisted, the bureaucratic form of organization facilitates if it does not positively require it. It is this fundamental aspect of academic work that we consider in this chapter.

There are, of course, some forces supporting autonomy in the very nature of scholarship and science. Professions based on theory and research are, it turns out, more efficiently pursued through collegiate than through 'line' management. Tension between these two working principles is a commonplace in industrial, civil, and military as well as academic service. But in England there has been an additional special factor—the historical existence and influence of the Oxford and Cambridge colleges. In both these universities it

---

[1] Much of this chapter (pp. 150–68) is taken from my chapter in Harrison (ed.) 1992, where references to internal papers of the university (omitted here) may be found.

would be no outrage to assert that there has been, at least until recently, no university. College endowments have bestowed autonomy on fellows who have shaped the government of the university in their own image. Can we then look to them as a model of resistance to the threat of proletarianization? We can answer conveniently by examining the Oxford response to the Robbins Report, which was crystallized by the Franks Commission of Inquiry (Franks 1966).

Oxford before Franks could be described as a central redoubt of what Henry Fairlie had dubbed 'the establishment', encircled by a complex of admiration, envy, and hostility. The Robbins Report of 1963 triggered expression of these mixed emotions. Oxford was challenged to explain itself to the outside world while responding to the many internal tensions resulting from its enlarging scale and modified shape. It was not a simple opposition of left and right. Oxford's critics attacked from all quarters. From the left the thrust was against a traditional bastion of privileged inequality. But *The Times* and *Encounter* also carried the views of a wider group who felt that Oxford was not responding adequately to the meritocratic requirements of the scientific and managerial professions.

Antipathy towards Oxford's role as a nursery of the ruling class, old or new, was merged with complaint from the right about the anti-industrial ethos of the ancient colleges. Criticism from the left, much of which was made respectable by Anthony Crosland, condemned the narrow basis of recruitment of the nation's leading administrators, politicians, and businessmen through the private (that is 'public') schools and the ancient universities (Guttsman 1963; Thomas 1968; Crosland 1956, 1962). Oxford seemed to be failing to meet both the social and economic needs of modern Britain—to be obstructing the national aspiration towards wealth and equality. She became a scapegoat for critics from every quarter of the political circumference, who sought either to explain or to rescue Britain from its fading position of imperial power, its faltering industrial competitiveness, and its stubbornly persistent class inequality.

Such critics ignored much of Oxford's piecemeal adaptation to the changing demand for its graduates and its research: the development of science and engineering, the search for talented recruits as staff and students, the reform of syllabuses, the gradual modernization of an Anglican collectivity of undergraduate colleges into a collegiate university of secular scholars and scientists. She was derided by her critics, both intramural and extramural, as the bearer of outmoded culture and the perpetrator of anti-modern principles and practices.

In reality, of course, both Oxford and the wider world of higher education had been changing rapidly. 'Doubling in a decade' had emerged in the later 1950s as the slogan of higher-education policy among the countries of the 'First World' and was reiterated in the endless conferences and reports of the OECD.[2] Investment in human capital was believed to be the key to economic growth and, coupled with the continuing clamour for more equal social opportunity, gave compelling impetus to plans for the expansion of universities. There had been commissions in Sweden, France, and Germany. The California Master Plan was widely regarded as a model for appropriate tertiary education in a modern country. The Robbins Committee report was enthusiastically accepted as the British version of a wider drive towards economic efficiency and popular opportunity.

Oxford had to adapt to these events. It had expanded over the previous forty years from its 4,000 students and 350 academic staff in the 1920s to 9,500 students and 1,127 academic staff in 1964–5. Its academic shape had also shifted significantly towards science and graduate study. In the forty years from 1923 to 1963, while student numbers had more than doubled, the proportion reading arts and social studies dropped from four-fifths to two-thirds. Concomitant shifts in the relation between the university and the colleges, between research and teaching, and between private and public funding were changing the anatomy as well as the face of Oxford.

Yet Oxford had not been thoroughly investigated since the 1870s. Since that time the universities in the provincial industrial cities had slowly developed, London University had grown, and (more recently) the new English universities and the Colleges of Advanced Technology had emerged. Universities, not excluding Oxford, had become larger, had incorporated science into their curricula, had begun to increase the number of their graduate students and to acquire larger, more specialized, and more

---

[2] The Organization for Economic Co-operation and Development was set up to renew the economy of western Europe after the Marshall Plan of 1948.

elaborately organized teaching and research staff. The growth of
state interest in the universities in the twentieth century and the
emergence of government as overwhelmingly the most important
source of funds had slowly produced a structure of universities and
colleges which Robbins explicitly recognized as a national system
of higher education. Oxford needed a defined place within this
system.

The Franks Commission was consequence not cause of these
transformations. The question in this chapter is how effectively the
chosen method of internal appraisal succeeded in turning piecemeal
adaptations into a planned and purposive programme. Was it an
effective diagnosis of ills and prescription of cure? Was it, as was
suggested at the time, a 'lightning conductor' of external storm? Or
was it a more fundamental proposal to renovate an ancient guild
into a viable alternative to the modern form of hierarchical and
bureaucratic management of academic work? Was Oxford essentially different after Franks because of Franks, or irrespective of
Franks?

When Robbins reported in October 1963 Harold Macmillan had
relinquished the premiership to Sir Alec Douglas Home, Oliver
Franks was the Provost of Worcester College and Walter Oakeshott
was Vice-Chancellor. In November, Oakeshott presented Hebdomadal Council with the Robbins challenge. It demanded that
Oxford and Cambridge either solve their problem—the inability to
reach rapid decisions, the obscure financial and administrative
arrangements, the over-payment of staff, and narrow social
recruitment of students—within a reasonable time or be the subject
of an independent inquiry (Robbins Report: para. 687). Over the
following three months the Oxford–Cambridge–London axis was
hyperactive. A royal commission? A statement replying to Robbins? A
motion in Congregation? A letter to *The Times*?

Change, then, seemed inevitable in the Oxford of the early
1960s. Its winds blew gustily in Africa. Externalities generated new
challenge for the imperial nation. As Prime Minister (1957–63),
Harold Macmillan had sought a post-imperial role for Britain: yet
as Chancellor of Oxford (from 1960) he was less inclined to bend.
The University was after all much older than the United Kingdom:
it had eight centuries of venerable survival behind it and retained an
enviable eminence among the world's leading centres of learning.
Such conservative figures as Robert (later Lord) Blake followed

Macmillan and instinctively resisted a proposal for either a new royal commission or an internal inquiry in response to Robbins.[3]

Blake later changed his mind (Blake 1986: 1). But, in any case, the external pressures were too strong. The compromise was an internal appraisal. Otherwise, it was believed in the central circle of Council and General Board members, another external commission was highly likely. In 1963 R. H. S. Crossman, the Shadow Minister of Education, was vigorously and ominously interested in reform of a kind unlikely to be friendly to Oxford and Cambridge, and a general election was impending. In any case, some dons in both Oxford and Cambridge wanted a royal commission in order to facilitate reform and to clarify the position of the ancient universities in the emerging national system: but R. A. Butler and some of his Cambridge friends were unconvinced.

In the end an external commission was blocked by Cambridge caution, Macmillan opposition, and governmental unresponsiveness. Lesser responses were judged inadequate, and Hebdomadal Council decided to ask a small committee to review Robbins's criticisms of Oxford and, if they found them justified, to propose terms of reference for a larger committee. The Committee did so and promptly recommended a *Commission of Inquiry* to report upon Oxford's present and future role in the United Kingdom's system of higher education, having regard to its position as both a national and an international university. And further detailed questions were to be considered, covering virtually every aspect of Oxford's funding, student admissions, teaching, research, and administration, and the relation of the university to the colleges.

Council adopted this recommendation and on 18 March 1964 appointed Lord Franks, with his wide experience of the political and business world and his skill as an investigator, to be chairman of a commission with six other Oxford men and women.[4] Response

---

[3] In Annan 1966, Lord Annan outlines parallel developments through the Bridges syndicate in Cambridge.

[4] The other members were Professor Sir Lindor Brown, Fellow of Magdalen College, Waynflete Professor of Physiology; Mrs J. Floud, sociologist and Fellow of Nuffield College; Sir Robert Hall, economist and Principal-Elect of Hertford College, Visiting Fellow of Nuffield College; Miss M. G. Ord, Fellow, Tutor, and Dean of Lady Margaret Hall, University Lecturer in Biochemistry; Mr M. Shock, Fellow, Tutor, and Estates Bursar of University College, and Mr J. Steven Watson, Student and Tutor in history at Christ Church. Mr B. G. Campbell, Fellow of Merton College, a Deputy Registrar of the University, was seconded to be Secretary to the Commission.

to Robbins had to be immediate. Reform for modernity had to be long-term. The problem was to state the essential nature of Oxford in twentieth- or even twenty-first-century terms. Both organization and minds needed transformation, and particular piecemeal changes were already in train through the committees of the early 1960s, on admissions, on fellowship entitlement, and on syllabus, which paralleled the Bridges syndicate and other reform mechanisms in Cambridge. Franks conceived of his task as an integrating process of collective reorientation. He thus followed a method of open hearings, maximal involvement of dons in their senior common rooms, college governing bodies, and departmental laboratories as well as in the formal university assemblies of sub-faculty, faculty, General Board, Council, and Congregation. There was a mounting drama of internal debate. Franks and his colleagues became a seminar of continuing education. From the chair he was adept at masterly summaries of inarticulate witness.

Whether the method was adequate to the task remained a disputed question. A shrewd editorial in the *Lancet* insisted on its weakness. The tone of the report was ineffably bland. 'It [was] almost as if the insiders were aware that unless they flattered their audience—the teaching masters of arts in Congregation—they would be unlikely to push through the real changes to which they were committed. One suspects that Lord Franks was instinctively aware of this and that his insistence on hearing all the evidence in public was a way of bringing home the facts to the university, well in advance of the report itself.' The conclusion was there drawn that the internal Commission 'must have postponed any serious consideration of many matters by an external and broadly constituted outside body' (*Lancet*, 21 May 1966: 1141–3). Sir Hans Krebs also thought that open hearings inhibited internal witnesses, especially those with embarrassing knowledge of Oxford's 'financial and administrative obscurities'.

The distinction between inside and outside pressure in the dynamics of the inquiry is perhaps unreal, given the scatter of Oxford graduates to positions of power and influence in the nation as well as in Oxford itself. Crossman, Crosland, Macmillan, and Blake were all, after all, Oxonians. Besides, Lord Franks repeatedly distanced himself from the university's daily practices and made himself the embodiment of an outside view. He sought criticism and suggestion from outside—from Lord Heyworth and the UGC, from Lord Robbins and the progressives of higher-education policy, and he delighted in the ensuing intellectual exchanges. A million words of written evidence were collected and published, a million and a half words of oral exchange were recorded, and a compendium of numbers on teaching and research in Oxford was compiled. Twice a week through the three terms of 1964–6 Franks presided as a regal, puritanical, and earnest commissioner over public hearings to discuss the written submissions. He was, in Sir Maurice Shock's phrase, 'both the mechanism and the lubricant'. As Franks himself told Congregation, 'Oxford was aroused to a reflective and constructive dialogue within itself', while the voices from outside were widely heard.

Method apart, we cannot expect any human inquiry to be omniscient. Two spectacular developments in the immediate aftermath of the Franks Commission illustrated its limited vision. One was the 'student troubles'. Franks noticed the Williams Committee on the disciplinary powers of the vice-chancellor and proctors. The Commission hoped that one result of the Committee would be 'the more effectual ventilation of grievances of the student body'. But Franks went no further, despite evidence received from the Student Representative Council. The demise of the single-sex women's colleges was also unforeseen, despite the wish expressed by New College in 1964 to become mixed (Ste Croix 1964) and the presence of two women on the Commission. The decision not to discuss the second issue was deliberate. Though a clear lead on mixed colleges might have averted later confusion, it seems clear that the Commission was influenced by the women's college principals (Dame Lucy Sutherland, Dame Janet Vaughan, and Lady Ogilvie) none of whom attached 'great importance to the value of shared residence in a collegiate society in a small city like Oxford'.

The report itself was in two volumes. The first comprises a reasoned statement of recommendations; the second is a digest of the relevant statistics: the whole constitutes perhaps the best sociological account of the working of a single university in this century. As Oxford's riposte to the charges of obscurity and inwardness it must be judged a distinguished success. No royal commission could have been more thorough or better informed. As a reform movement by collective self-education and sustained seminar, it reflected the personality of its chairman as a man of stern principle, worldly practicality, and mandarin resolve to incorporate criticism into conserved tradition. The attendant publicity certainly offered weapons to Oxford's foes but also gave comfort to its friends. It removed all excuse from the decision-making bodies if they failed to act, because it gave them comprehensive information and unambiguous if general guidelines. Perhaps Franks's gift for synthesis and generalization left too much detailed interpretation for subsequent internal administrative decision. But the bold outline of a future Oxford was admirably clear.

Ancient Oxford was to modernize its collegiate glories. The departmentally segmented and hierarchically controlled monolith was the dominant form in Germany, France, the United States, and in all countries which had inherited the European medieval university. Why, in the early modern and early industrial periods, the collegiate form survived vigorously in the ancient English universities while fading from the Catholic Europe which gave it birth remained something of a mystery. The modern starting-point for Franks was Oxford's distinctiveness. The collegiate university, as Franks understood that phrase, was a rare form of organized higher education. Indeed, Oxford was arguably unique despite the superficial resemblance of its design to that of Durham, Harvard, Claremont, London, Wales, or even Cambridge. It selected its students carefully, though still disproportionately from the type of school and social background which had hitherto maintained the established life and character of the university; it offered them education and not merely training in a small-scale residential community affording close contact of teachers with taught, a shared domestic life, and individualized teaching.

Nevertheless, modern conditions meant that collegiate ideals had to be reinterpreted. The colleges would have to change in response to the growth of the natural sciences and new methods of scientific research, the increasing presence of graduate students, and new demands for wider educational opportunity. And given that the riches of the colleges (though not all colleges were rich) had been increasingly augmented by state funds channelled through the university, greater public accountability for collegiate expenditure would also be required.

Franks took the problem of socially fair and academically meritocratic admission of undergraduates with methodical seriousness. The Commission recommended that Oxford should work towards reform within the emerging national system by instituting a single entrance examination, a streamlined college Admissions Office, by abolishing closed scholarships and restricting open awards on entry.

There was a historically close organic connection between the Oxford and Cambridge colleges and the 'Public Schools'. Earlier in the century these schools dominated admissions to the colleges. For example, 62 per cent of the men entering Oxford as undergraduates in 1938/9 came from the HMC boarding schools. The direct grant schools contributed 12.6 per cent and the private sector as a whole 74.6 per cent, leaving only 19.2 per cent for boys from maintained schools in the United Kingdom and a small 6 per cent recruitment from overseas. Among women the private sector was less closely connected but still dominant, 63.9 per cent being recruited from it, 32.6 per cent from the maintained schools, and 3.5 per cent from elsewhere.

These proportions became less socially skewed with the continuing improvement of the state secondary schools after the 1944 Act, and increasing pressure towards meritocratic selection. The maintained schools had increased their share to 40.2 per cent of the men's and 42.7 per cent of the women's places by 1965/6. The fact that the maintained schools in 1963/4 had produced 64 per cent of the men and 72 per cent of the women who intended going to the universities in Britain clearly raised the question of how far places in the Oxford and Cambridge colleges were being allocated on merit and how far there was a selective bias in favour of the private sector.

The Franks Commission concluded from the evidence that the qualifications of men entrants from the maintained schools had been better on average than those of entrants from independent boarding schools. Moreover, the independent boarding schools had provided the lowest proportion of Firsts and the highest proportion of Thirds in degree classification among men entering from the different types of school. The independent day and direct grant schools had contributed the highest proportion of Firsts, and the maintained schools the lowest proportion of Thirds. Thus the traditional 'Public Schools' were suspect in this crucial test of meritocracy at a time when Anthony Crosland was introducing a new initiative on the 'Public Schools' question. We cannot know how far the sensitivity fostered by Franks or the formal reforms introduced after Franks influenced the course of subsequent change. But we do know that in the 1970s Oxford made dramatic progress towards meritocratic entry as measured by A-level performance. She attracted the aspirations of less than 5 per cent of university applicants, but admitted a high and rising proportion of those with high A-level attainment. The universities collectively admitted 21.4 per cent with AAA, AAB, and AAC, or ABB in 1970. The Oxford figure was 58.6 per cent. But by 1980, while the figure for all universities had hardly moved (to 22.5 per cent), the Oxford figure shot up to 73.5 per cent, and still further, well above 80 per cent by 1990. Thus Oxford admissions progressed markedly toward severe selection on academic criteria.

The recruitment of senior members was also subject to criticism by Franks. While Oxford remained the collegiate university *par excellence*, the inherently centrifugal tendencies of modern teaching and research, which had elsewhere produced the 'multiversity' (Kerr 1963: ch. 1), were beginning to make it difficult for colleges to maintain high teaching standards and attractive careers for college tutors. Accordingly, the Commission's highly self-conscious effort to modernize a federation of colleges into a strong collegiate university involved proposals which were just as fundamental for the academic staff as for the students. The central core of Victorian Oxford had been a group of working tutorial fellows to which the growth of the university added professors, readers, and lecturers. The modernized collegiate conception would produce further convergence of the older structure of academic staff to the hierarchy of ranks which characterizes the Scottish and the English redbrick universities. Before Franks, the Oxford academic staff were divided between the colleges and the university with most wearing two hats, either as university staff with college fellowships or as college men and women with part-time university posts. Under the new proposals two hats were to become standard issue.

The Commission's scheme for fellow-lecturers, which was essential to the full participation of colleges in expanded graduate work, involved the proposal that all appointments should be advertised and then made jointly by the university and a college. In effect it was to propose greater university control over the internal affairs of colleges. A version of it was instituted in the 1970s. Likewise, faculty centres for the arts and social studies, which were seen by the Commission as essential to the development of collegiate participation in graduate teaching and research, were provided in the course of the following decade. There was, in short, some marginal shift of the academic centre of gravity away from the colleges towards the university.

The Commission envisaged a medium-sized university for the future, and its proposals on size and shape were approved. Oxford would grow in the 1970s and 1980s to accommodate 13,000 students, including 3,500 to 4,000 graduates. These targets were in fact reached by 1986–7 when there were 13,260 matriculated students of whom 3,530 were graduates. In the course of expansion, greater emphasis was to be place on the applied sciences, engineering, clinical medicine, and social studies. More generally the natural and social sciences were to be encouraged with 'compensating contractions', presumably in the arts. The Commission noticed that the expansion of Harvard and other leading American universities had involved the creation of large graduate schools and research centres, more or less separated from undergraduate schools. In rejecting this strategy of expansion the Commission may have misconceived the academic staffing of American universities as a two-tier profession of graduate and undergraduate teachers; but they correctly anticipated college opinion in Oxford. 'Our reasons', Franks told Congregation, 'were that we thought, first, that if they came into being in Oxford, undergraduate education would almost certainly be devalued. Secondly, it leads to a division in the academic staff between those who do research and teach graduates and those who teach undergraduates. We believe that this would be a bad thing in that society of equals to which Oxford aspires.' It was feared that the development of post-graduate schools would drive the colleges into a secondary place in Oxford, 'but since it was our purpose to preserve the life, the enterprise, the initiative and the responsibility of the colleges, we therefore turned away from separate great graduate schools'.

The Commissioners therefore set out to produce a plan in which new developments would be made to fit into or revolve around a modernized college system. They recognized all the contemporary threats to the viability of collegiate organization, not least the plight of the poorer colleges which had generated discreet unease inside the walls. They sought solutions making Oxford safe for commensality. The graduate student was to be incorporated, and income was to be redistributed from the richer to the poorer colleges. The university would support and integrate the work of the federated colleges, would streamline its own administration and government, and explain itself more quickly and more clearly to the UGC and the outer world by better statistical services. Oxford would justify itself to an egalitarian age by a reformed procedure for admissions, the abolition of closed scholarships, the encouragement of more women students, and the rationalization of dons' incomes. At the same time the claim to international standing was plainly asserted. 'Oxford', noted Franks, 'is a university with a higher than average concentration of talent, and . . . it is reasonable that this should be reflected in a higher than average salary, age for age, than is to be found in British universities taken as a whole.'

How, then, could increased numbers be fitted into the colleges? The Commissioners saw that 'in the collegiate university those who are not fully brought into college life inevitably suffer'. They therefore contemplated the creation of one or two new colleges. But how far could graduate students be integrated into the existing colleges? Given that many were married, and all were in pursuit of academic excellence, many argued that they would best fit into departments. Witness to this effect included the students themselves as represented by the Student Representative Council, the economists as represented by their sub-faculty, and some natural scientists who also wanted undergraduate teaching transferred from college to university. Rudolph Peierls thought that the tutorial system was 'highly wasteful of the time and energy of the staff' and doubted its benefits to undergraduates.

The nub of this problem was to ensure a proper distribution of students and staff between colleges. Graduate student numbers were increasing and they needed specialist dons. Yet unless all dons were to be involved with both graduate and undergraduate studies, research scholars might gain more status than those who taught only undergraduates. The Commissioners did not exaggerate when they said that 'if postgraduate training is to be brought into the system of college education and made part of the balance of life of the fellow-lecturer, the consequences will be a fundamental change in the nature of Oxford, and the magnitude of this change should not be underestimated'.

For the undergraduate, or at least for the arts undergraduate, the educational advantages of the traditional college were widely held to remain immense. However, these colleges had hitherto made no serious attempt to take over the university's responsibility for graduates and, with a few recent exceptions, had done little to offer them social amenities. If graduate teaching, a responsibility of the university, was now to be offered in colleges, at least one of the arguments for the traditional college had to be abandoned. Except in very small schools, the 'college-department' would tend to be either too big or fail to meet the requirement that a college is a microcosm of a wide range of studies.

There was, and still remains, no obvious way out of this dilemma. The Roberts Report, discussing the relevant section of the Franks Report in 1987, was saddened to see, on re-reading the selection of evidence provided, how little things appeared to have changed in twenty years (Roberts Report 1987: 7). Here, then, was an area where the Commission failed to provide sufficiently detailed guidance on how its aspirations could be realized. It left graduate admissions in the hands of the university but also proposed to leave the general organization of studies to the faculties and recommended the setting up of faculty centres to fulfil the same functions for graduate studies in arts as do the science departments for science subjects. It regarded 'the establishment of these centres as essential'. It was no more than tentative in its recommendation of specialization between colleges, despite the fame of the Nuffield College model of specialized graduate study. In fact most graduates continued to belong to the traditional undergraduate colleges. The Commission contented itself with advising that no college be allowed to admit a graduate unless someone in the college could look after him academically. Specialization was recommended but its extent was to be confined within the limits compatible with manageable size in what remained all-subject, undergraduate-centred colleges. Oxford was therefore left with awkward problems of duplication in the larger subjects and co-operation between colleges in the smaller and more specialized fields. In these respects, over the next decade very little collegiate progress was made.

The report came before Congregation on 31 May 1966 as a resolution to take note of the Commission's findings and as a signal of the beginning of a process of legislating changes in the statutes of the university. In the following two years Congregation approved new statutes arising out of the Report. Congregation, like the Commission, was mindful of the criticism made by the Robbins

Committee of 'the difficulty Oxford has in reaching rapid decisions on matters of policy with its present constitutional arrangements, and the general obscurity in which so many of its administrative and financial arrangements are shrouded'. The need for administrative reform was generally accepted. Despite protests organized in London by Jossleyn Hennessy (which were much discussed by Hebdomadal Council) all the powers of Convocation were abolished with the exception of its power to elect the Chancellor and the Professor of Poetry. The Hebdomadal Council became established by statute as the chief administrative body of the university. The central administrative services were unified under the Registrar, and additional statistical information and liaison services were established on a professional basis. And, most important, a four-year vice-chancellorship was instituted—beginning with the tenure of Alan Bullock, the Master of St Catherine's, in 1969. The Vice-Chancellor henceforth was to be elected by Congregation (on the nomination of a committee consisting of the Chancellor or Vice-Chancellor and representatives of Council, Congregation, and the colleges) from among the members of Congregation.

These administrative changes had been proposed by the Franks Commission in order to arrive at an optimal combination of democracy with decision. Yet on this crucial issue there were difficulties: Oxford dons were jealous of their ancient and established forms of democratic academic government. Over the centuries they had fought off or escaped control from without— from popes and prime ministers, bishops and bureaucrats, kings and capitalists. Were they to be defeated at last by a drive towards internal hierarchical efficiency? Could they maintain the alternative to bureaucratic hierarchy which we describe as the major trend of polytechnics and universities in Chapter 6?

In the event, the Commission's plan was seen as too radical and accordingly defeated at two crucial points. First, Congregation refused to give Council power to make decrees. Instead Congregation retained the power to annul, amend, or repeal decrees and regulations made by Council and reserved its right to pass resolutions which, if carried with at least seventy-five members voting in favour, would require Council to promote legislation giving effect to them. However, though academic democracy was thus preserved, it was made more effective in that henceforth any decision taken on a division at a meeting of Congregation could be submitted, if Council so decided or if at least fifty members of Congregation so required, for rejection or confirmation to a postal vote of all the members of Congregation. This procedure was followed for the first time in 1969 when opposition to the setting up of a new Human Sciences degree was rejected by 153 to 122 votes and was finally overcome through a postal vote by 540 to 491.

Second, the Commission was keen to strengthen the effectiveness of the General Board. It proposed to group the existing sixteen faculties into five 'super faculties' with up to eight sub-faculties under each faculty board. Professor Beloff argued before Congregation that the super-faculties would find it impossible to draft sensible agenda. Lord Franks argued in reply that 'seventeen bodies reporting to the General Board . . . is an administrative nonsense, as much of a nonsense as thirty-one colleges being in correspondence with the Hebdomadal Council'. But Beloff's nonsense was preferred by both Hebdomadal Council and the General Board, mainly because it seemed to them that the new faculty boards would have no clear function to perform and that the new sub-faculty boards (up to forty in number) would fragment academic administration too greatly. They advised rejection, and Congregation approved by 179 votes to 115. Franks had hoped for a streamlined academic senate of no more than fourteen. But the super-faculties never came and General Board membership became twenty-four in 1966–7.

Thus the Commission did not fully persuade Oxford of the need for administrative reform of the university's central bodies, though both the vice-chancellorship and the Registry were strengthened and, despite the Vice-Chancellor's non-attendance, the General Board became a more powerful mechanism of academic policy and resource allocation.[5] Looking back as retiring Vice-Chancellor in October 1985, Sir Geoffrey Warnock thought the criticism that Oxford was slow and cumbrous in her operations had somewhat died away. 'We have found ways,' he asserted, 'while remaining an essentially federal and inevitably rather complex system, of speaking with one voice when necessary and of acting when necessary with respectable decisiveness and celerity; we have found ways too of presenting ourselves, to Government and the UGC, and particularly perhaps to schools, as one university, and not a

---

[5] The Vice-Chancellor in 1988 (Sir Richard Southwood) did in fact begin to attend the General Board.

disorderly crowd.' Warnock's was the authentic and informed voice of collegiate Oxford two decades after Franks.

In presenting the Report of the Commission to Congregation Lord Franks was explicit about two principles which had guided him and his colleagues: 'our democratic form of government, whereby academics govern themselves, and the college system'. Frank's notion of democracy was Schumpeterian (the electorate chooses between competing élites), whereas dons were natural children of Rousseau (the 'town meeting' of citizens).

True, the Commission's scheme for internal taxation aimed at redistributing income between the richer and the poorer colleges was accepted, along with a series of proposals for rationalizing the keeping of college accounts. Nevertheless, both before and after Franks, defence of college autonomy was probably the most strongly held interest in Oxford. Under the Commission's recommendations a Council of Colleges would have been set up, under a statute of the university, with power to bind colleges by the votes of a majority of its members. Franks believed, and continued to believe, that the Council of Colleges would strengthen the democratic influence of colleges in the university and that the alternative was anarchy. Opponents saw it as a major constitutional change in the relationship between the university and the colleges, moving the balance of power still further towards the centre. Congregation would not have it, and set up a Conference of Colleges which met for the first time in November 1966 with no formal powers but providing a forum for the exchange of information and opinions.

From the Commission's point of view this outcome was a disaster: anarchy or fragmented democracy precluded purposive decision and clear policy. Far from strengthening the colleges, a conference as distinct from a council actually weakened college power by denying it a collective voice. Many dons subsequently dismissed the Conference of over sixty representatives as a useless body. It was Oxford's equivalent of the North American Indian's League of the Iroquois which shied away from the binding collective decision that would have held back the White Peril.

Must we then conclude that the Franks Commission failed to bring about a decisive shift of democratic power in Oxford? In retrospect it certainly seems that continuity rather than change ruled the transition. But we must ask 'power for what?' before delivering a verdict. The Commission was primarily concerned with enabling the central bodies to make decisions. Yet this was surely too narrow a view of where the important decisions in Oxford are in fact made: they are made in the college common rooms, the laboratories, and lecture halls as well as in the statutory committees of the university. To put the matter perhaps too simply, the coterie, the private lunch in a Fellow's rooms, the informal seminar, were the vehicles of charisma, the college was the custodian of custom and tradition, and the academic post the bearer of expertise. Each offered a base for innovation. Informal exchanges and *ad hoc* committees have always been the fertile seed-bed of change whether in practice or in statute. They have been the hidden multiple motors of Oxford's recurrent versatility.

Only within this pluralistic nexus of influence can we ask the narrower question of where power lay before and after Franks. Did the power of the Vice-Chancellor increase? Probably not, though it came slightly closer towards resembling the vice-chancellorship of a British redbrick or the presidency of an American university. Though acquiring no substantial financial power, the office remained one of persuasive influence but largely ceremonial authority. Until the 1960s it had rotated among the heads of colleges, each either refusing or taking a three-year term. Franks made it an elected four-year term as part of a plan to give central direction to the collegiate university, strengthening its foreign relations while a streamlined university administration would ensure internal integration.

Was, then, effective power put into the hands of the full-time university administrative officers headed by the Registrar and the Secretary of Faculties? Certainly not. These officials had no formal power at all. They were conceived, and conceived of themselves, in classical civil-service terms—serving, that is, the elected dons in their several offices just as Whitehall civil servants serve their ministers, though also influencing the composition of committees and sub-committees within the framework of Council and General Board.

Were, then, the heads of house the power élite? Again no. Colleges continued to be run by their governing bodies, comprising the Fellows, each of whom had a vote. The head of house was selected by the Fellows and controlled by them. He, or she, was unlikely to be currently a charismatic or expert leader in the teaching or research life of Oxford. If he came from outside he might become an important lay influence in Council: but only through competitive election by the dons' ensemble—Congregation.

Must we, then, look to the professors? At the time of the Franks inquiry there were 120 of them among the 1,400 dons. Each had convinced an electoral board that he or she possessed high expert distinction or exceptional promise. In the sciences especially, the professor could enjoy the considerable baronial power which is familiar on the American campus. But arts and social studies professors could be, and quite often were, without influence. Franks did nothing to change the fact that their access to Faculty Boards or the supreme General Board or Hebdomadal Council depended on election.

In simple constitutional terms, Congregation continued to rule. The Hebdomadal Council or the General Board might propose, but the assembled dons disposed. Congregation could, and occasionally did, say 'non placet' to the wishes of those it had elected to the formal heights of university authority. The ancient syndicalist arrangement survived and the central university bodies could still, justly if satirically, be described as the executive committee of the collegiate class. Franks left the public life of Oxford as he found it, quietly led and controlled by the private life of its colleges. Thus Oxford continues to stand as a collegiate alternative to the normal professorial and administrative hierarchy of university organization in Britain and internationally.

The Franks claim that Oxford deserved special consideration as a university of international standing was heard with much misgiving and some hostility by academics in other institutions. One of the more articulate voices was that of Charles Carter, the Vice-Chancellor of the new University of Lancaster.

Certainly we must not level the universities down to a dull mediocrity. But, before we can allow Oxford to get away with the argument, there are some awkward questions to be answered—to which the Report gives no attention at all. What is meant by calling Oxford an 'international university'? Taking a broad view of her activities, is she contributing more (per head of staff) to civilization than Manchester, or (dare we say it) Sussex? There are subjects to which Oxford, though apparently having a 'higher than average concentration of talent', is contributing little. There are important areas of study which Oxford has neglected. If the state is to be asked to use public money to maintain, say, two privileged centres of excellence, does it follow that the two should be sited at Oxford and Cambridge? . . . The 'centres of excellence' argument itself is suspect. The activities of a university grow, not like a single tree, but like a forest, with some fine and vigorous specimens and other stunted or in decay. It is not reasonable to expect that all will be vigorous at once, and a given sum of money may be better used in encouraging vigour where it is found in the university system, rather than in trying to raise the average quality of the single university. (Carter 1966: 381–8)

Here was an ultra-modern voice, speaking in terms not of separate universities but of a national system—with the implication that some form of central planning is desirable which would treat faculties, departments, or even smaller teaching and research groups as its units. The logic of this view is that there had to be one national university, or (better) one university system, on the grounds that 'in the contemporary and coming world no university or institution of higher education of any kind can be looked upon as an independent unit. Each and every one of them must be regarded as belonging to a network, a national network for the most part but one which has increasing connections and extensions abroad' (Carter 1966: 384). Future developments were to afford a comment on Charles Carter's view. The UGC in 1986, the UFC in 1989, and unofficial surveys of national academic opinion in 1976 and 1989 produced rankings of university departments which gave overwhelming evidence of Oxford's and Cambridge's continuing dominance. As a modern research university Oxford emphatically confirmed its repute among the world's leading institutions.

There was no Franks revolution. The Commission had staged an impressive performance of advanced organizational analysis and had met the Robbins challenges on external coherence and administrative dispatch. There were two years of absorbing drama. Franks had magnificently redesigned the collegiate ideal in contemporary costume. But the electric electoral atmosphere of 1964 passed, and the acrimony of 'outside' criticism softened. Oxford's conservative champions were already growing in self-confidence during 1963 (Griffin 1966: 220). Drama became momentarily farce in the Commission's confrontation with All Souls. Could this venerable institution find a justified role in twentieth-century Oxford? This college without undergraduates, pilloried as suffering from infirmity of purpose, after wobbling between deciding to take

in graduate students and merging itself with St Antony's, now
introduced visiting fellowships for academics from other institutions in Britain and overseas. Sixteen visitors came into residence
during 1966–7. By 1988 well over 300 foreign academics had
experienced Oxford in this way. Yet, for better or for worse, the
ancient anatomy was essentially undisturbed. When an Oxonian,
senior or junior, made a new acquaintance inside or outside the
university he or she could expect the same old enquiry: 'And which
college are you from?'

COLLEGIATE POWER

What then can be concluded about this rare form of higher
education? In its origins the collegiate university was both the
application of a pedagogical theory and at the same time a means of
social survival. The first colleges in twelfth-century Paris, the
Collège de Dix-Huit, and the Sorbonne which soon followed, were
partly a recognition of the successful academic discipline of the
monasteries and the Mendicant Orders. They also represented a
move by the secular priests in the struggle to wrest dominance of
the paramount School of Theology from the Regulars. At Oxford
subsequently the college also developed as an organization of
learning under discipline as well as a refuge in the chronic conflict
between the clerks and the laity. But it would be a naïvely idealistic
history which explained the collegiate form solely in terms of a
theory of learning. Much more is owed to social pressure. Indeed
the history of the colleges could plausibly be represented as a
sequence of binary oppositions. Struggles between Regulars and
Seculars, crown and mitre, town and gown, scholar and gentleman-
commoner, hearty and aesthete, and, not least, between university
and college. These are the conflicting interests which have shaped
college organization, the co-operation and competition between
colleges, and the Franks effort to modernize a federation of colleges
into a strong collegiate university.

Oxford still remains a distinctive milieu of teaching and research.
There is a binary relation of the university to the thirty-six colleges.
The overwhelming financial dependence of the university on the
State despite resolute private fund-raising in recent years contrasts
with the autonomy of the colleges as private, endowed corporations. The separated function of the university as the examining and
syllabus-setting authority automatically strengthens the bonds

between college tutors and pupils. The publication of the annual league tables of college performance in the university degree examinations, though its validity and consequences are disputed, is a market monitor of competing companies of scholars, examining each year incidentally not only the candidates but their mentors, and thereby rewarding or punishing the dons as teachers in the precious academic currency of reputation. It is not obvious why there should be research productivity in a place so obviously dedicated to teaching and apparently so cushioned by the elegant amenities of high table and senior common room.

Still less obvious is where power lies in a collegiate university. This is not a simple problem of the conventional antipathy of academics to administrators. They both know who really owns the cultural property, even when the academic is found in some insalubrious cubbyhole in a chemical laboratory, while the administrator dwells in sartorial splendour and marble halls. Admittedly, there is a particularly marked malice in the dismissively patrician reference of the Oxford college Fellow towards the Registry and the central administrative bodies—the General Board and the Hebdomadal Council. But these superficialities disguise attitudes more complex than can be conveyed by the word ambivalence. There is a background here of traditional organization, of cultural assumption, of changing external and material circumstances, and of anxiety in the face of threat which we have discussed as proletarianization.

The questions of academic leadership may be answered in part through the biographies of famous men and women: but they also require exploration of the institutional origins of authority and influence. Obituaries, appreciations, biographies, and autobiographies abound. Some are short and derogatory, as when the Chancellor and pre-Reformation Bishop of Oxford was described in Latin as 'a mitred hog and father of eighteen'. Some are long and exquisitely appreciative, as when Geoffrey Faber writes about Benjamin Jowett. Altogether, they record seven or eight centuries of a glittering community of the high-born and the gifted, the scholarly and the pedantic, the eccentric and the established. But this is no place to attempt an account of notable individual lives. A sociological account of leadership and authority is more appropriate and must stem from Max Weber's discussion of charisma and bureaucracy and his description of the social role of the Chinese literati. Weber is especially relevant to a discussion of power and control in collegiate Oxford precisely because he was interested in education for the élite or ruling strata of societies.

Most educational systems have been restricted to élites, and within such groups Weber distinguished three broad types of social personality: the charismatic leader, the 'cultivated man', and the 'expert'. The charismatic person is readily recognizable in the case of the distinguished biologist who summoned a younger colleague to his sick-bed in the university hospital. He wanted to explain that he had a solution to the zero growth problem in demography. The solution was less significant than its origins. It had come from the Almighty by prayer. This, the sick man claimed, was his major method in scientific discovery. Such men, presumably if they also know their biology, are powerful. The gift of grace is seldom expressed in such a direct and conventional form in the modern age. But we recognize the general phenomenon of the creative scholar or scientist who is possessed by the power of ideas on the frontiers of his discipline and, so possessed, possesses others along with a disproportionate share of the university's attention and resources.

One recognizes also the 'cultivated man'. A person of refined sensibility and comprehensive appreciation of the most prized elements of intellectual culture. There has been a long line of those whose influence over others is tied less to monumental achievement in a particular branch of science or scholarship than to a catholic and discriminating devotion to scientific and scholarly excellence in general. They are the bulwark against what Walter Metzger castigated as 'professionism' (Metzger 1987). They are the exemplars of learning for the rising generation.

The third type of social personality, the expert, is also apparent in the modern university. This is someone to whom habitual reference is made as 'the greatest living authority' on the subject, be it Coptic or psephology or antibiotics or the rise of the gentry in the sixteenth century. They are the specialist custodians of erudition and research.

These three social types tend to embody three types of power and authority. The charismatic leader is magically or divinely inspired and will create excitement, loyalty, enthusiasm, and effort whatever the formal organization and whether the milieu is military, religious, political, or educational. There is no organizational blueprint for the generation of charisma. No doubt tension *vis-à-vis* other powers, competition, a culture which invites emulation of past and present intellectual exploits, and normative expectations of excellence would all be important components. The charismatic tutor is a recognized figure since Socrates. If, as seems to be the case, Oxford has had a relatively high frequency of appearance of such leaders, perhaps they thrive in the collegiate environment. But what elements of college have been crucial? Celibacy perhaps? Many of the most celebrated coteries of scholars and aesthetes in Oxford and Cambridge seem to have had close emotional ties. Commensality? The sharing of a common table, the college as hotel as well as instruction centre, raises the probability of informal relations beyond the specificity and impersonality of the lecture room or the class. The tutorial system itself has the same *gemeinschaft* as opposed to *gesellschaft* quality on which charisma is more likely to flourish.

It is, however, the second type of personality, the cultivated person who carries authority sanctioned by custom and tradition, which is historically most characteristic of Oxford at least since the Reformation. Such values foster an education which prepares the pupil for the style of life of the ruling class of society, which means, in the case of Oxford up to the middle of the twentieth century, the amateur gentlemanly administrator of imperial Britain. And, again, as Weber insists, the curriculum of such a system is derived from the cultural norms and standards of the ruling group. So, given that the English aristocracy and gentry were as much at home in the saddle as at the desk, it is not surprising that dons in eighteenth- and nineteenth-century Oxford emphasized character as well as brains, were suspicious of specialization, insisted that the table be provided as lavishly as the library, and gave social honour as much to the rowing coach as to the professor. These sentiments have had to come to terms with meritocratic specialization in our own day. But the cultivated person remains an ideal, and the college, as distinct from the university, his refuge.

Yet the third type—the expert—is also, and necessarily, a presence in Oxford as on any campus with aspirations to international prestige. The power and influence of expert knowledge is associated with the rational and bureaucratic authority typical of advanced industrial societies. The professorial chair or the readership gives the expert an honoured place in the university, but with a place in the college which has been much more problematic.

Thus, all three social types are to be found in the quadrangles, laboratories, and lecture halls of Oxford, and all three forms of authority—charismatic, traditional, and rational-legal—are there to support them. All three co-operate and compete to form a unified, but many-faceted, whole. But in reality there are no pure types either of personality or organization. Both *people* and *principles* contend for power at every point.

If, as I have argued in the Oxford case, there is constitutional democracy and election is the key, who are the dons who fill the administrative offices in the colleges and in the university? Let us note first that virtually everyone holds some office at some time, though probably about one-fifth have *short* careers in this sense. Out of a determined monomania for teaching or for research, or because of idleness or spectacular incompetence, this minority will not be elected to chair a sub-committee, act as dean of degrees or secretary to a sub-faculty or any of the hundreds of petty offices to be found in Oxford's ramified plurality of colleges and university institutions. Sometimes expertise counts: an economist becomes investment bursar in his college, I became Keeper of the Gardens in mine. But the senior university officers—the faculty chairmen, the members of General Board and Council—being elected, must secure the confidence of their colleagues, and this guarantees in most cases a demonstrated competence. Are they charismatic, cultivated, or expert? Any of these three qualities enhances the probability of election, but none is essential. Far from charismatic, a chairman may be dull and reliable. Far from cultivated, he may be a militant philistine but prodigiously efficient. Far from expert, he may actually have come to hate his subject and the burden of tutorial teaching but be sharply intelligent, completely in command of past precedents and present issues, and a stalwart for academic standards in general if unwilling, or unable, to practise them in the teaching or research of his original discipline.

If we take one of the most influential positions in Oxford, the vice-chairmanship (now chairmanship) of the General Board, more than one man answering each of these descriptions has occupied the office in recent years. There has been no discernible relation of subject or academic rank. They have included a tutorial fellow in law, an engineer, a college tutor in languages, a university lecturer in chemistry, a college tutor in philosophy, and a university professor of physics. They all, however, have one significant, if negative, characteristic in common: none have been strongly university as opposed to college men. The quality they have shared is exceptionally high administrative competence of the kind required to run a business with an annual turnover of over £50 million. Perhaps this helps to explain the attitudes of dons towards professional, as distinct from amateur, academic administrators. Because colleges are essentially academic producer-co-operatives, because Oxford is organized as an ancient syndicalist federation, and because its resources of dons and money are sumptuous, there is a constantly renewed stock of proven and willing administrative talent. The corollary is a persistent disbelief in the need or the justification for administrative staff other than those who serve the amateurs.

But will it last? Certainly the idea of the college attracts tenacious loyalty from the three estates of the academy—the junior members, the senior members, and the old members. And the first two estates can appeal to a powerful social source of moral authority—merit. Student selection has moved far and fast towards A-level merito-cracy since Franks. And Founder's Kin and the Thirty-Nine Articles are long gone from the senior common rooms. On the other hand, meritocracy is by no means complete. A new egalitarian age questions the fairness of college elections with respect to education-ally disadvantaged groups—comprehensive pupils, women, blacks. And a new age of research technology questions collegiate efficiency.

In any case meritocracy is by itself not enough. Old members are also crucial in maintaining powerful external connections. Over the centuries the élitist democracy of the dons has fought off or escaped control from without. Today the colleges are threatened most by the State and the threat, left or right, is real, despite determined efforts to raise private funds and the fact that eight of the ten post-war ministers of education have been students or fellows of Oxford colleges. The threat to autonomous syndicalist government also comes from within. Though Congregation is the supreme expres-sion of the collegiate university as an academic producer-co-operative, it is constantly endangered by the failure of the resident dons to turn up at its meetings. There is the occasional grand occasion when a full house and spirited debate renew the consciousness of genuine self-government. But the norm is routine business played before an empty house. Hence anxiety is generated when, as in 1990, Hebdomadal Council set up a working party to see whether Congregation procedures should be changed. The alarm was sounded in the *Oxford Magazine* in the second week of Trinity 1991 by John Lucas, a stalwart defender of donnish dominion (Lucas 1991). In the same issue the editor, Professor Jim Reed, offered a judicious summary of the problem:

It would be bad to get this one wrong. For if the academic and the administrative standpoints in Oxford are formally far apart, they are not so distant substantively. There have not been many cases of a damaging divergence of opinion between the administration and the rank-and-file as to where the University's real interests and commitments lie—something that cannot by any means be said of all British institutions of higher education. (Reed 1991:1)

So the questions remain. Twenty-five years after Franks the collegiate university still commands wide and powerful affections and interests. But the world is now more competitive and more threatening. The collegiate idea is challenged from inside and outside Oxford. Will commensality survive and, if so, with what further modifications? And, finally, if *not*, what kind of effective university could be envisaged for the twenty-first century?

8

TEACHING AND RESEARCH

WE have traced the background of expansion in higher education associated with the Robbins Report of 1963. It has continued ever since, though at a varying and reduced pace and with alterations of shape, starting with the creation of new universities, and the incorporation of the former Colleges of Advanced technology as technological universities. Later came the founding of thirty polytechnics in England and Wales and several Central Institutions in Scotland which largely absorbed teacher-training, and finally the development of the Open University to form an elaborated hierarchy of institutions. Funding over the past thirty years has been transformed. We have described it from one angle as the proletarianization of intellectual labour, involving a smaller proportion of established tenured staff paid from general university funds, a relative decline of the professoriate, and the addition of a significant auxiliary group of contract researchers and part-time, mostly junior, teaching and research staff.

There have been ramified consequences vividly illustrated by the hundreds of comments we received in the responses to our 1989 survey questionnaire. A female professor of social studies in one of the new universities writes,

I work 60–70 hours per week, which is necessary in order to get any research or scholarly work done at all. This state of affairs comes about because of staff cuts and consequent increase in demands for student contact, and because of increasing administration demands. This has led me personally to seek early retirement so that I can get on with my work (the job has got in the way of the work). I observe serious overwork on the part of my colleagues at the same time that salaries are decreasing. It is very hard to maintain morale . . . attention to and investment in students is maintained, but research and scholarship suffer.

Others, especially in the natural sciences, were contemplating emigration rather than early retirement for similar reasons. Yet others deplore the consequences of under-funding for the nature of research itself. People are judged by 'the money they bring in from outside', research projects are chosen from fashion for short-term solution rather than long-term value. Short-term profitability replaces academically durable standards. 'Research funding on 2–3 year grants', writes a London medical professor, 'is all very well; but if soft money on short term is to be the only or main support one can only expect results from quick projects of very limited value. The dual funding system[1] was not a bad idea. To dismantle it by starvation will not help Britain in the long term.' For the polytechnic scientists and scholars, however, without the opportunity to enjoy it, the dual funding system is one they always longed to experience.

In this chapter we describe these changes as a possible modification of the beliefs and practices of the academic profession in Britain, which had traditionally distinguished itself from its foreign counterparts by the strength of its conviction that research and teaching must be tightly linked in the pursuit of scholarship and science. Between 1919 and its demise in 1989, the UGC acted as bridge and buffer between the universities and the State, carrying this academic interest and and protecting it against governmental control. The two academic 'products' were funded as if, like wool and mutton, they were delivered in harmonious joint supply. Half of a don's time was assumed to be devoted to research, and money for libraries and laboratories flowed in proportion to the number of students, geared to a tenaciously defended 8 : 1 ratio of students to staff. This arrangement served the academic interest. In the 1950s and 1960s, at least until the May Events of 1968, it was the privileged foundation of a period which Noel Annan (1991: 377) labelled 'the golden age of the don'. Much admired and envied in other countries, its attractive logic could never have survived expansion at the rate of 'doubling in a decade' nor persist from the sunlit post-war years through the inception of the polytechnics to the clouded new conditions of faltering economic growth after 1973.

The 1950s and 1960s were indeed a golden age. Scientists had little difficulty in convincing society and its political leaders that there should be a substantial national commitment to research,

---

[1] The dual support system divided responsibility between the UGC (for general funds in aid of the research time and equipment of academic staff) and the Research Councils (for responsiveness and initiative in particular branches of research activity).

including fundamental research. Technological (and thence economic) development was coming to be seen as dependent on a stock of basic discoveries which needed continuous replenishment. The university system had to train the large number of research scientists who would be needed by what was to be an increasingly research-based industrial system. 1963 was the year of Harold Wilson's famous speech 'Labour and the Scientific Revolution', heralding the beginning of a 'white-hot technological revolution' in British industry. Research was seen as essential to national prosperity as well as (echoing Truscot) an indispensable adjunct of university teaching.[2]

Full-time teaching and research staff in the universities doubled between 1960 and 1970, not counting the Open University nor the growing numbers of staff paid from non-university funds. Between 1955/6 and 1972/3 this central core of academic men and women increased by about 10 per cent each year. In the decade of the sixties, funding fully met the aspiration of the expanding university professions to maintain the traditional balance of teaching and research activities. Research money made available through the research councils (reorganized, and confirmed in their independence of government following the Trend Report of 1963) also grew at an average rate of 10 per cent in real terms (Blume 1982: 11). Furthermore, the belief that science had an intrinsic need for continuous growth (more funds for achieving the same rate of discovery), expressed by the term 'sophistication', was widely accepted and embodied in governmental science policy.

But the golden age soon came to an end. The values which had sustained its policies for higher education and for science met adverse conditions in the 1970s and 1980s. The potential conflict between aspirations and restraints, ideas and realities, became clear only after the post-war period ended. When the polytechnics were recognized in 1970 it was as institutions particularly responsive to the needs of local industry and government for applied research, despite the fact that most of their new recruits would inevitably have been nurtured in the traditional conceptions of research and teaching. The demand for a share in the research funding system was equally inevitable but was unrequited, even though Britain legislated no parallel institutional division of labour to that decreed

---

[2] Stuart Blume pointed all this out in the course of the Leverhulme Enquiry (a revisit to Robbins) in the early 1980s (Blume 1982).

by the California Legislature when implementing its Master Plan for higher education in 1960, which reserved the granting of doctorates and recruitment from the top one-eighth of high-school leavers to the university.

More generally the end of the post-war period was also the end of the earlier conditions of reasonably assured financial planning under buoyant economic conditions. Inflation rose steeply in the 1970s. Five-year planning—the quinquennium—was destroyed in 1972–7 and the universities as well as the polytechnics have lived ever since under conditions of chronic financial uncertainty as well as straitened funding.

In December 1973 Research Council funds were cut at short notice and in 1974–5 the Advisory Board for the Research Councils had to face a science budget which was reduced by 4 per cent in real terms. Given that the Research Councils for Agriculture, Medicine, and the Environment had significant commitments to their own tenured staff, the consequences included reduced grants to academic researchers, and the alpha-rated but unfunded project application became a notable feature of the British science scene. Moreover the same underlying financial stringency—issuing in the seventies from faltering economic growth, and later from the determination of the Thatcher government to reduce public expenditure—eroded the 'dual support' system of university research. The Research Councils now found themselves increasingly pressed to provide basic equipment previously made available from UGC funds. Thus the administrative frame within which teaching and research funds have been channelled to higher education has been changed fundamentally, and overall resources have deteriorated from pre-Robbins standards.

The tension between the political and the academic domain went beyond financial questions. The relation between the Conservative government and the university was dramatized in the early 1980s by the case of the predecessor to the Economic and Social Research Council (it was then called the Social Science Research Council). Sir Keith Joseph persuaded Lord Rothschild to subject the SSRC to an official enquiry (Rothschild 1982). There was uproar, which is summarized in the following paragraphs (Halsey: 1982):

> Lord (Joseph) tried to mend the electric light.
> It struck him dead; and serves him right

For 'tis the duty of the Wealthy Man
To give employment to the Artisan.

Lord Heyworth had invented the Social Science Research Council in 1965. In 1982 Lord Rothschild was invited to abolish it. It is doubtful whether the invention was ever fully accepted by the political Right. It is certain that the invitation was refused. Rothschild could have replied to Sir Keith Joseph in one short dismissive sentence. Instead, characteristically and in the public interest, he presented the Secretary of State for Education with a vigorously argued rejection of dismemberment and liquidation of the SSRC. It would be an act of 'intellectual vandalism' (Professor Barry Supple's phrase) and would have 'damaging consequences for the whole country—and ones from which it would take a long time to recover'.

Lord Heyworth was a practical man who rose to eminence in Unilever between the wars before the social sciences became established and when knowledge of both government and the governed was essentially amateur, a wisdom ascribed to politicians and civil servants. Only occasionally would some academic mandarin such as Keynes, or Beveridge, influence Westminster, Whitehall, and public opinion. For the most part practical men picked up their sociology, economics, and politics from experience, the Bible, and classical allusion. Business experience allowed Heyworth, for example, to induce the generalization that the *per capita* sale of soap was a reliable indicator of a country's level of civilization. But he was thoughtfully practical, came to appreciate the need for systematic and sustained study of an increasingly complex and unstable society, and was aware that freedom was threatened if people did not have access to collective self-knowledge independently of government. Accordingly, he proposed to set up another buffer organization, following British custom with respect to the public financing of activities which were to be controlled in practice by the beneficiaries—in this case the academic social scientists.

The upshot in 1965 was the formation of a Council designed to sustain social science, especially in the universities, where the teaching of economics, politics, and sociology was expanding to meet unprecedented student demand. The SSRC budget was tiny by comparison with those of the already established Councils for research in Science and Medicine: but it existed, and was insulated from political control in the traditional British manner. Then came two May events. The first, in 1968, demonstrated that the social sciences had entered the culture of many countries, including Britain, as a vocabulary of challenge to the social order of at least irritating, and potentially destructive power. Students, supported by the tax-payer, suddenly appeared, armed with sociological jargon, not as aspirants to but as subverters of suburban respect-ability. The second dramatic May, of 1979, carried into Downing Street a group of Conservatives, armed with stern nineteenth-century theories of society—pro-market and anti-State—deter-mined to restore a manageable order. Among them Sir Keith Joseph was convinced that low productivity, as well as antipathy towards business enterprise, patriotism, and familial piety, had been irresponsibly taught to students by left-wing dons. The SSRC was surely a most vulnerable quango. Could it survive the passing of consensus politics?

Of course, the incoming 1979 government had other and larger problems. Legislation to abolish the SSRC could not be high on the agenda. What could and did happen immediately through adminis-trative action was a sharp reduction in the flow of cash. The real resources of the Council both for research projects and postgraduate studentships were cut step by step. In 1979 (at 1980 survey prices) the SSRC received just over £20 million: by 1982 it was down by a quarter to £15.2 million. In that year the number of post-graduate student awards for the main social science disciplines was less than one half of what it had been in the mid-1970s. Moreover, pressure was also put on the Council to direct its activities towards the solution of problems of the national interest as understood in Whitehall and Westminster. Esoteric study of remote places and alien cultures must give way to urgent practicalities in a new age of austerity. The Council's Chairman, Michael Posner, took all this extremely seriously. For some, including me, the definition of problems was shifted too far out of the hands of the academic researchers and into the hands of the lay establishment. By 1982, of the nineteen Council members, only nine were academic persons.

Then, with the translation of Sir Keith Joseph to the Department of Education and Science, the ultimate solution came into view. Lord Rothschild was the author of something called the 'customer-contract principle' in his 1971 report *The Organisation and*

Management of Government Research and Development (Cmnd. 4814). Surely he could now be mobilized as the agent of abolition. According to press leaks Joseph wrote to Sir Geoffrey Howe suggesting that a report from Lord Rothschild could 'provide us with an effective basis for action—possibly action opposed by articulate and influential sectors of academic and political opinion'. Soon after in the House of Commons, Joseph announced Rothschild's agreement

to conduct urgently an independent review of the scale and nature of the Council's work, both in research and postgraduate training, having regard to the principles he enunciated in his Report . . . ; and in particular to advise (the Secretary of State for Education and Science):-

   i. Which areas, if any, of the SSRC's work should be done at the expense of the ultimate customer rather than the Exchequer;

  ii. Which areas, rightly supported by the Exchequer, could be done at least as well and as economically by other bodies, who would receive payment from the public purse either on a once-and-for-all or recurrent basis. The bodies concerned should be identified; and

 iii. Which areas, if any, at present supported by the Exchequer through other bodies could better be covered by the SSRC.

The trial began. Social scientists up and down the country bombarded Rothschild with encouragement to resist this destructive commission and braced themselves against a severe sentence. But no. Rothschild recommended that the SSRC be left in peace for at least three years with no reduction in its money and no more inquiries. Of course, he also wanted it sent to Swindon and to a school of plain English, and to undergo several other treatments for internal maladies of organization which were of no great public interest. But the main point was that he rejected the invitation to hostility of Sir Keith's first two questions and, with respect to the third, at least flirted with Professor Richard Layard's suggestion that some money be transferred from the University Grants Committee to the SSRC.

The Cmnd. 4814 question was the first one and the one that mattered. It was the original Rothschild formula, and a simplistic customer-contract answer could have obliterated SSRC. To be sure, Government departments could replace the Council if they were given the funds; bureaucrats could play customer to the social science professors as competing contractors. What is wrong with such a sturdy market solution to efficient distribution of scarcity? The answer is that the ultimate consumer is essentially our grandchildren. In any case Rothschild of Cmnd. 4814 had been misunderstood. He had never supposed that the customer-contract principle could be applied to the social sciences. 'There is . . . no doubt of the need for an independent body, such as the SSRC, to fund research, whether "pure" or "applied", for which no suitable "customer" exists.'[3]

Could it then, as Sir Keith's second question suggested, be some other body than the SSRC? The British Academy, the DES, and the UGC were canvassed, and Rothschild again came back with a firm rejection. 'Neither the British Academy nor the University Grants Committee have any money for this purpose; nor . . . would they be willing to undertake the task even if they had the money . . . It is highly likely, therefore, that if the SSRC were not to receive its grant, the research would not be done . . . '

These recommendations were reached by page four, at the bottom of which Rothschild wrote that 'the rest of this report develops these conclusions'. He meant, I think, that the other 109 pages were really padding to make up a document of the weight appropriate to the desk of a Secretary of State. Chapter 8, however, on postgraduate training, must be excepted from this criticism. Here a suggestion was made (p. 41) about the method of allocating students which usefully sharpened an issue much discussed by the universities and in a Working Party led by Sir Peter Swinnerton-Dyer (*New Society*, 8 Apr. 1982). In brief, it was that chosen degree

---

[3] In a letter to me (18 February 1982) Rothschild wrote: 'In retrospect I wish I had not been so brief in the infamous Rothschild Report on Government R&D; and I should probably not have used the phrase "customer-contractor", because so many people think of a woman buying a pair of tights at Marks & Spencer and of someone in overalls with a spanner in his pocket and a ladder on his shoulder. By the same token, although I did not say it explicitly, I did not believe the principle was likely to be applicable to the SSRC, for a variety of reasons with which you are familiar; but I saw no reason—and still do not—why scientists should be better qualified to assess national agricultural priorities than the ministry *if* the ministry backs up its economic data by having really good scientists in house. They did for a brief period but then gave it up. The good scientists are needed, of course, to stop people asking scientists to make perpetual motion machines.

'Unpopular as it is to say so, the same applies to medical research. But in both cases it only applies to a limited extent. One needs a mix of short, medium and long term studies, something I found also to be the case in the Government's Think Tank. The three parties interact with and stimulate each other'.

courses organized along the lines of American-style Ph.D.s (one year of courses plus two years on a dissertation) should be given a quota of awards. Then there should also be a separate competition for a pool of awards to be given to individuals in subjects not appropriately catered for by the American system. It was an excellence proposal on behalf of better research training and higher rates of completion.

Most of the rest was harmless superfluity. The discussion of the nature and significance of social science deserved applause. Even such a distinguished scientist as Rothschild faced a tall order in securing a firm grip on so vast a subject so quickly. The social sciences are centuries old, and he had three months. Far from carping at the result of his summary attempt to describe 'the scope and nature of the Council's work', one is compelled to admire the sense and lucidity of his general remarks. Nevertheless, carp I must, for his coverage was patently patchy. It was by an eminent layman for laymen. Professional social scientists inevitably found it too long to ignore, and too short to be definitive. Of the subjects listed in the SSRC's official catalogue, though social anthropology received handsome and favourable treatment, little or nothing was said about, for example, politics, geography, education, or linguistics. Worse, there was a whole chapter purportedly about sociology, as well as scattered remarks, and they were mostly unfriendly in the received establishment style. The lay reader would gain the impression that sociology was a pretentious mistake now discredited and replaced by more sensible, 'less ambitious and better established disciplines which are the heirs to the grander claims of sociology—for example, human geography, social psychology, and social anthropology'. This is a highly tendentious and ill-informed judgement. Far from inheriting, sub-disciplines like human geography are almost entirely debtors of sociology, borrowing ideas to enliven themselves. Indeed, a knowledgeable and dispassionate historian of the modern social sciences would instead describe sociology as the major source of ideas about social relations—so much so that neighbouring subjects including history, geography, and psychology, and not excluding economics, have absorbed sociological ideas to an extent which has transformed them.

Of course there were and are incompetent sociologists. A subject which carried excitement about important matters, and which was in rapid expansion after neglect, inevitably attracted some quacks. But the remedy lay in the maintenance of academic standards universally applied. It was gratuitous to recommend that the SSRC should withhold support for new or sub-standard sociology departments. The Council was not in that line of business, and did not have the money if it had the inclination. It was therefore to be hoped that this concession of Rothschild's to fashionable philistinism would not obscure his more general, more cogent, and more generous message that the case for fundamental or 'useless' science is, in the end, the faith of civilized people that they should expand rational enquiry to their own association, combined with the belief that this association is unable to express itself sufficiently through the market and must rely on a benign state. That some utility sometimes results in the short run is desirable and encouraging, but not essential to the case. To be sure the SSRC, its officials, and the researchers and students it aids, could all be improved. But if Britain had done away with them, she would afterwards and painfully have had somehow to re-invent them.

University and polytechnic staff are of course aware of these political incursions and increasing financial stringencies. Yet their response is somewhat paradoxical. They deplore the material circumstances but believe that both teaching and research standards have risen. These attitudes emerge clearly from our 1989 survey. Respondents were presented with the assertion that 'the quality of teaching (research) in my discipline in British higher education has declined over the past decade.' Three-quarters of them disagreed with respect to research and two-thirds with respect to teaching, in both the universities and the polytechnics. Dissatisfaction has grown, as both the survey statistics and the passionate comments appended make abundantly clear, not with the quality of their own performance but with the conditions of governmental control, salaries, and public respect under which they work.

Furthermore, for all the changes in their conditions and composition, academics remain firmly attached to the tradition of simultaneous interest in both teaching and research. The doctrine of interdependence is particularly marked in the universities. In 1964 we found nine out of ten academics subscribing to it. In 1976, with the addition of the polytechnics, there were greater proportions with interests heavily in either teaching or research, but the main body of academics still adhered to both. University staff had shifted towards a research orientation; a quarter of the polytechnic staff were heavily identified with teaching. Between 1976 and 1989 the trend continued as a further marginal shift towards greater research orientation in both universities and polytechnics. The research emphasis continued to be stronger in the universities compared with the polytechnics where over a quarter of the staff still gave heavy priority to their teaching duties. There is, of course, no mystery in this differential pattern of preferences. The universities have better funding, more favourable staff–student ratios, and superior plant as well as a longer research tradition. Polytechnic staff normally have a 17- to 19-hour-a-week teaching load in their contract. Their staff–student ratios have deteriorated from 1 : 8.4 in 1979/80 to 1 : 15 in 1989/90.

Attitudes are not, of course, necessarily identical with behaviour. We can begin to link them from the answers to our questions about the proportion of time spent on teaching, research, and administration, both ideally and in practice. Meanwhile it appears that looking back over the previous decade, our 1989 respondents believed that the quality of both research and teaching in their disciplines had risen. And it is also relevant to note that the assertion often heard that full-time researchers are typically people lacking the ability to obtain appointment to teaching posts was strongly rejected by 52 per cent of the university sample in 1976 and by 60 per cent in 1989. In this context the significant survey finding is that academics would ideally like to spend a greater proportion of their time on research than they actually do. The percentage allocations are set out in Table 8.1.

The 1980s have seen a sharp reduction in the proportion of working time spent on research in the university, without any shift in the balance of activities as ideally conceived. The ideal balance in the polytechnic gives less time to research (under a third compared with nearly a half in the universities), but here too there is a marked shortfall in the time actually spent on research activities. In both types of institution the pressures of administrative work have increased since the mid-seventies, and in the polytechnics undergraduate teaching now commands the lion's share of professional time. Moreover, over the whole period since 1964, the felt pressure to do 'more research than I would like to do' has increased. It was true for 18 per cent of the university staff in 1964 and was felt by over a third on both sides of the binary line in 1989. In short, the

Table 8.1. *Actual and (ideal) proportions of working time spent on teaching, research, etc., 1976 and 1989 (%)*

	1976				1989			
	University		Polytechnic		University		Polytechnic	
	Actual	(Ideal)	Actual	(Ideal)	Actual	(Ideal)	Actual	(Ideal)
Undergraduate teaching	26	(23)	27	(27)	26	(22)	43	(37)
Graduate teaching	10	(14)	7	(6)	12	(15)	7	(11)
Other teaching	—	—	13	(13)	—	—	4	(4)
Research and other creative activity	40	(45)	18	(29)	28	(43)	15	(30)
Administration, management, (examining, committees, admissions, etc.)	19	(10)	25	(14)	24	(12)	28	(16)
Other	—	—	—	—	10	(8)	3	(3)

Source: A. H. Halsey, 1976 and 1989 surveys.

subjective experience has been that scholarly and scientific ideals about teaching and research have persisted as a relatively stable expression of the traditional conception of the academic life through a period of expansion and vicissitude; but performance has in reality been at a lower intensity for both. A leaning towards the research life is more strongly defined as appropriate to the university than the polytechnic, though this expected bias is stressed more by university than by polytechnic lecturers, who tend to see research responsibilities as having more even claims in the two types of institution.

The three surveys may be used next to yield evidence on the research activity of the academics. A summary of the trends appears in Table 8.2. The trend is clearly towards greater output, although it may reasonably be suspected that the definition of a publication has been academically diluted in recent years as a malign by-product of the introduction of research productivity exercises by the UGC and the UFC from 1986. Moreover, the 1989 respondents

TABLE 8.2. *Trends in research output, 1964–1989*

	1964	1976		1989	
	Univ.	Univ.	Poly	Univ.	Poly
Currently engaged on research expected to lead to publication (%)	—	93	60	95	71
No papers ever published (%)	7	12	50	3	27
20 or more papers published (%)	27	26	2	53	10
Academic books published (mean)	0.1	0.8	0.3	2.4	0.7
Publications in last two years (mean)	—	3.5	0.9	6.3	2.0
No publications in last two years (%)	—	23	68	9	46

Source: A. H. Halsey, 1964, 1976, and 1989 surveys.

were an older group. Nevertheless, the surveys record that in 1964 more than two-thirds of the university staff had never published a book, whereas by 1989 this majority had fallen to a minority of 42 per cent.

We also have survey evidence on handicaps to research, as set out in Table 8.3. In the universities it appears that teaching commitments eased as obstacles to research in the period between 1964 and 1976, but then returned to obstruct research in the late seventies and the eighties. Other distracting duties pressed more heavily, though the terms as distinct from the vacations were lost to research for a declining minority. For the polytechnic lecturers the term is apparently lost to research for as many as 44 per cent because of these competing obligations. Although our 1989 respondents believed that standards of research had risen in the previous decade, it is perhaps not surprising that a majority (and an especially large one in the polytechnics) continued to disagree with the assertion put to them that 'an academic's first loyalty should be to research in his or her discipline: the teaching of students and the running of the institution should come second' and also to agree that 'promotion in academic life is too dependent on published work and too little on devotion to teaching'.

TABLE 8.3. *Handicaps to research, 1964–1989 (%)*

	1964	1976		1989	
	Univ.	Univ.	Poly	Univ.	Poly
Obstacle to research is					
1. teaching commitments	52	36	65	57	77
2. other commitments	54			76	77
Research during term					
substantial	24			27	13
little	43			49	43
almost none	33			24	44
Research is academics' *first loyalty*					
1. strong agree	4	4	2	11	7
2.					
3.					
4. strong disagree	23	27	51	25	49
Promotion too much *dependent on publication,* *too little on teaching*					
1. strong agree	32	24	28	33	35
2.					
3.					
4. strong disagree	5	6	6	6	5
Quality of research in my *discipline has declined in* *past decade*					
1. strong agree				10	8
2.				24	24
3.				34	34
4. strong disagree				32	34
Don't know				6	16

Source: A. H. Halsey, 1964, 1976, and 1989 surveys.

FUNDING AND THE GEOGRAPHY OF EXCELLENCE

What these survey findings reveal is an adaptation to two contending forces. On the one hand academics have a vision of a national array of autonomous institutions of higher education in which integrated research and teaching extend over the whole span of human knowledge and are funded according to their own inner logic. That logic, especially after Robbins, implied both great expense and rapid expansion. On the other hand stood the governmental paymaster with no assurance of economic growth, though Robbins had been informally told to assume an annual rate of 4 per cent (Annan, 1991: 382), no confidence that dons were an optimum investment, a commitment to reduced public expenditure, and beset by demands for money from many other Whitehall departments. An escape had to be found, and one route lay through selective funding after judging the merits of different university departments and institutions.

This was the situation that the UGC, with great reluctance, had to face in the 1980s. The geography of excellence had to be mapped. In 1981 it was a draconian foray which left Aston and Salford in devastation. In its Green Paper of 1985 (DES 1985) the government called for evaluation of research. Later that year the UGC embarked on a journey to chart the quality of all its cost centres (departments or sub-faculties) in the universities. Each cost centre had to send in a two-page description of its research achievements and its five best publications over the previous five years along with information on research grants, income from contracts, studentships, prizes, and honorific awards. The UGC sub-committees sat in judgement and secrecy to produce their cartography using this information and their own peer review assessments, by methods unknown to the anxious and suspicious inhabitants of what had hitherto been an academic *terra incognita*.

No wonder then that publication of the results aroused immediate and widespread criticism. 'Behind closed doors', absence of justified and precise criteria, bias against smaller and new departments, incompetent assessors, and hasty evaluations were all attacked by disappointed and sometimes outraged recipients of low ratings.

Here then was a dramatic moment in the decline of donnish dominion. Policy dictated it. The conflict between academic and state interests could not be resolved by traditional UGC buffering. The premiss of the new arrangements was disputed, and even if there had been agreement, the technical means of implementing funding decisions was primitive. The place of bibliometric and informational methods was contentious. Their use might threaten the more consensual principle of peer review.

Nevertheless the new arrangement for selective grant was to become a permanent feature of higher education. The UGC was deemed by the government to be an outmoded apparatus and was displaced by the UFC which immediately began a new ranking exercise, less hurried, and more valid and reliable, because prepared by sixty specialist committees. The results were published in August 1989 (*THES*, Sept. 1989), again to a chorus of criticism because assessment of 'the best places' is always uncertain and disputable, and the measurement of teaching as distinct from research quality has so far defied all attempts at convincing solution. A sober account of the process has been published by Peter Jones and John Sizer, and discussed by Ben Martin, Sir William Taylor, and others in a symposium held at Augsburg in 1990 (Daniel *et al.* 1990).

The interests of the central bodies in a public ranking of individual institutions was to justify differential funding over and above student numbers. The interests of others varied—from vulgar curiosity to the opportunity of making more informed choices for parents, students, employers, and academics themselves. None of the interested parties could be wholly satisfied. The science of measurement cannot be applied as more than one aid to judgement, and the basic controversy resided in a long war of attrition between academics pursuing their calling and politicians pursuing their own idea of the wealth of the nation.

Meanwhile the repercussions of changes in funding have to be traced into the wider pattern of a trend towards hierarchy in the system of higher education. Where are 'the best places'? The results of our 1976 and 1989 surveys can help towards understanding variations in research and teaching quality in the universities and polytechnics. Martin Trow and I wrote a portrait in 1971 which emphasized the historically determined hierarchical character of the university system both before and in the immediate aftermath of the Robbins Report. We explored the correlates of research orientation, partly through a sample survey of British university teachers in 1964 and partly through institutional analysis. I then repeated the survey in 1976 and in 1989, adding an explicit question about the location of the best departments in the respondent's discipline. Thus the 1976 and 1989 surveys yield reputational academics' rankings of their own subject on a wider set of self-defined criteria, not necessarily confined specifically to research quality. The respondents were asked 'Where are the best three departments in your subject, whether at universities or polytechnics?'

Before presenting the results of the ranking question, it is worth repeating that the foregoing analysis of the surveys carried out in

1964, 1976, and 1989 shows important trends in the research leanings and activity reported by university respondents. In 1964 only 10 per cent of the universities' sample claimed to be very heavily oriented to research as distinct from teaching, but this proportion doubled by 1989. Meanwhile, over the same period, those publishing at least twenty articles also roughly doubled from 27 per cent to 53 per cent, and the proportion who had published five or more books rose from 4 per cent to 13.5 per cent. Similarly, the proportion of people who agreed with the assertion that 'An academic's first loyalty should be to research in his discipline. The teaching of students and the running of his university should be second to this first duty of an academic career' rose from 4 per cent in 1964 to 11 per cent in 1989.

We cannot necessarily take these indications of opinion and behaviour entirely at face value. Both research orientation and research productivity are correlated with age, academic rank, and institutional affiliation, and all of these relations need further exploration. But it is noticeable that, if age is kept constant, measures of productivity still increase, that sex is related to productivity in a complex way which we examine in Chapter 10, and that there are major differences between universities in both the interest in and the performance of research. In general it appears that productivity is correlated with rank and with membership of institutions with high prestige. Thus 39 per cent of the Oxbridge dons reported in 1964 that they had published twenty or more articles compared with 33 per cent in London, 26 per cent in the major redbricks, and 6 per cent in the former Colleges of Advanced Technology which became technological universities. Looking again at the hierarchy in 1989 the Oxford figure rises to 56 per cent, the major redbricks to 55 per cent, and the technological universities to 40 per cent. In short the pyramid appears to be fairly stable over time, but with a rising level of research interest.

Against this background we can consider the pattern of answers to the question about 'best departments'. To present the results both briefly and fairly is difficult. Universities and polytechnics vary in size and subject coverage. Institutions of higher education are patchy, some departments having higher repute than others. Smallness of institution, subject, or sample reduce visibility and also increase the risk of measurement error. Largeness may exaggerate fame. Moreover, there is the problem of weighting which arises if second and third choices are allowed to count. Our solutions to all these problems are arbitrary but not unreasonable. A first choice is counted as 3 points, a second as 2, and a third as 1. This yields a *sum rate* for each institution and each subject, which is the number of mentions multiplied by the scores as defined. Second, we have excluded from overall assessment any university or polytechnic with a sum rate of 150 or less from the university respondents. A consequence is that no polytechnic and only twenty-one universities appear in the league of highly reputable research institutions.

The problem of large size arises in the case of London. But its famous colleges are virtually autonomous and LSE, Imperial, UCL, and King's are separately identified, though the London medical schools are grouped as one, leaving out other institutions. If London were treated as a single entity it would have a sum rate of 2,747 from the university respondents and therefore lead the list unless Oxford and Cambridge were to be combined as Oxbridge to replace it.

Another possible source of error comes from the known bias of respondents towards the merit of their own institution. This bias would have the effect of favouring the larger departments. We have therefore re-analysed the rankings excluding 'home votes'. But the results are virtually the same, particularly with respect to the dominance of Oxford and Cambridge.

OVERALL RATING

On these assumptions and cautions the 1989 league table of universities in the eyes of the academic staff and as a general assessment runs as in Table 8.4. The cut-off at 150 points is arbitrary. Below that the rankings become pretty meaningless in that less than eighty-two respondents recorded a first, second, or third choice in any subject for an institution with a sum rate below 150. The league table emerging from the judgement of university academic staff contains few surprises. Oxford leads with 1,920 points, followed closely by Cambridge. There is then a huge gap until Manchester takes third place. Edinburgh is fourth. The big London colleges are prominent and the eminence of Imperial and LSE is notable given their restricted subject coverage. The major redbricks retain their solid strength. The mild surprises are that Warwick has risen so rapidly to tenth place in its short career and that Lancaster and York are among the twenty-one leading places.

TABLE 8.4.   *Overall ranking of British universities, 1989*

Ranking	Institution	Sum rate 1989
1	Oxford	1,920
2	Cambridge	1,902
3	Manchester	678
4	Edinburgh	592
5	Imperial College, London	587
6	London Medical (combined)	536
7	Bristol	512
8	UCL	481
9	LSE	418
10	Warwick	366
11	Glasgow	268
12	Leeds	260
13	Nottingham	249
14	Southampton	243
15	Birmingham	218
16	Sheffield	205
17	Lancaster	173
18	Newcastle	169
19	Reading	159
20	King's College, London	157
21	York	151

This first simple assessment can be repeated using the polytechnic staff rather than the university staff as the judges. The result (not printed) is not wildly different. Of the top nineteen places as judged by university staff eleven are at the top of the polytechnic list, and again no polytechnic is included. Manchester Polytechnic came nearest with 86 points. Cambridge, Oxford, and Imperial are the leaders with Manchester fourth, LSE fifth, Warwick sixth, Bristol seventh, and Edinburgh eighth.

SUBJECT RANKINGS

A second step is to differentiate subject areas (Table 8.5). In the broad subject-groupings used in recent official statistics before the introduction of cost centres, and again using the sum rate and splitting London into its main colleges, it emerges that Oxford leads in the arts and social studies and Cambridge in the sciences. The London hospitals have the highest repute in medical studies and Imperial College in engineering and technology. Three smaller

TABLE 8.5. *Subject group best departments, 1989—university respondents*

Subject	Institution	Ranking	Sum rate
Arts	Oxford	1	255
	Cambridge	2	220
	Bristol	3	47
	Edinburgh	4	42
	Manchester	5	37
	East Anglia/		
	Warwick	6	34
Language/Literature,	Cambridge	1	277
and Area Studies	Oxford	2	255
	UCL	3	76
	Edinburgh	4	68
	York	5	55
Architecture and other	Reading	1	13
professional studies	Sheffield	2	11
	Cambridge	3	10
	Bath/Cardiff	4	9
Social, Administrative,	Oxford	1	382
and Business Studies	LSE	2	372
	Cambridge	3	244
	Manchester	4	173
	Warwick	5	162
Science	Cambridge	1	821
	Oxford	2	698
	Imperial	3	306
	Edinburgh	4	241
	Manchester	5	154
Agriculture, Forestry, and	Glasgow/Reading	1	39
Veterinary Studies	Edinburgh	2	32
	Bristol	3	31
	Nottingham	4	26
Engineering and Technology	Imperial College	1	253
	Cambridge	2	181
	Southampton	3	99
	Manchester	4	57
	Bristol	5	52
Medicine, Dentistry, and	London (combined)	1	680
Health Studies	Oxford	2	270

TABLE 8.5. (CONT.)   *Subject group best departments, 1989—university*
respondents

Subject	Institution	Ranking	Sum rate
	Manchester	3	201
	Cambridge	4	133
	Edinburgh	5	130
Education	London (combined)	1	104
	Exeter	2	45
	Leeds	3	24
	Warwick	4	20
	Loughborough	5	19

subject areas are also delineated. London leads in education. Glasgow and Reading tie for first place in architecture, forestry, and veterinary studies, and Reading leads in architecture and similar professional training. If however London is treated as a single entity it wins first place in six of the nine areas with a third in languages and literature, a third in the sciences, and a fourth in architecture and related training.

STABILITY OF RANKINGS

Third, the 1976 and 1989 surveys offer some indication of the stability of ranking of the different universities. The number of judges or 'voters' is sufficiently large in seventeen subjects and the outcome of ranking by university respondents is shown in Table 8.6. In this case only first choices are used, yielding a rank by the percentage of choice obtained. Only subjects with at least forty 'voters' are included except in the case of philosophy, where the number dropped to thirty in 1989.

This more detailed ranking of subjects confirms the two simpler pictures. Cambridge leads strongly in the sciences and Oxford equally strongly in the arts. The London School of Economics offers a strong challenge in the social sciences, attracting the highest number of votes in economics, sociology, and politics. Imperial College has a possibly more remarkable prestige, sustaining its first position in civil engineering as well as a third place in chemistry, mathematics, and physics. Moreover, the solid worth of the Victorian foundations in Manchester and Bristol remains manifest

TABLE 8.6. *Ranking stability, 1976–1989*

Subject	Survey date	1st	2nd	3rd	4th	5th	Other UFC top ratings
ENGLISH	1976	Oxford	Cambridge	UCL	East Anglia	York	
	1989	Oxford[5]	Cambridge[5]	York[4]	UCL[4]	Birmingham[5]	
FRENCH	1976	Oxford	Cambridge	Manchester	Bristol	Bradford	
	1989	Cambridge[5]	Oxford[5]	Aston	Bath/Bradford/Essex/Nottingham[5]/Reading[5]/Salford/Edinburgh[4]/Warwick[5]		
HISTORY	1976	Oxford	Cambridge	Edinburgh	LSE		
	1989	Oxford[5]	Cambridge[5]	SOAS[4]	Edinburgh[4]		UCL[5] Birmingham[5]
PHILOSOPHY[a]	1976	Oxford	UCL				
	1989	Oxford[5]	Cambridge[5]/Warwick[4]				
ECONOMICS	1976	LSE	Cambridge	Oxford	Edinburgh	Warwick	Birkbeck[5] Essex[5] S'hampton[5] York[5]
	1989	LSE[5]	Oxford[5]	Cambridge[4]	Warwick[5]		
LAW	1976	Oxford	Cambridge	LSE	Edinburgh	Kings	LSE[5]
	1989	Oxford[5]	UCL[5]	Cambridge[5]	Queen Mary[4]	Kings[4]	Bristol[5] Edinburgh[5]

GEOGRAPHY	1976	Cambridge	UCL	Bristol	Durham	Aberdeen/LSE	Leeds[5]
	1989	UCL[5]	Cambridge[5]	Bristol[5]	Durham[4] Manchester/Cambridge	Oxford[5]	Oxford[5] Warwick[5]
SOCIOLOGY	1976	LSE	Oxford	Essex			
	1989	LSE[4]	Essex[5]	Surrey[4] Lancaster[5] Cambridge[5]			
BIOLOGY	1976	Cambridge	Edinburgh	Sussex/Glasgow		Bristol/Liverpool	
	1989	Cambridge[5]	Oxford[5]	London (Med.)	Edinburgh[4]	UCL[4]	Warwick[5] Imperial[5]
PHYSICS	1976	Cambridge	Oxford/UCL	Imperial	Bristol	Birmingham	
	1989	Cambridge[5]	Oxford[5]	Imperial[5]			Birmingham[5] Bristol[5] Liverpool[5] Manchester[5] Nottingham[5] UCL[5]
MATHEMATICS	1976	Cambridge	Manchester	Oxford/Imperial		Edinburgh	
	1989	Cambridge[5]	Oxford[5]	Edinburgh[3]	Imperial[5]	Manchester[4]	Warwick[5]
CHEMISTRY	1976	Cambridge	Oxford	Imperial	Bristol	Leeds	
	1989	Oxford[5]	Cambridge[5]	Imperial[5]/Bristol[5]			Nottingham[5] Southampton[5]

TABLE 8.6. (CONT.) *Ranking stability, 1976–1989*

Subject	Survey date	1st	2nd	3rd	4th	5th	Other UFC top ratings
CIVIL ENGINEERING	1976	Imperial	Cambridge	Swansea	Leeds/UCL		
	1989	Imperial[5]	Cambridge[5]	Leeds[3]/Loughborough[3]/Nottingham[4]			Bristol[5] Newcastle[5] Swansea[5] UCL[5]
GOVERNMENT AND ADMINISTRATION	1976	LSE	Cambridge	Oxford	Leeds	Edinburgh	
	1989	LSE[5]	Oxford[5]	Manchester[3]	Essex[5]	Hull[3]	Warwick[5] Strathclyde[5] King's London[5]
PHYSIOLOGY	1976	Cambridge	UCL	Oxford	London (Med.)		
	1989	UCL[5]	Oxford[5] Cambridge[4]				

Notes: The superscript numbers refer to UFC categories.

5 = International excellence in many areas, National excellence in all others
4 = National excellence with some evidence of International excellence
3 = National excellence in a majority of areas or limited International excellence
2 = National excellence in up to half of areas
1 = Little or no National excellence

The last column notes universities with a 5 grading by the UGC who were not included among the institutions with the highest number of first choices by the 1989 survey respondents evaluating all departments in their own discipline.

[a] Only 30 'votes' appeared in 1989.

as well as the enduring excellence of Edinburgh. The quickly established positions of some departments in the new universities, notably Warwick, are also important features of the current university scene in Britain.

A conference in Augsburg provided an opportunity for further discussion of methods of ranking academic departments and the application of the general ideas to the exigencies of German universities. There was general agreement that peer review is the best principle of evaluation. From this point of view both the UFC exercise and this present survey have great advantages. Further statistics, including bibliometric indicators, should be seen as supplementing rather than supplanting professorial judgement.

My ranking was a by-product of the survey of conditions and opinions of British academics. It was not conceived as an alternative to the UGC or UFC evaluations. Its strength is its contribution to a sociological sketch of higher education in Britain. To use it as a precise measure of any particular department or institution would be a grave weakness. The outline of the scatter of research productivity and orientation in the British system comes out clearly. The hierarchical character of the system was hardly to be doubted and the peaks of Oxford and Cambridge and the major London colleges are prominent. But, below these high mountains, further differentiation is hazardous. Reliable discrimination for state funding of research or judgement on the present and future merit of particular departments would need much more refined information.

9

A SUCCESSFUL ACADEMIC CAREER

WE saw in Chapters 3 and 6 that career patterns for academics are entwined in an evolving hierarchy of institutions, with Oxford and Cambridge exerting a disproportionate influence at both the point of entry and as the preferred occupational destination. The ancient colleges are both prominent feeder institutions and also the refuge of an alternative to the chair at another university or a similar high position in a polytechnic. Thus the professorship in Britain is not unequivocally the zenith of an academic career, and there are in any case other high positions in institutions of higher education. The vice-chancellors, polytechnic directors, and heads of colleges often have relatively highly distinguished academic backgrounds. Nevertheless the chair is conventionally, and for the majority, the highest object of vocational ambition. We can therefore enquire into the conditions for success. What enables men and women to negotiate successful passage to this high point of an academic career?

The ingredients of success are not mysterious, but our survey data does not include them all. We collected information on sex, social origin, schooling, qualifications, attitudes to research and teaching, publication record, and subject area. But, as is usual in enquiry into social phenomena, the 'variance explained', i.e. the statistical measurement of the influence of our identified independent variables on the variation (yes or no) of the dependent variable (holding or not holding a chair or headship of a polytechnic department), falls far short of total explanation. We have not measured such important contributory qualities as animal energy, charm, luck, intelligence, or the chance of network connections, for example, which a knowledgeable observer of any actual professorial election would look for. Nevertheless, some enlightenment filters through the data we do have. The main outlines of the analyses are set out below.[1] It begins with a numerical description

---

[1] We have used logistic regression analysis for our purpose. A technical presentation and discussion by Muriel Egerton is at Appendix 2 below.

of the relation between membership of the professoriate (ie., university chairs and polytechnic headships of department) and certain characteristics of people and posts in the higher education system.

We are dealing with a sample of nearly 6,000 (4,226 university and 1,414 polytechnic) academic staff, taken at two points in time —1976 and 1989. The sample is divided between the professoriate and other academic staff. Each person is then classified by

1. Class of origin
2. Type of secondary schooling
3. Class of first degree and whether holding a higher degree
4. University group of graduation
5. Faculty or subject
6. Research and teaching orientation
7. Number of academic books and articles published.

We also distinguish men from women, but this we discuss separately in the next chapter (Ch. 10). Our model of the selection process rehearses the life and occupation cycle, assuming that class origin and schooling influence qualifications and thus indirectly the chances of promotion to professorial rank.

The percentages of the professoriate and of other academic staff in each of the relevant categories (independent variables) is set out in Table 9.1, columns 1 and 2. The percentages are a first rough indication of the importance of the variable in question in discriminating between those who do and those who do not take the successful path. The difference between the percentages in each row indicates how much the variable matters by showing the relative concentration of people with the characteristics specified who are found in the 'successful' and 'unsuccessful' group. However, this is a very rough approximation because in real life the characteristics are linked: they 'interact' with each other. The next step is to use the odds ratios shown in column 3. It must be remembered, of course, that even at this second stage, interactions between the purported causative variables are still not being taken into account. The odds ratio is, nevertheless, an advance on the simple difference between the percentages in columns 1 and 2. We express the results throughout this analysis in terms of odds ratios which are explained for the non-statistical reader in the first example below.

TABLE 9.1. *Correlates of career success, 1976–1989*

	Professoriate	Others	Odds ratio[a]
Service or intermediate class origin	86.7	82.8	1.36[b]
Manual class origin	13.3	17.2	0.73[b]
Private secondary schooling	39.2	36.5	1.10
State secondary schooling	60.8	63.5	0.90
Class of degree			
First	57.5	37.0	2.29[b]
Others	42.5	63.0	0.43[b]
Graduation			
Oxbridge	34.6	24.0	1.67[b]
Others	65.4	76.0	0.59[b]
Doctorate	60.3	57.9	1.06
Oxbridge doctorate	19.1	11.9	1.77[b]
Research orientation			
Research mainly	32.1	21.6	2.19[b]
Both teaching and research	32.5	25.0	1.94[b]
Teaching mainly	35.4	53.4	0.46[b]
Publications			
Articles: More than 20	68.4	24.9	6.54[b]
Articles: Less than 20	31.6	75.1	0.15[b]
Books (mean)	3.13	0.87	1.43
Sex			
Male	97.6	88.1	5.26[b]
Female	2.4	11.9	0.19[b]
Age (mean)	51.16	41.36	1.12[b]
Subject area			
Arts	20.4	19.0	1.04
Social Science	27.0	28.5	0.90
Natural Sciences	31.1	30.3	1.05
Engineering/Technology	12.9	14.4	0.86
Medicine/Health	6.9	6.3	0.96
Agriculture/Forestry/Veterinary Science	1.7	1.5	1.11

[a] These odds ratios are not controlled for the effects of other variables.
[b] Statistically significant at less than 0.05 level.

Source: A. H. Halsey, 1976 and 1989 surveys.

CLASS OF ORIGIN

Class of origin has some predictive value in identifying those who are promoted into the professoriate. One way of showing the relationship is to distribute each of the two academic ranks by class of origin. These are the column percentages shown below and in Table 9.1:

CLASS ORIGIN	ACADEMIC RANK (%)	
	Professors	Other ranks
Service/Intermediate	f_{11} 86.7	f_{12} 82.8
Manual	f_{21} 13.3	f_{22} 17.2
Total	100.0	100.0

Clearly the distribution is not random and this is confirmed by an ordinary Chi square test (x^2), testing the null hypothesis (i.e. that there are no significant differences in the population represented by the sample cells).

We now think of the association between the two variables in terms of odds instead of proportions. Odds are familiar in racing or other gambling circles. An odds is the ratio between the frequency (f) of being in one category and the frequency of not being in that category. It may be interpreted as the chance that an individual selected at random will be observed to fall into the category in question rather than into another category. We can first calculate the odds, called conditional odds, corresponding to a traditional percentage. Conditional odds are, in this case, the chances of coming from middle-class origins relative to working-class origins for professors or for other ranks. In Table 9.1 the odds on middle-class origin for professors is $f_{11}/f_{21} = 86.7/13.3 = 6.52$ and for other academic staff $f_{12}/f_{22} = 82.8/17.2 = 4.813$. Thus the odds on coming from a middle-class family are between one and a quarter and one and a half times greater among the professoriate than among the other academic ranks. In a traditional percentage table, two variables are unrelated if the percentages are identical or close for each of the rows. Similarly, in an odds table, the variables are not associated if all the conditional odds are equal or close to one another.

We can then take a second step to compare directly two conditional odds, a single summary statistic being calculated by dividing the first conditional odds by the second. This forms an odds ratio ($\frac{f_{11}/f_{21}}{f_{21}/f_{22}}$). The odds ratio in this case is 1.36. A member of the professoriate is significantly more likely to have sprung from the middle classes. Or to put it the other way round, a manual-class origin is less likely to lead to a professorial position, the odds ratio on this formulation being 0.73. It should moreover be remembered here that academics generally are heavily recruited from the service class (57.8 per cent), less so from the intermediate class (25.4 per cent), and least from the manual working class (16.7 per cent). But the odds ratio tells us also that the dice are loaded still further against those of manual-class origin after they enter the academic profession and compete for promotion to chairs in universities or headships of department in the polytechnics.

Given this explanation of the first association of academic rank with class origin it may be seen from Table 9.1 that there are significant associations with all of our independent variables except for secondary schooling and the possession of a doctorate. It also appears that, leaving sex to the next chapter, the stronger associations are with publications record, research orientation, and class of first degree. But again it is to be remembered that these measures are for each of the independent variables separately and do not take account of the obvious fact that these forces are interactive. Some sense of the pattern of interaction may be gathered from the following remarks, beginning with those factors which operate before entry into the academic professions.

SCHOOLING

Schools were classified into two groups; private (i.e. public and direct grant) and state (i.e. maintained grammar, secondary, modern, and other). We found no significant association between schooling and achieving a professorship (odds ratio = 1.10). But schooling is significantly associated with class for the academic professions as well as the population as a whole. People born into the manual class who became academics were one third as likely to have attended a private school as those who were born into the service class; and people born into the intermediate class were half as likely (0.48) to attend such schools as people born into the service class. Clearly then this association is mixed into the association we have noted between class of origin and academic rank.

Schooling was also significantly associated with class of degree—those who went to state schools are more likely to emerge with a First than people who went to private schools. The likelihood of achieving a First, having attended a private school, was 0.79 compared with the first-degree achievement of those who attended state schools. So here is a different ingredient of association among the independent variables. The strong association of first-class degrees with appointment to the professoriate runs counter to the effect of class origin. Moreover, the pattern becomes still more complex when we note that graduation from Oxford or Cambridge is also associated with a destination in the professoriate as well as being strongly associated with private schooling. Those who went to private schools were more than three times more likely to have graduated through Oxbridge than were those who went to state schools.

DEGREE CLASS AND WHERE GRADUATED

The outcome so far in the selection process is that professors were more than twice as likely (2.29) to have first-class degrees as those in the other academic ranks. They were also two-thirds more likely (1.67) to have graduated through Oxbridge. And people graduating through Oxbridge were one-third more likely (1.33) to gain a first-class degree than people who graduated elsewhere.

It turns out that holding a doctorate is not associated with admission to the professoriate, though we should also note that professors were three-quarters more likely (1.77) to have their doctorates from Oxford or Cambridge than were the other academic ranks. Doctorates from Oxbridge made up 22 per cent of all the doctorates held by our sample. Those who held a first-class degree had more than treble the chance (3.12) of doing their doctoral work in Oxford or Cambridge and this was especially so for those who had taken their first degree in either place. By doing so they increased the likelihood of going on to an Oxbridge D. Phil. or Ph.D. by fourteen times (13.69) compared to graduates from the other universities.

So a picture begins to emerge of the effects of class, schooling, and qualifications on success in the academic career. It is a complex picture, but focused around education at Oxford or Cambridge. The recruitment process can be visualized as passing through two stages. At the stage of undergraduate entry, pupils from private schools are at an advantage over pupils from state schools, and therefore over pupils born into the manual working class. However, pupils from private schools do relatively less well in their degree results compared with the selected pupils from the state schools. Students with first-class degrees who did not study at Oxbridge tend to migrate to the ancient universities at the Ph.D. stage where they join the considerable numbers of Oxbridge graduates with first-class degrees. Among students who got Firsts from a working-class background, 16.3 per cent graduated at Oxbridge and a further 5 per cent did a D.Phil. or Ph.D. there. Of other students getting Firsts, 31.7 per cent graduated at Oxbridge and a further 6 per cent went on to the doctorate in the same university group. In short, Oxford and Cambridge have played an important but not an especially meritocratic role in the recruitment of academics who finished their education before 1989. The effects of class and schooling can be put diagrammatically as in Figure 9.1.

The pathways are clearly differentiated as we have described them and a good deal more could be said about so complicated a web of social relationship. But above all it must be emphasized that all of these determinants of career success in the upbringing,

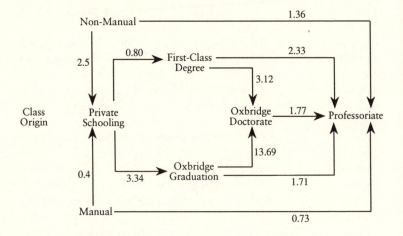

FIG. 9.1   *Paths to the professoriate (with odds ratios)*

education, and training of entrants to the academic professions are relatively weak compared with the determining characteristics that revolve around research interests and performance to which we now turn.

RESEARCH INTEREST AND ACTIVITY

We found that research attitudes and performance are strongly associated with entering the professoriate. Professors are more than twice as likely (odds ratio 2.19) as the non-professorial academics to give priority to research. They are also almost twice as likely (1.94) to value teaching and research equally as distinct from being oriented towards teaching compared with the other ranks. Publication records tell a similar story. A person who has published over twenty articles is eight times more likely (8.36) to be found among the professors than a person who has published less than ten articles. Between ten and twenty articles gives twice the chance of becoming a professor as publishing less than ten. Each book increases the odds on being a professor by 0.43 (1.43); thus three books more than doubles the odds.

None of these estimates take into account any connection with the other factors we have been considering or age or sex. Some of these associations deserve remark. Research orientation is linked to publication record. Research-oriented people are twelve times (12.23) more likely to have published twenty or more articles than their teaching-oriented colleagues. People who are equally inclined to teaching and research are approximately eight times (7.74) more likely to have published twenty or more articles than those who prefer teaching. Again, research-oriented people will have published on average 2.3 times more books than those who lean towards teaching.

Returning to the earlier factors we should also notice that qualifications are associated with variations in published work. People with first-class degrees are 1.74 times more likely than those without to have published more than ten articles, and 1.64 times more likely to have published more than five books. Oxbridge graduates are 1.36 times more likely to have published more than ten articles than non-Oxbridge graduates. People who have obtained their doctorate at Oxbridge are twice (1.94) as likely to have published more than ten articles and twice as likely to have published more than five books (2.05).

These findings are sufficient to demonstrate the great importance of the research dimension in determining who does and who does not receive promotion into the professoriate. The next step is to explore the effect of the variables we have mentioned net of their effect on each other. The analysis appears in Appendix 2. But two points emerge which deserve mention here in the body of the book. In our analysis we examine both the universities and the poly-technics and both the 1989 and 1976 surveys together. But further exploration shows, first, that neither attitudes to research nor publication records had as strong an association with headships of department in the polytechnics as with professorships in the universities. Second, it emerges that attitudes to research and actual publication record are less strongly associated with the professor-iate in the polytechnics in 1989 than in 1976, indicating that the pattern of promotion has been diverging on the two sides of the binary line with respect to research in recent years. There is, in other words, some indication that leadership in the universities continues to resist external pressure to assimilate itself to line management, to continue to seek academic meritocracy, while the polytechnics, in addition to inheriting their traditional technical college culture, are increasingly pressed towards a more bureau-cratic order.

So far we have dealt with the route to a head of a department post in a polytechnic or to a chair. We have noticed that a hierarchy of careers and career preferences evolved before Robbins and was later elaborated, above all by the development of the polytechnics. We have indicated the persistence of an alternative set of career preferences in, for example, Fellowships of the Royal Society (Table 3.1) and the British Academy (Table 3.2) and in the ratings of departments in the polytechnics and universities. We can now take a closer look at career opportunities by comparing experience and attitudes among individuals with varying degrees of contact with Oxford and Cambridge.

NATIVES, EXPATRIATES, AND UNCONNECTED

In the period since Robbins the influence of Oxbridge on academic careers has, in one sense, weakened. In 1964 over a third of all British university teachers had at some time studied or taught in the two ancient English universities. By 1976 the percentage had fallen to 29 and by 1989 to 26. To be sure it remained an impressively strong link in the context of the declining size of Oxbridge in the higher education system as a whole. At the beginning of the century Oxford and Cambridge together contained the largest group of university staff; by 1960 they made up 11 per cent, but after the polytechnics were incorporated, the Oxbridge proportion dropped further to below 6 per cent in 1976 and 1989. Apart from the appointment figures the extent of connection with Oxbridge suggests an influence beyond the walls of the colleges. In 1989 it was still the case that more than a third of university teachers and more than a tenth of polytechnic teachers had been students or teachers at one or other of the two universities. They fall into six groups: i. Oxford or Cambridge teachers who had also studied there as undergraduates (118 cases or 8 per cent of the 1964 sample; 165 cases or 5 per cent of the sample in 1989). ii. Oxford or Cambridge teachers who had not studied there as undergraduates (43 cases or 3 per cent in 1964 and 14 cases or 1 per cent in 1989). iii. Those teaching elsewhere but who had both studied and taught at Oxford or Cambridge in the past (70 cases or 5 per cent in 1964; 42 cases or 1 per cent in 1989). iv. Those teaching elsewhere who had studied but not taught at Oxford or Cambridge (226 or 16 per cent in 1964; 584 or 18 per cent in 1989). v. Those teaching elsewhere who had not studied but had taught at Oxford or Cambridge (45 cases or 3 per cent in 1964; 22 cases or 1 per cent in 1989). vi. Those teaching elsewhere who had never had any contact with Oxford or Cambridge at any point in their student or teaching careers (891 cases or 63 per cent in 1964; 2,403 cases or 74 per cent in 1989).

The sample numbers in groups ii, iii, and v are small, but reliable comparisons are possible for groups i, iv, and vi. In fact we have simplified the groupings into three, the 'Oxbridge natives', the 'Oxbridge expatriates', and 'the unconnected' in the other universities and the polytechnics, by combining i with ii and iii with iv and v. For the period from 1964 to 1989 these comparisons are set out in Table 9.2.

It can be seen from Table 9.2 that the Oxbridge natives and expatriates come more frequently from middle-class backgrounds, nearly three-quarters of their fathers having held white-collar jobs. This finding for the two main groups who have studied at Oxford or Cambridge is similar to that of many national studies showing

TABLE 9.2. Career-related characteristics of three academic groups, 1964, 1976, and 1989 (%)

	Oxbridge natives			Oxbridge expatriates			No Oxbridge connection		
	1964	1976	1989	1964	1976	1989	1964	1976	1989
Professorial/managerial origins	76[a]	66	76	75[a]	69	74	55[a]	54	55
Public or direct grant school	60	44	53	41	47	46	23	21	24
First-class honours	70	68	66	41	47	40	47	36	27
Doctorate	40	69	77	33	60	66	49	54	54
Research orientation									
Research	33	28	40	33	23	34	27	19	23
Research/teaching	42	35	36	33	25	32	35	22	28
Teaching	25	37	24	22	51	34	38	59	48
Publications: 20+ articles	39	51	57	26	28	46	19	22	32
Academic rank – Professor or head of department	12	13	10	20	17	19	11	9	11

[a] The figures are for white-collar paternal occupation.

Source: A. H. Halsey, 1964, 1967, and 1989 surveys.

that Oxbridge students come from a rather higher social background than at polytechnics or other universities. Secondary schooling follows a similar pattern, distinguishing the connected and the unconnected. These two indicators are, of course, two aspects of a common difference of social background which has persisted throughout the expansion period since Robbins.

When, however, we turn from background to qualifications, a different pattern emerges. The group with the highest proportion of first-class honours degrees is group i—those who both took their first degrees and now teach at Oxford or Cambridge. Over two-thirds of them have firsts. Next, but some distance behind, are the Oxbridge expatriates, and third are those who graduated elsewhere and have no connection with Oxford or Cambridge. Thus we again see that Oxford and Cambridge have considerable attractive power for the most able higher-education teachers as measured by this criterion, and they remain particularly successful in keeping their own best graduates. It is, however, interesting to note that while in 1964 there was a low proportion in group iv (not printed) which suggested that those without a first-class degree stood a slightly better chance of employment as university teachers if they came from Oxbridge rather than one of the other universities, by 1989 this differential advantage seems to have disappeared. In the old days this group had the lowest proportion of Firsts. More recently it has risen to an intermediary position in this respect.

For the academic profession as a whole it is clear that standards judged by possession of a first-class degree have seriously declined, while the hierarchy of institutional staff quality has steepened. In 1964 an Oxbridge teacher had 1.49 better chances of holding a First compared with the average 'unconnected' academic. By 1989 the ratio had climbed to 2.48. The pattern of doctorates has also changed significantly over the period. In 1964 the expatriates were least likely to have the Ph.D. qualification (suggesting that this group might have consisted in part of those who gained moderate degrees at the ancient universities and then retired to other universities, perhaps to teach, without so much interest in research or in further mobility). But the Oxbridge natives also had a lower proportion of doctorates than the unconnected. This can be explained by the custom of early election of students who had taken Firsts to fellowships or lectureships. However, by 1989 the pattern had moved to conform with the hierarchy of prestige. Over three-quarters of the natives held doctorates compared with two-thirds of the expatriates and not much more than half of the unconnected.

We have seen that the structure of rank at Oxbridge is different from that obtaining elsewhere and therefore the natives cannot be compared with the others in terms of membership of the professoriate. However, those who have an Oxbridge connection, and particularly those who move out as expatriates, have much better chances of a chair or headship of department—a pattern which has remained stable from 1964 to 1989. More detailed analysis shows that the chances of such promotion are particularly good among those with the closest connection in that they have had teaching experience at Oxford or Cambridge, and in this sense, they are the most significant members of the 'colonizing' force. In general any contact with Oxford or Cambridge improves the chances of reaching the highest academic rank elsewhere.

We have also noticed at various points in this study that the preferences of academics mean that Oxford and Cambridge tend to be 'terminal' rather than 'transit' institutions. So it is not surprising that less than 10 per cent of the Oxford and Cambridge natives want to move. It is also true that desire to move is strongest among the expatriates, 40 per cent of whom wish to leave their present post compared with 30 per cent among the unconnected and 9 per cent of the natives. The would-be movers were asked in 1964 and 1989 where they would like to go and their responses were repeated fairly faithfully in both years: 47 per cent preferred Oxford and Cambridge, 11 per cent London, 12 per cent the major redbricks, 7 per cent the minor redbricks, 9 per cent the new universities (a drop from 12 per cent in 1964), and 11 per cent chose Scotland.

Relative satisfaction, not surprisingly, reflected the hierarchy: yet this is not affected by expectations of promotion to the professoriate. The natives have easily the highest expectations. As many as 43 per cent believe themselves to be more likely than others of similar age and rank to be offered a chair and they are followed by the two smaller (not printed) groups iii and v where the percentages are 38 and 37 respectively. The least hopeful are the unconnected, where only 23 per cent see themselves as likely to be promoted.

Thus it is possible to repeat our observation on the 1964 survey that those 'whose experience has been confined to Oxford and Cambridge seem to be least affected in their conceptions of academic success by the idea of a hierarchy of professional

TABLE 9.3. *Career attitudes of three academic groups, 1964, 1976, and 1989 (%)*

	Oxbridge natives			Oxbridge expatriates			No Oxbridge connection		
	1964	1976	1989	1964	1976	1989	1964	1976	1989
Wish chose another profession		17	17		15	31		20	35
Have seriously considered leaving academic life	23		27	20		35	23		39
Have seriously considered taking an academic post abroad	31		47	38		38	36		34
Would prefer another British university	8	7	8	52	50	43	33	37	30
Would prefer to move to Oxbridge		73	55		65	64		33	37
Highest academic achievement									
Oxbridge, chair		53	60		34	39		14	16
Other university chair		34	33		45	48		56	64
Preferred of 4 posts									
Cambridge	68	68	69	39	45	44	23	27	28
Sussex	20	12	11	34	24	24	36	25	24
Leeds	9	8	9	13	17	18	23	28	30
London	3	12	12	13	14	13	19	20	17
Would not go to a polytechnic at more salary[a]		78	63		65	44	—	54	38
Would not got to a university at same salary[b]					18	21	—	25	31

[a] Question put to university staff.
[b] Question put to polytechnic staff.

Source: A. H. Halsey, 1964, 1976, and 1989 surveys.

expertise with the professorship at its apex. They are the clearest representatives of the older conception of an academic career—the working tutor who is a full member of his self-governing college' (Halsey and Trow 1972: 234). And again we can repeat that those with no Oxford and Cambridge contact are least inclined to move of all the groups except the Oxford and Cambridge natives, and least likely also to think of those two universities as destinations. They are also the most pessimistic about personal chances of a chair and thus appear to be the soldiers of the modern academic army (Halsey and Trow 1971: 235).

These 'soldiers', as may be seen from Table 9.3, are the group who most regret their choice of profession and who had most seriously considered leaving academic life. The proportions of the disappointed have been rising fastest among them. The natives were most shielded from such sentiments even though they included 27 per cent by 1989 who had given serious consideration to taking academic posts abroad.

Within the British system of higher education, the hierarchy clearly remains a strong determinant of preference. The Oxbridge natives have least desire to move, and if they do, the idea generally would be to go to 'the other place'. The expatriates, too, express less desire to move to an equivalent post in another university than they did in the earlier years, and among the would-be movers, two-thirds would prefer a move to Oxbridge. Equally noticeably, the unconnected are much less conscious of Oxbridge whether out of realism or genuine preference. It is significant that, when asked what would be the highest academic achievement for the respondent, the natives give their votes to an Oxbridge chair more than to a chair in another university, whereas the unconnected think much more about a chair outside Oxford and Cambridge, and the expatriates lie between.

As to the question of moving from a university to a polytechnic or vice versa, it is the natives who are most unwilling to move to a polytechnic even at a higher salary. This preference is less marked among the expatriates and still less among the unconnected. Significantly, too, in all groups reluctance has been diminishing between 1976 and 1989. Movement in the opposite direction, from a polytechnic to a university post, but at the same salary, would be refused only by minorities of less than a fifth among the polytechnic expatriates and between a quarter and a third among the polytechnic unconnected.

We asked about preference as between four posts in all three of the survey years, and Table 9.3 shows the distribution of preference between our three groups. Perhaps the most remarkable feature of this pattern is not so much that the natives would prefer the Cambridge lectureship to chairs in Sussex or Leeds or a readership in London but that the popularity of the Cambridge lectureship has risen for both the expatriates and the unconnected between 1964 and 1989. Sussex has lost the glamour of its earlier days for all three groups. The attractiveness of the Leeds chair with a headship of department attached has risen for both expatriates and the unconnected but remains unattractive to the natives. Thus the alternative conception of a successful career with its most prized destination in an Oxford or Cambridge college has survived expansion and development but has least attraction among the increasingly large majority whose earlier careers did not touch Oxford or Cambridge. Among that majority a chair in a university is the normal ambition whether in Oxbridge or in the larger system.

WOMEN AND MEN

THE participation of women in higher education is patchy, passionate, and peculiar because we are living through a period in which vigorous reforms are taking place with a view to establishing fair or equal chances in what remains, despite many slights and denials, one of the most attractive careers for women in paid employment in modern society. In one sense the establishment of an equal position for women in teaching is relatively easy in that such posts are culturally assimilable to the traditional 'caring' role of women in the domestic economy. Leonora Davidoff and Catherine Hall have written a beautifully detailed portrait of the role of the bourgeois wife in keeping her husband 'on stage' in a business career from behind the screen in the family home (Davidoff and Hall 1987). Historically, an educational career was one of the obvious paths out of domesticity into professional life for Victorian women. Marriage was, of course, the culturally favoured career. The nurse and the governess were relatively respectable alternative positions in society, while actresses, courtesans, and prostitutes were ancient but more or less scandalous, 'deviant' cultural figures.

This is not the place to detail either the history or the sociology of women's penetration into the educational world.[1] In her study of ten Victorian pioneers of the path out of domesticity into public professional life, Julia Parker has been at pains to emphasize the special qualities of both Victorian middle-class culture and the high resolve of those like Annie Besant, Octavia Hill, Florence Nightingale, or Beatrice Webb, who overcame a multiplicity of familial and social obstacles to their ambition. If we compare the circumstances of women moving out of domestic and family life in the last quarter of the twentieth century with those of the Victorian women discussed by Mrs Parker, 'what is immediately striking is the vulnerability of the women of the present day. The Victorian ladies had three important strengths: adequate material resources, strong family networks and, whether or not religiously inspired, a

---

[1] More detail may be had from Park 1991: ch. 1.

commitment to work which they could see as crucially important in bringing about a more just and merciful society' (Parker 1988: 194). Today both social circumstance and definitions of femininity are transformed: religious belief has declined, fertility has fallen, family networks have weakened, and the vocation of social service is less compelling. Modern women are subject less to the motives of the heroine and more to the mundane necessities of earning a living, even in the higher professions.

The modern female professional is also almost as different in her social position from her earlier twentieth-century forebears as described by Talcott Parsons (Parsons 1949). By the 1930s and 1940s, to be sure, a career in the professions had been made more acceptable as an alternative to marriage: but the cultural dominance of feminine domesticity was still overwhelmingly great. As Parsons put it:

The majority of married women, of course, are not employed, but even of those that are a very large proportion do not have jobs which are in basic competition for status with those of their husbands. The majority of 'career' women whose occupational status is comparable with that of men in their own class, at least in the upper-middle and upper classes, are unmarried, and in the small proportion of cases where they are married the result is a profound alteration in family structure. (Parsons 1949: 223)

For Parsons at mid-century the analysis of sex roles turned fundamentally on 'the interrelations of the occupational system and the conjugal family' (Parsons 1949: 223). For Julia Parker, writing of women in the 1980s, 'the step from domestic into outside work remains a difficult one when family responsibilities are also retained' (Parker 1988: 195).

Academic women provide an illuminating case in the study of the history and sociology of professional employment among women. The teaching role has been historically compatible with perceptions of femininity, by contrast, for example, with business: and therefore the educational career was relatively attractive to middle-class girls in Victorian times. Moreover, the motives of these girls were both material and cultural. As Josephine Butler remarked in 1868:

The desire for education which is widely felt by English women, and which has begun to find its expression in many practical ways, is a desire which springs from no conceit of cleverness, from no ambition for the prizes of intellectual success, as is sometimes falsely imagined, but from the conviction that for many women to get knowledge is the only way to get bread, and still more from that instinctive craving for light which in many is stronger than the craving for bread. (Butler 1868).

HIGHER EDUCATION AND THE VICTORIAN WOMAN

Attempts to change regulations governing the admission of women to university degrees, though dependent on improving the secondary education of girls, began to acquire momentum simultaneously with school reform. The key figure in many of these battles was the fanatically motivated Emily Davies. She had reacted to the failed attempt of Elizabeth Garrett to sit the London University matriculation examinations by petitioning various university boards to allow girls to sit their pre-university local examinations and, in 1863, Cambridge University allowed a trial examination to be held (Kamm 1966: 52). The trial became a permanency four years later and Oxford followed suit in 1870. But Emily Davies wanted to achieve a higher goal—that of the entry of women into the universities generally and, therefore, female access to formal degree qualifications. There was opposition from many sides, not only against the entry of women as such, but also in the guise of proposals that they should sit 'modified' examinations. It was on this latter basis that London University became the first to admit women in 1869. In the same year Emily Davies started a college in Hitchin within which women, though taking the same examinations as men in Cambridge, had no official status. In 1874 this college moved to Girton, Cambridge, and by 1881 its students were admitted to degrees.[2] By the end of the 1890s women were placed on an equal footing with men with respect to the granting of degrees in all the major universities and Girton, as a womens' college, had been joined in Cambridge by Newnham College. Like Somerville and Lady Margaret Hall in Oxford, the differences between these two women's colleges reflected the unease which continued to exist about the admission of women to sit examinations alongside men. Girton scholars, like those in Somerville, sat the same examinations as their male fellow students. Those at Newnham and Lady Margaret Hall were allowed to take a more

---

[2] Ironically Cambridge was, in fact, the last university to grant women full status; it was not until 1921 that women could receive even titular degrees and not until 1948 did they become co-equal with men.

'relaxed' approach and sit modified versions of the male examinations. Thus attitudes towards the higher education of women remained markedly ambiguous. The pioneers of the movement were anxious to allay the suspicions of the college authorities as well as to overcome the prejudices of male undergraduates against the supposed 'blue stocking' invasion. There was in other words a struggle to demonstrate both that 'college girls' were upright and respectable citizens and at the same time that they were not contaminated by pursuing high educational qualifications, disqualifying themselves from marriage (Delamont 1978).

THE EARLY FEMALE GRADUATES AND EMPLOYMENT

Resistance to the new and unfamiliar female graduate was based on a cultural distinction between the public and the private sphere defining distinctive male and female roles. This distinction proved to be one which education alone could not overcome. And the struggle of many middle-class women to enter the previously restricted public world of employment was, correspondingly, a long and bitter one. Teaching was one of the few professional careers open to the new graduates. It was mainly available in primary and secondary schools, and even here there were warnings that supply would exceed demand. Such warnings were thinly disguised anti-feminism. A late Victorian protest was apposite.

There are not yet 800 women graduates at London and Cambridge. Of these the majority are assistant mistresses in public or private schools, visiting teachers, lecturers, or head mistresses. There were in 1881, according to the census of that year, 123,000 women teachers and over 4 million girls between the ages of 5 and 20; and yet already this little handful of graduates is told that it is in excess of the demand and that it must take lower salaries in consequence. (Collet 1890)

So does monopsony reinforce cultural prejudice. Though women were becoming more acceptable as recruits to middle-class employment, the established conceptions of appropriate sex roles was stubbornly persistent.

It was no doubt plausible to argue, as did the International Federation of University Teachers in 1966, that 'women have always been admitted into the teaching profession, unhampered by any traditional prejudice against them; on the contrary, it is generally accepted that women have special gifts for educating the young, teaching them and forming their character' (International Federation of University Women 1966: 20). Nevertheless, the entry of female graduates into the higher levels of teaching was contested and limited. The leap from the lower to the higher professions was never an easy one, and the following comment made at the beginning of the twentieth century is still often echoed today:

In most of the new co-educational universities, teaching positions were nominally open equally to women with men, but in practice a woman had to be exceptionally well qualified and much more distinguished than a man in order to gain an appointment. (Holcombe 1973: 66)

Some, like the early Somerville graduate Lillian Faithfull, who became Vice-Principal of the 'Women's Department' at King's College London in 1894, went on to have successful academic careers (Spender (ed.) 1987: 351). But many found themselves confined in their academic employment to women's colleges. Change was slow and limited. A woman could take a medical degree by 1885 in Edinburgh but not in many of the London colleges and was refused membership of the BMA until 1893. Careers in law remained firmly closed until the passing of the 1919 Sex Disqualification (Removal) Act, and it was not until 1925 that the Civil Service opened its administrative grade examinations to women (Kamm 1966: 203). Moreover, all these professions, including school-teaching, operated marriage bars which disqualified women from working once they were married.

WOMEN STUDENTS AND THE EXPANSION OF HIGHER EDUCATION

We have already described the expansion of student numbers in the British universities and, more recently, the polytechnics (Table 4.6). The number of male full-time undergraduates in 1988/9 was an increase of 11,400 on the 1970 figure, while the number of female undergraduates went up by 52,700 in the same period. The emergence of the polytechnics in the 1970s pushed the proportion of women students in higher education further still. The polytechnics specifically targeted groups unlikely otherwise to enter higher education and, at least in their initial stages, were particularly attractive to women. The Secretary of State for Education in the mid-1960s, Anthony Crosland, declared:

There are two categories of students whose importance to the nation can hardly be overestimated. First, there are the tens of thousands of students who want to do a full-time course which, although not of degree standard, leads to one or other of the many professional qualifications marked by a certificate or an associateship. Secondly, there is the huge and growing army of part-time students at all levels, almost all of them already in employment. Now the universities cannot cater for these without a complete transformation of the university system of a kind which would not be practicable for many years . . . (Robinson 1968: 252)

Here was a vast, unsatisfied demand and, in the first years of the new polytechnics, female full-time students outnumbered males by some 11,000. Over the next decade, however, men drew level, and the 1988/9 figures show the numbers of men to be slightly greater at 147,900 compared to 146,700 women. The continued rise in the student population in the 1980s was largely confined to the polytechnic sector, with the numbers entering the universities rising much more slowly. The Open University, as we have seen, also provided more opportunities, especially for part-time women students. Between them the polytechnics and the Open University gave spectacular increases in part-time opportunities for women. By 1990 women made up 43 per cent of all students in higher education—an increase of about 10 percentage points in less than twenty years.

These advances are impressive, but it should also be noticed that women are distinguished from men in their academic interest and their qualifications. There is still a high propensity for women to enter areas linked to traditional sex roles or stereotypes such as nursing, teaching, and the arts. They are accordingly heavily outweighed by men in the sciences and applied sciences including engineering. In this respect there has been little change since the 1960s, when women formed 42 per cent of arts students, 22 per cent of medical students, and 3 per cent of those studying technology (International Federation of University Women, 1966: 6).

WOMEN IN THE SENIOR COMMON ROOMS

Despite the large increase in female students in higher education, barriers against an academic career remained, with the consequence that the numbers of women in the higher ranks of teaching are disproportionately low (Table 10.1), just as they are in law and medicine. The gap between the sexes is narrowing, but its persistence deserves explanation.

TABLE 10.1. *Men and women in British universities (1989/90), distribution by rank, full-time academic staff (%)*

	Men	Women
Professors	11.4	1.7
Readers/Senior lecturers	22.3	8.9
Lecturers	57.5	65.5
Others (research, teaching, etc.)	8.6	23.9
TOTAL	100.0	100.0
(No.)	(38,098)	(9,488)

Note: These figures include 10,836 men and 4,995 women employed in research only.

Source: USR, *University Statistics*, 1989–90, table 29.

Are the differences caused by prejudice? Sex discrimination is widely complained of. It is denounced in the AUT publication *AUT Women*. The 1990 Hansard Report was heavily critical of the universities, describing them as 'bastions of male power and privilege', arguing that, in certain cases, the under-representation of women in top positions represented a situation worthy of examination by the Equal Opportunities Commission (Hansard Society 1990: 68). It can reasonably be replied that universities and polytechnics try to be good employers and are willing practitioners of the statutory policy of equal opportunity between the sexes. But women are well known to be a minority in the senior common rooms. They constituted 10 per cent of the university staff in 1964. By 1976 that percentage was marginally increased to 11.6 and in polytechnics it was 13.6. In 1989 our sample numbers indicated a further rise to 14 per cent among those with full-time posts carrying both teaching and research duties (that is, excluding research-only staff) in the universities and 21 per cent in the polytechnics. The USR census for 1989, however, with its wider definition of full-time and part-time staff, and including those with research duties only, indicates that the proportion of women employed in university academic staffs was 20 per cent. Thus significantly more women have entered the senior common rooms in recent decades. But, as we shall see below, inequalities of rank persist in that men have tended to retain the more secure and more senior positions.

In pursuit of explanation we can begin with an empirical map of the similarities and differences between the women and men we find in the senior common rooms of polytechnics and universities. Their origins, their domestic position, their distribution between university groups, subject areas, and academic ranks are set out in Table 10.2 for the higher education system as a whole, and the further differences between the universities and polytechnics appear in Table 10.7.

To put the statistics into context, we should note that if social background, marital status, household income, faculty member-ship, rank, and university group were unrelated to sex, the percentages would be equal in each row of Table 10.2. If the whole system were equally and equally competently staffed by men and women, all the odds ratios would be equal to 1. They are not.

The academic professions remain predominantly male. There is strong social selection in the passage from junior to senior common room. The juniors are now over 40 per cent women, the seniors 20 per cent. But what kind of selection? Genetic capacities may presumably be ruled out. The relatively high female proportions in education, literature, language, and social studies suggest continued differential socialization. The proportions run in the universities and the polytechnics from approaching half in language and literature departments of polytechnics to as low as 2 per cent in the engineering and technology departments of universities. Explana-tions for such uneven distribution presumably lie in the experiences of girls in their families and schools. Sex differences in recruitment among university groups are not wide, though the relatively low figures for Scotland and the older redbricks invite explanation. The rank and tenure distributions in both universities and polytechnics suggest further selective processes. In both sectors women are scarce in the upper ranks and the secure appointments and concentrated in the lower teaching ranks and in the army of research workers on fixed-term contracts (see Tables 10.2 and 10.7). Again, the explanations are not obvious.

There are differences too in the career patterns and connections to family life. Women academics are on average three years younger than men. They are more likely to come from middle-class origins, though there is little difference in their schooling.

ACADEMIC WOMEN AND FAMILY

More men than women are married. A higher proportion of women are cohabiting or are separated or divorced or widowed or never

TABLE 10.2. *Women and men in higher education in Great Britain, 1989: origins and distribution*

	Men	Women	Odds ratio or significance of difference
Age (mean years)	46.4	43.5	$p<0.00$
Social background (%)			
Origin in service or intermediate classes	83.1	89.6	1.75[a]
Origin in manual classes	16.9	10.4	0.57[a]
Private secondary schooling	30.2	28.9	0.94
State secondary schooling	69.8	71.1	1.05
Marital status (%)			
Married	80.9	58.3	0.32[a, b]
Living as married	5.8	9.9	1.87[a]
Separated/Divorced	5.4	12.0	2.31[a]
Widowed	0.7	1.6	2.57
Never married	7.2	18.2	2.85[a, b]
Household income (mean %)			
Salary	72.7	61.8	$p<0.001$
Other earnings	7.0	3.8	$p<0.001$
Spouse's income	16.8	31.0	$p<0.001$
Subject area (%)			
Arts	15.3	24.7	1.85[a]
Social Sciences	27.5	41.3	1.83[a]
Natural Sciences	28.2	13.5	0.39[a]
Engineering/Technology	15.6	3.7	0.20[a]
Medicine/Health	11.6	16.0	1.41[a, b]
Agriculture/Forestry/Veterinary Science	1.8	0.9	0.51
Rank (%)			
Professoriate	15.3	3.9	0.22[a]
Reader/Sen. lecturer/Principal lecturer	42.2	38.1	0.83
Lecturer	42.5	58.0	1.89[a, b]
University group (%)			
Oxbridge	4.0	3.4	0.89
London	10.3	12.4	1.13
Old redbrick	16.0	11.5	0.69[a]
New redbrick	7.1	5.5	0.77
New Robbins	8.0	8.5	1.04
Technological	5.9	4.6	0.77

TABLE 10.2 (CONT.). *Women and men in higher education in Great Britain, 1989: origins and distribution*

	Men	Women	Odds ratio or significance of difference
Scotland	9.9	5.7	0.56[a]
Wales	3.7	2.1	0.55
Polytechnics	34.6	46.3	1.62[a]
Terms of employment (%)			
Full-time	96.0	92.7	0.51[a]
Part-time	4.0	7.3	1.95[a, b]
Contract terms (%)			
Till retirement	79.0	67.4	0.54[a]
No specific term	11.7	16.4	1.53[a]
Fixed term	5.4	12.7	2.48[a]
Probationary	2.4	3.2	1.40
Other	1.5	0.2	0.16[a]

[a] Statistically significant at the 0.05 level or less.
[b] Distribution differs between universities and polytechnics.

Note: Odds ratios and probabilities (*p*) are not controlled for the effects of other variables. N varies slightly on different variables due to missing values and is approx. 1861 for men and 298 for women.

Source: A. H. Halsey, 1989 survey.

married. These differences hold even when age (women being somewhat younger than men) is taken into account. Although the numbers of 'unpartnered' people are low they include separated or divorced women (who may have responsibility for child care) as well as those who have never married.

Those women who are in a partnership appear to function as secondary bread-winners. If we examine the percentage of household income that comes from the salary of the respondent it turns out that less than half of the household income enjoyed by partnered women comes from their own salaries compared with over two-thirds (69.6 per cent) of the income accruing to partnered men. Women also tend to earn less from other sources, though this form of income is minor for both sexes according to our data.

More women work part-time in their academic appointments than do men (Table 10.2). And this is true for the partnered more than the unpartnered women. The differences are however fairly small. Well over nine out of every ten of men and women in both the universities and the polytechnics are full-time. It is simply that our samples included 6.8 women against 5.2 per cent men part-timers in the universities and 8.3 women against 1.7 per cent men in the polytechnics. It is also clear that women are much more likely to have less secure contracts than men. Over three-quarters of the men compared with two-thirds of the women among the full-time employees of universities or polytechnics have tenure until retirement. None of this description is new or surprising. We already know that women in paid employment in general are likely to have lower rank, to be paid less, to be more likely to be part-time or temporary, and to be secondary bread-winners to their partners (Purcell 1988).

ACADEMIC WOMEN AND CAREERS

This outline of the structural position of women in the academic professions reflects their late and uncertain entry as well as the continuing struggle to adapt to the conflicting pressures of the formal as distinct from the domestic economy. We must now ask how this struggle impinges on the performance of women in their professional role (Table 10.3). Purcell suggests that because women see themselves as secondary bread-winners they are inhibited from seeking career advancement in the way to which men are habituated. The general view is that women in work are more concerned about working conditions and the social relations of employment than with advancement in their career.

In addition it has been found (Rose and Fielder 1988) that if a promotion involves change in geographical location, married women are expected to follow their husbands, even if this involves demotion or job loss for the wife. The converse does not hold true to the same extent.

There is some evidence of such predispositions among academic women at the present time. We have already noted the general pattern of attitudes towards mobility between institutions and posts. If we look at sex differences from this point of view we find from responses to questions about preferred posts which were asked of the university sample that social or family considerations are more important to women than to men in making decisions about moving from one job to another (Table 10.4 and Appendix 2).

There are congruent patterns of response to related questions. As Park has pointed out (Park 1991: 26), women express more discontent with working conditions than do men, who are more inclined to grumble about salaries. University women are also more dissatisfied with academic life than either university or polytechnic men. University women more frequently give lack of job security as a reason for wanting to leave academic life and this presumably is partly a reflection of their less secure contracts. In general it may be that women are less satisfied because their conditions are typically worse, not because they are women.

Purcell also suggests that women tend to be marginalized into 'caring' rather than decision-making roles in their profession. Talcott Parsons noticed much earlier in the century (Parsons 1949) that a sexual division of labour was characteristic of professional employment such that, for example, women doctors were disproportionately engaged in paediatric as against surgical specialisms. There is a general tendency for professional and domestic roles to be assimilated to each other. This is borne out by our finding that women in 1989 spent a greater proportion of their time than men teaching undergraduates (Table 10.3) and correspondingly they spent rather less of their working time in research activity. This pattern holds in the polytechnics as well as the universities, even though polytechnic teachers generally give proportionally more time to teaching than to research whatever their sex. In this connection it is significant that there is little difference between the sexes in the percentage of time *ideally* allocated between the teaching and research functions. It should, however, be emphasized that these differences are small and in any case they are subjective estimates which may themselves be the outcome of differences in male and female consciousness.

On the other hand it is objectively true that men do more supervising of research students than do women. In the universities 70 per cent of the men compared with 56 per cent of the women were currently (in 1989) supervising research students. The comparable figures in the polytechnics were 34 and 23. Such a difference of activity may well be reflected in greater opportunities for men to publish, and this is particularly likely in that men are more concentrated in the sciences where research students are more likely to be cast in the role of apprentice researchers than they are in the humanities where the women tend to gather. At all events women more than men see the teaching burden as an obstacle to

TABLE 10.3. *Women and men in higher education, 1989: teaching and research*

	Men	Women	Odds ratio or significance of difference
Allocation of time (mean % adjusted for age)			
Teaching undergraduates	33.1	35.2	$p<0.05$
Doing research	23.22	20.8	$p<0.01$
Would like to teach undergraduates (%)	28.3	30	n.s.
Would like to do research (%)	37.4	35.4	$p<0.05$
Supervision of research students (%)	59.7	47.1	0.61^a
Insufficient time for research because of teaching commitments (%)	64.3	81.8	$2.49^{a,\,b}$
Index of career-related activities (mean adjusted for age)			
All	5.69	4.82	$p<0.001^b$
Non-professors	5.16	4.72	$p<0.01$

Notes: As for Table 10.2.

Source: A. H. Halsey, 1989 survey.

research. In the universities three-quarters and in the polytechnics still more of the women thought that teaching commitments left insufficient time for research (Table 10.3).

Other career-related activity was pursued more vigorously by men according to an index constructed from our questions (Appendix 2 contains the details). This may, however, be not so much a sex difference as a consequence of the fact that women, carrying greater domestic responsibilities, are less visible and high ranking in their profession. Hence their lower participation in such activities as refereeing applications for grants, speaking at other institutions, and so on. However, there are also other causative factors at work: when this analysis is refined to exclude professors and to control for age, differences between men and women are seen to be slighter. So a general picture emerges of academic women as somewhat but not enormously more involved in the teaching side of the work of the polytechnic or university rather than in research or in the associated activities of the academic professional life.

TABLE 10.4. *Women and men in higher education, 1989: careers and attitudes*

	Men	Women	Odds ratio or significance of difference
Academic attitudes (mean)			
Binary equality (factor score)	−0.18	1.10	$p<0.001$
Élitist teacher orientation[a]	−0.11	0.67	$p<0.05$
Élitist research orientation[a]	−0.14	0.93	$p<0.01$
Career			
Promotions over past decade (mean)			
Age below 35	0.75	0.61	$p<0.10$
Age 35–49	0.53	0.45	$p<0.05$
Age 50+	0.20	0.29	$p<0.10$
Give non-career reason for moving to another institution[b]	−1.28	−0.86	$p<0.001$
See themselves as likely to obtain a chair[b] (%)			
More likely	26.3	15.4	0.49[c]
Less likely	25.3	38.3	1.87[c]
Have seriously considered leaving academic life (%)	35.8	41.4	1.27[c]

Notes:
 [a] Controlled for subject and age.
 [b] Universities only.
 [c] Statistically significant at the 0.05 level or less.

Source: A. H. Halsey, 1989 survey.

From studies of the labour market generally, Purcell also suggests that women are less likely to be involved in trade union activity, although she states that this is not the case for the academic professions. In our survey women's union membership is slightly greater than that of men, and women record holding union office as frequently as men. Thus 74.2 per cent of the women and 69.8 per cent of the men were members of a union and 24 per cent of women compared with 23 per cent of men had held some kind of office. Perhaps women's interest in union activity results, as Purcell suggests, from a political perspective which is at once both consensus-seeking and more radical. There is some evidence in our survey to support this generalization in the case of the academic professions (Table 10.5).

TABLE 10.5. *Women and men in higher education, 1989: trade union activity*

	Men (%)	Women (%)	Odds ratio or significance of difference
Trade union member	70.1	74.0	1.23 n.s.
Trade union office-holder	22.9	24.6	1.13 n.s.

Source: A. H. Halsey, 1989 survey.

A FACTOR ANALYSIS OF SEX DIFFERENCES

At this point, we can look at another major theme of our general analysis of academic attitudes—the question of the binary division between polytechnics and universities. Factor analysis can illuminate the issue in terms of sex differences. Using this method Muriel Egerton shows six factors which together explained more than half the variance (reported in more detail in Appendix 2).

Analysis of the factors in terms of sex differences shows that men and women differ most conspicuously in their attitudes to the binary divide. Women are relatively much keener on its dissolution. Out of the six factors this factor, relating to the equalities and inequalities between universities and polytechnics, accounted for most variance (18 per cent). The difference between university women and men was much greater on this factor than that between polytechnic men and women, with university women being relatively more favourable to dissolving the binary divide (Table 10.7).

No sex differences were found on a second factor, relating to the importance of teaching as against research. However, men and women did differ with respect to a third factor, related to the autonomy of universities and polytechnics against industry and government. This suggests that women are more inclined to adopt an élitist teaching orientation than men. Sex differences were also found in a fourth factor, suggesting that women are more inclined to favour an élitist researcher orientation than men. The latter two factors, which indicate support for the autonomy of higher education, and separate teaching from research, while valuing both, can be interpreted as reflecting traditional academic values. Women are concentrated in the humanities and social sciences, and these subjects may be more 'traditionalist' than the pure or applied sciences, where research is more frequently carried out in collaboration with industry. However, even when discipline was taken into account, women were somewhat more inclined to adhere to the more traditional positions. No differences between men and women were found on the final two factors, related to the expansion of higher education, and to the status and conditions of academic employment.

Finally, we may examine directly the effects of sex on the probability of promotion into the professoriate and so complete our discussion of career success from Chapter 9, where we ignored the distinction between the sexes. The correlates of career success are set out for men and women in Table 10.6. The corresponding table without sexual distinction is Table 9.1. As before, it must be remembered that the odds ratios (or probabilities) do not take into account any linkages or 'interactions' between the variables we include in the analysis and, also as before, the analysis of *net* effects appears at Appendix 2. We should also again remember that staff with only research duties are not included in this analysis. The differences between men and women in promotion chances are related significantly to doctoral qualifications, research orientation, and research performance. Men more frequently hold doctorates and have more frequently taken them in Oxbridge, though first degree Firsts and place of graduation do not differentiate between the sexes. The research discriminations, both attitudes and performance, are real but not large. Men are on average more research-minded and more productive with consequently better chances of promotion. The pattern of predictive associations will look different when net effects rather than gross correlations are considered: for example, qualifications are better predictors in the context of all the factors identified for women than for men, as also high productivity in research. Both of these effects, it may be surmised, stem from the fact that women academics generally are relatively less involved in research and lean more towards teaching. The outstanding woman researcher is therefore more visible to selection committees appointing candidates to chairs.

With respect to research productivity it appears that women do have a higher proportion of non-producers and lower proportions of very high producers, and this difference obtains also for the record of publications in the last two years—a measure which

TABLE 10.6. *Correlates of career success: differences between men and women, 1989*

	Men (no. = 1,861)	Women (no. = 298)	Odds ratio or significance of difference
Qualifications			
1. Degree class			
(*a*) First class (%)	33.9	29.5	0.83 n.s.
2. Graduation			
(*a*) Oxbridge (%)	24.3	20.1	0.77 n.s.
(*b*) London (%)	17.9	17.6	0.99 n.s.
3. Doctorate (%)	61.1	46.3	0.54[a]
(*a*) Oxbridge (%)	11.7	8.4	0.68[a]
(*b*) London (%)	12.4	10.6	0.82 n.s.
Research orientation			
1. Research mainly (%)	27.8	20.5	0.65[a]
2. Both teaching and research (%)	28.7	27.5	0.96 n.s.
3. Teaching mainly (%)	43.3	52.1	1.42[a]
Publications			
1. Articles			
(*a*) 20+ (%)	43.3	21.0	0.36[a]
(*b*) Controlled for age of subject and binary type			0.51[a]
2. Books			
(*a*) Number (mean)	2.26	2.28	$p = 0.914$ n.s.
(*b*) controlled for age and binary type	2.24	2.37	$p = 0.783$ n.s.
Index of career-related activities (mean adjusted for age)			
All	5.69	4.82	$p < 0.001$[a, b]
Non-professors	5.16	4.72	$p < 0.01$[a, b]

Notes: As for Table 10.2.

Source: A. H. Halsey, 1989 survey.

TABLE 10.7. *Sex differences between universities and polytechnics, academic staff, 1989*

	Universities			Polytechnics		
	Men (n=1618)	Women (n=234)	Odds ratio	Men (n=854)	Women (n=202)	Odds ratio or significance of difference
Marital status						
Married	82.3	54.7	0.25[a]	78.4	62.0	0.45[a]
Never married	7.2	22.0	3.67[a]	7.4	14.0	1.99[a]
Subject area (%)						
Health/Medicine	11.4	12.9	1.35	1.5	5.3	5.52[a]
Rank (%)						
Lecturer	49.0	77.3	2.88[a]	31.6	43.6	1.49[a]
Part-time	5.2	6.8	1.34 n.s.	1.4	8.0	5.36[a]
Full-time	94.8	93.3	0.74 n.s.	98.3	92.0	0.19[a]
Teaching and research (%)						
Insufficient time for research because of teaching commitments	56.3	81.4	2.82[a]	79.5	86.9	1.57[a]
Index of career-related activities (mean)	6.47	5.49	$p<0.000$	4.28	4.11	$p<0.02$
Binary equality (factor score)	−3.32	−0.98	$p<0.001$	4.29	4.54	n.s.

Notes: As for Table 10.2.
Source: A. H. Halsey, 1989 survey.

offsets the tendency for women to be relatively recent recruits. In sum the male performance is superior but not spectacularly so. And the university/polytechnic difference certainly dwarfs sex differences in higher education as a whole.

Summing up we may in general say that our portrait of academic women is very similar to the picture which has emerged from studies of women in employment generally. There is only partial assimilation, there is some tendency towards a sexual division of labour, the direction is one which assimilates professional to domestic roles in that teaching in some aspects is, so to say, *in loco parentis*. The outcome is that women in this privileged profession put themselves, or are put, at a disadvantage in the competititon to produce research. They are partially subordinated to men. Yet, to repeat, we cannot offer a comprehensive explanation of the markedly poorer prospects of professorial promotion which have so far been women's lot. All that we can do is to point to a continuing problem. A female professor of arts wrote to us: 'I am not a feminist of any school, but it is a fact that the percentage of women in academic posts decreases as you go up the ladder. I am frequently the only woman . . . on committees of the university, though (it) has a respectable number of women professors.'

11

ACADEMICS AND POLITICS

THE staff of polytechnics and universities are well known to be an electoral oddity. They behave in terms of political party support, not like a cross-section of the professional classes to which they are assimilated by income and style of life, but as if they were a fair sample of manual workers. Martin Trow and I showed all this in detail for the 1960s (Halsey and Trow 1972). The three surveys together now afford a serial picture of party identification from 1964 to 1989. In 1964 it appeared that, if dons only were enfranchised, Labour would have led the Conservatives by 7 per cent. The comparable figures in 1976 was 12 per cent and in 1989 19 per cent. And by that time in the polytechnics the gap had become 26 per cent. There was, in other words, a strengthening of anti-Conservative feeling in the British academic professions over a period of a quarter of a century. These trends are spectacularly different from the concurrent electoral history of the nation at large and therefore deserve closer scrutiny. They are outlined in Appendix 1. A more detailed examination can begin in Oxford where the balance of political feeling among academics has recently been disputed.

In 1990 Brian Harrison proclaimed six New Year resolutions in the *Oxford Magazine*, (Harrison 1990). The first was 'never to allow wishful thinking to distort our assessment of Oxford opinion', a rebuke to Colin Matthew, who had asserted that support for the government in Oxford 'has always been small and, in the latter part of the decade, [the 1980s] negligible' (Matthew 1990). Harrison asked how Matthew knew 'because he cites no polls of donnish opinion, only the vote against Mrs Thatcher's honorary degree in 1984 and the lack of support for student loans in a recent Congregation debate'. Our surveys supply some evidence for resolving the disagreement between the Matthew and the Harrison descriptions.

In 1964 we asked a random sample of university teachers in Britain what party they generally supported. The answer from 8 per cent was none. Of the rest 38 per cent supported the Conservative Party, and the figure for Oxford and Cambridge dons was exactly the same. At the General Election in that year the Conservatives obtained 43 per cent of the national vote. Thus, British academics as a whole lent slightly to the left (Table 11.1). By 1976 the Oxbridge Conservative vote had dropped to 31 per cent while that for the other universities had fallen still further to 26 per cent. Among polytechnic teachers the Conservative percentage was 25. The question this time was which party had been supported in the 1974 General Election. Nine per cent said they had not voted at all. The percentage for the electorate as a whole was 38. An anti-Conservative gap had opened to separate academic from national opinion, but least so among the dons of Oxford and Cambridge. Mrs Thatcher came to power in 1979 on the strength of 43.9 per cent of the total vote. But in the following ten years the Conservatives suffered a drastic loss of support among dons and academics generally. When asked in 1989 which (if any) political party they felt closest to, 11 per cent answered none. Among the rest the Conservative support was 15 per cent in Oxbridge, 18 per cent in the other universities as a whole, and 18 per cent in the polytechnics, while polls of the national electorate were wobbling between 34 and 38 per cent.

Thus, over the period since Robbins, support for the Conservative Party among academics had dropped sharply. The Labour lead in the universities other than Oxford and Cambridge was 7 per cent in 1964, rising to 9 per cent in 1976 and 17 per cent in 1989. In Oxford and Cambridge comparable figures for Conservative support descended still more sharply: Labour led by 2 per cent in 1964, 5 per cent in 1976, and as much as 26 per cent in 1989. Matthew was perhaps exaggerating slightly in that the 1989 Oxbridge 15 per cent support for the Conservatives is not negligible, but he was nearer the mark than Harrison.

The leftist tendency of the academic professions in Western democracies is well known. We should however note that in Britain in 1964 and 1976 the Oxbridge dons showed no great tendency to prefer the Labour to the Conservative Party. Oxford and Cambridge were in this respect contrasted with similar institutions like

TABLE 11.1. *Party support by university and polytechnic academic staff, 1964–1989 (%)*

	1964		1976			1989		
	Oxbridge	All other Univ.	Oxbridge	All other Univ.	Poly	Oxbridge	All other Univ.	Poly
Conservative	38	38	31	26	25	15	19	18
Labour	40	45	36	35	44	41	36	44
Liberal (SLD)	15	15	25	25	22	29	25	18
SDP	—	—	—	—	—	6	11	7
Green	—	—	—	—	—	8	7	11
Other	7	1	7	14	9	1	3	3

Note: Non-voters are omitted.
Source: A. H. Halsey, 1964, 1976, and 1989 surveys.

Harvard or Princeton in the United States where support for the
party of the left is characteristically greater than in other less
prestigious universities and colleges. The fate of Labour and Liberal
Party support also deserves remark. University support for Labour
has also fallen since 1964. It was lower then in Oxford than in the
universities generally but has remained stable in the ancient
universities while being boosted in 1989 by the 44 per cent support
of the polytechnics. The Liberals, over the same period, have gained
support both in universities generally and in Oxford. But the 'house
party', the SDP, had largely collapsed by the summer of 1989 and
not least at its university point of invention in Oxford. A national
poll (Observer/Harris), taken on 23–5 January 1990, estimated a
2 per cent support for Dr Owen's connection in the nation at large,
with 6 per cent for the Liberal Democrats, 49 per cent for Labour,
and 36 per cent for the Conservatives. The Greens had 5 per cent
and the Nationalists were level with Dr Owen. In short the trends
from polling samples, making due allowances for their unreliability,
do suggest that a consensus hostile to Mrs Thatcher's government
had been building up in the nation, that the universities were
among the leaders of this movement, and that Oxford senior
members contributed enthusiastically to academic political opinion.

GRANTS AND LOANS

The question of types of student support is, of course, hotly debated
inside and outside academic circles. In the 1989 survey we put the
matter crudely, asking respondents to agree or disagree with the
statement that 'students should be maintained by grants alone
rather than by loans or any mixed system.' Matthew had used the
vote in Congregation at Oxford as evidence for an anti-Conservative consensus. Our survey shows that 60 per cent of Oxford dons
agreed with the statement either strongly or with reservations,
compared with 74 per cent of academic staff in other universities
including Cambridge. Again Matthew seems to be closer to
Harrison's resolve to be empirically objective than does Harrison
himself. Opinion on this point of educational policy is shifting and
will, no doubt, shift in future. But for the time being it is clear that,
wisely or unwisely, Oxford was strongly opposed to the Thatcher
government.

THAT THATCHER VOTE

As to granting an honorary doctorate to Mrs Thatcher, the 1989 survey does not speak directly. But there were two relevant items. There was the statement 'universities ought to resist being too responsive to the needs of modern industry and commerce.' Here Oxford opinion was more strongly in agreement (67 per cent) than was university opinion in other places (60 per cent). There was also the statement that 'universities ought to be less under the control of central government.' Both Oxford (88 per cent) and the other universities (89 per cent) agreed overwhelmingly with this sentiment. This evidence is further comfort to Matthew's view. I would add, from direct observation of the occasion in Congregation in 1984, that the opposition to granting Mrs Thatcher an honorary degree was, as Matthew wrote, an expression of 'the unacceptability of educational policy', in which the speakers saw themselves as Oxford representatives of the 'Education party' which covered the interests of all those who seek a more enlightened nation from the kindergarten to the graduate school. They came from the laboratories, the departments, and the colleges not as partisans for the political parties but to make a gesture of solidarity for the life of scholarship and science and a protest against its crude subjection to a particular and negative theory of the responsibilities of government.

So by agreeing with the Harrison resolve to rely on fact rather than wishful thinking in our assessment of Oxford opinion, we are likely to be led to Matthew's view that in 1990 Oxford dons were mostly opposed to the Conservative Government and even more hostile to the associated educational policies.

We cannot, however, safely leave the question of the relation between academia and government as one adequately covered by a debate in Oxford which, at least in the sense that Mrs Thatcher was a chemist from Somerville College, may have been a parochial storm rather than a deep fissure between academic opinion and Conservative political doctrine. Our 1976 and 1989 surveys can be used for two wider purposes. They can show the distribution of political allegiance among university and polytechnic teachers and among the different university groups, and they can also show the connection between political and academic attitudes towards various aspects of the public and private life of higher education amidst the turmoil of the later 1970s and the 1980s.

TABLE 11.2. *Party support among various academic groups,*
1976 and 1989

		Conservative	Labour	Centre	Other
All university staff	1976	26	35	24	16
	1989	18	37	35	10
All polytechnic staff	1976	25	44	21	10
	1989	18	44	25	14
Oxbridge	1976	31	36	23	11
	1989	14	40	37	9
Other universities	1976	26	35	24	16
	1989	19	37	35	10
Polytechnics	1976	26	44	21	10
	1989	18	44	25	14
Arts (Univ.)	1976	21	38	16	17
	1989	9	46	32	13
Arts (Poly)	1976	15	58	17	10
	1989	4	59	20	17
Social Sciences (Univ.)	1976	17	48	20	14
	1989	10	51	27	10
Social Sciences (Poly)	1976	22	48	20	11
	1989	15	51	22	12
Natural Science (Univ.)	1976	24	33	26	17
	1989	19	28	45	8
Natural Science (Poly)	1976	38	34	27	16
	1989	30	33	31	14
Engineering Tech. (Univ.)	1976	38	27	22	13
	1989	32	28	36	6
Engineering Tech. (Poly)	1976	36	33	21	10
	1989	27	28	25	19
Medical (Univ.)	1976	38	24	24	14
	1989	32	24	34	10
Medical (Poly)	1976	29	37	29	5
	1989	17	57	20	7
Agric./Vet. (Univ.)	1976	38	18	26	18
	1989	26	21	43	9
Agric./Vet. (Poly)	1976	—	—	—	—
	1989	—	—	—	—
University professors	1976	35	—	—	—
	1989	25	30	39	6
Polytechnic	1976	33	—	—	—
heads of department	1989	22	49	24	5

Source: A. H. Halsey, 1976 and 1989 surveys.

In reading Table 11.2 it must be borne in mind that the political centre of gravity moved towards the centre between 1976 and the summer of 1989 in all groups. Thus among university teachers the proportion of Conservative voters dropped from 29 to 18 per cent, and among polytechnic teachers from 28 per cent to 18 per cent. Similarly, in the case of Labour support, there was a fall among university teachers from 41 to 37 per cent and among polytechnic teachers from 47 to 44 per cent. The centre gained. Liberal (SLD) voting in the universities rose from 27 to 28 per cent, though it fell from 23 to 18 per cent among polytechnic teachers. The SDP did not, of course, exist in 1976, but attracted 10 per cent of the university and 7 per cent of the polytechnic vote in 1989, and, again similarly, the Green Party (arguably not of the centre but at any rate neither Conservative nor Labour) appeared in the 1980s to take 7 per cent of the university and 11 per cent of the polytechnic vote in 1989.

Who, then, were the academic supporters of the various parties? In 1976 relatively heavy, though still far from dominant, support for the Conservative party was to be found among the professors in the universities and especially among engineers, technologists, polytechnic scientists, and university medical faculties (Table 11.2). Labour support was heaviest among the social science faculties and the arts departments of polytechnics. The different university groups did not have markedly different political complexions. Oxford and Cambridge were not unduly inclined towards political conservatism: they were relatively inclined *also* to Labour voting. The one rather glaring exception to this political homogeneity of the university world, in the mid-1970s, was the very marked support for Labour among the new universities, where the Labour lead was three times as great as elsewhere. The polytechnic staff were more inclined to vote Labour than the university staff.

But by 1989, though Labour continued to dominate the polytechnics and, as we have noted, the Conservative vote had fallen drastically throughout the higher education system, the Liberal and Social Democratic centre was the most popular political position among the university professoriate and in Oxford and Cambridge. The most resilient centres of Conservative support were the university medical faculties (polytechnics had only non-clinical health-related studies) and the engineering and technology faculties. Even so the technology departments of the polytechnics showed a slender Labour lead by 1989. But Labour led most clearly among the arts and social science staff, as it had in 1976, while the greatest gains went to the centre or other parties, especially among the science faculties. Not surprisingly, union members in both the universities and polytechnics tended to lean towards the left and were still more inclined in this direction by 1989. A similar stance and shift was also to be found among the older members of the academic professions.

ATTITUDES TO STUDENTS

Attitudes to students—their quality and their participation in the life of the college or university—is clearly correlated with political predispositions (Tables 11.3A and 11.3B). In both 1976 and 1989, Conservative voters showed themselves to be distinctly more pessimistic about the quality and the motivation of their students. In 1976, looking back over the expansion of the previous decade, 47 per cent of Conservative-voting university staff but only 33 per cent of Labour voters thought that the average level of ability of their students had dropped. Labour voters were more ready to involve students in staff appointments, undergraduate admissions policies, the determination of type and content of courses and examination procedures and standards.

Differences in student appraisal persisted up to 1989, but in the mean time academics of all political shades were beginning to adopt more cheerful views. Optimism expressed itself most clearly with respect to the proportion of the relevant age-group which should be deemed suitable for higher education. Over three-quarters of the Conservatives in both the universities and the polytechnics believed in 1976 that we had reached the point where pretty well all school-leavers capable of profiting from a university (polytechnic) education had the chance to receive one. But by 1989 these proportions had dropped to just under 50 per cent in the polytechnics and to 40 per cent in the universities (Table 11.3B), while among Labour supporters less than 10 per cent on either side of the binary line thought that Britain had reached the limit. During the same period a similar change of opinion took place with respect to the admission of mature students. Conservative voters had been largely traditionalists on this matter in 1976, but by 1989 were almost unanimously in favour of encouraging mature entry—while Labour voters had moved to the same view from a point where half of them had been traditionalists. An overwhelming 85 per cent of university Conservatives in 1976 would have expelled or suspended students who disrupted the functions of a university or polytechnic, compared with 44 per cent of the Labour voters. During the following fifteen years, however, the threat of student militancy faded and both Conservatives and Labour supporters became more relaxed in their attitude towards this kind of discipline of the students.

THE CONDITIONS OF WORK

Various measures of the attitudes of academics to the conditions under which they work and their career prospects reveal a process of increasing defensiveness about working conditions (Tables 11.3A and 11.3B). Though more militant than in 1976 in protecting staff–student ratios, the Conservative voters found themselves being joined in 1989 by voters for other parties to form a two-thirds to three-quarters majority in opposition to this crucial element of government policy.

The binary division is similarly a feature of higher education related to party political preference. But the relation is also strongly affected by institutional affiliation. Thus, 76 per cent of the university Conservatives in 1976 would not give university status to any of the polytechnics, compared with 56 per cent of their Labour colleagues and 50 per cent of their polytechnic counterparts of either political persuasion. Conservative opinion has shifted sharply in more recent years. With respect to the provision of libraries and laboratories, and residential facilities, the institutional interests of the polytechnic Conservatives override their political instincts and they favour equality. It is only in the universities that political difference emerges in the shape of greater Labour sympathy for the polytechnic case.

In 1989 the same blurred distribution of opinion obtained on the question of whether the quality of degree work in the polytechnic measures up to university standards (Table 11.3B). There is only minority support generally for the idea that universities should restrict themselves to the traditional academic subjects leaving the newer and more vocational subjects to the polytechnics: but Conservatives in both polytechnic and universities incline a little more to this view.

TABLE 11.3A. *Political party preference and academic attitudes, 1976 (%)*

	Conservative		Labour	
	Univ.	(Poly)	Univ.	(Poly)
Expansion has lowered the average level of ability of my students in recent years	47	(—)	33	(—)
The average level of academic motivation of my students has decreased in recent years	43	(—)	33	(—)
We have now reached the point where pretty well all school-leavers capable of profiting from a university (polytechnic) have the chance to attend one	78	(76)	45	(42)
Students who disrupt the functions of a university (polytechnic) should be expelled or suspended	83	(85)	44	(40)
The increased participation by students in academic governance has introduced inappropriate criteria into academic decision-making	55	(52)	22	(22)
Students should play little or no role in				
Staff appointments	86	(78)	65	(46)
Undergraduate admissions policy	70	(57)	47	(29)
Type and content of courses	15	(19)	7	(8)
Examination procedures and standards	45	(43)	21	(19)
Promotion should be based in part on formal student evaluation of their teachers	19	(26)	41	(51)
Admissions policies should be biased in favour of mature students	30	(40)	53	(52)

Staff–student ratios must not be allowed to deteriorate further even if this means turning away qualified students	65	(54)	49	(49)
A professorship (principal lectureship) ought to be part of the normal expectation of an academic career and not a special attainment of a minority of university (polytechnic) teachers	21	(54)	23	(55)
University (polytechnic) teachers, being among the better-paid members of the community, should moderate their demands for higher salaries	31	(55)	47	(54)
Because it is non-professional conduct, university (polytechnic) teachers should not engage in militant actions such as strikes or picketing	72	(84)	34	(32)
Polytechnics should not be given university status	76	(50)	56	(51)
Universities should have better staff–student ratios than polytechnics	65	(54)	49	(49)
Degree-level work in the polytechnics is rarely of the same standard as that in the universities	78	(25)	62	(53)
There should be equal academic provision (e.g. libraries and laboratories) in polytechnics and universities	45	(92)	61	(96)
There should be equal non-academic provision (e.g. residential accommodation) in polytechnics and universities	63	(89)	77	(93)
Universities should restrict themselves to the traditional academic subjects, and leave newer and more vocational subjects to the polytechnics	32	(43)	26	(32)

Source: A. H. Halsey, 1976 survey

TABLE 11.3B. *Political party preference and academic attitudes, 1989 (%)*

	Conservative		Labour		Centre	
	Univ.	(Poly)	Univ.	(Poly)	Univ.	(Poly)
Student quality in my subject has fallen over the past decade	26	(50)	25	(27)	28	(42)
More has meant worse	23	(42)	20	(23)	26	(37)
All who can profit from HE now enter	40	(48)	6	(9)	17	(19)
Students who disrupt should be expelled (strongly agree)	61	(48)	13	(19)	34	(34)
Admission policies should encourage mature students	95	(98)	98	(98)	98	(98)
Staff–student ratios should not be allowed to deteriorate even if this means turning away qualified students	72	(71)	66	(74)	70	(76)
Professorship (principal lectureship) should be normal expectation of an academic career and not an attainment of a minority	25	(64)	34	(73)	29	(67)
HE teachers should moderate salary demands	24	(22)	9	(5)	13	(6)
HE teachers should not engage in industrial action	69	(72)	19	(13)	47	(44)
Research interest is essential to a good university teacher (strongly agree)	50	(36)	61	(43)	49	(33)
Degrees in polytechnics seldom up to university standard	66	(22)	55	(16)	64	(18)
Equal academic provision in polytechnics and universities desirable	65	(92)	71	(95)	62	(97)
Equal non-academic provision desirable	84	(96)	88	(95)	84	(98)

Source: A. H. Halsey, 1989 survey.

The structure and conditions of the academic career do not divide the academics along political lines so clearly as attitudes to students or even to the binary line. There is a firm majority drawn from all political quarters in favour of retaining the university chair as an attainment of the minority. The principal lectureship is thought by rather more than half the polytechnic staff to be a status which ought to be made part of the normal career, but the agreement is bipartisan.

During the fifteen years of material decline, militancy over salary levels has grown greatly, especially among Labour voters. However, the Conservatives have remained sharply divided from Labour colleagues by their unwillingness to engage in 'industrial action'. Moderation in salary claims is a leftish opinion in universities, but not in polytechnics. Antipathy to militant action on the other hand is very much a conservative attitude in both universities and polytechnics. That universities should enjoy better staff–student ratios was agreed by half the polytechnic teachers in 1976, but the opinion was, not surprisingly, more strongly held in the universities, and is a conservative majority opinion in both institutions.

THE INTELLECTUALS

So political and educational opinions are intertwined. How academic people see the future shape and scale of higher education may be fairly accurately predicted from their party sympathies. But these party divergencies must be understood in the wider frame of two deeper influences on the social consciousness of British scholars and scientists. First this somewhat heterogeneous collection of increasingly specialist professions is, in a cultural sense, conservative. This conservatism reflects in part the distinctive character of secure attachment to the State and the social order which has earned the description of the British 'key' profession as pragmatic and useful—a ready servant of government administration and industrial need. No one wishes to be labelled an intellectual, and worse, the intelligentsia is a dated, obscure class of foreign dissidents. Anti-intellectualism in this sense has been a feature of British culture at least since the reform and revival of the universities by the Victorians. The structure of British society has offered continually renewed support for these sentiments. There are professional rewards for specialists both within the academy and outside in the House of Lords, the boardrooms of industrial companies, the mass media, the governing bodies of quangos, and even the political parties. There have been, in short, powerfully integrating forces working to make scientists and scholars 'at home' in their society. Alienation has been a foreign word for largely incomprehensible foreigners. The remarkable contribution of Jewish refugees from Hitlerite or Stalinist persecution to the intellectual life of the British universities is an especially illuminating example of the absorptive capacity of the establishment in the twentieth-century United Kingdom.

But second, there has been a contrary force. In addition to the small and firmly marginalized groups of intellectuals who have existed outside the establishment, for example the Marxist eccentrics clustered round the *New Left Review*, there has also developed a much more general discontent within official society. It is a complex movement with diverse manifestations. In polytechnics and universities it is expressed by our survey findings—a widespread resentment of political intrusion into traditional autonomy, a protest against deteriorating salaries and working conditions, an anger with philistine disrespect for the dignity of academic labour. Elsewhere it shows itself in high rates of movement out of the civil administration into lucrative posts in private industry, in right-wing nostalgia for a lost empire or a lost entrepreneurial culture, in disillusion with the two great political parties, in the fitful rise and fall of the Social Democratic Party, and even a general despair over the power of politics as such. The most obvious expression of this contrary force is the very steep decline of support in academic circles for the Conservative Party.

Are we then to interpret this second force as the new social base in Britain for a distinctive class of intellectuals? Or is the older and voluminous literature on the subject a relic of history finally put to rest by the wholesale collapse of the Communist regimes? A preliminary answer must surely be that the dramatic 'suicide note' from Marxism which leaves liberal capitalist ideologies in at least temporary command of the field of political argument poses more questions than it solves. There is here not only the mushroom growth of seminars and centres on East/West European comparison in politics, economics, and society but also the long tradition of social criticism which has existed in British universities, in the political parties, in literary circles, and in the performing arts, which together makes up an opposition to the currently dominant idea of capitalist, market, or free society. It expressed itself in the past as ethical socialism or Fabianism or New Liberalism, and figures in present day environmentalism, feminism, green politics, internationalism, humanism, and many other new, often chaotic, debates over the desired constitution of post-capitalist society. Institutions of higher education may be expected to contribute to these debates, especially as a challenge for scientific specialists to find common language with philosophers, economists, and sociologists who concern themselves with political argument.

Ideas are of interest in this context only in so far as they move the world. Mendel's genetic discoveries, for instance, lay in a social vacuum for a century until they were rediscovered in 1900. Subsequently taken up by universities, they have reshaped society, for example, by tightening control over pigs and corn, by influencing the procedures of educational selection, and by modifying the perception of race and sex. Universities, linked to business and government, thus realize ideas. What was originally the intellectual amusement of a monkish recluse eventually became an organized industry and an administration capable of transforming man and nature.

This example signals the profound significance of the subject, but does not describe the literature on intellectuals, which is mainly more narrowly focused on the relation between intellectuals and the political order. In the tradition of liberal thought the primary concern has been with freedom of enquiry. Among Marxist writers the preoccupation has been with the role of intellectuals in class conflict. The two traditions are not, of course, hermetically sealed, and indeed over the past thirty years have tended to converge on to the idea that intellectuals themselves form a class: but in neither tradition are the definitions clear.

On the class issue, however, two things are clear. In the twentieth century the division of intellectual labour has become one of vast scale and complexity, and institutions of higher education have come to occupy a central role in it. Daniel Bell has elaborated these developments into the thesis that the university in post-industrial society has displaced the business enterprise in classical industrial society as the central institution guiding production and distribution. In tacit agreement, some Marxist or Marxisant writers have depicted the campus as the locus of class struggle in terms reminiscent of Marx and Engels describing a nineteenth-century Manchester factory.

At all events the university domain has been dramatically enlarged since the noun 'intellectuals' began to have wide currency in reference to the nihilistic Russian university students of the 1860s or the Dreyfusards of the 1890s in France. University graduates then constituted a tiny 1 or 2 per cent minority; now developed countries offer post-secondary education to a quarter, or, in countries like the USA or Canada, more than a half of their young people. Thus the intellectual class, if it is a class, has become a sizeable force in our time. And in the process the university has evolved out of its medieval European origins as the principal sustaining institution of the intellectual community. Even Wittgenstein, for all his hatred of university life, found it compellingly convenient to live in one.

The attraction may be ebbing now. Public sector institutions, at any rate, are under widespread fashionable attack (ironically in the name of a version of early nineteenth-century doctrines which created the liberal university). Sir Keith Joseph, when Secretary of State for Education, was prone to believe that the liberal polity and free business enterprise had been undermined by left-wing dons. Historians like Martin Weiner or Corelli Barnett were habitually cited in evidence. True, it is difficult to conceive of either a culture of high technology without a university system, or of a university system without heavy State patronage. Yet intellectuals are always prone to fall out with the powers, as Hobbes saw when he examined the reliability of the dons in seventeenth-century England. Of course, they always represented a potential threat to any *status quo*—thought can be critical.

But in the past they have found other patrons than princes. Churches, armies, Grub Street, and coffee-houses, even the garret and the begging-bowl, have sheltered and fed them. Edward Shils's writings (Shils 1972) remind us of the long sweep of institutional support which has succoured intellectual labour down the ages from Christian troubadours and Brahmin *pandits* to contemporary professors, columnists, and best-selling authors.

No wonder then that the definition of intellectuals is difficult. Shils distinguishes them from the unreflective lay majority as 'persons with an unusual sensitivity to the sacred, an uncommon reflectiveness about the nature of their universe and the rules which govern their society'. He thus establishes connections and continuities between priest and professor, pundit and political theorist.

But the definition also raises two problems, first that of the relation between its two elements, concern with the normative and curiosity about the existential, and second, given the increased scale of intellectual work which is linked to the expansion of the modern universities and polytechnics, the relation between the 'clerisy' and the 'laity'. The two problems together raise questions as to how ideas which originate in a secular discipline such as nuclear physics or genetic theory are to be socially applied when they generate normative problems of tremendous significance such as nuclear war or the political control of individuals. Whoever are to be counted among the intellectuals, the character of their institutional attachment and support becomes crucial in determining the influence of their ideas. One, but only one, way of tackling the issue is to ask whether twentieth-century intellectuals are, or are becoming, an independent class, the agents of some other class, or classless individuals.

Two features of British discussion in this context deserve immediate remark. Britain and its universities have been remarkably successful in winning Nobel prizes compared with other countries. Trinity College, Cambridge houses twenty-eight Nobel Laureates compared with seven in the whole of Japan. And yet Britain has always refused to take its intellectuals very seriously, again compared with other countries, especially France. We have already noted Peter Scott's characterization of the British academic professions as a body integrated with government and business interests, pragmatically servicing national needs. On the other hand we have described the idea of higher education in Britain as dominated by Victorian élitism, at least until the Robbins report of 1963.

What, then, is the problem? The clue, I think, is in Bernard Crick's quotation from H. M. Hyndman referring to 'the furious prejudice stirred up in those days among the educated middle class against anyone who took *the side of the people* in earnest . . . ' (my italics) (Crick 1982), and in Raymond Williams's reference to 'art and thought as belonging, from the beginning, *to the people as a whole* . . . ' (again, my italics) (Williams 1982).

This is the problem—ideas by whom and for whom? In whose interest is high intellectual work carried on? Answers are to be sought by locating ideas in social structure and by analysing the origins, nurture, support, and consciousness of their bearers. Our survey results can offer no more than a small empirical footnote to this extensive task. Following Shils in defining the intellectuals as producers of ideas and accepting that institutions of higher education are their major institutional location, we can use a crude operational definition—persons holding chairs who have published voluminously compared with their university and polytechnic colleagues.[1]

The universities house the specialisms of the highly educated rather than what Bell calls 'the custodians of critical and creative thinking about the normative problems of their society'. The Church of England, the BBC, the House of Lords, and Fleet Street also have their claims. The director of the London School of Economics could have been in the sample, but not the Archbishop of Canterbury, or the Chief Rabbi. Sir Karl Popper is in, but Bernard Levin or Hugo Young are out.

Nevertheless, the high professors, defined to include the leading one-tenth of academic staff, are at least relevant and arguably of the essence. Raymond Williams, in commenting on the view of 'English backwardness' as an explanation of the resistance to the idea of an intelligentsia, makes the acid point that those who could be called intellectuals in other countries are in Britain mostly brought up in a system of private education designed for a class which includes the leading politicians, civil servants, company directors, and lawyers (Williams 1982).

All the relevant sociological enquiry supports that generalization. Our surveys shows that over one-fifth of the high professors had been through the private schools compared with 15 per cent of other academics and only 5 or 6 per cent of the population as a whole. And as we saw in earlier chapters, Oxford and Cambridge, with their close ties both in recruitment from the well-to-do and as suppliers to the elevated metropolitan institutions of State and industry, are also dominantly the nurseries of both the intellectuals and the powers. Such a pattern of connection has undoubtedly given Britain an integrated establishment of political, economic, and cultural management, and may account for such paradoxes as Nobel prize winning combined with anti-intellectualism, scientifically innovatory but ailing technology, and 'high-culture' television drama succeeding spectacularly in the American market, while American vulgarity dominates the British screens.

---

[1] See Table 11.4 for details of the definition.

But the full story is more complicated. First, educational systems everywhere translate parental advantage into filial opportunity—and this is as true in Russia or Yugoslavia as in the USA or Britain. Second, by international comparison, the British offer opportunities to enter the class of 'workers by brain' more widely than most countries, for example, France, the Netherlands, or Germany.

The high professors in 1976 and 1989, though disproportionately drawn from the suburban classes, are also meritocrats. Half of them hold first-class degrees compared with less than a third of the ordinary run of university teachers and less than one in five of polytechnic staff. Though their intake is socially skewed and much intellect is wasted on the way to their gates, the British universities are unquestionably meritocratic in their internal distribution of honour and rank. The scientific civil service is similarly constituted, by contrast with the socially narrower recruitment of the legal and administrative branches.

Moreover, the outlook of the academic leadership is more meritocratic than is the norm for all university and polytechnic teachers. The high professors are not typically extinct research volcanoes. They have had markedly more books and articles accepted for publication in the last two years, and they continue to give research preference over teaching and administration *after* their promotion to a chair. Though Oxbridge-connected, they are not as Oxbridge-bound as their lesser colleagues. The latter as a group saw a Cambridge lectureship and fellowship as more desirable than a London or Sussex chair; the high professors take the reverse view, even though their group view of Oxbridge is the same in that more than one-third of them as well as their colleagues agree that 'Oxford and Cambridge have preserved their dominance in practically everything that counts in academic life.' The important point is that more than half of the highly productive academics disagree with this statement. They dominate the research life of British higher education, editing journals, refereeing articles and grant applications, travelling abroad to conferences, advising industry, and appearing on television more than their less eminent colleagues. They are more conscious of a decline in public respect for academic people and distinctly more tempted to join the migrants to American universities and research centres (Table 11.4).

Can we then conclude that the intellectuals are a class—their property being the cultural capital of recognized and rewarded

TABLE 11.4. *The high professor's background and attitudes, 1976 and 1989 (%)*

	High Professors		Other University and Polytechnic Staff	
	1976	1989	1976	1989
Born into professorial, managerial classes	64	58	58	55
Went to independent/'public' schools	21	22	14	15
Got a first-class degree	67	51	39	31
Strongly believe in student grants not loans		37		54
Believe universities should be less controlled by Government	71	90	62	89
Believe strongly that public respect for academics has declined	1	57	—	48
Strongly believe academic salaries too low to attract staff of requisite calibre	69	—	68	
Have seriously considered accepting an academic post abroad	—	52	—	34
Believe Oxbridge has preserved predominance	38	44	37	44
Believe research in Britain would be more effective if concentrated in a few 'research universities'	—	19	—	18
In last three years have:				
Served as a paid consultant to a government department or international government agency	47	40	11	13
Ditto to a business or industry	40	52	29	40
Written or appeared on mass media	—	59	—	33

Attended a conference abroad	79	91	33	48
Served as editor or member of editorial board of an academic journal	63	77	12	23
Refereed manuscripts for a journal	89	97	38	54
Refereed grant applications	79	84	18	12
In last two years have:				
Published one or more books or articles	95	99	64	74
Prefer the Cambridge lectureship among the four posts	28	30	35	38
Self-placement on political spectrum				
Far left	2	2	5	5
Moderate left	34	36	40	44
Centre	36	37	32	34
Moderate right	26	25	22	17
Far right	1	1	1	1
Party support				
Conservative	36	26	25	17
Labour	30	29	39	40
Liberal	24	40	24	31
Other	10	5	12	12

Note: High professors are professors who had published 4 or more books, or 11 or more articles in 1976, or 20 or more articles in 1989.

Source: A. H. Halsey, 1976 and 1989 surveys.

merit and their vanguard the high professors? Lipset and others have shown in the case of America that academics of higher attainment and recognition are more likely to be left or, in the American sense, liberal than their colleagues: and the more intellectually eminent, the more likely to be critical of their government.

The British survey evidence shows a pattern which in one important respect is different. As may be seen in Table 11.4, the high professors are somewhat to the *right* of their colleagues both in their subjective place on the political spectrum and their voting record. Nevertheless, they also, like their American counterparts, are more heavily engaged in government consultancies and more worried about the subjection of the universities to the State.

The position is therefore that university teachers generally are politically much more to the left than the non-university middle class; their profile of party allegiance resembles more that of the manual working class. But within this 'class-deviant' political position the academic leadership leans back towards the norm of the middle-class laity.

The standard-bearers of intellectualism at least in Britain in the 1970s and 1980s were not the agents of the working class. Nor were they solidaristic scribes of middle-class interests. And most certainly they were not a class in themselves, being far too differentiated by salary and political opinion to act together. Some believed in the early 1980s that the Social Democratic Party would unite them: that party was, after all, essentially their invention. But it collapsed and the normative debates to which we have referred are wooed by but have no secure home in any of the parties.

No. The fact is that intellectuals, academic or other, are not a class. They are a loosely knit array of overlapping hierarchical status groups seeking honour and reputation mainly from each other. They are overwhelmingly State employees, albeit often reluctant and sometimes recalcitrant. But some can always be found to serve Mrs Thatcher or Mr Major and (not always others) Mr Kinnock or Mr Ashdown. That is not a class. If there has been *une trahison des clercs*, it has been a betrayal of the classes as well as themselves. Could there then be Raymond Williams's intelligentsia for the people? A completely meritocratic tendency might make it possible. It could happen, and it could serve as the high intellect

of 'the people as a whole' on one simple but difficult condition—
that the democratic state is for 'the people as a whole'. The
unfinished programme of expansion in higher education may turn
out to be a vital foundation for such a society.

12

RETROSPECT

THE decline of donnish dominion was written in the stars from the moment that the ancient civilizations of the Near East began to form an abstract alphabet (Goody 1968). Literacy thereby became potentially a democratic possession. Access to human capital became intrinsically available to all. Nevertheless, a long and incomplete evolution has been needed to turn potential into reality. The history of popular communication from usable alphabet through the printing press to modern information technology has been a very slow process, albeit accelerating in our own time. The process has been slow because to democratize communication also requires transformation of virtually every aspect of social structure. People are bound together by power and authority, by interest and sentiment, by habituation and learning, as well as by words and numbers. Vast changes of human society were therefore required to work out all the implications of this original linguistic revolution. Nor is the journey complete. The scope and reach of higher learning never ceases to unfold. It is built into the modern social project of ever-increasing human command over nature, prolonging life, ceaselessly hungering after economic growth, and permitting more widespread leisure. The pull of professional needs and the push of democratic demands for access continually press for expansion in face of limited public and private resources. Higher education comes at the end of the process as the conspicuous international growth industry of the twentieth century. It is a worldwide phenomenon with ancient roots. We have been concerned in this study with its record in a particular country: but the background of transition out of pre-industrial to industrial society deserves a brief review as it is now, following Max Weber, the standard interpretation of social development among sociologists of education.

Behind this interpretation lies the yet wider one of a general characterization of industrial society by contrast with an earlier agrarianism. Agrarian society was characteristically static, segmented in its structure, and with separate special languages attached to its various functions. Hunting, cooking, tool-making, ritual, and territorial defence all had identified groupings and specialized knowledge passed on and made personal by apprenticeship. Each unit was capable of perpetuating its own social reproduction. Training and education therefore, as Weber emphasized, was also segmented and hierarchical. The family and quasi-familial community organizations passed on the common culture, smiths taught their children special skills, and a class of priests and literati were the guardians of high culture, working in the interests of the dominant strata. As Ernest Gellner has put it in the perspective of the social anthropologist, 'it may be useful to distinguish between one-to-one, intra-community training and call it acculturation, and specialized *exo-training* (on the analogy of exogamy), which calls for skills outside of the community, and call that education proper' (Gellner 1983: 31).

Exo-training is therefore the origin of both the rise and fall of academic power. Modern industrial societies aim to turn everyone into a member of the educated class of participating workers and citizens. The distinction between the clerisy and the laity is eroded and institutionally, as we have noted, the university has a monopoly of nothing. In that context the decline of donnish dominion is simply the inverse of the rise of meritocracy. Modernization entailed nationalizing the reproductive as well as the productive functions. National systems of education and training eventually emerged, and achievement, at least on the surface, displaced ascription as the means whereby individuals found their place in the occupational structure, itself continually changing and becoming more complex.

Gellner's macroscopic view of the evolution of industrial society has nationalism as its focus. He presents a model of modernity with education and mobility built in as essential features. 'A society has emerged based on a high-powered technology and the expectancy of sustained growth, which requires both a mobile division of labour, and sustained, frequent and precise communication between strangers involving a sharing of explicit meaning, transmitted in a standard idiom and in writing when required. . . . The level of literacy and technical competence . . . required of members of this society, if they are to be properly employable and enjoy full and effective moral citizenship, is so high that it simply cannot be provided by the kin or local units . . . ' Only a modern national education system will serve. 'At the basis of the modern social order stands not the executioner but the professor' (Gellner 1983: 34). An industrial society requires universal literacy and general sophistication. 'Its members are and must be mobile, and ready to shift from one activity to another, and must possess that generic training which enables them to follow the manuals and instructions of a new activity or occupation.' Since they are normally required to be able to communicate with strangers, communication has to be explicit, impersonal, context-free, and in a shared and standardized language.

In agrarian medieval Europe the conditions for international communication were established by the *lingua franca* of Latin in advance of the industrial conditions which required and facilitated mass participation. Abelard or Erasmus could be famous and peripatetic teachers. Students could travel between *studia generale* by donkey, barge, and bark from Edinburgh to Rome. The 'nations' of a university campus prefigured the retreat to nationalism of a culture extending throughout Christendom in the Middle Ages and there were struggles between kings and pope for authority over the curriculum and organization of originally ecumenical institutions. But by and large and for the time being, the dons were masters of their own house, essentially because they lived on the economic margins of a society where the nation state had yet to intervene as the main strategic agent of economic growth and popular participation.

The subsequent development of science lay at the centre of successive industrial transformations. A shared and standardized language linked researchers into international networks permitting competitive co-operation in the global advance of physical, chemical, and biological knowledge. The university was the major instrument of this development; the academic was accordingly held in high esteem. But scientific advance translated into technological development in industry meant breaching the walls of the academy and extending knowledge, or at least its use, throughout society.

Thus Gellner emphasizes that:

The educational system which guarantees this social achievement becomes large and is indispensable, but at the same time it no longer possesses monopoly of access to the written word: its clientele is co-extensive with the society at large, and the replaceability of individuals within the system by others applies to the educational machine at least as much as to any other segment of society, and perhaps more so. Some very great teachers and researchers may perhaps be unique and irreplaceable but the average professor and school master can be replaced from outside the teaching profession with the greatest of ease and often with little, if any loss. (Gellner 1983: 35–6).

In short, the academic becomes both indispensable and also deprived of his former privileged position. This is something of a paradox. The highly educated are both central to the working of a dynamic, endlessly innovating, mobile, and wealthy society, but graduates and cognitive activity are dispersed to all the other institutions of society—business enterprise, recreational organizations, social administration, even the family and local social groups. So the university, as Daniel Bell has argued, has become the gatekeeper to the higher occupational positions in a complex society in which new technical élites reshape the class structure and the populist reaction is to demand greater 'equality', usually meaning educational expansion, as a defence against social exclusion (Bell 1973).

We have looked in detail at the expansion of higher education in Britain both before and after the Robbins Report of 1963. In this narrower and more recent context it is the more obvious that such a vast infra-structure is so expensive that its maintenance, as Gellner claims, 'is quite beyond the financial powers of even the biggest and richest organizations within society such as the big industrial corporations'. Only the State can sustain and control it. It is worth noting Gellner's emphasis in view of the contemporary dispute over the role of the State *vis-à-vis* higher education and also to correct a serious misreading of his work by the most recent contributor to the discussion, Sir Douglas Hague, who twice quotes Gellner on the replaceability of the average professor but fails to notice his insistence on the primacy of the State in financing and controlling organized education. Hague is thus freed to advance his own solution to the problems of innovation and organization of learning —the extensive, indeed exclusive, use of the market.

We come to Hague's proposals for reform below. Meanwhile and more centrally, Gellner's version of the Weberian thesis is that the universal necessity of high standards of education is not only national but must be of a generic character preceding and topped by further specialist training. This is indisputable, but Gellner then claims that the additional skills consist only of a few techniques that can be learned fairly quickly. That gloss is arguable. The implication that there has been a narrowing of the distance between the most advanced modern specialist and the comprehensive school child by comparison with the university medieval schoolman and the peasant of late agrarian Europe is contentious. Cognitive possession of difficult intellectual work at the frontier of the natural and social sciences is one thing, while power to use this body of knowledge in daily life is quite another. And the problem of the institutional means for developing and passing on scientific knowledge is yet a third question which has to be left open.

Indeed, the character of an educational system in relation to the participation of citizens cannot be adequately described by distinguishing only between the general and the specialized. No individual can possess comprehensive knowledge of the whole of the culture available to him in society. Some degree of participation, often combined with dependency and possibly exploitation, clearly exists. I can switch on the electric light without generalized knowledge of the theory of circuitry. My brother can produce exquisite Brussels sprouts from his allotment without even GCSE-level botany. Certainly a generalized scientific culture must exist in modern industrial society with the implications for both the structure of knowledge and the organization of social relations which Gellner so brilliantly sketches. He shows convincingly that a cognitive epistemological revolution was necessary, and supplied by the philosophers Hume and Kant, as a pre-condition for the development of both the knowledge itself and its social use. He is equally convincing in his argument that a necessary consequence was the superimposition of national and indeed international ordering of both production and reproduction in industrial society. In that context the decline of academic power is what Weber referred to as the disenchantment of the world.

We have focused in this study on the outcome of the ensuing battles, so characteristic of both the public and the private life of contemporary higher education, which turn on the place of the academic in the organization of scientific culture. But there are wider implications for citizenship which Gellner's bold and simple distinction between generalized and specialist knowledge short circuits. In reality both intimate, personal and standardized, generic, scientific knowledge coexist and compete at all levels, just as citizenship and class together determine the social distribution of power. My brother and Dr Stefan Buczacki both find a place in horticulture; the use of log linear models in social science involves both those non-mathematical practitioners who learn by experience and those mathematicians who deduce procedures from abstract mathematical theory. Weber illustrated how easy it is to misinterpret modern scientific culture when he pointed out that its existence did not mean that his audience in the lecture room in Munich knew more of the conditions of life under which they existed than had an American Indian or a Hottentot. 'Unless he is a physicist, one who rides on the street car has no idea how the car happened to get into motion. And he does not need to know. He is satisfied that he can "count" on the behaviour of the street car . . . The savage knows incomparably more about his tools' (Gerth and Mills 1947: 139).

Who dominates either in the academy or in the society at large is a question that can only be resolved in the political and organizational context. The organization and passing of such a culture rests on traditional structures of kinship and community as well as the inventions of the national institutions which have allowed it to emerge. A place for the *cognoscenti* has to be found within it. Both traditional and 'scientific' learning are embodied in it at all levels; and some pattern of transition for individuals out of learning into occupation has to be fashioned. So if economic liberal reformers like Douglas Hague, preoccupied with present-day British problems, try to abolish universities and polytechnics, or at least put them into competition with private sector organizations, they are talking about political power in a given country as much as about the essence of the culture of industrialism.

In other words Gellner's profundity becomes dangerous when translated into Hague's unsociological proposals. Gellner quotes Veblen to good effect, but does so by reference to *The Theory of the Leisure Class* as an aside from the main argument that generalized education precedes specialist training in our own time. He refers to 'the "gentlemanly" or leisure class element in higher education' as, in effect, a false claim to high status for specialized training at the end of a long education in face of the paradox that terminal and specialized instruction at an early age has negative prestige (Gellner 1983: 27). Hague seizes on this aside and invokes Gellner's support for the flat assertion that academics are 'the last guilded manifestation of Thorstein Veblen's leisure class' (Hague 1991: 31). He draws the inference that entirely new structures of intellectual life are required for the future—not a 'sheltered system, shielded from competitive pressure by two types of monopoly: natural monopolies of brain-power and of certain physical resources, like libraries or laboratories; and man-made monopolies bestowed by government, first through restrictions on the power to confer degrees and, second, through the university cartel' (Hague 1991: 31). What he fails to notice is that Veblen (in a quite separate book specifically dealing with Hague's problem of reform) wrote his elaborately satirical commentary on the culture of the senior common room 'conducted by businessmen' (Veblen 1918) precisely to attack the very solution that Hague puts forward.

Moreover, and above all, Durkheim's preoccupation with *l'education morale* is highly relevant to the understanding of the transmission of modern culture from one generation to another. The ancient and the modern institutions work in complex interaction. The external mark of certification is an outcome of both ascription and 'achievement', which explains the stubbornly persistent inequality of the social distribution of the certificates of entry into an ever-changing and more specialized division of labour. The efficient worker has to acquire appropriate attitudes to punctuality, duty, the calculation of reward for effort, and so on, and these attributes pass from fathers to sons and mothers to daughters through every kind of social encounter and not solely through the formal educational system. Here again lie the roots of continuing social inequality. And against a background of declining religious belief, increasing frailty of family and community, and the search for new legitimacies in the social order, the role of the professorial expert at the apex of the education system is both strengthened and undermined. The question of how these moral as well as cognitive authorities are to be socially organized cannot possibly be appropriately resolved by simple market solutions. Only a complex process of politics can properly determine the duties and privileges of professions, including the academic professions. Contemporary enthusiasm for the use of the market disguises a politics which permits a wide range of alternatives.

Similar arguments apply to organizing research and its application. Market competition is no guarantee of innovation. It may explain the success of the German universities in the middle of the nineteenth century, but equally fails to explain the remarkable successes of British academic innovators in the period between Hume and Rutherford. Humility about the conditions that foster creativity should give us pause before we apply any simplistic reform.

Experience should have taught us that institutions of higher education have multiple ends. Yet contemporary argument is frequently narrowed on to problems of efficient and economical means towards the ends of innovation and the formation of 'human capital'. These are important considerations. We have discussed them as teaching and research in the earlier chapters. Parsons and Platt have portrayed the university or polytechnic as the institution-alization of rationality ('the core value of the university is cognitive rationality'), and few would reject that definition (Parsons and Platt 1973: 26). Nevertheless as we have insisted, and as our earlier discussion of the idea of a university illustrates, many different values have hitherto been sought. Efficiency is one, but apart from the debatable question about its relation to market organization, other ends, such as fair access and freedom of research and teaching, also have legitimate claims. Thus, for example, efficient management might settle the struggle between the dominant form of monolithic departmental hierarchy and the alternative form of producer co-operation described in Chapter 7. But even if this were so, it could still be argued that self-government is an end in itself which ought to be preserved, even at some cost to efficient decision-making.

Another prized value in higher education, especially perhaps with respect to women, ethnic minorities, and disadvantaged classes, is equality. Should poor chances in lower education be compensated in higher education by some form of quota or positive discrimina-tion, for example? Should the strict principle of meritocracy be modified by recognizing that women rarely compete on equal terms in research because of childbearing and persisting habits of domestic division of labour? Hague is concerned at various points with the search for equality or fairness. He is impatient with it as 'part of the British disease' (Hague 1991: 53). And he thinks it is probably vain. He caricatures the peer review system for research funding as 'the infuriating belief that if only more and more people in appropriate academic disciplines spend more and more time evaluating longer and longer applications . . . then research grants would be allocated with precise fairness' (p. 53). He bemoans the neglect of managerial efficiency, while acknowledging its inevitable tension with 'constitutional propriety' in a democracy. He leaves us in no doubt of his own managerial sympathies. He believes that 'the ethos of the universities is itself too egalitarian' and wants to see the end of national pay scales (p. 78). He notes that 'many polytechnics yearn to become universities and, if the present system survives, one day some politician will be daft enough to let them' (p. 71). The printer's ink was scarcely dry on Hague's pamphlet before Mr Major and Mr Clarke announced the ending of the binary line. So we may now assume that Hague, successful in his demand for the demise, or at least cutting back, of the UFC and its replacement by a 'free market', will be a no less fervent advocate of freedom for any other 'knowledge business' to call itself a university if it so wishes.

For my own part I would not wish the end of efficiency to be bought, if it could be so bought, at the price of equality, as expressed in either self-government or in open access. Universal access to post-compulsory education is a noble modern aim. But the historical openness of the British higher education system can easily be misunderstood. There is ample evidence in the foregoing chapters that the system is a very restricted one—governed traditionally by sponsored rather than contest mobility, with expansion as the increasingly urgently recommended solution. Yet in another important sense the system is relatively open by comparison with other European countries. Walter Müller has demonstrated that, on the counterfactual assumption that a group of nine European countries have the same class structure of occupations, England and the other British countries (Scotland and Northern Ireland) are among the less socially selective: 'at the highest educational level we find the countries spread along a considerable range, the extremes of which are represented by France and England. In France more than 55 per cent of graduates have grown up in one of the two service classes [middle classes]; in England only 35 per cent' (Müller and Karle 1990: 10).

Nevertheless the equality drive has by no means run its course, and if the pathway leads, as many reformers expect, through some carefully engineered expansion along the lines laid down by the best practice of the American states, then some further components of donnish dominion may well be justifiably sacrificed. The age of 'faculty' domination in colleges, universities, and schools had to end with the rise of mass systems of higher education. Burton Clark has described the process in the USA. It is no simple secular decline but a splintering of the academic professions by opposing forces to produce a hierarchy of institutions pursuing different, if complimentary, aims. We have traced hierarchical differentiation in Britain in the earlier chapters. Burton Clark has depicted the American version as follows:

the upper part in a hierarchy of prestige become more professionalised: it is more fully based on arcane knowledge, more involved in peer judgement, more independent of clientele demands, and related market forces. The bottom half, especially the bottom one quarter, becomes less professionalised: it is committed to introductory materials that many can teach, more dependent on student reaction than peer approval, and heavily driven by market demands. Not far from the 'shopping mall high school' we find the shopping mall community college. Up the hierarchy we find inner-directed organizations in the hands of professors; down the line we observe other-directed organizations that are client-driven. Perhaps it cannot be otherwise in a system of higher education that simultaneously seeks to function under a populist definition of equality, where all are admitted, and also tries to serve the gods of excellence in the creation and transmission of all rarefied bodies of knowledge (Clark 1987: 261–5).

In Britain the fragmentation of the academic professions has come later and more dramatically out of an entrenched system of ancient establishment with its restricted access, its ideology of sanctuary for outstanding minds, its position in a mature class system, and its traditionally close kinship and affinity with the national ruling classes. Noel Annan's *Our Age* (1990) is a personal account of this British transformation. His golden age of the don is partly ironic, partly nostalgic, partly celebratory. It was preceded by a golden age of the undergraduate in Cambridge or Oxford from 1914 to 1950—a privilege remembered by him and his contemporaries out of the public schools, who went on to enjoy 'laughter and the love of friends' assured of an elevated social position and equipped with access to European high culture (Annan 1990: 337). Dons, especially for students destined for the academic succession, were friends as well as guides and philosophers. Oxford and Cambridge provided a network of intimate tutelage to the manners and morals of the dominant class. Its claims were status claims. The market was shrouded discreetly behind the brilliant screen of high social connection. The golden age passed to the dons themselves after the Second World War. A programme of expansion assuaged the guilt of exclusion of the mass of working-class compatriots, liberated the excitement of new discovery in letters and science, and involved academic people in advice to governments, in power over social and scientific policy. It was an interlude of academic licence to govern colleges and universities and to build new ones without serious financial restraint or lay interference. The dons grasped their opportunity in the fifties and the sixties with almost reckless abandon. For disciplinarians and interdisciplinary enthusiasts, for élitists and expansionists, teachers and researchers, everything seemed possible in a benign state and a respectful society.

The first clouds gathered fast and broke precipitously in 1968. Britain was on the edge of the storm which had its centres in Berkeley, Paris, and Tokyo. But the climate soon became global and was frozen more sharply in Britain than other competing countries by relatively sluggish economic growth and relatively firm political determination to curb and question the value of British higher education. The very fact of élitist restriction of access contrasted the UK and the USA, in that Britain lacked anything parallel to the American political constituency of educational interest and support. Anthony Crosland, in the mid-1960s, constantly met demands for faster expansion by severe reminders that education was very low in popular political priorities. Shirley Williams's later plea for thirteen points of economy in universities was largely ignored. Malcolm Bradbury's *History Man* became a novel stereotype of the modern don. And Corelli Barnett's *Audit of War* argued offensively that the Oxbridge tradition had robbed Britain of the entrepreneurial spirit, substituting indolence and impracticality. So far from enjoying a supporting constituency, higher education in Britain faced a hostile public led by stridently anti-academic politicians convinced of the truth of monetarism. That the origins of the doctrine were themselves academic—a revival of theories which were born early and were thought to have died late in the nineteenth century at the hands of the new liberals—was an irony largely unnoticed.

So the prestige of academic people in the eyes of both the politician and the populace has plummeted. There is a short-term and real meaning to be attached to the decline of donnish dominion in Britain since the middle of the twentieth century. We have sadly portrayed deteriorating conditions of intellectual work. The autonomy of institutions has declined, salaries have fallen, chances of promotion have decreased. The dignity of academic people and their universities and polytechnics has been assailed from without by government and from within by the corrosion of bureaucracy. Dons themselves have largely ceased to recommend the academic succession to their own students. They see themselves as an occupational group losing its long-established privileges of tenure and self-government, pressed to dilute its tutorial methods, hampered in control of syllabuses, and restricted in its research ambitions by chronic shortage of funds. And these worsened conditions are not simply the outcome of justified pressure to raise the educational standards of the majority of the populace—that after all is a central concern of the key profession—but also, and above all, the melancholy consequence of disapprobation. They are unloved by their political masters.

In this book we have placed this recent and continuing process in a larger frame. Decline was incipient from the dawn of a civilized culture. The rise of industrial society further undermined the monopoly of the educated and accelerated open access to knowledge while driving expertise into greater specialization. Institutions of teaching and research thereby became more bureaucratic. Utility for government and business in harness with political pressure for more democratic access led to expansion of university provision, but changed the shape as well as the size of the system of higher education. Systems of higher learning have diversified. In Britain the particular and paradoxical outcome has been a more elaborate pyramid of prestige, with Oxford and Cambridge never more securely placed at the apex on the basis of academic merit but retaining the inheritance of more sumptuous amenities and superior social connections. Accordingly the British version of decline has had the double face of élitist institutions which also successfully lay claim to modern legitimacy. Perhaps the greatest irony is that collegiate Oxford and Cambridge are still the sturdiest stalwarts of democracy in the internal management of their academic affairs.

The outlook for British higher education is bleak. It is adapting, belatedly and reluctantly, to the legitimate demand for expansion. The demand is legitimate socially because modern citizenship requires access on fair terms to the cultural inheritance; and it is legitimate economically because a viable modern economy requires a labour force that is competitively equipped to use advanced technology. But the attack on an admittedly restricted and expensive traditional system of higher education is conducted on the basis of dogmatic preference for market solutions and is further distorted by an urgent search for political survival and advantage.

In the welter of argument it is easily unnoticed that the old system defends internationally recognized excellence. It also carries the heavy ballast of commitment to autonomy for institutions, freedom for individuals, and financial independence for organized bodies of teachers and researchers. All have been undermined by government action in the drive towards expansion. Yet the framework is of doubtful wisdom. The hierarchy is elaborating basically in the image of the American system, but without three vital conditions for success. They are first, that major financial support must come from the State, second, that legislation has to provide limitations on the functions of particular kinds of higher-education institution, and third, that an underlying social support of belief in education, expressing itself in a strong political constituency, has to be established.

An enlarged and diverse British system of higher education, based on these three conditions, would no doubt give first priority to universal access for 16- to 19-year-olds to a wide range of relevant training for tomorrow's economy. And it would go further to make a reality of citizenship through the various forms of *l'education permanente*. But it would also, if it were to arise, secure a place for the university as Victorian idealists like Mark Pattison or Edwardian dreamers like Veblen desired. There would be a place for scholarship and science insulated from the market-place with respect to both worldly rewards and practical curricula. In such a system some institutions would be both austere and élitist in their insistence on high standards. And such institutions would be somewhat distanced from political power and radically removed from the rewards offered to businessmen.

The attack on academic autonomy, or as we have described it the demand from the state that intellectual labour be proletarianized, has been conspicuously aggressive in the past decade. The counter-attack has been surprisingly mild and perhaps this is a tribute to yet another value nurtured in higher education—the tolerance of hostile ideology and the patience to pursue reasoned argument. Perhaps also it has been a case of bewilderment—the conservatism that finds proposals for radical change incredible. Yet beneath the surface there is deep bitterness which the replies and especially the free comment attached to our survey questionnaires rather tragically illustrate. For they are so often patiently dogged by reaffirmation of faith in the academic calling.

13

PROSPECT

THE future of higher education in Britain was, at least in the legislative sense, settled by the Further and Higher Education Act of April 1992. Yet financially, socially, educationally, and politically this law left everyone in a state of great uncertainty. It was, of course, predictable that the binary system was over when I laid down my pen in 1991. The government had already announced the absorption of the polytechnics into the mainstream system and had invited them all to choose a new name for their own new university. The furore and the manœuvrings in this nominal exercise need not detain us. Where is De Montfort or Glasgow Caledonian or London Guildhall? The complete list of polytechnics becoming universities appears below, together with seven other new degree-granting institutions. There were 33 English and Welsh polytechnics and 15 Scottish Central Institutions before the transforming merger began. There are now 88 UK universities (123 institutions counting separately the constituent colleges of the universities of London and Wales).

Old polytechnics	*New university name*
Anglia Polytechnic	Anglia Polytechnic University
Bournemouth Polytechnic	Bournemouth University
Brighton Polytechnic	University of Brighton
Bristol Polytechnic	University of the West of England, Bristol
Birmingham Polytechnic	University of Central England in Birmingham
Coventry Polytechnic	Coventry University
Leicester Polytechnic	De Montfort University
Derbyshire College of Higher Education	University of Derby
Polytechnic of East London	University of East London
Polytechnic of Wales	University of Glamorgan

Old polytechnics	*New university name*
Glasgow Polytechnic merged with Queen's College, Glasgow	Glasgow Caledonian University
Thames Polytechnic	University of Greenwich
Hatfield Polytechnic	University of Hertfordshire
Huddersfield Polytechnic	University of Huddersfield
Humberside Polytechnic	University of Humberside
Kingston Polytechnic	Kingston University
Lancaster Polytechnic	University of Central Lancashire
Leeds Polytechnic	Leeds Metropolitan University
Liverpool Polytechnic	Liverpool John Moores University
City of London Polytechnic	London Guildhall University
Luton College of Higher Education	University of Luton
Manchester Polytechnic	Manchester Metropolitan University
Middlesex Polytechnic	Middlesex University
Napier Polytechnic of Edinburgh	Napier University
Polytechnic of North London	University of North London
Newcastle upon Tyne Polytechnic	University of Northumbria at Newcastle
Nottingham Polytechnic	Nottingham Trent University
Oxford Polytechnic	Oxford Brookes University
Paisley College of Technology	University of Paisley
Polytechnic of the South West	University of Plymouth
Portsmouth Polytechnic	University of Portsmouth
Robert Gordon Institute of Technology	Robert Gordon University
Sheffield Polytechnic	Sheffield Hallam University
South Bank Polytechnic	South Bank University
Staffordshire Polytechnic	Staffordshire University
Sunderland Polytechnic	University of Sunderland
Teesside Polytechnic	University of Teesside
Polytechnic of West London	Thames Valley University
Polytechnic of Central London	University of Westminster
Wolverhampton Polytechnic	University of Wolverhampton

Other degree-awarding institutions
Dundee Institute of Technology
Bath College of Higher Education
Bolton Institute of Higher Education
Cheltenham and Gloucester College of Higher Education
The London Institute
Queen Mary College, Edinburgh
West Surrey College of Art and Design

In 1990/1, universities in the United Kingdom had full-time academic staff totalling 51,261 of whom 10,800 were women. There were 4,591 part-time staff. Of the full-time total 31,861 were wholly university-financed and 2,530 were in clinical medicine. Academic professors amounted to 10 per cent and readers and senior lecturers to 20 per cent of the full-time staff. These universities had 404,518 students, apart from those at the Open University and those on continuing education courses. Full-time students amounted to 352,574. Undergraduates numbered 297,641 and graduates 106,877 of whom 59 per cent were full-time. About 16 per cent of full-time students were from overseas, accounting for 10 per cent of all full-time undergraduates and 42 per cent of all full-time postgraduates. In October 1992 over a quarter of a million new entrants were recorded, and in 1990 84,990 students completed undergraduate courses (77,163 receiving first degrees). Graduate students totalling 44,512 completed their courses.

Expansion, then, is in something like triumphant progress. But underlying governmental resolve there is debate of growing urgency concerning the use of the market or the State as the source of funds, and, even more important perhaps, a search for the most appropriate model of organization. Commentators like Martin Trow, even if they are impeccably American in their opposition to the State, none the less insist that a university is not a business enterprise. We shall return to this point. But in advance a querulous editorial on 'Professing' from the Hilary 8th Week 1994 issue (No. 104) of the *Oxford Magazine*—the most obvious citadel of anti-market conceptions of the academic calling—deserves quotation: 'the authorities—including vice-chancellorial authority, no less— have come clean about certain recent happenings. While we were quietly sleeping in our beds, "emergency decisions" were being taken, originally in a single case but then "repeated on a number of occasions" to secure an invitee for this or that statutory chair who would otherwise have said no. Without the exercise of discretion in such instances, "serious academic damage would be done". Damage? Well, "a major opportunity would be missed." '

What it comes to is that the editor decried the professorial salary of £34,984 as 'hardly enticing', and quoted the *Daily Telegraph* to the effect that the salary is less than that of the head of even the smallest comprehensive school. So the question arises as to whether merit should be rewarded (as the government insisted for 1988) and indeed whether the whole concept of a basic Oxford professorial stipend is sustainable. The editor tells us that to abandon the basic principle of the professorial stipend 'would go well beyond any helpful flexibility and take us straight into an American "star professor" system'.

'Not (of course) a slippery slope, more an abyss. Whether we could ever pinch enough from Peter to entice Paul is only a practical doubt. More important is what it would feel like once all the Pauls were assembled. An academic culture is a precarious balance put at risk by altering the warmth of its collegiality by a couple of degrees. We already have less of a safety margin than we had. A radical change here would accelerate other changes. It would necessarily pre-judge the debate still pending on other matters of academic conditions.' But the editor is clear that 'although Oxford by sustained effort may remain one of the large handful of international research universities, it should at least pause before pursuing that aim at the cost of a culture which makes it one of a smaller and more distinguished group still: a group you don't need all the fingers of one hand to count.' He means, of course, a university in which strength is not to be measured simply by the professors, but one which has depth and doesn't rely wholly on its top-of-the-order people. The market, in short, threatens ancient collegial organization and the general quality of a university.

On the other hand the issue of the market verses the State cannot be entirely separated from the underlying problem of social ends for education. The question can be put as that of whether the experience of the United Kingdom points the way to simultaneous survival of both world-class excellence and a mass system. We have already seen that the last chairman of the UGC did not believe that any modern government had demonstrated willingness to face this issue, not even, as I had suggested, the state of California. We could, therefore, ask whether excellence in higher education is doomed to be sacrificed on the altar of satisfying popular demand. One way out is to pursue the distinction between teaching and research and then to classify universities according to their teaching and research functions or, as the French do, to devise a separate CNRS system. We shall return to this question and also to the further question of whether excellence has to reside in the 'private' sector. Can autonomy be a bargain between academics and government?

There are three other points commonly made by reviewers of the first edition. First, no one greeted with any enthusiasm my incorporation of the evolutionary theory offered by Weber and Gellner. It was not to be taken too seriously and certainly not as an explanation based on defensible comparative method. It was however, I thought, a suitable background against which the proposals put forward by Douglas Hague for further privatization ('half the dons on twice the salary') represented a catastrophic misreading of both the nature of higher learning and of the historic role of the State in its promotion.

A second noticeable reaction from reviewers as serious and knowledgeable as Harold Perkin and John Roberts was that there was an air of sadness about my review of the British universities in this century. I think that this reaction, or criticism if such it be, is fair. I want very much to see a viable system of mass higher education but I am also convinced that the preservation of excellence in universities has been a distinguished and precious feature of university life in the United Kingdom in modern times.

The third characteristic of reviews of the first edition is only barely worth remark. This is that there remains a widespread hostility to sociology, especially when applied to the understanding of the academic vocation. I remember being both amused and outraged in the early 1970s when Martin Trow and I produced our *British Academics* and the Professor of Greek at the University of Oxford recoiled from the survey numbers and somehow imagined that the book advocated Black studies in US campuses. The same spirit is still alive. *The Times* asked Professor Philip Thoday, about to retire from the Chair of French Literature in the University of Leeds, to write a review. He obliged with insouciant self-confidence, cheerfully dismissing painstakingly assembled survey data where it did not happen to coincide with his own experience and prejudices. It is, I fear, doubtful whether any serious progress has been made by sociology in persuading others that it has a powerful apparatus of analysis to offer.

THE BROAD VIEW

Some of my reviewers, as I have said, have been less than enthused by the evolutionary theory of declining dominion for dons which I derived from Weber and Gellner (pp. 258–64). It is true, of course, that a single series of observations offers no base for generalizations through the comparative method: but the implicit democratization of writing, which flowed from alphabetic simplification in Greece in the seventh and sixth centuries before Christ, is a landmark of huge importance along the road to mass modern higher education. The earlier evolution need not concern us. The essential point is, as I have argued, that while knowledge is power, the university has a monopoly of nothing and accordingly the privilege and prestige of the professor, as it emerged especially in nineteenth-century

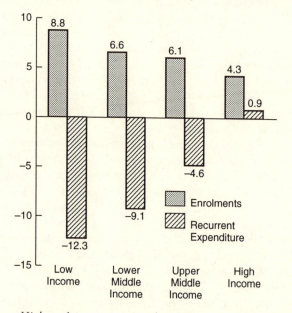

FIG. 13.1   *Higher education enrolment and public expenditure on higher education. Average annual growth rates by country income group, 1980–8 (%). Source: Salmi 1993*

Germany, is forever fragile. My interpretation is that, in our time in Britain, we saw its fall in the context of a rapid and institutionally explicit expansion of post-secondary opportunities for adolescents.

If, however, my interpretation is correct then comparable developments should be found in other countries where the power of science is harnessed either to enhance the economy or to open the society: and there are relevant cases. What used to be called the first, the second, and the third worlds all provide them. The erstwhile first world to which Britain has belonged has assembled a vast documentation and study, not only nationally but also through such international agencies as the OECD. Thus, for example, vigorous efforts are now made by OECD to record the development of higher education in the twenty member countries in comparable statistical terms. *Education at a Glance* is one useful outcome. From it may be discerned a common pattern with particular national variations of combined expansion for students with decline in distinctiveness and conditions of service for academics. The common pattern is that higher education contributes heavily to economic development through research and through training professionals. The correlation is high. Enrolment rates in the OECD countries average 51 per cent, in middle-income countries 21 per cent, and in low-income countries 6 per cent.[1] Between 1965 and 1990 enrolment percentages rose from 1 to 9 in North Africa, 8 to 16 in the Middle East, 7 to 21 in Latin America, and 8 to 17 in East Asia.

Nevertheless, the World Bank report insists that higher education is in crisis throughout the world. Higher education everywhere is heavily dependent on government funding and unit costs are high relative to other sectors of education. Given widespread fiscal constraints, the challenge is to maintain or improve quality in higher education. The poorest countries have found this impossible and the typical view from the senior common room is one of overcrowded and deteriorating physical facilities, inadequate staffing, poor library resources, and insufficient scientific equipment and instructional materials. Putting the two trends together, expanding student numbers and contracting public expenditure per student, Dr J. Salmi has produced the figures shown in Figure 13.1.

---

[1] J. Salmi, World Bank, *Higher Education: Issues and Options for Reform* (July 1993).

To illustrate the gravity of the crisis we can point to the decline in real terms of teacher salaries. Academics either leave the universities for better pay in other sectors or they moonlight to augment this total income. In Nigeria, for example, university salaries in 1992 were only 10 per cent of their value in 1978. A survey of thirty-one sub-Saharan African countries showed that the average number of books per student held by university libraries fell from 49 in 1980 to 7 in 1990.

Latin America

A similar story may be obtained with respect to Latin America. Thus, Professor Orlando Albornoz came to Oxford and put together a short book on an increasingly large subject—education and society in Latin America.[2] He includes the Caribbean in his region. He is probably talking about 700 institutions of varying sorts and sizes up to Mexico's 400,000 students at the Universidad Nacional Autonoma de Mexico. But he narrows the focus to universities and their special sensitivity to politics. Underlying it all, of course, is the understandable and continuing preoccupation with development. Can education (human capital) yield economic growth? If so, how is it that the State has virtually given up trying to control education in the region? He is pessimistic, not so much because he doubts the 'education-leads-to-development' thesis in general, but because he looks sadly across the Latin American universities and finds them mediocre, corrupt, politicized, bureaucratic, lethargic, not possessed of the research spirit, and recruiting staff and students by non-meritocratic criteria. High culture in Latin America belongs to literary, not academic, notables.

Why this melancholy scene? Albornoz, in a somewhat repetitive fashion, begins to sketch an interesting answer. First, the sixteenth-century Spanish colonizers set up teaching rather than research institutions: they were from a country already isolated from the European university mainstream, and they did not export Salamanca. Their mission was to train priests and professionals, not to seek universal knowledge. Second, the response to modernity was late: it was led by Cordoba in 1918 in Argentina, offering a 'Latin American' type of university, and it failed. Third, there was the American influence, especially in Mexico, which was something

---

[2] O. Albornoz, *Education and Society in Latin America* (London: Macmillan, 1993).

like an extension of the land grant colleges (though the author doesn't explicitly say so) minus a resolute applied research impulse and oriented strongly towards a market for professional graduates. Market organization along American lines, private, public, or mixed, was in any case more political than economic and largely confined to Mexico, until Chile, after Allende, encouraged its universities to discourage the Cuban tendency. Then fourth, and finally, Cuba itself developed universities and schools in the image of the Soviet Union—not a model that has commended itself elsewhere in the region, especially since the collapse of the Berlin Wall. Thus a complexity of failure has so far emerged.

If there are lessons from Latin America for Europe they are two. First, there is historically no effective substitute for State patronage of education. Privatization and markets guarantee neither development nor democracy. Of course, as Albornoz accepts and Daniel C. Levy has argued in his work[3] on private universities and the Latin American State, complete control whether by the state or by the market cripples high learning. The rise of secular private universities was a reaction to perceived failure to deal with social class, political and economic demands in Latin America. Including the Catholic universities, the private sector grew from 14.2 per cent of all enrolments in 1955 to over 34 per cent in 1980. The region had had baleful experience of state monopoly exercised by authoritarian governments. And some private universities have been too ready to be subservient to the interests which have supported them. No one claims that private expansion is the solution to Latin American ills or that further privatization is desirable. Nevertheless, the net effect of private initiative has been to show a correlation with improvement of standards and commitment to democracy in recent times. It is incidentally odd that Albornoz has apparently ignored Émile Durkheim, the great prophet of State-led educational development in the French Third Republic.

Second, the mystery that liberal centres of research came out of the European medieval university and transplanted themselves all over Asia, North America, and parts of Africa becomes all the more intriguing in the light of South American failure. And tragic too when the pathway to privatization in rich countries is being followed everywhere because the State no longer wishes to shoulder the burden. A revenge for Latin America? No wonder Albornoz

[3] D. C. Levy, *Higher Education and the State in Latin America* (Chicago, 1986).

looks with humility at his universities and prefers to admire the likes of Gabriel Garcia Marquez.

Eastern Europe

Nor is this discouraging story confined to the third world. For example, the *Times Higher Educational Supplement* (16 July 1993) reported the staging of a protest meeting at the Moscow State University where Igo Aotlobovsky, President of the University's Joint Union for Faculty and Students, said, 'we have the situation where a cleaning lady gets paid more than a university professor . . . we have lost 25% of faculty members over the past five years and things are getting worse.' The anecdote no doubt caricatures the reality of a fast changing scene, and academic differentials were typically smaller in Eastern than in Western Europe after 1917: but the trend echoes world-wide tendencies.

As to the current trends in the United States, a most useful contribution has been edited by Sheldon Rothblatt, *The OECD, the Master Plan and the California Dream* (Berkeley, Calif., 1992). This small book began from the OECD publication *Higher Education in California* (Paris, 1990) as one of the series of reviews of national policies for education which OECD undertakes. In this case it was written by me with my two co-examiners Michio Nagai and Pierre Tabatoni. As is customary, there was a 'confrontation' meeting in Paris attended by the examiners, the Californian participants, and representatives of the OECD countries as well as the OECD administrators. We then had, in 1990, a further conversazione in Berkeley. Rothblatt has put together the result including contributions from me, Patrick Callan, Burton Clark, Clark Kerr, and Martin Trow.

My view of the possibility of California as a model for the future of higher education in Britain and the OECD countries of Europe is reproduced below.

CALIFORNIA AS OECD FUTURE[4]

In the body of the Examiners' report we described the Californian system of postsecondary education, its place as a variant of

---

[4] 'Part One: The Examiners' Report, Chapter 9, Challenges for the Future', in *Higher Education in California*, OECD (Paris, 1990), 81–5.

arrangements in the fifty American States, its structure of power, its mechanisms for planning and its problems of finance, labour supply and promotion of mobility through educational opportunity. We began with a flattery: California was, for millions in our childhood, the hope of progress. We continued with a description: California has an advanced system of postsecondary education related to an advanced economy. We added a salutation: California is the exemplar of postindustrial society. We end now with a question: Is California the model for OECD futures? It is an ambiguous and could be a deeply political question. Models can be ideals or ideal types, i.e., they can be aims to be sought or avoided with passion, or they can be conceivable social states which social scientists can attempt to analyse in terms of the conditions and probabilities of their emergence. The distinction is crucial, for the one implies advocacy while the other, in principle, presupposes value neutrality.

We cannot pretend to be fully qualified for either mode of discourse. We carried with us to California a lifetime of more or less sophisticated prejudices from England, France, and Japan concerning ideals of society, economy, and education. And those who gather to discuss our report, whether Californians, Europeans, or representatives from OECD countries bordering the Pacific, will be burdened or enlightened by attitudes from their own experience. H. L. Mencken once remarked that if you hear a man praising his own country you may depend on it that he expects to be paid for it. We, by and large, have found much to praise in another country. Others may or may not concur. All that we can hope to do is to offer an honest report of our impressions, drawing attention to the priorities over which reasonable people may honourably disagree.

As to the other mode of discourse—futurology—we need no reminder of the intellectual difficulties. The history of social science is littered with inaccurate preductions and, indeed, is all too prone to convey false prophecy. Moreover, our visit to California was short, our study of its institutions brief and our mastery of its documents incomplete. Furthermore, even though—as we have remarked—information on Californian economy and education is as voluminous as anywhere in the world, it too falls short of offering a complete test of such theories of social change, of the impact of education on economic and social development, and of the structure of post-industrial society, as are available to us. Again, all we can do is to arrange limited evidence for rational discussion. In short, we cannot ourselves presume to present advice to other OECD countries as to whether they could or should make California their mentor.

We can none the less affirm that we have found some preconceptions in California which are fundamentally similar to those of other educational policymakers in OECD countries: they all subscribe to a value consensus; they want their people to be free, to be prosperous and to live in civilised accord. To be sure, this consensus may not extend to total agreement about the characteristics of a civilised person or an ideal society. The values of freedom, equality, and order, in their shifting balance, are more or less compelling to different observers at different times in different countries. And cultural standards are intrinsically contestable. Some, like . . . [me], tend towards the absolutism which assumes that a Mozart symphony is more valuable than a rock concert, that astronomy is more truthful than astrology, and that Henry James writes better prose than Harold Robbins. Others are more cautious, believing with Professor Tabatoni that Mozart in his exuberance would have approved of jazz and even rock. Certainly, cultural relativism sets continuing problems for those who would shape educational curricula. Nevertheless, the operative consensus among policymakers in California, as in other OECD countries, is that they urge tolerance on each other and desire earnestly that all citizens are incorporated as owners of all that is best in their humanistic and scientific inheritance. This is the faith of teachers everywhere. Disagreements turn more on means than on ends. And policy disputation is confused by uncertainty as to how potent formal education can be in reshaping or improving a civilization.

Nowhere more than in California has the vision of the progressive educationist been more clearly, perhaps even naively, expressed. Both the official ideology, and the daily utterances of presidents and provosts, announce the ideal of a democracy of skilled producers and educated consumers. Nowhere is there more optimistic determination that schools and colleges can deliver such an elevated society.

If, then, we examine the possibilities of completing the journey to the 'Californian dream' while mindful of the difficulties and of our own deficiencies, we shall thereby most effectively answer the general question of how much can be learned by OECD from the western coast of America.

The first point to accept about the map of the future is that there are immovable demographic contours. Most obviously, a population which has clearly moved into the new demographic regime of low fertility and increased longevity, combined with the recent and continuing influx of young immigrants, must give particular direction to educational policy. We would point to two such demographically based constraints on future progress. First, the cultural and economic background of the immigrants must imply priority of attention less to the postsecondary than to the (primary) K-12 stage of education. This will inevitably give rise to difficulties with the raising of resources and their allocation. The quality of postsecondary education is challenged not only by its own future needs for staff and facilities but even more by the quality and quantity of the 18-year-olds whom it aspires universally to admit. Nor is this problem a leisurely preoccupation for the twenty-first century. Already in the 1990s the first demographic wave of relatively ill-prepared minority group children will come of postsecondary age.

Moreover, there is a second demographic difficulty. *The Twenty-First Century*[5] details the approaching high rate of retirement of existing teachers. This phenomenon is a consequence of the educational expansion of the 1950s and 1960s. It poses the challenge of replacement, not only in simple numerical terms but also in the recruiting of a teaching force which reflects the social and ethnic composition of the new generation of students. Hence, the need for accelerated identification, training and promotion of ethnic minority teachers is already urgent.

A different set of constraints can be thought of as economic. The Californian aim is not only for a multicultural society but for a prosperous one in which production is based on a scientific culture. It therefore follows that a high output of both scientists and science must be part of the programme, that talent has to be mobilised whatever its social origin, and that future generations as a whole must be nurtured in a scientific culture which at the same time carries a universal consciousness of collective interdependence. The curriculum, from infancy through all the stages of upbringing and advanced education, is challenged to offer a wide cultivation in

[5] A background report by Clive Condren, *Preparing for the Twenty-First Century* (California Postsecondary Education Commission, 1988) and summarized in Part Three of the OECD Review. This compilation of fact was an invaluable guide to us as Examiners.

science, the social studies and the humanities so that all may know and appreciate the culture by which they live, and at the same time ensure the scientific advance and the technological skill that postindustrial society requires. Policies adequate to match this ambition will be a stern challenge to both teaching and research and will extend far beyond the boundaries of conventional or formal education to include the educative dimension of family life, the mass media and experience in the workplace.

Third, there are recognisable political constraints. Against the background of the dream of equity there are already clamorous demands from the relatively disadvantaged groups. Political support for an education system which may well be seen by some of the ethnic minorities as having denied them real opportunity in the past could easily be withheld in the future.

Given these demographic, economic, and political difficulties, we can describe the Californian future as a dramatic challenge to both resolve and resource. The scale of the problems is such that the issue of balance between planning and market forces is surely a crucial one. There is no question, of course, of subsuming educational planning into the kind of command economy . . . that previously existed in . . . Eastern Europe.[6] . . . California belongs with all other OECD countries to those political economies in which an optimal balance is sought between governmental and private enterprise and funding. The practical questions come in one form or another of the issue of how to articulate state and private interests. Discussion of these balances with respect to student support, the operation of schools and colleges, the funding and direction of research, the application of science to technological advance, and the cooperation of educational with industrial enterprise, can be usefully pursued in all OECD countries on the basis of what we have learned in California.

Debate on this broad issue of planning and the market is in any case especially opportune, given two facts: first, many if not most Californians are committed to the minimisation of state expenditure and the maximisation of private funding. Second, some OECD countries, especially in Western Europe, have been moving their policies in the same ideological direction against a tradition of strong state management in educational affairs. It is true that decreasing taxes provide, in particular, resources to people, who

[6] Referred to in ch. 2 of the OECD Review.

can therefore decide to allocate them partly for their personal education strategies in the schools of their choice. These tax rebates can complement public funding or substitute for it; but they are lightly effective for the less privileged groups and even the lower middle class, as they do not pay much tax, and they therefore rely on the political promises of free education for all, and thus for their own children's schooling: an historical cornerstone of Californian citizenship. This is where the priorities are, and they imply strong public support for education.

Our own tentative view is that the challenge of developing citizen opportunity in a multicultural society, of offering high quality education in science and the humanities to all, and of ensuring the renewal of scientific and technological culture in competition with the rest of the world, is one which cannot hope to be met without extension of resources for education and therefore more systematic overall policies and planning at all levels of the education system, and particularly at the state level which has to allocate public funds. Such policies might also be addressed more actively to the problems of reconciling the search for better performances in teaching the mass of Californians and the necessity to save scarce financial resources and human expertise.

Much of what we have written may be held to support this general view. Thus, though we have admired Californian science and technology, we have also observed dissatisfaction with basic education, especially in the high schools. Similarly, though we have been hugely impressed by the expansion of opportunity, we have also noted the differentially high dropout rates among Hispanic and Black students in high schools and from undergraduate courses. The mission of the community colleges has also commanded our respect for its audacious universalism. But the community colleges are in difficulties with respect to financial support, and are plagued with the threat, as Joshua Smith (then Chancellor of the California Community Colleges system) has expressed it, of being a parking lot for students and educational tasks left by other segments. They also have a patchy and unsatisfactory record in their attempt to develop effective transfer programmes to the four-year colleges.

If we lean towards shifting the balance in favour of political rather than private effort, our theoretical reasoning turns on the distinction between public and private goods. . . . [S]cience is a public good, technology more of a private good; technology can be appropriated, science belongs to us all. It follows that the nurturing of science is a collective responsibility and therefore appropriate to the political process and to public funding. Similarly, education is at least in part a public good; and training like technology, is a private accomplishment or property which can be bought or sold according to the preferences of buyers and sellers. Education on the other hand, through its 'neighbourhood effects', is a public good: in a postindustrial and multicultural society education is an essential feature for both the integration and further progress of any country which lives by it.

Of course, the line between public and private, which perhaps the distinction between education and training only partly captures, is hard to draw. We might reasonably argue that education as a consumption or as a positional good should be thought of as private, and that only education as a production good be entitled to a place in the public realm. But at all events, all countries consciously or unconsciously make political decisions about this distinction when they construct their policies for taxation and educational expenditure. Present patterns in California can be looked at in this light, and again our tentative suggestion is that the nurturing of scientific culture, and the aims of universal access with equity between different social groups, must imply considerable support by government to education as a public good.

Whether or not this general view is justified, we must expect considerable debate about the Californian future in terms of governmental responsibility. All postsecondary institutions would like greater public support in order to face their future responsibilities for larger numbers of admissions and higher expectations of successful retention and of improvements in co-ordination with other schools and colleges. Not everyone is satisfied with the pattern of grants and loans, especially those who are most anxious to improve the ratio of educated people of ethnic minority. Private colleges are particularly worried about the growing tuition gap. They advocate more generous public support to students, which would leave them freer to use their own funds. Public institutions, and especially the community colleges, seek larger institutional grants to enable them to raise the quality of their offering.

Yet the sources of public finance remain severely limited in California by the constitutional constraints introduced by Proposition 13 and the Gann ceiling. Together with similar policies at the federal level, the state thrusts heavy responsibility on to private charity and private willingness to buy educational products. Of course, economic growth and a growing class of graduates give California a fertile soil for the cultivation of private generosity to the universities and colleges. But it may be questioned whether private funding is adequate to the educational ambitions that the Californians have set themselves and whether the expected increasing competition for private funding will not, in the end, prove to be disadvantageous to public universities.

The Californian state budget links growth of real expenditure to the average rate of population growth. It thus ignores the special ethnic and age structure of the population from the point of view of educational demand. Moreover, there are other areas of public expenditure which are not equitably calculated from average population growth, for example social services to the elderly or penal services to a country afflicted by growing rates of crime. In consequence, education will have to compete more sharply for public funds and will itself be a divided house, given the claims of the three public segments and those of the fourth, the independent colleges and universities.

Finally, whatever the outcome of debate about public sources of finance, and quite independently of it, the case may be made that the co-ordinating activities of the state are too weak to guarantee the administration of the journey to the Californian dream. First, it may be questioned whether CPEC (California Postsecondary Education Commission) provides sufficiently strong co-ordination and even whether its admirable and continuing analyses of the state of the system are illuminating enough to show Californians exactly where they stand in relation to their aim to integrate their diverse peoples into a solidary, equitable, and free society. It is not possible, for example, from existing studies to gauge exactly how open Californian society is in terms of educational achievement or occupational placement for men and women of different ethnic and social backgrounds.

Co-ordination between the postsecondary segments is largely based on cooperative procedures and dependent on the good will of the interested parties. Collective decision-making is incremental and undoubtedly CPEC has given substantial aid in long-range planning and in evaluation. It is, however, a reasonable object of

debate as to whether arrangements could be improved through a
clearer hierarchy (of objectives), a better demonstration of different, cumulative and sensitive factors which might create emergency
situations, and of combined ways to cope with them through a
clearer definition of the functions of CPEC and the Round Table [a
voluntary committee of business and educational leaders]. How far
can monitoring and control be separated? Is there a case for more
active communication and persuasion of the public through the
mass media in favour of the general educational interest, and is this
a job for CPEC?

We do not know, and are far from suggesting that the world be
made over to bureaucrats. We do not take it for granted that the
central ministries in Europe serve education better than the mixed
advisory bodies, or that private supporters best serve California.
We do, however, incline to the view that social science analysis has
not been mobilised, even in California, to the task of informing
civic and political leaders of the pathways and their pitfalls towards
what has to be recognised as a magnificently ambitious educational,
social and economic goal.

A POST-MORTEM IN BERKELEY

In the spring of the year following the OECD meeting in Paris, we
had a kind of return match at Berkeley in May 1990. Whereas in
Paris, Americans were more than usually conscious of the community of higher education, especially the historically common origin of
the 'four years institutions' (the medieval European university and
the Germany research heritage), now in Berkeley awareness of
difference became prominent. The question of whether Californian
development constitutes a model for OECD futures was not
ignored. Indeed, Professor Burton Clark conclusively offered 'no' as
an answer while others, out of diffidence or sensitivity to the perils
of California's own future, in effect invited the visitors to refuse to
take 'yes' for an answer.

Kerr, Trow, Callan, and Clark criticized my view from various
points of view and I replied as follows in Rothblatt's book.[7]

President Clark Kerr

It was highly appropriate that Clark Kerr, who was President of the
University of California before the formulation of the Master Plan,

---

[7] S. Rothblatt 1992.

should have taken a major part in our conversations. In 1990 he was elegantly at pains to de-mythologize the story of 1960. A plain American come to do a job of work was how he preferred to remember his role in the original Californian commission. Treaty between hard-headed spokesmen for competing, legitimate, but different interests was the fortunate outcome, avoiding a nightmare of under-funded chaos rather than elaborating a dream or unfolding an Olympian blueprint for the educational development of all nations. It was a practical exercise in parochial politics, not a pace-setting venture into mass or universal higher education.

In one sense Kerr's account is endearingly preposterous. He is no plain American, and many of the other parties to the treaty were also educationists, politicians, or administrators of high distinction. Kerr himself is after all the author of *The Uses of the University*, the Godkin Lectures of 1963 delivered at Harvard, which clearly broke new ground in the international conception of the possibilities of a fully modern system of higher education. One only has to think of the contrasted reception of Kerr's with Flexner's earlier message of the 1930s in *Universities: American, English, German* to realize that an entirely new 'idea of the university' had been born. Flexner was urging the USA to follow the model of English Oxbridge restriction. Kerr simply described 'the multiversity', pointed to its comprehensive affinity with advanced industrial society, and left it to make its own persuasive way through the international world. No wonder then that Flexner was forgotten while Kerr's book was a constant reference source for the European progressives in education who had adopted the slogan of 'doubling in the decade' and for the Pacific Rim countries who saw that economic growth necessarily presupposed a vast development of education and training beyond school.

In another and equally obvious sense the former President was 'telling it like it is'. Californian development is characteristically pragmatic—the outcome of individual enterprise, mediated from time to time, and usually reluctantly, by collective agreement which is embarrassed to call itself planning. The Plan, after all, is what defines an underdeveloped or a communist country. It was not at all that Kerr was unaware of the need for firm definition of the sphere and function of the university, the state colleges, and the junior (community) colleges or of the immediate pressures of immigration and natural increase that might easily engulf the campuses and colleges. He assumed something like a transition from mass to universal higher education but wore this theoretical clothing lightly and concentrated on the exigencies of short-term survival. There was in any case also a felt threat to the autonomy of higher education in its three state and one private sectors. Legislative activity and power might subjugate educational autonomy to the political process. So suspicion of Sacramento added urgency to the task of treaty-making between the sectors. Reading Kerr's reflections from thirty years on, this passion for autonomy has undiminished echoes and, I would suggest, tends towards defining OECD as a latter-day super-Sacramento and super-Washington that might be yet another agent of political bureaucracy liable to stifle the grass-roots sources of vitality on which Californian education essentially depends.

Yet in a third sense the President is again mistaken. He was, despite contradictory affirmation, dreaming the Californian dream. True he was sleep-walking, as practical reformers habitually do. But the Californian dream was his inheritance from older American commitment to Jeffersonian equality of opportunity, to Benjamin Franklin's insistence on 'useful knowledge', to John Maynard Keynes's balanced economy, and to James Madison's vision of power shared between relatively autonomous institutions. The Californian dream is a vigorous variant of that wider and deeper philosophy of the good society. If it is relatively unselfconscious this is because swift social change promotes practical problem-solving rather than academic and theoretical contemplation. The latter luxury was more sumptuously available to an OECD Examiner, especially thirty years later. But its principles, as Kerr himself indicates, guided the practical action of men and women under the pressure of present circumstances.

Burton Clark

Professor Clark was asked to address himself to the question of the exportability of the Californian system to other OECD countries. He is sceptical to the point of rejecting the possibility of such an international transfer. To make his case he believes that the original analysis offered by the Examiners has to be amplified in two directions—to bring back the nation and the local unit so as to expose the dynamics of a vast, decentralized system. It is for others, not me, to judge the deficiency of the Examiners' Report in these two respects. Certainly Clark's own description of what he insists is a 'bottom-up' system of higher education is completely persuasive. He brings out admirably its five primary characteristics: large size (3,500 institutions of virtually infinite variety); extreme diversity; radical decentralization; intense competition; and a high degree of institutional initiative. Few will quarrel with these distinguishing features of both American and Californian arrangements.

The question is rather how much these attributes are weaker or even absent from the systems of other OECD countries. I would suggest that he exaggerates both the historical and contemporary differences. Thus, for example, it is misleading to suggest that England had only two places in the first half of the nineteenth century, Oxford and Cambridge, while America was developing hundreds of colleges by local initiative. On American definitions there were dozens of English and Scottish foundations at that time, including four (or five) ancient Scottish universities and Durham, as well as the mechanics institutes and Nonconformist academies. The point is that they were obscured by the fame and magic of the ancient English colleges and lacked the fervent support of local communities and national élites which was so marked a feature of the American continent. And the first industrial nation did not share the faith of the first new nation in the power of formal education either as an engine of industrial advance or as a redemptive instrument of cultural modernization.

What is more spectacularly different is the British and European trust in the benevolent potential and social responsibility of the State compared with the preference of the Americans for market solutions. It is market competition as opposed to aristocratic patronage that informs the contrasted paths of development on the two sides of the Atlantic. At the same time it is of importance to exact understanding that, rhetoric and culture notwithstanding, we keep in view the central role of the State in the funding and fostering of education in all countries, including the United States of America. In the 1980s economic liberal ideas have notably increased their influence on both public and private institutions including hospitals, insurance schemes, public utilities, and prisons as well as schools and colleges. These trends towards privatization, with their most spectacular eruption into the political economies of eastern Europe and the former Soviet Union since 1989, are in effect an assimilation of social and educational organization in these countries to the model of American society. They have, incidentally, dated the classification of the political economies of education which I extracted from the literature to form a context for the examination of California in that year. The 'command economy' end of the spectrum has virtually passed into history. Yet the importance of State activity in education remains paramount.

Thus any appraisal of California has to include competition for the federal dollar in the conduct of research activities, and the funding activities of the Californian State Legislature have to be seen as an essential political underpinning of the competitive effort of the Californian Higher Education business. Viewed from that angle, President (as he then was) David Gardner and the leaders of the State University sector and the presidents and chancellors of the individual public and private universities and colleges are both businessmen and politicians. What makes their dual role distinctive is that they are also guardians of the autonomy and academic integrity of their several institutions. And it is the effectiveness with which they play that distinctive part that gives us the key to understanding the character and powerful dynamic of the 'bottom-up' system that might, in some form, be exported to other quarters of the world.

It is not, or at least not only, that competition is absent in Europe. Hunting for funds in the private sector, though primitive in its organization by comparison with Harvard or Stanford or UCLA, is now an established feature of the European scene. Competitive entry to different universities and colleges has traditionally been organized in Europe through both the State and the market. An intriguing object of speculation for the future is the growth of European Community funds—a nascent United States of Europe—which might play a parallel role to that of the federal government in Washington and induce politically backed competition for European federal funds among the member states of the European Community. An 'American' future for Europe may already be in the making, with or without conscious attempts to transpose the lessons of California. The underlying dynamic, I believe, is the logic of mass higher education. Its structure is inevitably shaped by the history of each country and the assumptions about the nature of higher education that are embodied in its institutions. Variations in the forms of competition illustrate both the force of history and the easily unforeseen consequences of simplistic administrative borrowing. The lessons of California are accordingly more than the opportunity to be sophisticated by close attention to the experience of an alternative human laboratory.

Patrick Callan

Patrick Callan's caustic essay on the frailty of the Californian Master Plan still further reinforces my feeling that the difference and distance from Sacramento to London or Brussels is rather overestimated by Bob Clark. He puts emphasis on the bias towards aggregation when the State controls; but surely recent movements contain the tendency towards disaggregation through market forces and the distinctive feature, at least of the British case, is that governmental action is directed towards the creation of markets or quasi-markets, for example in the use of the 'customer-contract' principle of research funding.

The realization of the ideals of wide and equal access turn everywhere and increasingly on the use of political-administrative skill. A great feature of the California Master Plan was the negotiation, legislation, and preservation of separate missions for the segments of higher education—a politically sanctioned restriction of the market that is possibly more secure in California than in Europe. But it is precisely at this point that Callan is most critical and gloomy about the Californian prospect. His gloom has been further justified by subsequent events. The economic recession has continued to plague Californian efforts to go on with educational expansion. In 1991 it became increasingly clear that the capacity of the state to meet rising demands for expenditure is threatened in the remaining years of this century by a growing gap between those demands and the tax revenues that are currently forecast. An alarming analysis was published by the State's Department of Finance in November 1991 and still more alarmingly publicized by *The New York Times* under the headline 'Amid Cuts, California is Curtailing College Dreams'. The essence of the financial report is that, even assuming normal recovery from the current slump, California faces a deteriorating ratio of taxpayers to 'tax receivers' throughout the 1990s because of rapidly growing numbers of dependants at both extremes of the age spectrum. Immigration and a recent surge in fertility have driven up the number of children; low birth rates in the 1960s and 1970s together with out-migration of the high-earning 45 to 64 age group has slowed down the growth of the working population.

To the extent that these demographic trends continue, California faces continuing budgetary difficulties. No matter how strong its economic recovery, the state will not be able to fund existing programs at current levels within projected tax revenues. With rapidly increasing case loads, the imbalance between taxpayers and tax receivers could result in a $20 billion budget gap in the year 2000.[8]

It is rather that the structure of competition is different (and also differs between the European countries). We can bring out the transatlantic difference by contrasting the USA and the UK. American higher education is market-driven conspicuously at two points—student entry and faculty recruitment. American student consumer sovereignty is aided by modular courses, credit transfer, and electives. Traditionally the British universities have been a State-regulated and unitary system aided by totally defined degree courses for three-year, full-time undergraduates, not transferable between institutions. Entry has been a national competition at exit from secondary schools and a further national competition for a class of degree standardized nationally by the system of external examining. In both systems the agent of competition has been the individual, but in America the arena of competition has been the college while in Britain it has been the nation.

Similarly for academic staff America has run an elaborate market (with Michaelmas fairs reminiscent of the hiring of shepherds and servants in agrarian England) while Britain, especially since World War II, has had in effect a State bureaucracy with a rigid age-wage national salary scale. The British, and indeed the European systems generally, are moving towards the American market system. But meanwhile the differences tell us a great deal about the values that underlie two different organizations of higher education. Bureaucracy is combated in America primarily by reliance on 'exit', i.e., use of the market. In Britain more reliance is put on 'voice', i.e., there is more academic self-government, especially in Oxford and Cambridge. And a further consequence is greater institutional 'loyalty'. Such are the pros and cons of market and State organization. With respect to competition in research, it must be recognized that reputation is just as ferociously sought in Europe as in America. The management of a market for research funds by the State is becoming an increasingly prominent feature of arrangements on both sides of the Atlantic.

[8] *The New York Times* (10 Nov. 1991).

Vulnerable Californian programmes include higher education. Already all three state segments of higher education have suffered budget cuts with consequential freezes of faculty salary, elimination of classes, worsening staff–student ratios, and raised student fees. The promised tenth campus of the University of California has been postponed. President Gardner, in effect reiterating his previous remarks in Paris, told the Regents in October 1991 that admission standards might have to be raised to cut enrolments with the anticipated consequence of heightened ethnic tension if Asians and whites are refused admission to preserve the affirmative action programme in favour of African Americans and Hispanics. In short the Master Plan which legislated the Californian dream is patently at risk.

Callan points to the evidence of poor state leadership, weak bureaucracy, and adversary relations between collegiate and state authority in a 'post-Proposition 13 era . . . increasingly dominated by the state'. He deplores the fact and cannot explain why 'California has had so little success in developing effective mechanisms of governance over the last three decades'. He suspects that politicization 'saps the energy and willingness of boards and administrators to take the initiatives and risks that are the essence of leadership'. In consequence he is far from sanguine about the capacity of California to solve its urgent problems of rising demand for enrolment, falling supply of funds, and shortage of qualified higher education staff. So one plausible interpretation of his remarks is that if there is a Californian model to export it has to be different in the 1990s than it was in the 1960s. No doubt this is true. Progress cannot be merely extrapolation of past policies.

But more fundamentally I think that what Callan is raising is the abiding question of how politics and enterprise can interact to maximize educational quality under new political and economic conditions. Putting the problem in that way permits the possibility of a reverse flow of lessons from Europe and/or Japan to California. Even so I believe that the Master Plan is unlikely to become an antiquity but, on the contrary, to remain a principled guide. That guide, we should note, is not unequivocally an instruction simply to go on expanding. It also contains a traditionally 'European' lesson —that higher education standards in both teaching and research must be maintained. So it was that in Paris both the President of the University and the Chancellor of the State

University affirmed that, if forced by economic recession or failing financial support, the universities would choose quality rather than quantity, thus presumably shifting the burden of response to popular demand out of their two segments on to the private colleges and the community colleges. Incidentally we should note here that, quite apart from the priority given at present to affirmative action on behalf of certain minorities and other social groups, because the Californian four segments are not, in fact, fully autonomous, a pure meritocracy can never emerge. Again, we see here a commonality of commitment of American and European educational leadership with an ironically converging trend—the Europeans for the time being more sensitive to the need to take in greater numbers, the Americans more anxious to preserve the traditional meaning of higher education.

Martin Trow

Martin Trow challenges the Examiners' Report at a quite different level. Kindly and correctly he appreciates that my own contribution to the analysis proceeds from a position in political and social philosophy—the standpoint of an English ethical socialist—which is different from his own commitment as an American liberal. His essay is an elegant reaffirming statement of the view he shares with many Americans of the dynamics that underlie the expansive centrality of education in the search for our common goals of prosperity and freedom. He is surely right in distinguishing between two different philosophies and in separating both from Marxism, especially in its orthodox historicist form. He and I do differ, not with respect to the value of freedom nor as to our rejection of Marxist historicism as its most potent enemy in recent history, but rather with respect to both our conceptions of equality and the means of its attainment through collective action. It is not clear to me how far we differ, if at all, on the third of the trilogy of Western social values—fraternity or solidarity—but there can be no doubt that he sees the underlying (and for me logically anterior) idea of *koinonia* as one with radically different origins in America compared with European experience. For me fraternity or solidarity is rooted in an ancient Judaic-Christian collectivist conscience. From the Pauline premise that we 'are all members one of another' flows the inference that equality and sensitivity to the freedom of others must be the central guide for personal action and public policy.

Thus the horizontal bonds to which Trow refers are the fundaments of good society as well as the model of an always improvable person, and it is the task of education to bind the individual into these collective as well as personal goals. In John Steinbeck's fiction Tom Joad's notion of individual and collective consciousness is that of the European socialist; Trow's alternative script is that of the American liberal, and the idea of educational policy that is to be derived from the two starting points is radically different. For me also as a Briton the contextual assumptions are made that class is a divisive force against the integrating influence of citizenship and that the State is a relatively benign and reasonably uncorrupt instrument of democratic will. For Martin Trow the binding force of society is ambition tolerated between free individuals. Social consensus relies on shared hope for the future rather than on sad lessons from the past. And the State is more suspect than the market as an instrument for delivering human preferences.

More specifically, Trow argues three propositions. First, that American ambition shaped by American liberalism enjoins the individual to rise out of, not with, his class. Second, that class analysis of education is of dubious relevance to the Californian case and is in any case not empirically possible. Third, that the equivalent to European guilt about class inequality is, in America, race or ethnicity.

I would want to weaken all three of these propositions, arguing instead that Europe and America are more alike than they suggest and still more that the two continents are converging. American exceptionalism is a time-honoured but none the less unproven thesis. True that neither Steinbeck's *Grapes of Wrath*, nor any other work of fact or fiction, will ever destroy the historical truth that America never had a coherent working-class movement. But the knowledge we have of comparative social mobility, whether in the older and cruder measures offered by Seymour Martin Lipset and Reinhard Bendix and their associates[9] or in the more recent and highly sophisticated work of their successors. Otis Dudley Duncan, Beverly Duncan, Robert M. Hauser, David L. Featherman, Michael Hout, and Donald J. Treiman, as well as the

[9] *Social Mobility in Industrial Societies* (Berkeley and Los Angeles, 1959).

European class analysts associated with the CASMIN (Comparative Analysis of Social Mobility in Industrial Nations) group at Mannheim, lends no support to the idea that *relative* individual intergenerational mobility rates are higher in the USA than in Europe. The modern social scientific consensus is, to use Robert Erikson's and John Goldthorpe's title, one of *Constant Flux*. In the sense of relative mobility America is an open society but no more so than the western or eastern European countries. The differences, and they exist within Europe as well as between. Europe and America, stem from differences in the development of the occupational structure of distinct industrialisms, not from differences in the openness or fluidity of these societies. There are, in other words, historically determined differences in *absolute* rates of mobility but a commonality of underlying mobility regimes as revealed by comparison of *relative* mobility rates.

As to educational equality of opportunity, there are again intercountry variations. But the essential differences stem from different patterns of recruitment to jobs or careers at any given level of educational qualification. Perhaps the most important research finding here is that of Hout[10] showing that the tie between socio-economic origins and destinations weakened in America by one-third between 1972 and 1985 and that this trend is related to the proportion of workers who are college or university graduates. The older assumption that class origin influences job destination irrespective of educational qualification is now seen to be false in the case of degree holders.

Thus the Californian programme of college expansion appears to be a powerful engine of what Europeans used to call 'class abatement'. Nevertheless, important as these shifts in the class structure are in their implications for the openness of society and the use of educational policy for equalization of opportunity, they are emphatically not a demonstration of the irrelevance of class. Class stratification exists or does not exist independently of whether the Californian state collects statistics about it, whether or not sociologists can agree about its measurement, and whether or not the citizenry feels guilty about it. Certainly ethnic guilt is a distinctive American social sentiment (and one cannot but be amazed that Harriet Beecher Stowe's *Uncle Tom* ever became a

---

[10] 'More Universalism, Less Structural Mobility: The American Occupational Structure in the 1980s', *American Journal of Sociology*, 93 (May 1988), 1358–1400.

term of abuse—there is surely no more dramatic case of the triumph of particularistic over universalistic morality). Yet it is surely significant that the current right-wing attack on affirmative action in the form of D'Souza's *Illiberal Education*[11] repeatedly insists that poverty rather than colour must be the legitimate claim to affirmative support from the State. Nor is the USA different from other OECD countries in its record of achieving relative equality of income distribution whether through educational or other social policies. The USA is a country of high relative income inequality. The shape of class stratification has and will alter, but we have no grounds on which to declare its premature demise.

Fact and ideology are at odds here. Why? It is partly a difference of cultural tradition: Europeans tend to hide while Americans proclaim their upward ascents. But it is also true that Trow overstates the difference in attitudes to education. Social elevation through education has always been recognized on both sides of the Atlantic as an individual phenomenon (social mobility, incidentally, has been greater in the 'class ridden' British islands than in France or Germany). It is an intrinsically vertically rather than horizontally bonding experience as Trow remarks. I would add that this individualized opportunity structure is probably growing faster in Europe than in America. There is convergence.

Educational reform, so vigorously publicized by OECD, has led the European countries towards raised popular aspirations for the education of their children. In the past the management of ambition has been markedly different on two sides of the Atlantic. American cheerfulness has vastly encouraged educational aspiration. First the comprehensive secondary or high school and, since World War II, the college has been made the normal popular prize of American citizenship, and the consequences for the idea of higher education in terms of its admission standards and curriculum have been but lightly regarded. A much looser connection of education to the occupational hierarchy has been an accepted feature of the economic order. The higher educational institutions have been great social integrators of American life with both the towering secular cathedrals of Harvard, Chicago, and Berkeley as well as the modest chapels of a thousand community colleges and two thousand four-year institutions offering collectively virtually universal hospitality to any conceivable liberal or vocational study. In

[11] Dinesh D'Souza, *Illiberal Education* (New York, 1991).

Europe by contrast the hierarchy of institutions has been tightly held in a strait-jacket of class stratification. Education has been tied to strongly defined and class-linked styles of life. Mobility through education has been, in Ralph Turner's distinction, sponsored from early selection in contrast to the American structure of contest with its second, third, and nth chances. Hence, among many other things, the uniquely American phenomenon of the community college: and the American process identified by Burton Clark of 'cooling out'.

Today it all seems to be changing and converging as educational expansion becomes globalized. The European countries are in process of broadening the definition of a university, inventing the equivalent of community colleges in two-year institutions like the French IUTs, recognizing British polytechnics as universities, and developing many new vocational, short-cycle, part-time courses in such institutions as the Open University.

This convergence is another facet of the Americanization of Europe. The final question is then whether it also spells the end of class society. Trow seems to suggest that it does. California legislators do not demand class equality of access, and Californian statisticians do not collect figures on the class composition of different student bodies. But surely this does not dispose of the problem. Subjective perceptions of class may be looser, less pervasive, and linked in more complicated connection to race and ethnicity in America compared with Europe. But the objectivity of power and advantage remains. European class consciousness may be different—though here too there is clear evidence of change, not least the dramatic re-emergence of ethnic consciousness in western as well as eastern Europe. Nevertheless, for all their cultural emphasis on individualism, Americans are also class conscious and also aware of the (Weberian) class implications of different educational levels and pathways. As Jackman and Jackman summarize their study of Class Awareness in the United States.

Our results offer no support for the often-heard claim that the United States is a classless society. Nor do we find evidence that America is a society where class conflict is undermined by crosscutting affiliations and loyalties. On the other hand, the structure of subjective class does not conform to the dominant analytic formulations of class. Subjective classes do not capture a single distinction between owners and workers, between those with and those without authority, or between manual and white-collar workers. . . . Evidence throughout the book supports our view that social life is organized into a graded series of groups that behave like Weberian status groups but which have their basis in configurations of socioeconomic criteria. These groups we call social classes.[12]

And, with particular reference to the mission of the community college, the American case is summarized by Brint and Karabel:

What the junior college vanguard and their successors proposed to these students was, in effect, that they renounce their goal of gaining access to the higher rungs of the occupational ladder in exchange for short-range mobility and the security of stable employment in middle-level jobs. By offering vocationalization as a solution to the problem of the gap between the aspirations of junior college students and the opportunities available to them, community college administrators were pursuing their own organizational interests in finding a distinctive function and a secure market niche for their institutions. But they were also, it must be stressed, expressing a genuine concern for the welfare of the large numbers of students who entered the community college only to emerge with neither the credits necessary for transfer nor any marketable skills. If this dilemma continues to be with us, it is because it is woven into the fabric of a society that is striving still to reconcile the democratic promise of upward mobility through education with the stubborn reality of a class structure with limited room at the top.[13]

In short the relevance of class, freed from any assumption of the Marxist theory of history, remains essential to an understanding of education in an advanced industrial society. Martin Trow raises the fundamental question of horizontal bonding in such a society. In California this form of integration has instead its brave attempt at multicultural society through basic universalization of educational opportunity. Yet, as Trow emphasizes, in campus practice ethnic identity through separate group experience and learning is fundamentally inconsistent with the ideal of an individualized claim to occupational and other life-chances for which education is its publicly offered preparation. I fully share his vision and his fear. Ethnic division would undermine Californian and American solidarity. And so too, I believe, could class. So I would insist that *koinonia* must remain the yardstick of the good society with class as well as race as its still powerful and potent sources of social division.

[12] Mary R. and Robert W. Jackman, *Class Awareness in the United States* (Berkeley and Los Angeles, 1989), 216–17.
[13] Steven Brint and Jerome Karabel, *The Diverted Dream, Community Colleges and the Provision of Educational Opportunity in America, 1900–1985* (New York, 1989), 213.

THE BRITISH CASE

So much for the discussion of educational models and particularly the relevance of the California system as it was left in Sheldon Rothblatt's book. Returning finally to a direct appraisal of the recent British experience in an international context, it is difficult to disagree with Martin Trow that over the past ten or twelve years British higher education has undergone a more profound reorientation than any other system in the industrial world. He has recently emphasized one aspect of the revolution—a transformation of university life which we can now see as more significant than Rothblatt's *Revolution of the Dons* in Victorian Oxbridge—the emergence of 'managerialism' in the government's own direction of British universities where managerialism is understood by central government as a substitute for relations of trust. This question of autonomy, linked as it is to the funding of teaching and research, is at the heart of current debate.

There have been two debates in the House of Lords, as usual obscured by the fatuous 'noble Lord' obsequies.[14] One was a staged question by Noel Annan (formerly provost of King's, Cambridge and Vice-Chancellor of the University of London) asking what action will be taken by Her Majesty's government to reduce bureaucratic burdens on universities: he had in mind four such burdens inflicted in the previous three years.

They all came from the Higher Education Funding Council: first, the requirement that universities create mechanisms for ensuring the quality of teaching; second, requiring a separate assessment by another quango of the quality of each subject taught; third, requiring the quality of research in each department to be assessed; and fourth, requiring the costs of such research to be calculated in what Annan could only call 'a grotesquely complicated way'.

Much satire and more sarcasm followed from Max Beloff, Frederick Dainton, Maurice Peston, and others. Annan summed up the decline of donnish dominion himself. 'The truth is, at the very moment when the universities have been screwed financially and need every penny to keep teachers in post and research on the boil, a vast new administrative burden has been put on their shoulders

---

[14] *Hansard*, 6.12.93, pp. 788–808 (I use the word 'obsequies' as an oblique reference to funeral rites or ceremonies, given the threatened demise of the second chamber of the Palace of Westminster), and ibid. 2.4.94, pp. 1307–52.

that removes what money they can cobble together for teaching and forces the teachers to become low grade administrators.'

Underlying all this is a tragedy. The present government does not trust the universities to do either research or teaching. The old fiduciary relation which gave birth to the UGC in 1919 is dead and buried. Instead of a buffer the HEFC was deliberately formed as an arm of government and in the process the British system, which was internationally admired and imitated for its quiet administration, its devotion to teaching, and its high-quality research, has joined the downward spiral of all the venerable institutions of public government—parliament, civil service, police, and judiciary—from a once high plateau of envied political democracy and freedom. An avalanche of illustration followed and finally a reply from Baroness Blatch, a minister of state for education, feebly offering the usual assurance of minimum governmental interference and maximal autonomy in the context of a grant for 1994–5 to 143 higher educational institutions and 76 further education colleges amounting to £3,322 million, including compensation for institutions for the 45 per cent reduction in tuition fee levels announced by the Secretary of State for Education in 1993.

The other House of Lords debate (on 2 February 1994) may also be remarked in that it allowed Lord Walton of Detchant (formerly a prominent physician and Warden of Green College, Oxford) to draw attention to the report of the National Commission on Education, which, as we have noted, was formed when the government rejected Claus Moser's plea for a royal commission. The discussion on this occasion ranged widely, and often equally fatuously, over all the stages of education, but Walton explained that in 1990 the percentage qualifying at 18-plus for entry to some form of higher education was 68 in Germany, 48 in France, 80 in Japan, and 29 in England, and that the UK nevertheless spent almost twice as much per capita on higher education as did many other countries. The explanation was largely that of student grants. Though not starkly put, the NCE has not given priority to higher education. No doubt rightly the first place is given to nursery provision (since rejected by the government) and after that to training (in a new regime for post-14-year-old children of substituting for A levels a modular general education diploma). The drive here is perhaps an anticipation of a unitary system of post-compulsory (perhaps to be called higher) education when the post-binary system has settled down. In higher education itself the commission advocates a major shift for student grants and loans to be funded from the private rather than the public purse.

Though we do not have a detailed social analysis of the staff of the new unitary university system, we do have for 1992/3 an analysis by the University Statistical Record of the 52,152 full-time academic staff in those universities which had previously been funded by the University's Funding Council. In 1992/3 there were 50 universities in Great Britain (counting the various colleges and institutions of the University of London as a single university and including the six colleges of the University of Wales, the London and Manchester Business Schools, the University of Manchester, Institute of Science and Technology as separate institutions; but excluding the Open University and the independent University of Buckingham). Between 1988/9 and 1992/3 the number of full-time non-clinical staff who were not paid wholly from university general funds increased by 23 per cent compared with an increase of 7 per cent for those staff who are paid wholly from university general funds. The proportion of women among full-time academic staff continued to grow and was in fact 22 per cent in 1992/3 compared with 14 per cent ten years previously. The number of part-time academic staff actually fell slightly to 4,270 compared with the previous year but rose by comparison with the 3,400 part-timers in 1988/9.

It should be noticed that the academic professions continue to age, at least in their central core of full-time people wholly financed by the university general funds. Despite the special early retirement schemes of the middle and late 1980s the proportion of this core staff aged 55 years and over increased from 14 per cent to 17 per cent in the ten years up to 1992/3. Meanwhile the average age of all full-time academic staff was 45 years for those who were paid wholly by university general funds and only 33 years for those who were not so paid but employed on 'soft money', i.e. temporary funds.

There are, to repeat, two fundamental trends behind the dramatic merger of the binary into a unitary system. The first is financial cutback. In 1980 the staff–student ratio was 1 to 8; in 1990 it was 1 to 14, and the outlook for 1994 and later is 1 to 17. At the same time there has been such a tremendous growth of student intake that the government has decreed a standstill over the next three years. In effect the growth plan for the year 2000 has already been achieved.

What then are the consequences? First, and never to be forgotten, we have at last seen the emergence of the basis for a genuine mass higher education system. Thus is an ancient educational dream realized. But, in the same process and under the pressure of the two trends, we have seen the introduction of powerful managerial pressures from the centre as the two sides of the divide have converged. Pressure from above, of course, always meets cultural resistance. The commitment of academic professions to what Martin Trow has always called a private life of teaching and research is more stubbornly resistant than the public shape of the system, i.e. its formal governance and relations to government.

What is perhaps least appreciated (and did not for me fully emerge until I had read hundreds of comments from the respondents to the 1989 survey) was that the rhetoric of business models and market relations—the language of customers, competition, efficiency gains, 'value for money', etc.—could be so totally substituted for relations of trust. To put it bluntly, academics were invited to believe that an impoverishment of the staff–student ratio could be counted as an efficiency gain: and some, like Douglas Hague, apparently believed it. Others of us remain or indeed become increasingly sceptical of the capacity of the government through the Funding Council either to measure teaching or research efficiency or to do substantive justice through centralized control of the minutiae of the private teaching and research life of universities, their faculties, and their departments. Noel Annan may have overdone the satire but he was essentially right.

But again the underlying problem is the extraordinary political weakness of organized education. The National Commission only demonstrates the point. As we noticed above on pp. 10 and 268 there is no serious political constituency in Britain compared with the United States, and what there is is more tender in its attitudes towards lower than towards higher education. There is even a certain amount of guilt which is residual from the older and easier days of a UGC liberal establishment. It was easy for the incoming economic liberals to divide and conquer. It was easy for them to bribe the better established universities with the hint if not the promise of becoming research universities. That issue still remains unsettled in that the ex-polytechnics are encouraged rather than refused formal access to research funds. What is certain is that the old dual system has gone. We can even speculate that the propaganda conducted by Lord Joseph and his economic liberal friends has succeeded in the universities while failing in the economy as a whole. Oxbridge indifference and university aspiration generally towards gentlemanly status, it is alleged, undermined the entrepreneurial spirit in Britain. In fact, of course, the opposite thesis can at least as plausibly be maintained. But that is an argument for another place. In the meantime, at least immediately, we have a government which has had four general election victories and which, at every step, has grown in self-confidence with respect to centralization and privatization, almost in proportion though inversely to its decline in public support at the polls and in the common rooms.

We need not despair. Roderick Floud, who took over as Provost of London Guildhall University, told me in July 1994 that he remains 'constantly impressed by the dedication of most university staff to their past and to their students'. One of his greatest managerial difficulties is 'that of restraining the enthusiasm of academic staff for the design of new, better, and additional courses, while being unwilling to give up any of their existing activities.' It is in any case appropriate to end on a note of cheerfulness. Britain has after all at last launched itself into a mass or democratic phase in tertiary education. Poor morale in the senior common rooms is an understandable consequence as are scandals about financial management and the selling of bogus degree courses. Yet, as John Roberts rightly insisted in his review, 'preservation of the best should surely be in some ways easier in a system which recognises and positively encourages diversity, a spectrum in which different kinds of university can fulfil different tasks and uphold different traditions. There lies the possibility of giving the majority of our fellow-citizens for the first time a stake in and an interest, in every sense of the word, in their universities—of making them theirs, as much as ours.'[15] I agree with the Warden of Merton that it is about time we did.

[15] *Oxford Review of Education* (19 Apr. 1993), 560.

This appendix has four elements. First, there is a brief description of the 1989 survey of academic staff in British universities and polytechnics. Second, there is a reproduction of the 1989 survey questionnaire. In the actual survey a 'university' and a 'polytechnic' version was sent out: but here, to save space, they are amalgamated. Third, we have inserted the percentage (or where appropriate mean) answers to each replicated item. This yields five columns of figures on the 1989 version of the questionnaire, detailing the results for the universities in 1964, the universities and the polytechnics in 1976, and the universities and polytechnics in 1989. The figures are 'marginals', i.e., do not include any breakdown by other variables such as university group, academic rank, sex, etc. Such tables are confined to the body of the book. Then fourth and finally, we have put in a cross-reference guide to all three surveys—1964, 1976, and 1989—to make clear the content of each survey and to let the reader see how far the three 'sweeps' were replications.

THE 1989 SURVEY

I asked the director of the Social and Community Planning Research (SCPR) to collaborate in carrying out a postal survey of polytechnic and university teachers and researchers in 1989 to follow up our 1964/5 and 1976 surveys. Lindsey Brook of SCPR was in charge of the field operations and has written a detailed technical report. Some essentials are reproduced here together with the questionnaire and the main responses (i.e., 'marginals') of the two samples described.

The Sampling Frames

For university staff, an adequate sampling frame exists in the form of the Commonwealth Universities Yearbook, updated and published annually by the Association of Commonwealth Universities (ACU). The data are stored on tape, and we investigated the possibility of sampling direct from the datatape. For technical reasons, this proved not to be feasible. Instead, the sample was drawn from page proofs of the 1989 edition of the Yearbook which the ACU kindly made available to us. (The latest *published* issue was that of 1988, based on entries compiled in summer 1987, which was nearly two years out of date at the time our survey was launched.)

For polytechnic staff, no sampling frame of comparable quality was available. Instead, it was decided to use the tactics adopted in 1976—to write to each of the thirty-five English and Welsh polytechnics and Scottish Central Institutions to ask them to provide an up-to-date list of academic and research staff on their 'establishment'. The approval of the Committee of Polytechnic Directors (CPD) was obtained, and Professor Halsey wrote personally to each of the Directors (or Rector, Principal, or Provost, as appropriate) for the necessary information. All the polytechnics and institutes complied. One, however, required us to draw the sample from a list of employee identification numbers, and sent only the names of those sampled.

Oversampling and Sampling Intervals

The decision was taken to oversample two groups in the universities sample: professors and women academics (the latter group could be identified because the Yearbook gave the forename(s) of all women listed, but only the initial(s) of the male academics). For analyses of the universities sample as a whole, the data were to be corrected by applying weights.

The sampling intervals decided upon were:

Male professors: every fourth name
Female professors: all
All other women academics: every fourth name
All other academics: every tenth name

There was no oversampling in the polytechnics samples. Here, every seventh name was selected.

Response

Response to the survey is shown in Table A1.1. As can be seen, it was (as in 1976) rather higher among university than among polytechnic staff. It is possible that the transfer of polytechnics from control by the local authorities affected response. This took place at the beginning of April 1989, just before the present survey was launched, and we understand that there was an unusually high level of staff changes at that time. So many of the polytechnic academics to whom we wrote may have left by the time the questionnaires reached their institution.

Gross response rates only are shown. In random samples using face-to-face interviewing techniques, we can calculate net response rates with a considerable degree of accuracy, because the number of ineligible and non-responding sample members is by and large known. In postal surveys, we cannot know how many of those who failed to reply are ineligible to take part. All we can say with confidence is that the net response is likely to be considerably higher than the gross rates shown.

TABLE A1.1. *Overall response, 1989*

	Universities sample		Polytechnics sample	
	No.	%	No.	%
Issues	5,121	10.0	2,544	10.0
Did not respond	1,664	32.5	1,064	41.8
Responded	3,457	67.5	1,480	58.2
(Assumed to be) ineligible				
no longer in academic life	70		20	
no longer at address/left (no further information)	62		43	
not known/envelope returned (no reason given)	55		29	
has honorary/consultant post only	45		1	
retired	36		8	
on sabbatical/abroad	23		4	
has administrative post only	19		2	
other non-academic post	5		3	
died	4		1	
ill	3		1	
other ineligible	7		2	
Total (assumed to be ineligible) (gross)	329	6.4	114	4.5
Total (assumed to be eligible) (gross)	3,128	61.1	1,366	53.7
Unproductive				
refused	244	4.8	61	2.4
promised to return questionnaire but did not do so	18		4	
incomplete questionnaire (unusable)	12		5	
Total unproductive (gross)	274	5.4	70	2.8
Total productive (gross)	2,858	55.8	1,296	50.9

Weighting

As in the universities sample three groups—male professors, female professors, and other women academics—were oversampled, so the data had to be weighted to restore correct population proportions. It was also decided to apply another series of weights to the universities sample to correct for differential response among the different types of institution.

To correct for differential response, the overall response rate of 55.81 per cent was divided by the response rate for each type of institution (= WT1):

Oxford and Cambridge	55.81/46.47
London	55.81/55.22
Old redbrick	55.81/55.90
New redbrick	55.81/56.78
New Robbins	55.81/63.97
Ex-CATS (technological)	55.81/53.93
Scottish	55.81/56.28
Welsh	55.81/55.93

The weighted base is 2,858 if only WT1 is applied.

All items were included for both the university and the polytechnic sample except where indicated by the absence of a figure in the appropriate column. Note particularly the questions appended which were asked only of polytechnic respondents. An indication of the overlapping but different coverage of the 1964 and 1976 surveys may be had from the cross-index at p. 311 below and from the absence of a figure in the appropriate column. Most of the figures are percentages for the whole of the university or polytechnic sample. The other figures are means and are so indicated.

Survey among Academic Staff

Letter on Face Sheet

This is a survey of academic staff in universities and polytechnics designed to bring up to date attitudes towards higher education practice and policy from previous surveys in 1965 and 1976

Anonymity is guaranteed.

The funding is from the Spencer Foundation—an American charity which supports educational research. The survey is being administered by the SCPR—an independent non-profit institute specialising in social surveys.

My intention is to write a book on British higher educational developments since Robbins. I depend on and shall be most grateful for the time and trouble that I am asking my colleagues to take.

Professor A. H. Halsey
Nuffield College, Oxford

April 1989

Questions

	Univ. 1964	Univ. 1976	Poly 1976	Univ. 1989	Poly 1989
1a What is the name of your faculty, department, school or other unit (Centre, Institute, Laboratory etc)?					
IF YOU ARE ATTACHED TO MORE THAN ONE, PLEASE GIVE FULL DETAILS OF EACH					
b Are you at present head of, or do you chair, any of these					
Yes – Please answer Q.1c		10	10	15	11
No – Please go to Q.1d		90	90	85	89
c Which ones?					
IF YOU HEAD MORE THAN ONE, PLEASE WRITE IN EACH					
d Has your faculty (department, school, unit) been reorganised in the past ten years?					
PLEASE TICK ONE BOX					
by amalgamation with other departments or faculties				39	54
by dispersal among other departments or faculties				4	7
or, in some other way				29	31
IF 'OTHER' PLEASE DESCRIBE					

	Univ. 1964	Univ. 1976	Poly 1976	Univ. 1989	Poly 1989
2a What is your broad teaching and/or research discipline?					
b And what is your particular subject specialism?					
3 Compared with about a decade ago, is the number of students in your subject, at your university (polytechnics)					
larger now				50	78
smaller now				16	11
or, has it stayed about the same?				35	11
Not applicable: subject not taught then					
Don't know					
4a How would you describe the academic ability of the students applying to take your subject at your university (polytechnic) over the same period?					
PLEASE TICK ONE BOX UNDER a BELOW					
b How would you describe their academic ability at graduation?					
PLEASE TICK ONE BOX UNDER b BELOW					
It has become a lot worse — at entry	1			4	8
— at graduation				1	2
It has become a little worse — at entry	20	6		23	30
— at graduation				15	16
It has remained about the same — at entry	63	35		40	26
— at graduation		46		48	22

		16	14		
It has become a little better	at entry			23	25
	at graduation			25	32
It has become a lot better	at entry			10	11
	at graduation			11	18

5a   At present about 16 per cent of eighteen year olds in Britain go on to higher education at universities or polytechnics. If you were advising on higher education policy for 10 years from now, what proportion would you recommend?

PLEASE ASSUME PRO RATA ADJUSTMENT IN STAFF AND OTHER RESOURCES TO COPE WITH ANY CHANGE

	20+		28	30
Proportion of 18 year olds who should be going on to higher education 10 years from now (mean)				

5b   And should the balance in numbers be . . .

PLEASE TICK ONE BOX

more towards the universities than it is now	17	4
more towards the polytechnics than it is now	18	49
or, should the balance stay about the same as now?	65	46
Don't know	15	16

6   Here are some possible functions of universities and polytechnics. For each please tick one box to say which you think is particularly appropriate for universities to provide, particularly appropriate for polytechnics, appropriate for neither or equally appropriate for both.

AGAIN PLEASE ASSUME PRO RATA ADJUSTMENT TO COPE WITH ANY CHANGE

PLEASE TICK ONE BOX FOR EACH

For 1989 only

		UNIV.			POLY			
		Univ.	Poly	Neither	Both	Univ.	Poly	Neither	Both
a	To offer vocational courses	3	47	2	48	1	60	2	37
b	To offer sandwich courses	1	52	1	46	0	52	1	46
c	To develop links with business and industry	3	16	2	80	0	26	1	73
d	To offer part-time courses	1	31	1	67	0	45	1	54
e	To conduct fundamental research	79	0	0	21	52	1	0	48
f	To conduct applied research	21	7	0	71	5	22	0	73
g	To offer graduate courses	52	0	0	48	8	3	0	90
h	To award doctoral degrees	73	0	0	27	27	1	0	73
i	To offer access courses to prepare mature students for higher education	1	41	14	43	0	47	19	35
j	To offer courses to mature students	4	6	1	90	0	24	0	76
k	To educate academic high fliers	76	0	0	23	44	1	1	54
l	To provide courses in classical and humanistic education	61	0	1	37	53	1	2	44
m	To educate students with 'non-traditional' qualifications	4	15	2	80	1	42	2	55

7a   Thinking of the way higher education will develop over the next decade, do you think that

PLEASE TICK ONE BOX FOR EACH

	Univ. 1976	Poly 1976	Univ. 1989	Poly 1989
Polytechnics will become more like universities		37	45	45
Universities will become more like polytechnics			69	72

PLEASE TICK ONE BOX FOR EACH

	Univ. 1989	Poly 1989
Polytechnics should become more like universities	27	44
Universities should become more like polytechnics	16	47
The distinction between them should disappear	24	63

c Why do you think that?

8 How would you view the opportunity to join the staff of one of the polytechnics (universities)

a at your present salary? PLEASE TICK ONE BOX UNDER a BELOW
b at a higher salary? PLEASE TICK ONE BOX UNDER b BELOW
c at a lower salary? PLEASE TICK ONE BOX UNDER c BELOW

		Poly 1976	Univ. 1989	Poly 1989
I would not consider going to any of them —	Present Salary	24	73	30
	Higher Salary		42	10
	Lower Salary		94	82
I might go to some but not others —	Present Salary	53	25	62
	Higher Salary	65	52	63
	Lower Salary		5	16
I would accept such an offer from almost any of them —	Present Salary	41	2	9
	Higher Salary	11	7	27
	Lower Salary	6	1	2

9 How much do you agree or disagree with each of the following statements?

PLEASE TICK ONE BOX FOR EACH

		Univ. 1976	Poly 1976	Univ. 1989	Poly 1989
a	An active research interest is essential if a person is to be a good university teacher.				
	strong agree	52	42	54	38
	agree	35	40	36	48
	disagree	10	14	7	10
	strong disag	3	4	3	5
	Don't know	2	3	0	1
b	An active research interest is essential if a person is to be a good polytechnic teacher.				
	strong agree	25	31	14	26
	agree	40	39	43	47
	disagree	29	23	35	18
	strong disag	6	8	9	10
	Don't know	9	2	8	1
c	Universities should have more staff per student than polytechnics.				
	strong agree	23	4	31	2
	agree	39	2	35	8
	disagree	24	29	20	19
	strong disag	14	55	14	71
	Don't know	7	6	10	3
d	Salaries of university academic staff should be higher than those of equivalent academics in polytechnics.				
	strong agree			24	1
	agree			27	3
	disagree			26	13
	strong disag			23	83

laboratories) in polytechnics and universities.

strong agree	22	70	33	81
agree	33	24	34	14
disagree	31	5	25	3
strong disag	14	1	8	2
Don't know	6	2	3	1

f There should be equal non-academic provision (e.g. residential accommodation) in polytechnics and universities.

strong agree	34	70	54	82
agree	38	21	31	14
disagree	20	7	11	2
strong disag	8	2	3	2
Don't know	6	3	5	2

g First degree work in the polytechnics is rarely of the same standard as that in the universities.

strong agree	22	6	17	4
agree	48	19	43	14
disagree	25	32	28	27
strong disag	6	43	12	55
Don't know	17	5	21	6

h University academic staff tend to have higher qualifications than academics in polytechnics.

strong agree			40	13
agree			51	52
disagree			7	19
strong disag			2	15
Don't know			18	13

i It is very difficult for a person to be promoted in any university (polytechnic) if he or she does not have administrative skills.

strong agree			8	23
agree			25	40
disagree			34	22
strong disag			33	15
Don't know			8	11

10a   Is your present post or contract

PLEASE TICK ONE BOX

	Univ. 1976	Poly 1976	Univ. 1989	Poly 1989
until retirement age, but dismissible with notice	76		74	74
for no specific term			9	17
fixed term			12	8
probationary			4	1
or, do you hold it under some other arrangement			1	1

IF 'OTHER' PLEASE SPECIFY

b   IF 'FIXED TERM' OR 'PROBATIONARY' AT Q.10a
What is the length of the contract?

	Univ. 1976	Poly 1976	Univ. 1989	Poly 1989
PLEASE WRITE IN MONTHS OR YEARS (mean)			3.4	2.1

c   Is your present post or contract

	Univ. 1976	Poly 1976	Univ. 1989	Poly 1989
Full-time			94	96
or Part-time			6	4

11a   In this academic year, are you supervising any research students doing graduate degrees (wholly or mainly) by thesis or dissertation?

INCLUDE PART-TIME STUDENTS

	Univ. 1964	Univ. 1976	Poly 1976	Univ. 1989	Poly 1989
Full-time	54		18	68	32

12a   Are you currently engaged in any scholarly or research work which you expect to lead to publication?

INCLUDE REPORTS WITH RESTRICTED CIRCULATION (E.G. FOR PUBLIC BODIES OR INDUSTRY)

	Univ. 1976	Poly 1976	Univ. 1989	Poly 1989
Yes	93	60	95	71
No	7	40	5	29

b   How many papers have you ever had published in academic book and journals?

INCLUDE ANY PAPERS WHICH YOU CO-AUTHORED
PLEASE TICK ONE BOX

	Univ. 1964	Univ. 1976	Poly 1976	Univ. 1989	Poly 1989
None	13	12	50	3	27
1 or 2	39	14	23	5	20
3 or 4	39	13	12	7	14
5 to 10	22	20	9	14	18
11 to 20	17	16	4	18	11
More than 20	22	26	2	53	10

12c   How many books of an academic nature have you ever had published?
INCLUDE ANY WHICH YOU HAVE EDITED, CO-EDITED, OR CO-AUTHORED

	Univ. 1964	Univ. 1976	Poly 1976	Univ. 1989	Poly 1989
Books (Mean number)	0.1	0.8	0.3	2.4	0.7
None	69	67	87	42	70

d   How many of your professional writings (papers, articles, or books), have been published, or accepted for publication, within the last two years?

	Univ. 1976	Poly 1976	Univ. 1989	Poly 1989
(Mean number)	3.5	0.9	6.6	2.0
None	23	68	9	46

INCLUDE ANY WHICH YOU HAVE EDITED, CO-EDITED, OR CO-AUTHORED. EXCLUDE ANY NEWSPAPER AND MAGAZINE ARTICLES

13 We are interested in the percentage of your working time which you actually devote to teaching, research, and university (polytechnic) adminstration. We also would like to know what percentage you consider ideal for yourself.

In the left hand column, please estimate how you actually spend your time, averaged over the current academic year.

In the right hand column, please estimate how ideally you would like to spend it. Write in a percentage, even if it is a zero. Please check that the percentages add up to 100% in each column.

'TEACHING' INCLUDES PREPARATION AND SUPERVISION BUT EXCLUDES EXAMINING

		1989 SURVEY ONLY Univ.	Poly
Undergraduate teaching	(actual—mean)	26	43
	(ideal—mean)	22	36
Graduate teaching	(actual—mean)	12	7
	(ideal—mean)	15	11
Research and other creative activity	(actual—mean)	28	15
	(ideal—mean)	43	30
Polytechnic/university management & administration (e.g. committee work admissions, examining, references)	(actual—mean)	24	28
	(ideal—mean)	12	16
Other	(actual—mean)	10	3

PLEASE TICK ONE BOX

	Univ. 1964	Univ. 1976	Poly 1976	Univ. 1989	Poly 1989
Very heavily in research	9	17	5	19	8
In both, but with a leaning towards research	51	36	15	38	19
In both equally	1	25	21	22	16
In both, but with a leaning towards teaching	36	17	37	14	31
Very heavily in teaching	3	5	24	6	26
Other				1	1

IF OTHER PLEASE DESCRIBE

b   Do you feel under pressure to do more research than you would like to do?

PLEASE TICK ONE BOX

	Univ. 1964	Univ. 1976	Poly 1976	Univ. 1989	Poly 1989
Yes, under a lot of pressure	5	6	7	13	7
Yes, under a little	14	16	20	23	27
No	81	78	73	64	66

c   What are the main obstacles that you experience in carrying on research?

PLEASE TICK ONE BOX FOR EACH TO SHOW WHETHER OR NOT IT APPLIES TO YOU

		Univ. 1964		Univ. 1989	Poly 1989
i	insufficient time because of teaching commitments	(applies)	57	57	77
ii	insufficient time because of commitments other than teaching	(applies)	52	76	77
iii	slowness of machinery for obtaining equipment, books, etc.	(applies)	12	20	23
iv	insufficient contact with others working in my field	(applies)	24	27	40
v	insufficiencies in my university/polytechnic library	(applies)	8	27	26
vi	inadequacies in my university/polytechnic computing facilities	(applies)		6	11
vii	unresponsiveness of the university/polytechnic adminstration to my research needs	(applies)	15	23	36
viii	unresponsiveness of my department [or college] administration to my research needs	(applies)	2	22	32
ix	inadequate funding by Government, Research Councils, and similar bodies	(applies)	35	66	53
x	Difficulties in recruiting research staff of the necessary calibre	(applies)		37	21

15a Apart from time, how adequate in general are the resources available to you (library, laboratory, research staff, etc.) for the kind of scholarly or scientific research you are doing? Are they

PLEASE TICK ONE BOX

	Univ. 1964	Univ. 1989	Poly 1989
excellent	16	17	7
adequate	43	51	50
somewhat inadequate	32	26	33
or highly inadequate	9	6	10

b Are you able to carry on research during term?

	Univ. 1964	Univ. 1976	Poly 1976	Univ. 1989	Poly 1989
Yes, a substantial part of it	23			27	13
Yes, but only a little of it	47			49	43
Almost none of it	31			24	44

16a Comparing your own faculty (department, school, unit) with similar ones in other British universities/polytechnics would you describe it as above average, average, or below average in

PLEASE TICK ONE BOX FOR EACH

	Univ. 1964	Univ. 1976	Poly 1976	Univ. 1989	Poly 1989
its teaching of undergraduates? (above average)	58	58	58	62	66
its teaching and supervision of graduate students? (above average)	22	35	27	46	30
the research and scholarship carried out by the staff? (above average)	28	38	20	52	24
its responsiveness to new ideas? (above average)	44	38	40	43	37
its quality as a whole? (above average)	52	47	46	59	51

b Where are the best three departments in your discipline in Britain, whether at universities or polytechnics?   See Chapter 8

PLEASE LIST THE INSTITUTIONS ACCORDING TO YOUR ESTIMATE OF THE OVERALL QUALITY OF THE DEPARTMENTS

Highest in my estimate
Second highest in my estimate
Third highest in my estimate

17 How much do you agree or disagree with each of the following statements?

PLEASE TICK ONE BOX FOR EACH

		Univ. 1964	Univ. 1976	Poly 1976	Univ. 1989	Poly 1989
a	An academic's first loyalty should be to research in his or her discipline; the teaching of students and the running of the institution should come second					
	strong agree	4	4	2	11	7
	agree	29	24	9	27	14
	disagree	43	45	39	38	31
	strong disagree	24	27	51	25	49
	Don't know	2	5	3	1	1
b	Promotion in academic life is too dependent on published work and too little on devotion to teaching					
	strong agree	35	24	28	33	35
	agree	43	45	45	40	43
	disagree	18	25	22	21	17
	strong disagree	4	6	6	6	5
	Don't know	2	4	4	2	3
c	Promotion should be based in part on formal student evaluations of their teachers					
	strong agree		6	7	13	15
	agree		26	34	44	51
	disagree		28	25	25	21
	strong disagree		41	34	19	13
	Don't know		2	2	2	2
d	Students who severely disrupt the functions of a university or polytechnic should be expelled or suspended					
	strong agree		35	23	32	30
	agree		37	37	44	45
	disagree		27	27	16	19
	strong disagree		11	14	8	6
	Don't know		3	3	5	4
e	We have now reached the point where more or less all those school-leavers capable of benefiting from higher education have the chance to do so					
	strong agree		23	22	5	4
	agree		38	36	13	15
	disagree		21	17	26	26
	strong disagree		18	25	57	54
	Don't know		3	3	5	3
f	Admission policies should encourage mature students					
	strong agree		10	9	61	71
	agree		36	35	35	27
	disagree		40	39	3	1

strong disagree	14	16	1	1
Don't know	4	3	1	1

g   If I had the opportunity to start afresh, I would choose another discipline

strong agree	25	10	9	14
agree	25	15	14	17
disagree	75	23	21	24
strong disagree	75	52	56	46
Don't know		3	7	8

h   If I had the opportunity to start afresh, I would choose another profession

strong agree	7	9	14	14
agree	12	12	17	17
disagree	25	21	24	24
strong disagree	55	50	46	38
Don't know	4	4	7	7

i   University education in Britain puts too little emphasis on vocational training and too much on the education of widely cultivated men and women

strong agree	5		6	12
agree	27		23	36
disagree	48		38	24
strong disagree	21		34	18
Don't know	3		3	6

18a   What is your opinion of the relative amount of support given in British higher education to different areas of research and teaching?
PLEASE TICK ONE BOX FOR EACH

		Univ. 1989	Poly 1989
Engineering and Technology	too little	43	45
	too much	7	9
	right	22	19
	don't know	28	26
Built Environment	too little	20	29
	too much	4	4
	right	17	17
	don't know	59	50

	Univ. 1989	Poly. 1989
Science		
too little	53	47
too much	8	10
right	20	19
don't know	20	24
Information Technology and Computing		
too little	27	28
too much	16	18
right	32	33
don't know	25	22
Business and Management		
too little	16	20
too much	29	24
right	24	28
don't know	32	28
Medicine, Dentistry, and Veterinary Science		
too little	32	28
too much	9	10
right	32	25
don't know	27	37
Health and Social Services		
too little	38	42
too much	7	7
right	21	17
don't know	34	35
Humanities, Social Sciences, and Law		
too little	38	33
too much	11	16
right	24	22
don't know	27	30
Art, Design, and Performing Arts		
too little	33	35
too much	10	13

	Univ.	Poly
right	21	18
don't know	37	34
too little	37	48
too much	8	6
right	25	20
don't know	31	25

Education

b In your opinion, which particular subject or subjects if any, are given too little support?

PLEASE WRITE IN UP TO THREE OR TICK BOX FOR 'NONE'

19 How much do you agree or disagree with each of the following statements?

PLEASE TICK ONE BOX FOR EACH

	Univ. 1989	Poly 1989
a There should be more representatives of industry and business on the Polytechnics/ Universities Funding Council		
strong agree	8	11
agree rese[1]	24	32
disagree rese[2]	34	32
strong disag	35	26
don't know	8	11
b The traditional system of tenure for staff is essential to the quality of university education		
strongly agree	23	
agree rese	39	
disagree rese	29	
strong disag	9	
don't know	2	

[1] Agree with reservations.   [2] Disagree with reservations.

		Univ. 1989	Poly 1989
c	The traditional system of tenure for university staff is essential to maintain academic freedom		
	strongly agree	32	
	agree rese	37	
	disagree rese	23	
	strong disag	7	
	don't know	2	
d	Research in Britain would be made more effective if it were concentrated in a few 'research universities'		
	strong agree	3	5
	agree rese	13	17
	disagree rese	29	27
	strong disag	55	52
	don't know	2	4
e	Students should be maintained by grants alone rather than by loans or any mixed system		
	strong agree	50	56
	agree rese	23	21
	disagree rese	20	16
	strong disag	7	7
	don't know	3	2
f	Polytechnics/universities ought to resist being too responsive to the needs of modern industry and commerce		
	strong agree	21	12
	agree rese	40	35
	disagree rese	28	34
	strong disag	12	20
	don't know	1	1
g	The quality of teaching in my discipline in British higher education has declined over the last decade		
	strong agree	8	6
	agree rese	19	18

disagree rese	35	35
strong disag	40	38
don't know	16	12

h The quality of research in my discipline in British higher education has declined over the last decade

strong agree	8	10
agree rese	24	24
disagree rese	34	34
strong disag	34	32
don't know	16	6

i Public respect for academic staff in British universities and polytechnics has declined over the past decade

strong agree	46	51
agree rese	44	38
disagree rese	8	8
strong disag	3	2
don't know	11	10

j Academic salaries are now too low to attract and hold staff of the necessary calibre

strong agree	65	71
agree rese	28	24
disagree rese	6	4
strong disag	1	1
don't know	2	2

k Many universities have become too dependent on fees of overseas students to balance their books

strong agree	52
agree rese	36
disagree rese	10
strong disag	2
don't know	17

Now there are a few questions about your present post and how you see your future.

20a What post (or posts) in your university do you hold at present?

PLEASE GIVE FULL TITLE(S) OF ALL POSTS HELD

b Are you a member of a College in your university?

	Univ. 1964	Univ. 1976	Poly 1976	Univ. 1989	Poly 1989
Yes—please answer Q.20c				20	
No—please go to Q.21			N/A	14	N/A
Not applicable: no collegiate system				65	

c What post (or posts) do you hold in your College?

PLEASE GIVE FULL TITLE(S) OF ALL POSTS HELD

21 IF YOU ARE A PROFESSOR, PLEASE GO TO Q.24
IF YOU ARE A READER OR A SENIOR LECTURER, PLEASE GO TO Q.23
IF YOU ARE A LECTURER, OR HOLD SOME OTHER ACADEMIC POST, PLEASE ANSWER Q.22 AND Q.23 FOLLOWING

22 Do you expect to be offered a Senior Lectureship or Readership, here or at another British university?

PLEASE TICK ONE BOX

	Univ. 1964	Univ. 1976	Poly 1976	Univ. 1989
Already offered	7	3		4
Yes, within 5 years	32	25		31
Yes, in 5–10 years	33	26		20
Yes, in 10 years or more	19	25		11
No, never	9	22		34

23a How likely do you think it is that you will eventually be appointed to a Chair at your present university.

PLEASE TICK ONE BOX

	Univ. 1964	Univ. 1976	Poly 1976	Univ. 1989
Already offered		1		1
Almost certainly	1	1		2
Quite probably	5	5		8
Possibly but not probably	26	23		33
Almost certainly not	68	70		57

b How likely do you think it is that you will eventually be offered a Chair at another British university?

	Univ. 1964	Univ. 1976	Univ. 1989
Already offered—Please go to Q.24	3	2	3
Almost certainly	3	2	3
Quite probably	14	12	17
Possibly but not probably	40	36	38
Amost certainly not	40	48	39

c Do you think of yourself as more likely or less likely than other university teachers of your rank and age to be offered a Chair eventually?

PLEASE TICK ONE

	Univ. 1964	Univ. 1976	Univ. 1989
More likely	16	19	25
About the same	52	50	46
Less likely	29	30	27
Already offered a Chair outside Britain	3	5	2

24a   Is there any other British university in which you would prefer to hold a post roughly equivalent to the one you hold here?

	Univ. 1964	Univ. 1976	Univ. 1989
Yes—Please answer Q.24b & c	30	37	32
No	52	63	69
Don't know	17	13	9

b   Which one?

MORE THAN ONE, GIVE HIGHEST PREFERENCE

c.   Why do you prefer that university?

PLEASE WRITE YOUR REASONS

25a   Which of the following would be most attractive to you personally? Which next? And which next? (This question was first asked in 1964 and we repeat it for purposes of comparison).

PLEASE MARK THEM 1, 2, 3, 4 IN ORDER OF PREFERENCE

	Univ. 1964	Univ. 1976	Univ. 1989
University lecturer and college fellow at Cambridge	33	35	40
Professor at Sussex	30	27	25
Professorial head of a department at Leeds	21	23	27
Reader in the University of London	16	19	17

PLEASE GIVE THE TITLE OF THE POST AND THE INSTITUTION (IF ANY IN PARTICULAR)

27a Since taking an academic post in Britain, have you seriously considered applying for, or accepting, a permanent post in higher education or research abroad?

PLEASE TICK ONE BOX

	Univ. 1964	Univ. 1989	Poly 1989
Yes, given it serious consideration—Please answer Q.27b		40	29
Yes, considered it, but not seriously	36	27	29
No	64	33	42
Not applicable: came from abroad		—	—

b To which country, or countries, have you considered going?

PLEASE WRITE IN ALL CONSIDERED

28a Have you considered leaving academic life permanently?

PLEASE TICK ONE BOX

	Univ. 1964	Univ. 1989	Poly 1989
Yes, given it serious consideration—Please answer Q.28b	23	37	39
Yes, considered it, but not seriously	28	31	33
No	49	32	27

b   Why is that?

PLEASE WRITE IN YOUR REASONS

29   How much do you agree or disagree with each of the following statements?

	Univ. 1964	Univ. 1976	Poly 1976	Univ. 1989	Poly 1989
a Staff–student ratios must not be allowed to deteriorate further, even if this means turning away qualified applicants					
strong agree		20	17	25	35
agree rese[1]		36	34	44	40
disagree rese[2]		36	37	26	20
strong disag		9	13	5	5
don't know		4		3	1
b British universities ought to have a common degree standard to safeguard excellence					
strong agree		11		32	
agree rese		27		42	
disagree rese		42		19	
strong disag		20		6	
don't know		10		4	
c Oxford and Cambridge have preserved their predominance in practically everything that counts in academic life					
strong agree		9		11	16
agree rese		28		30	33
disagree rese		34		33	28
strong disag		30		26	23

d A professorship ought to be part of the normal expectation of an academic career and not a special attainment of a minority of university teachers

strong agree	12	7	10	38
agree rese	27	16	20	31
disagree rese	36	38	40	22
strong disag	25	34	30	9
don't know	3	3	3	3

e Universities ought to be less under control of central government

strong agree		23	52	
agree rese		39	37	
disagree rese		31	9	
strong disag		7	2	
don't know		6	2	

f University/polytechnic teachers should moderate their demands for higher salaries

strong agree		9	3	2
agree rese		32	11	7
disagree rese		31	27	27
strong disag		28	59	64
don't know		4	2	1

g Polytechnic/university teachers should not engage in 'industrial action'

strong agree		25	17	14
agree rese		28	25	20
disagree rese		25	26	28
strong disag		23	33	38
don't know		3	1	2

h There is no valid way of appraising the quality of university (polytechnic) academic staff

strong agree		7	5	4
agree rese		19	19	18
disagree rese		42	46	46
strong disag		32	31	33
don't know		4	1	3

¹ Agree with reservations.   ² Disagree with reservations.

	Univ. 1964	Univ. 1976	Poly 1976	Univ. 1989	Poly 1989
i Junior academic staff have too little to say in the running of my department					
strong agree		13	14	11	6
agree rese		22	21	22	27
disagree rese		34	36	35	33
strong disag		31	30	32	24
don't know		4	3	3	5
j By and large full-time researchers in universities are people who haven't sufficient ability to obtain teaching appointments					
strong agree		2		3	
agree rese		11		9	
disagree rese		36		29	
strong disag		52		60	
don't know		8		12	

In this last part of the questionnaire, there are some questions about your background and career pattern, and other classificatory items.

30 Are you

	Univ. 1964	Univ. 1976	Poly 1976	Univ. 1989	Poly 1989
male	90	89	86	86	79
or female	10	11	14	14	21

31 When were you born?

	Univ. 1964	Univ. 1976	Poly 1976	Univ. 1989	Poly 1989
	1926[1]/1930	1937	1936	1942	1944

information can be coded according to Census classification and we can then make comparisons with the background of people in other professions.

What type of job did your father have when you were 14 years old?

IF YOUR FATHER DID NOT HAVE A JOB THEN, PLEASE GIVE THE JOB HE USED TO HAVE

PLEASE TICK ONE BOX

Classifications

	1989	1976	1964		Univ. 1964	Univ. 1976	Poly 1976	Univ. 1989	Poly 1989
Manager or administrator (e.g. company director, manager) Professional or technical (e.g. doctor, social worker) Farmer or Farm Manager			Hope-Goldthorpe Classes 1 and 2	(Service Class)	58	61	51	61	47
Clerical (e.g. secretary, book-keeper, clerk) Sales (e.g. shop assistant, commercial traveller)			Hope-Goldthorpe Classes 3, 4, 5	(Intermediate)	42	23	27	27	32
Skilled Manual (e.g. plumber, train driver, fitter) Semi-skilled or unskilled Farm worker Other			Hope-Goldthorpe Classes 6, 7	(Manual)		16	22	12	21

33   In what kind of school did you receive the major part of your secondary schooling?

PLEASE TICK ONE BOX

	Univ. 1964	Univ. 1976	Poly 1976	Univ. 1989	Poly 1989
Independent/public	19	15	9	20	11
Direct Grant	10	15	11	15	12
Maintained Grammar	57	51	58	47	50
Comprehensive		38	12	6	10
Secondary Modern		9	7	3	9
School overseas	13	2	3	8	6
Other				—	

IF 'OTHER' PLEASE DESCRIBE

34   Please record below all your degrees or other post-secondary qualifications

PLEASE WRITE IN

a   The degree or other qualification taken

b   If a first degree, its class

c   The institute at which you took the degree/qualification (and, if not in the UK, the country)

35   Please record in chronological order all the posts, including non-academic ones, you have held since April 1979. This biographical information over the last ten years will provide valuable data about the career patterns of those in higher

Include any part-time posts. If you held two posts simultaneously at the same institution, please enter both.
PLEASE WRITE IN THE TABLE BELOW

a   Name or grade of the post (e.g. lecturer, research assistant) or other activity. If you have held two posts in succession or simultaneously at the same institutions please show them separately.

b   Institution. If a university, polytechnic or other educational institution, give its name and, if not in the UK, the country. If not an educational institution indicate one of the following sectors: National Health Service, state-owned industry, private industry, commerce, civil service, local authority, international agency. If another sector, please specify.

d   Year in which left. (Please leave blank if still in position).

36   Have you taken part in any of the following activities in the last three years?

PLEASE TICK ONE BOX FOR EACH

	Univ. 1964	Univ. 1976	Poly 1976	Univ. 1989	Poly 1989
a Speaking to a seminar or lecturing at another university		64	25	82	58
b Speaking to a seminar or lecturing at a polytechnic or college		18	28	38	38
c External examining at another polytechnic/university		30	6	47	22
d External examining at a polytechnic/university or college		9	6	18	10
e Attending an academic or professional conference within the UK		90	64	94	90
f Attending an academic or professional conference abroad		44	12	67	27
g Holding office in an association connected with your academic work		30	23	49	33
h Serving as an editor or member of an editorial board or committee of an academic journal		18	5	38	12
i Serving as a referee for one or more manuscripts submitted to an academic journal		49	9	77	27

	Univ. 1964	Univ. 1976	Poly 1976	Univ. 1989	Poly 1989
j Serving as a referee for one or more grant applications to any grant-giving body		25	5	50	14
k Serving as a paid consultant to a government department or an international governmental agency (e.g. UNESCO)		15	7	28	13
l Serving as a paid consultant to a business or industry (including state-owned industry) or private organisation		15	34	37	48
m Giving unpaid advice to any organisation outside the higher education system				62	64
n Writing for or appearing on the mass media (television, radio, press, magazine)				41	29
o Serving on a CNAA committee		3	8	3	9
p Visiting another institution to take part in an academic review				14	18

37a   Do you take part in any kind of public or voluntary service activities, outside your university/polytechnic duties, that occupy an appreciable amount of your time?

Yes—Please answer Q.37b   31
No—Please goto to Q.38a   69

IF YES AT Q.37a

b   What are they?

PLEASE DESCRIBE THESE BRIEFLY

38a   At present are you

	1964	Univ. 1976	Poly 1976	Univ. 1989	Poly 1989
married		82	83	78	72
living as married				6	8
separated or divorced				5	8
widowed				1	1
or, never married	22			10	12

b   Has your spouse/partner graduated with a degree or diploma from a university or polytechnic?

	Univ. 1964	Univ. 1976	Poly 1976	Univ. 1989	Poly 1989
Yes	40*	51	61	63	78
No	60	—	—	37	22

* University graduate

39a   Are you at present a member of a trade union or staff association?

DO NOT INCLUDE PROFESSIONAL ASSOCIATIONS

Yes—Please answer Q.39b–d
No—Please go to Q.40a

b   Which one?

PLEASE TICK ONE BOX FOR EACH

Yes—1
No—2

	Univ. 1964	Univ. 1976	Poly 1976	Univ. 1989	Poly 1989
Association of University/Polytechnic Teachers (AUT/APT)		47	17	98	35
Manufacturing, Science, and Finance Union (MSF)		2		4	
National Association of Teachers in Further and Higher Education (NATFHE)			43		86
Other		2	5	10	32

IF 'OTHER' PLEASE SPECIFY

c. Do you attend any union or association meetings?

PLEASE TICK ONE BOX

	Univ. 1964	Univ. 1976	Poly 1976	Univ. 1989	Poly 1989
Regularly		11	18	17	20
occasionally		33	37	65	62
or, never		—	—	18	17

d Have you ever served as a union or association officer or branch committee member?

Yes		10	15	19	30
No		90	85	81	71

40a Which (if any) political party do you feel closest to?

PLEASE TICK ONE BOX OR WRITE IN YOUR ANSWER

	Univ. 1964	Univ. 1976	Poly 1976	Univ. 1989	Poly 1989
Conservative	32	29	27	18	18
Labour	43	40	48	37	44
SLD/Democrat	16	27	23	25	18
SDP/Social Democrat				10	7
SNP/Scottish Nationalist		3		2	1
Plaid Cymru		1	0	1	0
Green party			0	7	11
Other party	1			0	1
None	8	12	8	11	11

IF 'OTHER' PLEASE WRITE IN

40b   Where would you place yourself in the following political spectrum?

	Univ. 1964	Univ. 1976	Poly 1976	Univ. 1989	Poly 1989
Far Left	5	4	6	4	5
Moderate Left	48	40	41	43	45
Centre	28	33	30	35	33
Moderate right	18	21	23	18	17
Far right	1	1	—	—	—

41   For the last tax year (ending April 5th, 1989), please estimate as accurately as you can, the percentage of your household income that came from each of the following sources.

% of household income

	Univ. 1989	Poly 1989
Your own university (polytechnic) and/or college salary (including allowances)	70	70
Your other earnings (e.g. from consultancy work, royalties, other fees)	7	5
Your spouse's/partner's salary	19	21
All other income (e.g. investments, rents, child benefit etc.)	4	3
TOTAL (please check)	100	100

Thank you very much. We have asked a lot of questions. But you may think that we have missed vital points. If so, we should be most grateful for any further comments you might like to make. Please write them on the back page of this questionnaire.

Poly 14b
Have you applied for any research support from your polytechnic within the last three years?

Yes—Please answer Q.14c&d
No—Please go to Q.14e

Poly 14c
What did you apply for?

PLEASE TICK ONE BOX FOR EACH UNDER C) BELOW

Poly 14d
Was the application successful or unsuccessful?

	Poly 1976	Poly 1989
i Released time to work on a degree applied (successful)	85 (15)	31 (74)
ii Released time to work on research not connected with degree applied (successful)		49 (76)
iii Research assistance applied (successful)	84 (16)	54 (70)
iv Capital expenditure on equipment applied (successful)	76 (24)	51 (71)
v Support for data collection or analysis applied (successful)		32 (75)
vi Informal reductions in teaching applied (successful)		46 (66)
vii Sabbatical terms/years applied (successful)		35 (74)

Poly 21

Where do you see yourself in five years' time?

PLEASE TICK ONE BOX

	Poly 1976	Poly 1989
Same post in my present polytechnic	35	38
Present polytechnic but with promotion	36	23
Teaching in another polytechnic	10	3
In a management position in a polytechnic	6	7
Teaching in a university	6	7
In some other branch of education		3
In industry or commerce	4	7
In public services	2	1
Retired		
Other	12	12

IF 'OTHER' PLEASE SPECIFY

Poly 24d
There are many university degree courses which would not get past a CNAA panel.

	Poly 1989
strongly agree	45
Agree	43
Disagree	9
Strong disagree	3
Don't know	3

NB. Brackets around question numbers indicate that these questions were worded differently in earlier rounds of the survey series.

1989 Univ.	1989 Poly	Summary of question	Equivalents in 1976 Univ.	Equivalents in 1976 Poly	Equivalents in 1964 Univ.
1a	1a	Faculty, department, school	2, 3	2	2
b	b	Do you head/chair it?		4	
c	c	IF YES AT c) Which? (IF 1+)			
d	d	Has it been reorganised in last 10 years?	(5)		
2a	2a	Broad teaching/research discipline	(1)	(1)	(3)
b	b	Particular subject specialism			
3	3	No. of students larger/smaller than 10 years ago			
4a	4a	Assessment of academic ability of applicants	(8)		(6)
b	b	Assessment of academic ability of students at graduation			
5a	5a	Proportion of 18-year-olds who should be going on to higher education 10 years from now			(10)
b	b	... and should balance be towards universities or towards polytechnics?			
6a–m	6a–m	Function of universities and polytechnics		(5, 6)	
7a	7a	How higher education will develop over next decade		(7)	
b	b	... and how it should develop?			
c	c	... and reasons for thinking that			

| 1989 | | Summary of question | Equivalents in | | |
Univ.	Poly.		1976 Univ.	1976 Poly.	1964 Univ.
8a–c	(8a–c)	Views about joining staff of one of the polytechnics/universities at present salary/higher salary/lower salary	(27)	(10)	
9a	9a		32a	29a	
b	b		32b	29b	
c	c		(32i)	(29j)	
d	d		(32j)	(29k)	
e	e	Battery of attitudinal items on agree/disagree scale	32m	29n	
f	f		32n	29o	
g	g		(32o)	29p	
h	h				
i	(i)			(29i)	
10a	10a	Arrangement under which present post held	(4)	(3)	
b	b	IF RELEVANT: Length of contract			
		. . . is post/contract full- or part-time?			
11a	11a	Whether supervising any research students	6	13	
b	b	. . . IF SO: How many students?	6a	13a	
12a	12a	Whether engaged in any research expected to lead to publication	13	20	(42)
b	b	No. of papers ever had published	(14)	(22)	(40)
c	c	No. of books ever had published	15	23	41a–c
d	d	No. of professional writings published in last 2 years	16	24	
13	(13)	How working time actually spent; how ideally time should be spent	(33)	(31)	
14a	14a	Whether interests lie mainly in teaching or research	29	15	(17)
b	e	Whether feels under pressure to do more research	17	25	19
c	f	Main obstacles to carrying on research			(18)

15a	15a	Adequacy of resources for research	(11)	(18)	(20)
b	b	Whether able to carry on research in term-time	(10)	(17)	(21)
16a	16a	Rating of own faculty in comparison with similar ones in other universities			(16)
b	b	Best 3 departments in respondent's discipline in Britain			
17a	17a	Battery of attitudinal items on agree/disagree scale	(18a)	(11a)	(49i)
b	b		18b	(11b)	49vii
c	c		18d	11d	
d	d		(18e)	(11e)	
e	e		(18f)	(11f)	
f	f		(18g)	(11g)	
g	g		(18l)	(11k)	
h	h		(18k)	(11l)	
i	i				
18a	18a	Relative amount of support given in higher education to different areas			(49ii)
b	b	Subject(s) given too little support			(50)
(19a)	19a	Battery of attitudinal items on agree/disagree scale			
b	b				
c	c				
(d)	d				
e	e				
f	f				
g	g				
h	h				
	i				
	j				
	k				

1989 Univ.	1989 Poly.	Summary of question	1976 Univ.	1976 Poly.	1964 Univ.
20a	20a	University post(s) held at present	(43a)	(39a)	4
b		Whether member of college at university			
c		IF YES: College post(s) held			
21		[FILTER INSTRUCTIONS]			
22		IF LECTURER: Expectations of Senior Lectureship or Readership	(25)		37
23a		IF NOT ALREADY PROFESSOR: Expectations of a Chair at present university	22		34
b		. . . and of a Chair at another British university	23		35
c		. . . and likelihood of being offered a Chair eventually compared with his/her peers	24		36
24a		Whether would prefer to hold equivalent post in another British university	26		26
b		IF YES: Which one?	26a		
c		. . . and the reasons	26b		
25a		Which of four university posts would be most attractive?	21		(33)
b		. . . and the reasons			
26	22	Academic post regarded as highest achievement	(28)	(27)	
27a	23a	Ever considered permanent academic post abroad?			32
b	b	IF YES: In which country/countries?			
28a	24a	Whether ever considered leaving academic life permanently			(38)
b	b	IF YES: Why?			

Item	Description			
29a b c d e f g h i j	Battery of attitudinal items on agree/disagree scale	(32c) (32f) 32h 32p (32s) (32t) (32u) 32w 32z	(29c) (29g) (29u) (29v) 32x	49iv
30	Gender	37	41	
31	Date of birth	36	40	
32a	Father's occupation	(39)	(35)	(55)
b	...and whether self-employed/employee			
c	...and whether supervisor/foreman			
33	Type of secondary school attended	40	34	62
34a	Degree or other qualifications	(41)	(36)	
b	...and their class			
c	...and the institution where taken			
35a	In last 10 years ... posts held	43	39	
b	...institution/sector			
c	...year took up post			
d	...and year left			
36	Professional and other activities	(9)	(16)	

1989 Univ.	1989 Poly	Summary of question	1976 Univ.	1976 Poly	1964 Univ.
			| Equivalents in		
37a	33a	Public or voluntary service activities undertaken			} (48)
b	b	IF YES: What are they?			
38a	34a	Marital status	(38)	(42)	
b	b	IF (LIVING AS) MARRIED: Whether spouse/partner has degree/diploma			(61)
39a	35a	Whether trade union or staff association member	(31)	(28)	
b	(b)	IF YES: Which one?			
c	c	...and how often attends meetings			
d	d	...and whether ever served as officer or committee member			
40a	36a	Party political identification	(34)	(32)	(53)
b	b	Where placed in political spectrum	35	33	54
41	37	Source of household income in last year	45	44	
		Additional questions on polytechnics questionnaire			
	14b	Whether applied for research support in last 3 years			
	c	IF YES: What applied for?		(21)	
	d	...and whether or not application was successful			
	21	Where respondent sees him/herself in 5 years' time		26	
	25d	Agree/disagree that there are many university degree courses that would not get past a CNAA panel			29t

1. Logistic Regression Equations predicting membership of the Professoriate (Chapter 9)

The logistic regressions reported in this appendix were carried out using the Generalised Linear Interactive Modelling system (GLIM, release 3.77).

The sampling frames for 1976 and 1989 differed somewhat in their definition of researchers. Therefore these analyses excluded research-only staff and were carried out on teaching and research staff.

As stated in Appendix 1, in the university sample professors and women were oversampled. The data was sampled, using the SPSSX sampling procedure, so that the university sample conformed to the population structure. No comparable population statistics exist for the polytechnics. However, the proportion of professors/heads of department to other ranks was similar to, although lower than, that in the university sample. Excluding researchers, the proportions of professors/heads of department to other ranks is as follows:

	Universities		Polytechnics	
	Men	Women	Men	Women
	15%	4%	11%	3%

The variables of interest to the analysis discussed in Chapter 9 were qualifications and research interest/activity. Age and sex were entered first in order to control for their effects. The effects of gender were explored further in Chapter 10. Variables were entered cumulatively, that is to say, age and sex were entered first, then qualifications, then research orientation and research activity as measured by publications.

A number of qualification variables were of interest; class of degree, further degree, and the institutions in which these qualifications were obtained. It was found that, as reported in Table 9.1, first-class degrees, Oxbridge graduation, and Oxbridge doctorates had statistically significant relationships with membership of the professoriate. However, as discussed in Chapter 9, these variables are closely related, and are also predictive of research interest and publications. When all variables are entered into the equation, class of degree and Oxbridge graduation, but not Oxbridge doctorate, remain statistically significant, at the 0.05 level or less. This suggests that the two variables which remain significant have effects which are independent of their relationship to research. Similarly, research orientation remains statistically significant at the 0.05 level after publica-

TABLE A2.1. *Logit model for professoriate: combined university and polytechnic samples, 1976 and 1989 (excluding research-only staff)*

	Odds ratio	s.e. of estimate	ChiSq	(df)	p
Constant	0.00	0.484			
AGE	1.11^a	0.005	678.8	(1)	<0.001
SEX: Female	0.22^a	0.267	65.4	(1)	<0.001
QUALIFICATIONS					
1. Degree class: First	1.80^a	0.096	81.8	(1)	<0.001
2. Oxbridge graduation	1.27^a	0.103	16.6	(1)	<0.001
RESEARCH					
1. Research orientation					
(a) Both teaching and research	1.47^a	0.120	98.1	(2)	<0.001
(b) Research-oriented	1.32^a	0.125			
2. Publications					
(a) Articles: 1–10	1.77 n.s.	0.299	166.7	(3)	<0.001
11–20	2.43^a	0.310			
over 20	5.34^a	0.295			
(b) Books	1.21^a	0.010	117.8	(1)	<0.001

N = 5,581.
Log-likelihood, 2942.7 (df 5570).
Log-likelihood with constant only, 4167.9 (df 5580).

  [a] Statistically significant at the 0.05 level or less.

tions have been entered, indicating the effects of research-related activities other than publications.

The equation finally arrived at is given in Table A2.1. Interactions between surveys (1976 and 1989) and institutions (universities and polytechnics) were examined for all the independent variables in predicting membership of the professoriate. Interactions were entered at the end of the total equation.

Interactions which were statistically significant at the 0.05 level were found on three variables: research orientation, articles published, and books published.

Research Orientation

The interaction between institution/research orientation and professoriate was statistically significant at the 0.001 level (ChiSq=14.0, df 1). The direction of the coefficient indicated that research orientation was a stronger predictor of a professorship in the universities than in polytechnics. The interaction between research orientation, institution, and survey was also statistically significant at the 0.01 level (ChiSq=10.5, df 1). The direction of the coefficient indicated that research orientation had become a more powerful predictor for the universities relative to the polytechnics in 1989 than in 1976.

Articles Published

The interaction between articles published and institution was statistically significant at the 0.001 level (ChiSq=21.3, df 1). The direction of the coefficient indicated that published articles were a stronger predictor for a professorship in universities than in polytechnics. The interaction between articles published, institution, and survey was also statistically significant at the 0.05 level (ChiSq=4.5, df 1). The direction of the coefficient indicated again that publication of articles had become a stronger predictor for the universities compared with the polytechnics in 1989 than in 1976.

Books Published

The interaction between books published and institutions was statistically significant at the 0.01 level (ChiSq=8.2, df 1). The direction of the coefficient indicated that book publication is a stronger predictor of the professoriate in universities than in polytechnics. The interaction between book publication, institution, and survey was not statistically significant at the 0.05 level (ChiSq=0.0, df 1), indicating that institution differences remain stable over the two surveys.

As stated earlier, these variables are inter-correlated to a greater or lesser extent. The entry of two-way and also three-way interaction causes multicollinearity, thus distorting the coefficients.

Therefore it was decided to fit the equation predicting professoriate separately for universities and polytechnics in 1976 and 1989. The four equations found are tabled below and differences in the coefficients can be examined visually. It should be noted that too few university professors had published fewer than ten articles to make it feasible to carry out an analysis using all four categories of articles (none, 1–10, 11–20, and more than 20). Therefore articles published was recoded to combine none and 1–10, the base category becoming none to 10.

2. Construction of Scales used in Chapter 10

The following scales were constructed to analyse career-related gender differences.

TABLE A2.2. *Logit model for professoriate: university sample, 1976 (excluding research-only staff)*

	Odds ratio	s.e. of estimate	ChiSq (df) p		
Constant	0.00	0.647			
AGE	1.14[a]	0.009	584.4	(1)	<0.001
SEX: Female	0.23[a]	0.434	26.0	(1)	<0.001
QUALIFICATIONS					
1. Degree class: First	2.23[a]	0.153	34.3	(1)	<0.001
2. Oxbridge graduation	1.63[a]	0.156	15.2	(1)	<0.001
RESEARCH					
1. Research orientation					
(a) Both teaching and research	2.17[a]	0.184	67.0	(2)	<0.001
(b) Research-oriented	1.46[a]	0.191			
2. Publications					
(a) Articles: 11–20	2.99[a]	0.242	124.4	(2)	<0.001
over 20	6.43[a]	0.202			
(b) Books	1.29[a]	0.032	67.8	(1)	<0.001

N = 2,789.
Log-likelihood, 1223.9 (df 2779).
Log-likelihood with constant only, 2107.0 (df 2788).

[a] Statistically significant at the 0.05 level or less.

1. An index of promotions
2. An index of career versus non-career reasons for changing jobs.
3. An index of career-related activities
4. Factor scores were extracted from a factor analysis of academic attitudes.

1. Index of Promotions

Work histories for the ten years prior to 1989 had been recorded. The ranks associated with job changes were coded in detail. Therefore it was possible to determine whether a change of job involved a promotion or a demotion in rank. The number of promotions and the number of demotions was calculated, and demotions were subtracted from promotions in order to give an overall index of promotions. No distinction was made between internal promotions and changes in rank which were associated with moving to another institution. The resultant scale was a 6-point scale with a minimum of −2 and a maximum of 3.

TABLE A2.3. *Logit model for professoriate: polytechnic sample, 1976* *(excluding research-only staff)*

	Odds ratio	s.e. of estimate (df)	ChiSq (df)	(df) p
Constant	0.02	1.253		
AGE	1.07[a]	0.015	33.7	(1) <0.001
SEX: Female	0.14 n.s.	1.020	6.4	(1) <0.01
QUALIFICATIONS				
1. Degree class: First	1.82[a]	0.307	5.0	(1) <0.05
2. Oxbridge graduation	1.07 n.s.	0.361	0.0	(1) n.s.
RESEARCH				
1. Research orientation				
(*a*) Both teaching and research	0.67 n.s.	0.438 ⎱	0.2	(2) n.s.
(*b*) Research-oriented	1.01 n.s.	0.552 ⎰		
2. Publications				
(*a*) Articles: 11–20	1.20 n.s.	0.575 ⎱	2.3	(2) n.s.
over 20	1.94 n.s.	0.565 ⎰		
(*b*) Books	1.26[a]	0.099	5.7	(1) <0.05

N = 582.
Log-likelihood, 366.5 (df 572).
Log-likelihood with constant only, 419.7 (df 581).

[a] Statistically significant at the 0.05 level or less.

2. Index of Reasons for Changing Jobs (Universities Only)

This scale was constructed from open-ended responses to Q24c (Why an equivalent post in another university would be preferred) and Q25b (Why a particular post out of a list of posts would be preferred).

Five reasons were considered to be career- or achievement-oriented reasons:

1. Status, prestige, reputation
2. Academic reputation
3. Good place for research
4. Good facilities or resources
5. Challenge, scope, potential.

Two reasons were considered to be person- or socially oriented reasons;

1. Good place for teaching
2. Family/social reasons.

Career-oriented reasons were given minus scores and person-oriented reasons were given plus scores. First reasons were weighted by 1, second by

TABLE A2.4. *Logit model for professoriate: university sample, 1989 (excluding research-only staff)*

	Odds ratio	s.e. of estimate	ChiSq (df)	p
Constant	0.00	0.911		
AGE	1.11[a]	0.011	153.0 (1)	<0.001
SEX: Female	0.23[a]	0.502	21.9 (1)	<0.001
QUALIFICATIONS				
1. Degree class: First	1.85[a]	0.172	15.9 (1)	<0.001
2. Oxbridge graduation	1.12 n.s.	0.182	1.5 (1)	n.s.
RESEARCH				
1. Research orientation				
(a) Both teaching and research	2.47[a]	0.242	60.8 (2)	<0.001
(b) Research-oriented	2.54[a]	0.241		
2. Publications				
(a) Articles: 11–20	1.89 n.s.	0.438	64.8 (2)	<0.001
over 20	6.11[a]	0.359		
(b) Books	1.24[a]	0.028	64.4 (1)	<0.001

N = 1,453.
Log-likelihood, 873.4 (df 1443).
Log-likelihood with constant only, 1256.0 (df 1452).
  [a] Statistically significant at the 0.05 level or less.

0.8, third by 0.6, and fourth by 0.4. These reasons were then summed to create a scale. The scale had 61 points, most of which were fractions. Therefore the scale was recoded on a percentage basis into a 7-point scale with −4 as the minimum and +2 as the maximum. The plus or minus values of the original scale were preserved.

3. Index of Career-Related Activities

This scale was constructed from a list of activities in which respondents might have participated in the past three years (Q36 universities, Q32 polytechnics). The activities were as follows:

1. Speaking to a seminar or lecturing at another polytechnic or college.
2. Speaking to a seminar or lecturing at another university.
3. External examining at a polytechnic.
4. External examining at a university.
5. Attending an academic or professorial conferences within the UK.
6. Attending an academic or professorial conference abroad.

TABLE A2.5. *Logit model for professoriate: polytechnic sample, 1989 (excluding research-only staff)*

	Odds ratio	s.e. of estimate	ChiSq	(df) p
Constant	0.03	1.143		
AGE	1.03[a]	0.019	6.3	(1) <0.05
SEX: Female	0.25[a]	0.603	9.1	(1) <0.01
QUALIFICATIONS				
1. Degree class: First	1.43 n.s.	0.343	2.8	(1) n.s.
2. Oxbridge graduation	1.43 n.s.	0.387	0.7	(1) n.s.
RESEARCH				
1. Research orientation				
(a) Both teaching and research	0.70 n.s.	0.360	2.1	(2) n.s.
(b) Research-oriented	1.03 n.s.	0.425		
2. Publications				
(a) Articles: 11–20	1.81 n.s.	0.471	23.5	(2) <0.001
over 20	4.34[a]	0.346		
(b) Books	1.18[a]	0.054	8.8	(1) <0.01

N = 845.
Log-likelihood, 369.2 (df 834).
Log-likelihood with constant only, 427.9 (df 844).

[a] Statistically significant at the 0.05 level or less.

7. Holding office in an association connected with your academic work.
8. Serving as an editor or member of an editorial board or committee of an academic journal.
9. Serving as a referee for one or more manuscripts submitted to an academic journal.
10. Serving as a referee for one or more grant applications to any grant-awarding body.
11. Serving as a *paid* consultant to a government department or an international governmental agency (e.g. UNESCO).
12. Serving as a *paid* consultant to a business or industry (including state-owned industry) or private organization.
13. Serving on a CNAA committee.
14. Visiting another institution to take part in an academic review.

'Yes' responses to these items were summed to create a 15-point scale with a minimum of 0 and a maximum of 14.

4. *Factor Analysis of Academic Attitudes*

Twenty-two items from batteries of attitudinal items were entered into a factor analysis. The items were on 4-point Likert-type scaling, 1 equalling 'strongly agree' and 4 equalling 'strongly disagree'. The items were as follows;

Q9a   An active research interest is essential if a person is to be a good university teacher.

Q9b   An active research interest is essential if a person is to be a good polytechnic teacher.

Q9c   Universities should have more staff per student than polytechnics.

Q9d   Salaries of university academic staff should be higher than those of equivalent academics in polytechnics.

Q9e   There should be equal *academic provision* (e.g. libraries and laboratories) in polytechnics and universities.

Q9f   There should be equal *non-academic provision* (e.g. residential accommodation) in polytechnics and universities.

Q9g   First-degree work in the polytechnics is rarely of the same standards as that in the universities.

Q9h   University academic staff tend to have higher qualifications than academics in polytechnics.

Q9i   It is very difficult for a person to be promoted in *any* university if he or she does not have administrative skills.

Q17a   An academic's first loyalty should be to research in his or her discipline; the teaching of students and the running of the institutions should come second.

Q17b   Promotion in academic life is too dependent on published work and too little on devotion to teaching.

Q17e   We have now reached the point where more or less all those school-leavers capable of benefiting from higher education have the chance to do so.

Q17f   Admission policies should encourage mature students.

Q17i   University education in Britain puts too little emphasis on vocational training and too much on the education of widely cultivated men and women.

Q19a   There should be more representatives of industry and business on the Universities/Polytechnics Funding Council.

Q19d   Research in Britain would be made more effective if it were concentrated in a few 'research universities'.

Q19e   Students should be maintained by grants alone rather than by loans or any mixed system.

Q19f   Universities ought to resist being too responsive to the needs of modern industry and commerce.

Q19i Public respect for academic staff in British universities and polytechnics has declined over the past decade.

Q19j Academic salaries are now too low to attract and hold staff of the necessary calibre.

Q29a Staff–student ratios must not be allowed to deteriorate further, even if this means turning away qualified applicants.

Q29c Oxford and Cambridge have preserved their predominance in practically everything that counts in academic life.

Four further variables were entered into the analysis:

Q14a Do your own interests lie primarily in teaching or research (1 equals 'very heavily in research', 5 equals 'very heavily in teaching')?

Q5a At present, about 16 per cent of eighteen year olds in Britain go on to higher education at universities or polytechnics.

If you were advising on higher education policy *for 10 years from now* what proportion would you recommend? (Proportions were recoded as follows: 1 '40+', 2 '30 to 39', 3 '20 to 29', 4 '10 to 19', 5 'less than 10', to create a 5-point scale.)

Q8a How would you view an opportunity to join the staff of one of the polytechnics (for university staff), universities (for polytechnic staff) at your present salary. (The initial codes were 1 'would not consider going to any of them', 2 'I might go to some but not others, 3 'I would accept such an offer from almost any of them'. For polytechnic staff, 1 was coded to 3 as a polytechnic choice, 2 remained as 2, and 3 was coded to 1, as a university choice. The university codes remained as they were, so that 1 equalled to university choice, 2 equalled to 2 'some but not all' and 3 equated to polytechnic choice.

Scores on the 26 items were intercorrelated. The correlation matrix was factored and six principle components, all with eigenvalues in excess of 1.10, were rotated to an equamax solution. Factor loadings in excess of 0.30 are reported in Table A2.6. Factor scores were extracted for each factor.

The following analyses were carried out on these variables on data which had been sampled or weighted to conform with the population statistics.

i. Index of Promotions

It was predicted that women would have fewer promotions than men. *t*-tests were carried out on the Index of Promotions, with sex as the grouping variable. Three different age-groups were selected as it was believed that the impact of domestic responsibilities would show its greatest effect in the middle years (see Table 10.4 for means). The prediction was confirmed for

TABLE A2.6. *Summary of factor loadings for factors 1 to 6*

Variable	Factors					
	1 = Binary equality	2 = Teaching research	3 = Traditional teaching	4 = Traditional research	5 = Expansion	6 = Public respect
Q9c	−0.792					
Q9d	−0.784					
Q9e	0.698					
Q8a	0.646					
Q9g	−0.620					
Q9h	−0.548					
Q9f	0.530					
Q9i	0.472					
Q9b	0.415					
Q14a	−0.307					
Q17b		−0.699				
Q17a		0.684				
Q14a		0.645				
Q9a		0.487		0.637		

Q19a			0.719			
Q17i			0.606			
Q19e			−0.488			
Q19d				−0.613		
Q29c				−0.477		
Q5a					−0.682	
Q17e					0.661	
Q17f					−0.524	
Q29a					0.391	0.320
Q19j						0.748
Q19i						0.705
Eigenvalue	4.51	2.46	1.71	1.50	1.34	1.11
% variance	18	10	7	6	5.4	4.5

the middle age-group. Interestingly, after the age of 50, women have more promotions than men.

> Age less than 35
> $t = 1.52$(df 252) one-tailed $p = 0.075$
>
> Age 35 to 49
> $t = 1.72$ (df 1637) one-tailed $p = 0.043$
>
> Age 50+
> $t = -1.64$ (df 988) one-tailed $p = 0.0505$

ii. *Index of reasons for Job Change*

It was predicted that men would give more achievement-oriented reasons for changing jobs. This prediction was confirmed, $t = 3.32$ (df 1826) one-tailed $p = 0.000$ (see Table 10.4 for means).

iii. *Index of Career-Related Activities*

An ANOVA with sex and binary membership as independent variables and age as covariate was carried out on the Index of Career-Related Activities. It was predicted that women would participate less in these activities and this prediction was confirmed (see Table 10.3 for means). It was found that the difference between men and women was much greater in universities than in polytechnics (see Table 10.7 for means). In these analyses the means reported are adjusted for other independent variables and covariates using SPSSX MCA statistics.

> Sex $F = 12.69$(df 1, 2760) $p < 0.000$
> Binary membership $F = 353.59$(df 1, 2760) $p < 0.000$
> Sex × binary $F = 6.70$(df 1, 2760) $p < 0.01$
>
> *Universities*
> Sex $F = 31.001$(df 1, 1987) $p < 0.000$
>
> *Polytechnics*
> Sex $F = 5.343$(df 1, 1294) $p < 0.05$

Since some of the activities in the activity index tend to be carried out by those who have already achieved eminence in their profession, it was decided to run an analysis excluding professors. The differences between men and women were smaller, but still statistically significant at the 0.01 level.

> *Index of Career-Related Activities (excluding Professors)*
> Sex $F = 9.571$(df 1, 2523) $p < 0.01$

iv. *Academic Attitudes*

Of the six sets of factor scores extracted from the factor analyses, the means of 3 were different by sex at a level of statistical significance of 0.05

or less. These were binary equality, traditional teaching orientation, and traditional researcher orientation.

For purposes of presentation these variables were multiplied by 100, truncated, and then divided by 20, to give scales ranging from approximately -15 to $+15$. The scaling on binary equality was reversed so that plus scores represent positive attitudes to binary equality (see Tables 10.4 and 10.7 for means).

An ANOVA was carried out on binary equality with sex and binary membership as independent variables and age as covariate.

Sex	$F = 23.765 (df\ 1, 1323)\ p < 0.000$
Binary Membership	$F = 1501.72 (df\ 1, 1323)\ p < 0.000$
Sex × Binary	$F = 15.29 (df\ 1, 1323)\ p < 0.000$

Universities: binary equality
Sex $F = 33.75 (df\ 1, 778)\ p < 0.000$

Polytechnics: binary equality
Sex $F = 0.642 (df\ 1, 547)$, n.s.

ANOVAs were carried out on traditional teaching orientation and traditional researcher orientation, with sex and binary membership as independent variables and age and subject as covariates.

Traditional teaching
Sex	$F = 3.96\ (df\ 1, 1318)\ p < 0.05$
Binary membership	$F = 19.39\ (df\ 1, 1318)\ p < 0.000$
Sex × binary	$F = 1.13\ (df\ 1, 1318)\ n.s.$

Traditional researcher
Sex	$F = 7.54\ (df\ 1, 1318)\ p < 0.01$
Binary membership	$F = 14.48\ (df\ 1, 1318)\ p < 0.000$
Sex × binary	$F = 0.371\ (df\ 1, 1318)\ n.s.$

3. LOGISTIC REGRESSION EQUATIONS PREDICTING MEMBERSHIP OF THE PROFESSORIATE FOR WOMEN AND MEN.

It was not possible to apply the career formula described in Chapter 9 to the sample which had been adjusted to conform with the population, as there would have been too few women professors ($n = 17$) to make the analysis viable.

It was decided therefore to carry out separate analyses for men and women, using the data which had been oversampled for women and professors.

Polytechnics and universities were combined in their analysis. This means that the final equations arrived at are dominated by the university samples. They are larger than polytechnic samples in the first instance and have been oversampled for professors. For separate analyses of polytechnics and universities see Tables A2.2 to A2.5.

London qualifications were included in the analysis as it was known that for women both London graduates and London doctorates predicted professorships at a statistically significant level, when uncontrolled for other variables. However, these effects cease to be statistically significant when other variables are entered into the equation. Although it can be noted that for university women, a London doctorate remains a statistically significant predictor of the professoriate when the full equation has been fitted.

The equations arrived at are tabled below:

TABLE A2.7. *Women—Logit model for professoriate: combined university and polytechnic sample, 1989 (excluding research-only staff)*

	Odds ratio	s.e. of estimate	ChiSq	(df) p
Constant	0.00	1.831		
AGE	1.18[a]	0.027	415.8	(1)<0.001
QUALIFICATIONS				
1. Degree class: First	3.70[a]	0.377	7.5	(1) <0.01
(a) Oxbridge graduation[b]	—		0.7	(1) n.s.
(b) London graduation[b]	—		1.1	(1) n.s.
2. Doctorate	1.63[a]	0.404	7.7	(1) <0.01
(a) Oxbridge doctorate[b]	—		0.0	(1) n.s.
(b) London doctorate[b]	—		2.4	(1) n.s.
RESEARCH				
1. Research orientation				
(a) Both teaching and research	0.94 n.s.	0.480	20.9	(2) <0.001
(b) Research-oriented	2.36[a]	0.476		
2. Publications				
(a) Articles: over 20	3.58[a]	0.430	43.2	(1) <0.001
(b) Books	1.25[a]	0.072	21.0	(1) <0.001
3. Index of career-related activities	1.29[a]	0.077	11.7	(1) <0.001

N = 600.
Log-likelihood, 215.1 (df 591).
Log-likelihood with constant only, 415.8 (df 599).

[a] Statistically significant at the 0.05 level or less.
[b] Oxbridge and London graduation and doctorates were removed from the equation as they were not statistically significant when entered after degree class and doctorate, and being correlated with degree class and doctorate distorted the estimates of the latter.

TABLE A2.8. *Men—Logit model for professoriate: combined university and polytechnic samples, 1989 (excluding research-only staff)*

	Odds ratio	s.e. of estimate	ChiSq	(df)	p
Constant	0.00	0.632			
AGE	1.09[a]	0.009	283.8	(1)	<0.001
QUALIFICATIONS					
1. Degree class: First	1.75[a]	0.135	40.8	(1)	<0.001
(a) Oxbridge graduation[b]	—		17.4	(1)	<0.001
(b) London graduation[b]	—		0.0	(1)	n.s.
2. Doctorate	0.92 n.s.	0.164	39.6	(1)	<0.001
(a) Oxbridge doctorate[b]	1.58[a]	0.179	8.5	(1)	<0.01
(b) London doctorate[b]	—		1.5	(1)	n.s.
RESEARCH					
1. Research orientation					
(a) Both teaching and research	1.47[a]	0.175	100.2	(2)	<0.001
(b) Research-oriented	1.40 n.s.	0.176			
2. Publications					
(a) Articles: over 20	1.68[a]	0.173	174.8	(1)	<0.001
(b) Books	1.14[a]	0.023	123.7	(1)	<0.001
3. Index of career-related activities	1.53[a]	0.030	242.1	(1)	<0.001

N = 2,188.
Log-likelihood, 1500.6 (df 2178).
Log-likelihood with constant only, 2526.6 (df 2187).

[a] Statistically significant at the 0.05 level or less.
[b] London graduation and doctorates were removed from the equation as they were not statistically significant when entered after degree class and doctorate, and being correlated with degree class and doctorate distorted the estimates of the latter. Although Oxbridge graduation had a statistically significant Chi-Square it was correlated with Oxbridge doctorate, making the coefficients for both non-significant, and was excluded from the analysis as Oxbridge doctorate had a stronger effect, both when controlled for other variables and when not controlled.

BIBLIOGRAPHY

Access and Opportunity: A Strategy for Education and Training (1991), Cm 1530 (presented to Parliament by the Secretary of State for Scotland).

ANNAN, N. (1966), 'The Franks Report from the Nearside', *Universities Quarterly*, Sept.

—— (1967), 'Higher Education', in B. Crick, (ed.), *Essays on Reform, 1967: A Centenary Tribute* (Oxford).

—— (1990), *Our Age* (London).

ASHBY, E. (1961), 'On Universities and the Scientific Revolution', in A. H. Halsey, *et al.* (eds.), *Education, Economy and Society* (Chicago).

ARROW, K., (1973), 'Higher Education as a Filter', *Journal of Public Economics*, 2. 3. 193–216.

BALL, C. (1990), *More Means Different: Widening Access to Higher Education*, Royal Society of Arts, Final Report (May).

BARKER, E. (1953), *Age and Youth* (Oxford).

BELL, D. (1973), *The Coming of Post-Industrial Society* (New York).

BERDAHL, R. O, MOODIE, G. C., and SPITZBERG, I. J. (1991), *Quality and Access in Higher Education: Comparing Britain and the United States* (SRHE, Buckingham).

BLAKE, R. (1986), Transcript of his 'The Structure and Government of the University since 1945' (History of Oxford University seminar, 7 Mar.).

BLAU, P. M., and DUNCAN, O. D. (1967), *The American Occupational Structure* (New York).

BLOOM, A. D. (1987), *The Closing of the American Mind: How Higher Education Has Failed Democracy and Impoverished the Souls of Today's Students*, (New York).

BLUME, S., (1982), in G. Oldham (ed.), *The Future of Research* (SRHE, London).

BOUDON, R. (1974), *Education, Opportunity, and Social Inequality: Changing Prospects in Western Society* (London).

BOURDIEU, P., and PASSERON, J-C. (1977), *Reproduction in Education, Society and Culture* (London).

BRONSON G. *et al.* (1971), *Patterns and Policies in Higher Education* (London).

BUTLER, J. (1868), 'The Education and Employment of Women', in D. Spender, (ed.), *The Education Papers: Women's Quest for Equality in Britain* (London, 1987).

Carnegie Council (1980), *Three Thousand Futures: The Next Twenty Years for Higher Education* (San Francisco).

CARSWELL, J. (1985), *Government and the Universities in Britain* (Cambridge).

CARTER, C. F. (1966), 'The Franks Report from the Outside', *Universities Quarterly*, 20. 4. 381–8.

CDP (1974), *Many Arts, Many Skills: the Polytechnic Policy, and requirements for its fulfillment* (London).

CLAPHAM, B. N., and BRUNNER, E. (1944), 'A Study of Oxford Undergraduates: Their School and University Records' (Nuffield College, Oxford, unpublished paper).

CLARK, B. R. (1983), *The Higher Education System: Academic Organisation in Cross-National Perspective* (Los Angeles).

—— (1987), *The Academic Life: Small Worlds, Different Worlds* (New Jersey) 261–5.

Cmnd. 3006 (1966), *A Plan for Polytechnics and Other Colleges* (HMSO).

COLLINS, R. (1979), *The Credential Society: An Historical Sociology of Education and Stratification* (New York).

COLLET, C. (1890), *The Economic Position of Educated Working Women: A Discourse* (London).

CRICK, B. (1983), 'The Brains of Britain', *THES*, 14 Jan.

CROSLAND, C. A. R. (1956), *The Future of Socialism* (London).

—— (1962), *The Conservative Enemy* (London).

CROSS, M., and JOBLING, R. G. (1969), 'The English New Universities', *University Quarterly*, 2. 172–81.

CUMMINGS, W. K. (1980), *Education and Equality in Japan* (New York).

CURZON, G. N. (1909), *Principles and Methods of University Reform* (Oxford).

DAICHES, D. (1964), *The Idea of a New University: An Experiment in Sussex* (London).

DANIEL, H. *et al.* (1990), *Beiträge zur Hockschulforschung*, Proceedings of the Symposium on the University Funding Council's 1989 Research Assessment Exercise, Augsburg, 26–7 July 1990 (Munich).

DAVIDOFF, L., and HALL, C. (1987), *Family Fortunes* (London).

DAVIE, G. (1961), *The Democratic Intellect in Scotland and her Universities in the Nineteenth Century* (Edinburgh).

—— (1986), *The Crisis of the Democratic Intellect: The Problem of Generalization and Specialization in Twentieth Century Scotland* (Edinburgh).

DELAMONT, S. (1978), 'The Domestic Ideology and Women's Education', in S. Delamont and L. Duffin, *The Nineteenth Century Woman: Her Cultural and Physical World* (London).

DES (1985), *The Development of Higher Education into the 1990s*.

—— Department of Employment, Welsh Office (1991), *Education and Training for the 21st Century*, 2 vols., Cm. 1536.

DORE, R. (1976), *The Diploma Disease* (London).

DURKHEIM, E. (1893), *The Division of Labor in Society* (Glencoe, Ill.).

—— (1969), *L'Evolution pedagogique en France* (2nd edn., Paris).

EVANS, B. E. (1953), *The University of Wales: A Historical Sketch* (Cardiff).

FABER, G. (1957), *Jowett: A Portrait with Background* (London).

FLEXNER, A. (1930), *Universities: American, English, German* (New York).

FLOUD, J., and HALSEY, A. H. (1958), 'The Sociology of Education', *Current Sociology*, 7. 3.

FRANKS, O. (1966), *Report of Commission of Inquiry*, 2 vols. (University of Oxford).

FRIEDMAN, M. (1955), 'The Role of Government in Education', in R. A. Solo (ed.), *Economics and the Public Interest* (New Brunswick).

FULTON, O. (ed.) (1981), *Access to Higher Education* (SRHE, Guildford).

GELLNER, E. (1983), *Nations and Nationalism* (London).

GERTH, H., and MILLS, C. W. (1947), *Essays from Max Weber* (London).

GLENNERSTER H., and LOW, W. (1990), 'Education and the Welfare State: Does it add up?' in J. Hills (ed.), *The State of Welfare* (Oxford).

GOODY, J. (1968), *Literacy in Traditional Societies* (Cambridge).

GREEN, V. H. H. (1957), *Oxford Common Room* (London).

GRIFFIN, J. (1966), 'A Neglected Moral Function of the University', *Oxford Magazine*, 2 (Hilary Term).

GUTTSMAN, W. L. (1963), *The British Political Elite* (New York).

HAGUE, D. (1991), *Beyond Universities: A New Republic of the Intellect* (Hobart Paper, IEA, London).

HALSEY, A. H. (1961), 'A Pyramid of Prestige', *Universities Quarterly*, 15. 4.

—— (1977), 'Towards Meritocracy? The Case of Britain', in J. Karabel, and Halsey (eds.), *Power and Ideology in Education* (London).

—— (1979), *Higher Education in Britain: A Study of University and Polytechnic Teachers* (Final Report to SSRC).

—— (1982), 'The Decline of Donnish Dominion?', *Oxford Review of Education*, 8. 3.

—— HEATH, A. F., and RIDGE, J. M. (1980), *Origins and Destinations: Family, Class, and Education in Modern Britain* (Oxford).

—— and TROW, M. (1971), *The British Academics* (London).

—— *et al.* (1984), 'The Political Arithmetic of Public Schools' in G. Walford (ed.), *British Public Schools* (London).

—— *et al.* (1990), *Higher Education in California: Review of National Policies for Education* (OECD, Paris).

Hansard Society (1990), Report of the Hansard Society Commission on Women at the Top (London).

HARRISON, B. (1990) *Oxford Magazine*, 54.

——(ed.) (1992) *History of the University of Oxford*, viii (Oxford).

HERKLOTS, H. G. G., *The New Universities: An External Examination* (London).

Higher Education: A New Framework (1991), Cm 1541 (White Paper presented to Parliament).

HIRSCH, F. (1976), *Social Limits to Growth* (Boston).

HOLCOLME, L. (1973), *Victorian Ladies at Work: Middle-Class Working Women in England and Wales 1850–1914* (Newton Abbot).

HOWARD, A. (1954), *Oxford Magazine* (28 Apr.), 12.

International Federation of University Women (1966), *The Position of the Woman Graduate Today: A Survey* (London).

JENKINS, R. (1983), 'Pisgah sighting', in G. Jones, and M. Quinn, *Foundations of Praise: University College, Cardiff, 1883–1983* (Cardiff).

JOWETT, B. (1860), in J. Parker, (ed.), *Essays and Reviews* (London).

KAMM, J. (1966), *Rapiers and Battleaxes* (London).

KELSALL, R. K. (1957), *Applications for Admission to Universities* (Report on the inquiry commissioned by CVCP): 9.

KERR, C. (1963), *The Uses of the University* (Cambridge, Mass.).

KOGAN, M. (1971), *The Politics of Education* (London).

—— and KOGAN, D. (1983), *The Attack on Higher Education* (London).

KOTSCHNIG, W. M., and PRYS, E. (eds.) (1932), *The University in a Changing World* (London).

LADD, E. C, and LIPSET, S. M. (1976), 'The Growth of Faculty Unions', *Chronicle of Higher Education*, Jan 26.

LEAVIS, F. R. (1943), *Education and the University: A Sketch for an 'English School'* (London).

LÔWE, A. (1941), *The Universities in Transformation* (London).

LUCAS, J. R. (1991), 'Congregation', *Oxford Magazine*, 70 (Trinity), 6–7.

McPHERSON, A. (1973), 'Selections and Survivals: A Sociology of the Ancient Scottish Universities', in R. K. Brown (ed.), *Knowledge, Education and Cultural Change* (London).

MANSBRIDGE, A. (1923), *The Older Universities of England*, (London).

MARSHALL, A. (1872), 'The Future of the Working Classes', in A. C. Pigou, (ed.), *Memorials of Alfred Marshall* (London 1925).

MARSHALL, T. H. (1950), *Citizenship and Social Class* (Cambridge).

MATTHEW, C. (1990), *Oxford Magazine* 53 (Hilary).

METZGER, W. P. (1987), 'The Spectre of "Professionism"', *Educational Researcher*, 16, 6, 10–19.

MOBERLY, W. (1949), *The Crisis of the University* (London).

MORSE, E. (1990), *British Universities 1914–1940* (Ph.D. thesis presented at University of California, Berkeley).

MOSER, C. (1988), 'The Robbins Report 25 Years After—and the Future of the Universities', *Oxford Review of Education*, 14, 1, 5–20.

—— (1990), *Our Need for an Informed Society* (Presidential Address to British Association for the Advancement of Science).

MÜLLER, W., and KARLE, W. (1990), 'Social Selection in Educational Systems in Europe' (Paper presented to the meetings of the International Sociological Association Research Committee on Social Stratification, World Congress of Sociology, Madrid, 9–13 Jul.

NEWMAN, J. H. (1959), *The Idea of a University* (London, 1853–73; Image Books edn.).

NISBET, R. (1972), *The Degradation of the Academic Dogma* (London).

PARK, A. M. (1991), 'Women Working in Higher Education' (M.Phil. thesis, University of Oxford), ch. 1.

PARKER, J. (1988), *Women and Welfare: Ten Victorian Women in Public Social Service* (London, 1988).

PARSONS, T. (1949), 'Age and Sex in the Social Structure', in *Essays in Sociological Theory Pure and Applied* (Chicago), 218–32.

—— and PLATT, G. M. (1973), *The American University* (Cambridge, Mass.).

PAYNE, C. D. (ed.) (1987), *Generalised Linear Interaction Modelling System* (NAG, Oxford).

PERKIN, H. (1969), *Key Profession: The History of the Association of University Teachers* (London).

PESTON, M. (1969), 'The Future of Higher Education', *Oxford Review of Education*, 5. 2. 129–35.

PRATT, J., and BURGESS, T. (1974), *Polytechnics: A Report* (London).

PRICE, R., and BAIN, G. S. (1988), 'The Labour Force', in A. H. Halsey (ed.), *British Social Trends Since 1990* (London).

PURCELL, K. (1988), 'Gender and the Experience of Employment', in D. Gallie (ed.), *Employment in Britain* (Oxford).

REED, T. J. (1991), Editorial, *Oxford Magazine*, 70, 1 (Trinity).

Robbins Report (1963), *Higher Education: Report of the Committee Appointed by the Prime Minister under the Chairmanship of Lord Robbins 1961–63*, Cmnd. 2154.

ROBBINS, LORD, and FORD, B. (1965), 'Report on Robbins', *Universities Quarterly*, 20. 1. 13.

Roberts Report (1987), *Report of the Committee of Inquiry Into Provision for Graduate Students* (University of Oxford, 1987), 7.

ROBERTS, S. C. (1935), 'College Alliances', *Oxford Magazine*, 2 (Summer).

ROBINSON, E. (1968), *The New Polytechnics* (London).

—— (1970), *The New Polytechnics: The People's Universities* (London).

ROSE, J., and ZIMAN, J. (1964), *Camford Observed* (London).

ROSE, M., and FIELDER, S. (1988), 'The Principle of Equity and the Labour Market Behaviour of Dual Market Earners', Working Paper 3, *The Social Change and Economic Life Initiative* (Oxford).

ROTHBLATT, S. (1963), *The Revolution of the Dons: Cambridge and Society in Victorian England* (London).

—— (1968), *The Revolution of the Dons* (London).

ROTHSCHILD, V. (1971), *The Organisation and Management of Government Research and Development*, Cmnd. 4814.

—— (1982), *Report on the Social Sciences Research Council*, Cmnd. 8554.

SCOTT, D. (1971), *A. D. Lindsay: A Biography* (Oxford).

SCOTT, P. (1983), 'The State of the Academic Profession in Britain', *European Journal of Education*, 18. 3. 247.

—— (1984), *The Crisis of the University* (London).

SHILS, E. (1955), *Encounter*, 4.

—— (1972), *The Intellectual and the Powers* (Chicago).

—— (1981), *Tradition* (London).

SIMON, B. (1987), 'The Student Movement in England and Wales during the 1930s', *History of Education*, 16. 3.

SLEE, P. (1987), *Higher Education Quarterly*, 41. 2.

SPARROW, J. (1967), *Mark Pattison and the Idea of a University* (Cambridge).

SPENDER, D. (ed.) (1987), *The Education Papers: Women's Quest for Equality in Britain* (London).

STE CROIX, G. E. M. (1964), 'The Admission of Women to New College', *Oxford Magazine*, 1 (Michaelmas).

STEWART, W. A. L. (1989), *Higher Education in Post-War Britain* (London).

TAPPER, T., and SALTER, S. (1978), *Education and the Political Order* (London).

THOMAS, H. (ed.) (1968), *Crisis in the Civil Service* (London).

THUROW, L. C. (1975), *Generating Inequality: Mechanisms of Distribution in the US Economy* (New York).

—— (1981), 'Equity, Efficiency, Social Justice and Redistribution' in OECD, *The Welfare State in Crisis* (Paris), 137–50.

TROW, M. (1961), 'The Second Transformation of American Secondary Education', *International Journal of Comparative Society*, 2. 144–66.

—— (1987), 'Comparative Perspectives on Higher Education Policy in UK and US', *Oxford Review of Education*, 14. 1.

—— (1988), 'Higher Education Policy in UK and US', *Oxford Review of Education*, 14, 1, 81–96.

TRUSCOT, B. (1945), *Redbrick University* (London, 1943; Pelican edn.).

TURNER, R. H. (1960), 'Sponsored and Contest Mobility and the School System', *American Sociological Review*, 25. 855–67.

UGC (1968), *University Development 1962–67*, Cmnd. 3820, para. 554.

VEBLEN, T. (1918), *The Higher Learning in America* (New York).

WALKER, D. (1991), 'Our Polyprofs are Just as Good as your Professors', *Independent* (3 Jan.), 15.

WARWICK, D. (1990), *AUT Bulletin*, 173 (June), 9.

WHEWELL, W. (1837), *On the Principles of English University Education* (London).

WHITELEY, L. D. (1933), *The Poor Student and the University* (London).

WILLIAMS, R. (1983), 'Intellectuals Behind the Screens', *THES*, 21 Jan.

WINDOLF, P. (1985), 'Mass Universities for the Many: Elite Universities for the Few', (paper presented to the Anglo-German Conference on Educational Expansion and Partisan Dealignment, Frankfurt).

YOUNG, M. (1958), *The Rise of the Meritocracy, 1870–2033* (London).

INDEX